HANDBOOK OF

PARTIAL

HOSPITALIZATION

HANDBOOK OF PARTIAL HOSPITALIZATION

By

Geoffrey Angelo Williston DiBella, M.D.,

G. Wayne Weitz, A.C.S.W.,

Dorothy Poynter-Berg, C.S.W.,

and Judith L. Yurmark, A.C.S.W.

BRUNNER/MAZEL, *Publishers* • *New York*

Library of Congress Cataloging in Publication Data
Main entry under title:
Handbook of partial hospitalization.

Bibliography: p.
Includes index.
1. Psychiatric hospital care. 2. Partial
hospitalization. I. DiBella, Geoffrey
Angelo Williston, 1941-
RC439.2.H36   362.2′ 1   81-12231
ISBN 0-87630-270-3   AACR2

Published by
BRUNNER/MAZEL, INC.
19 Union Square
New York, New York 10003

MANUFACTURED IN THE UNITED STATES OF AMERICA

Preface

Partial hospitalization entered the new decade of the 1980s after about 45 years of existence and enthusiastic dedication to patients and after 25 years of mushrooming growth. Now is the time for organized synthesis. This will yield the highest levels of forcefulness and effectiveness when added to the caring concerns of the many participants. Quality partial hospital programs are more crucial than ever as key elements in a comprehensive system of psychiatric services offering continuity of care. Essential to quality development is a unified source of knowledge and concepts. This book provides such a source in order to significantly promote a comprehensive professional competence. In so doing this volume contains the most recent, complete, and integrated statement of the present state of the art and science of partial hospitalization for the 1980s.

There has still been no adequate definition of partial hospitalization. With this in mind, the definition herein is essentially as follows: *Partial hospitalization is a psychiatric treatment program of eight or more hours per week, for a group of six or more ambulatory patients, provided by two or more clinical staff, and consisting of interconnected therapies within a therapeutic milieu.* (See Chapter 2 for further details.) Typically, however, a partial hospital is a program of 20-35 hours per week and 20-25 regularly attending patients, with a staff numbering between five and seven people.

This work tends to focus on programs for the adult with the primary diagnosis of a "functional" mental disorder without substantial substance abuse; however, the authors believe the principles elucidated hold true for the treatment of all types of patients.

Throughout the book the reader will find the abbreviation, PHP; this stands for partial hospital program or partial hospitalization program. Many say it also means people helping people.

BACKGROUND AND PHILOSOPHY

This volume has arisen from our many years of interest in, experience with, enthusiasm over, responsibility for, and teaching about helping people with problems through partial hospitalization. Before this writing it was easy to become worn and bewildered because of a lack of a comprehensible book that dealt with all aspects of partial hospitals. Even though the quantity of PHP articles and chapters had risen from almost zero before 1955 to a rate of about 20 a year by 1960 (and continuing so through 1980), unfortunately, these were mainly cursorily descriptive and lacked systematization and comprehensiveness of coverage (author's analysis of Maxey, 1980).

In 1946 Cameron (1947) had the only partial hospital in the Western World, and he first used the term "day hospital" in the title of a paper. By December, 1979 there were over 1600 estimated in the U.S.A., and in England and Wales there were about 420 more (Edwards and Carter, 1979, pp. 36-59). A more precise number is due from a survey being completed in 1981 by the U.S.A.'s National Institute of Mental Health.

Despite this explosive growth, PHPs are still underutilized. Only 38 percent of state and county hospitals have partial hospitals (Witkin, 1979). PHPs provide just three percent or less of the total patient care episodes in the U.S.A. (Witkin, 1980), although there are many advantages and benefits to partial hospitals! The U.S.A. could probably use five to ten times the present number of PHPs. The era of partial hospitalization seems yet to come.

FORMAT, CONTENT, AND METHODS USED

How have the above concepts and purposes for PHPs been implemented? In general, an attempt is made to encompass all areas crucial to a well rounded, thriving, proficient partial hospital and to reflect the many significant contributions to and influences on partial hospitalization. Thus, this volume includes fundamental theory and philosophy underlying skills, day-to-day clinical problems, and such pragmatic issues as funding, accreditation, and community acceptance.

There are always limitations of time and space. For example, the authors especially felt the constraints that had to be applied to Part IV, concerning clinical techniques and issues. This part seemed infinitely expandable. There was also a tendency to place emphasis on what seemed the most current; changes are likely in the future. Included is the pertinent literature on PHPs through 1980, as found in Index Medicus and Psychological Abstracts.

Every chapter was specifically written for this volume in order to maximize pertinency. The preface, table of contents, appendix, and chapters 2, 4, 9, 11, 13, 14, 16, 20, 22 (first 2 sections), and 23 were done primarily by DiBella. Chapters 5 (jointly with P-B), 6, 7, 8, 21 (jointly with J.Y.), 22 (last section), and 25 (jointly with P-B) were done primarily by Weitz. Chapters 5 (jointly), 10, 17, 18, 19, 22 (fourth section), and 24, and 25 (jointly) were done primarily by Poynter-Berg. Chapters 1, 2 (part on other models), 3, 4 (on underutilization), 12, 15, 21 (jointly), 22 (part on research) were done primarily by Yurmark. Nonetheless, integration was maintained by each piece of the book being reviewed many times and augmented by each author.

A multidisciplinary input occurred for each section of this book. Just as no one profession is adequate to staff a partial hospital, the authors felt that no single professional would be adequately equipped to write a comprehensive book on partial hospitalization. The authors also consulted with all other types of professionals involved with partial hospitalization in an attempt to maximize inclusiveness, balance, and accuracy.

The target group of readers is expected to be those individuals learning about partial hospitalization. This group would include those in or about to enter partial hospital work, students in the mental health professions, and others interested in understanding partial hospitalization. In addition, this book would be useful to supervisors of all types of psychiatric programs, because of the comprehensiveness of coverage of all issues involved in program development and maintenance.

Stylistically, the following terms are used throughout. The word patient is interchangeable with client and recipient. All indicate the receivers of mental health services from staff. "Member" may refer to either patient or staff; both groups are members of the PHP "community." In deference to less awkward writing, only a single female or male gender of pronouns will be used, rather than use he and she or s/he, etc. The use of only one gender is not meant to disparage either gender.

ACKNOWLEDGMENTS

There are so many individuals who kindly assisted us. First of all, we are indebted to our patients; they have been so many things, including such sources of learning, inspiration, and motivation. Without them this book would be meaningless. In addition, our families and friends have provided crucial encouragement and understanding support. Professional colleagues have also contributed. Geoffrey DiBella benefited from many stimulating discussions with Olin West, M.D., John Casarino, M.D., and Rudolph Gross, M.D.

Judith Yurmark wishes to thank Marcy Yurmark for her constant support and editorial assistance; Goldy Uslan for her superior secretarial skills; and Dr. Ella Lasky, Suzanne Stone, and Stephen Williams for their constant encouragement.

Wayne Weitz is grateful to Dr. Joseph D'Afflitti, Judy Gregorie D'Afflitti, Judy Rosenfeld, David Hall, and E.N. Cohan for their review and valued feedback on various drafts of the work.

In addition, thanks are due to Mary M. Wilson and Barbara S. Russek, original PHP staff who helped and encouraged the program and this endeavor.

Dorothy Poynter-Berg expresses special appreciation to Stephen and Joshua Berg for their patience and understanding during the writing of this book and to Professor Alex Gilterman and the late Hyman J. Weiner for their helpful suggestions.

Finally, it has been a joy to work together; it has been one of our most satisfying team efforts ever.

Contents

II. THEORY: THE BASIC FOUNDATIONS OF PARTIAL HOSPITAL TREATMENT

Contents

HANDBOOK OF

PARTIAL

HOSPITALIZATION

I

Overview and Establishing PHPs

1

Partial Hospitalization:
Historical Roots and Development

The purpose of this chapter is to trace the origins and development of partial hospitalization and to understand its place within a historical view of the mental health field. It also outlines the social, humanitarian and economic forces that fostered the search for treatment alternatives, examines theoretical antecedents which encouraged development of PHPs, and summarizes the problems in its beginnings.

HISTORICAL ANTECEDENTS

To understand the development and impact of partial hospitalization, it is appropriate to review the difficulties of the severely mentally ill and the extraordinary variety of treatment approaches to which they have been subjected throughout history. Exorcisms, eugenics, bloodletting, chains, jails, and other tortures were once attempted in the name of treatment (Schwartz and Swartzburg, 1976, Meltzoff and Blumenthal, 1966).

Pinel in France, Dix in the United States, Muller in Germany, and Tuke in England are all well-known names in the "moral treatment era" and their valiant efforts are chronicled (Schwartz and Swartzburg, 1976). Despite their efforts in the 18th and 19th centuries, the treatment of the severely mentally ill was to remain primarily that of custodial care until the 1930s and 1940s.

With the late 19th and early 20th centuries came the development of the medical model in psychiatry, which included the one-to-one relationship of doctor and patient. Unfortunately, the shortage of trained personnel precluded the application of this approach to the myriad of patients in mental institutions. By the 1930s, these hospitals were virtually bursting at the seams. Urbanization, industrialization, economic depression, and the consequent pressures of living contributed to increases in hospital populations. Staffing and training were highly inadequate, providing, at best, minimal custodial care. Treatment of the severely mentally ill was viewed with much less interest than treatment of *good*, insight-oriented neurotic patients.

The hospital model for treating physical illness was still in use for severe

3

psychiatric illness, that is: 1) a hospital is the place where the patient goes to bed; 2) a hospital is a place where the patient stays until he is well, or as well as the doctor can make him; and 3) a hospital is a place where only the patient is treated (Cameron, 1956). The mentally ill patient was seen in the same light as the physically ill patient. The doctor would cure the patient and the patient, in turn, had little responsibility for his own care (Daniels, 1964) except to comply with the doctor's orders. Hospitals provided safe environments, where minimal demands were made, presumably to remove the acute stress precipitating admission. Care was often provided in peaceful rural settings which removed patients from view and responsibility of family and community.

The hospitals had a dual responsibility: to protect the patients from themselves and to protect the family and community from the patient. However, the hospitals kept patients in institutions, for which the public paid huge sums, increasing yearly, for which there was little return, except that of secluding patients. Overall, the patients benefited little. Instead, they were more often victimized by this approach. Goffman's *Asylums* (1961) described the institution's infrastructure which encouraged the status quo. Hospitals reinforced isolation and withdrawal since the rural setting discouraged family visiting and community contact. Dependency needs were fostered rather than more independent functioning encouraged. More effective and efficient treatment approaches were needed. Services outside the hospital were virtually nonexistent for those without substantial financial resources, or other extraordinary situations. Insulin coma, lobotomy, hydrotherapy, and electroconvulsive therapies seemed of some limited value in treatment, but did not in themselves encourage returning patients to family and community.

ALTERNATIVE TREATMENTS

A variety of other trends in treatment, within and outside the mental hospital, would pave the way for PHP development and growth. Among them, the emergence of group psychotherapy, modern family therapy and the development of the therapeutic milieu concept will be briefly discussed in this section.

The origin of American group psychotherapy is credited to Joseph Pratt, an internist, who worked as early as 1905 with tuberculosis patients to encourage them to deal more effectively with the emotional aspects of physical illness. He believed that patients could learn to overcome the discouragement and pessimism resulting from their illness, and to relinquish secondary gain and replace it with increased self-confidence and self-esteem. His groups were primarily didactic and directive in orientation, offering lectures stressing physical health rather than illness. L. Cody Marsh and Edward Lazell later applied these techniques to psychiatric patients (Rosenbaum and Berger, 1963).

Parallel developments occurred in Europe under the leadership of Jacob L.

Moreno, Alfred Adler, and others. Adler is credited with being the first European psychiatrist to use group methods (Rosenbaum and Berger, 1963), wanting to bring psychoanalytic concepts to the working classes. Trigart Burrow, Alexander Wolf, Paul Schilder, and Louis Wender encouraged the development of psychoanalysis in groups.

A.A. Low (1950), who organized Recovery, Incorporated, began an approach fostering group identification, support, socialization, and a decrease of isolation for mental patients. His groups led the way for other movements such as Synanon, Alcoholics Anonymous, and Overeaters Anonymous.

Joshua Bierer (1948), a follower of Adler and an early developer of PHP, began the *therapeutic social club* in England in 1938 for mental patients. Using social activities, patients were taught to relate to the outside world and to acquire social and behavioral skills needed for community adjustment. Samuel Slavson's *activity group* therapy, while begun in 1934 with children, was later applied to adult psychotic patients (Rosenbaum and Berger, 1963). Small group research flourished during this period. Behavioral, occupational, and recreational therapies were also added to groups at this time. (For further discussion of group treatment, see Chapters 6 and 7.)

Family treatment, begun in the early 20th century, encouraged the search for alternatives for hospitalized patients. Families were now seen by a few as resources for patients. As a result of this and of group therapy advances, much research highlighted the family as a group and family disturbance as a major factor in mental illness (Ackerman, 1958; Lidz, 1960).

Careful study of the organization of mental hospital facilities illustrated the overwhelming need for reform and restructuring. As a result, principles of social psychology, which had received much stimulus from World War II, were applied to mental hospitals, in an effort to humanize the institutions and to encourage the development of alternatives.

The "therapeutic community" concept, popularized by Maxwell Jones (1952) in England after World War II, offered an alternative to the custodial treatment in institutions. It proposed a restructuring of the hospital setting to try to make it more therapeutic. T.F. Main (1946) seemed to be the first to use, in a modern way, the term "therapeutic community." He believed in the importance of re-directing toward the outside world, changing the authoritarian role of the physician to a less directive "treatment facilitator," and rejecting the hospital as a refuge from society (see Chapter 7).

Main and Jones used other patients as therapeutic agents and supported the use of peer group support, believing that patients had a role in their treatment and in the treatment of others. Such a radical approach would later pave the way for increased belief in patient responsibility and the concept of "mutual treatment responsibility" (see Chapter 19). Although for years patients worked in the institutions without pay (in laundries, food services, etc.), it was finally realized that this showed that patients *could* step out of their illness and develop usable skills. The development of these techniques and concepts and the recognition of patients' strengths were shared through the growing professional associations (APA, AGPA, NASW, etc.) and publications in the field.

Paralleling these developments was the introduction of phenothiazines, open-door policies in hospitals, halfway houses, and mental hygiene clinics which were providing an outpatient alternative to hospital care. Their successes supported the belief that mental illness is treatable. "Patients have been permitted more of the privileges of normal life, as professionals have become more hopeful about their ability to control difficult, degrading, and sometimes dangerous behavior in the community" (Engle and Sabin, 1970). More and more mental health professionals learned of these concepts while discovering that removal of patients from family and community was deleterious to rehabilitation. As mental illness became more understandable and curable, alternative treatment was attempted.

With the rise in sophistication of mental health professionals and of society in general, particularly through the influence of mass communications, fear and ignorance lessened. Beginning in the 1940s, media exposed the ills of institutions, while portraying patients as people with feelings, thoughts, and needs, not simply as "the insane." Thus, the above developments generally supported the deinstitutionalization movement.

THE BEGINNINGS OF PARTIAL HOSPITALIZATION

Dzhagarov (1937) is credited with beginning the first "hospital without beds" in Moscow in 1933, due to a bed shortage and lack of funds for a larger institution to aid primarily psychotic patients, rather than due to a change in treatment philsosphy. His program served 1,225 patients in the years between 1933 and 1937, 80 patients at a time, for an average two-month stay. However, for the most part his program consisted of work therapy. His program was not known outside Russia at the time and probably had no influence on initial developments in the Western world.

Other informal precursors of the partial hospital include Adams House for neurotics established in Boston in 1935, and Lady Chichester Hospital set up in Hove, England, in 1938, among others. However, the first organized day hospital in the Western world was not introduced until 1946 by Cameron, in Montreal, Canada. He offered his program a complement to full-time hospitalization and to reduce the *need* for 24-hour care, not necessarily to replace the hospital, as Dzhagarov proposed. Bierer's program, in 1948, the first begun in England, was based on a psychoanalytic perspective, and included group and individual therapy, recreational and occupational therapies, psychodrama, art, physical treatment, and social club therapy. His program treated both children and adults, not as a replacement for inpatient care but as a transition between in- and outpatient services. He also questioned the use of the term "day hospital," suggesting it be used only when the program replaced inpatient care. Thus, from its beginnings, terms and functions of PHP have been controversial (Cameron, 1947, 1956; Bierer, 1948, 1962; Kramer, 1962).

Yale University Clinic, in 1948, Menninger Clinic, in 1949, and Massachusetts Mental Health Center, in 1952, followed quickly with programs to ease the transition from the hospital, but again, not to totally replace inpatient care, even though they had day and night services. They offered a *special intensive treatment* for those who were not actively suicidal, homicidal, or undomiciled (Kramer, 1962; Meltzoff and Blumenthal, 1966; Epps and Hanes, 1964).

The greatest single spur to PHP in the United States was the Community Mental Health Act of 1963, which mandated and provided funds for partial hospitalization. This legislation received much impetus from *Action for Mental Health*, a report of the Joint Commission of Mental Illness and Health in 1961. The report recommended an innovative approach encouraging community-based aftercare and rehabilitation programming, for chronic as well as acute patients.

The legislation brought financial support and consequently a large increase in the development of PHPs. Accordingly, PHPs increased from 112 in September 1963 to 142 in May 1964 (Zwerling, 1966), to over 300 by 1969 (Glaser, 1969). In 1980, there were approximately 2,000 in the United States and United Kingdom.

An analogous process occurred in England as a result of the Mental Health Act of 1960 (Bennett, 1964; Farndale. 1961), encouraging the de-institutionalization movement and growth of partial hospitalization.

Engle and Sabin (1970) describe the philosophical changes brought by PHP and the needed treatment changes, including socialization, vocational rehabilitation, and development of daily life skills:

> The philosophy of partial hospitalization is guided by the principle, the less hospitalization the better. Hospitalization invites regression, often severely taxes the diminished adaptational capacities of the patient and frequently costs in frustration and money more than it is worth. The purpose of partial hospitalization is to take as little away from the patient as possible. He keeps everything from his wallet, keys and driver's license to his citizen's rights, personal belongings and family. He continues to deal with personal social realities. We do not try to replace those individuals in the community he is accustomed to deal with: his personal physician, dentist, lawyer, and other associates. Our purpose is to supplement what the patient already has and increase his capacity to deal with it.

Traditional inpatient or outpatient care had little opportunity to provide these services. Medication was helpful, but could not address the need for lifestyle changes to maintain the patient in the community. However, PHPs enabled the patient to structure his day and to lessen the burden on his family. They offered these intensive services without the expensive "hotel" function of full-time hospitalization.

PHPs offered a new service incorporating a nontraditional treatment approach, including involvement of family, community, and environmental influences on the patient. Cameron (1947) wrote that PHPs challenged the three premises of the existing medical model: 1)deemphasizing the importance of the bed; 2) including family and environment in treatment focus; and 3) viewing the hospital as a part of the treatment process where the patient may begin the difficult and lengthy process of treatment, the bulk of which is offered upon discharge from the hospital through a PHP.

Partial hospitalization brought a shift from the existing traditional biomedical model with its hierarchical organization of power to a biopsychosocial team treatment model.

Interconnected and comprehensive multiple group psychotherapies (including groups with recreational and daily living skills, educational and occupational emphases, along with the more traditional verbal groups) appeared to be the nucleus of PHPs. Groups were seen as having advantages over individual therapy (see Chapter 6).

This innovative approach was fraught with ambiguity and with role-blurring (see Chapter 5). Much work awaited the PHPs in defining and designing programs to incorporate this new biopsychosocial team treatment, still in its infancy. Maxwell Jones's therapeutic community concept was just one model; furthermore, it was used in treatment of psychopathic patients and would need modification for other populations.

Many other aspects of PHPs have been debated within the movement. The value of individual treatment, ongoing or as needed, has been discussed and disputed (Daniels, 1964; Gootnick, 1975; Lamb, 1976a; Meltzoff and Blumenthal, 1966). However, a working relationship with families is usually encouraged. Crisis intervention has been a function of PHP since its inception. Indeed, PHPs use all treatment modalities.

Over the years, PHPs have grappled with such issues as defining populations to be served, daily schedules and programming, program functions and goals, staffing, funding, medications, outreach, physical plants, relations to other facilities, and length of stay. Team approaches and processes are also chronicled. The literature has been descriptive rather than theoretical, and less evaluative than would be helpful; it often fails to define and recognize principles and functions of PHPs (Guy and Gross, 1968). That PHPs can and do suceed is clear to their staff and patients, but more research is required to obtain appreciation by others outside the PHP field (see Chapter 3).

In the United States, partial hospitals have a professional organization, the American Association for Partial Hospitalization. This began in 1965 as the

Federation of Partial Hospitalization Study Groups. It has printed a newsletter since 1973 and has published its proceedings of annual conferences since 1976. Membership for each PHP is recommended, both for information, program sharing and development, and for increased recognition of PHPs within the mental health field.

2

Toward a Science of Partial Hospitalization: Basic Definitions and Theoretical Models

Any science is based on a terminology and concepts with precise, commonly accepted definitions. Unfortunately, partial hospitalization is still floundering without such a basis. Clinical staff working in different PHPs always waste considerable time each occasion they get together, because they need to clarify what exactly they are talking about. *All* mental health disciplines suffer from imprecise use of vague terms. When disciplines try to work together (as demanded in PHPs), the problem is greatly magnified. Examples of terms with so many different definitions as to be meaningless are "therapeutic community" (see Chapter 7) and "countertransference." Thus this book tries to adequately define all necessary PHP terms. Optimally definitions are operationalized; an operational definition is a statement giving meaning to something by explaining it in terms of what it concretely and observably does, thus also allowing it to be measured reliably and accurately.

CURRENT DEFINITIONS OF PHP

Some have looked upon the PHP as a waiting room, alumni club, hospital, social club, and (metaphorically) a bus, school, and others (Rodgers, 1967), but PHP is none of these.

The publications of The Joint Commission on the Accreditation of Hospitals (1981), The American Association for Partial Hospitalization (Cutick, 1979), the American Psychiatric Association (Werner, 1980), the National Institute of Mental Health (1979), and Luber (1979) were scrutinized in an attempt to find background and a satisfactory definition. In addition, the work of the U.S.A. Veterans Administration and the British system were examined, since they have been the most consistent in using certain terms for PHPs (Glasscote, 1969). None was completely adequate. Thus, the following is offered.

SUGGESTED DEFINITION OF THE GENERIC TERM "PARTIAL HOSPITALIZATION"

Partial hospitalization is the most general all-encompassing term that can be used; thus it can designate all types of programs. PHP can indicate "partial-day" (JCAH, 1981), evening, night and weekend hospitals, centers, care, programs, etc.

The term "partial hospitalization" seems to be so solidly entrenched that efforts to change it are doomed to failure. This is unfortunate since it has certain negative implications as a piece-of-a-hospital. DiBella feels a more positive generic term for these psychiatric programs would be "community milieu treatment (or programs)."

The question arises whether the term "partial hospital" (or "partial hospitalization") can designate anything but a program primarily for patients with a mental disorder. Although the authors are not aware of such expanded use presently, in the future the meaning of "partial hospital" may also include programs for patients with mainly physical disorders. If this expansion in usage of the term does occur, clarity will necessitate prefacing "partial hospital" with additional descriptive terms, such as "psychiatric" or "non-psychiatric medical."

Herein, "psychiatric PHP" is initially used; thereafter only PHP will be used throughout the book, with the understanding that psychiatric PHP is meant.

A psychiatric partial hospital (or psychiatric partial hospitalization) is a psychiatric treatment program of eight or more waking hours per week, designed for improvement of a group of six or more ambulatory patients, provided by two or more multidisciplinary clinical staff, and consisting of carefully coordinated, multi-modality, interconnected therapies within a therapeutic milieu. This program also emphasizes the regular participation of the patient in the entire program, which occurs almost always during at least two days per week for at least three weeks, with most of the treatment periods of at least three hours but less than 24 hours (see further discussion below).

Briefly, PHP includes all the unique ambulatory treatment programs under medical supervision that provide a careful combination of potentially all psychiatric treatments and a therapeutic milieu and that are of intermediate intensity between the level of 24-hour inpatient care and "traditional outpatient care." (See Chapter 14 for program varieties.)

The reader may notice that the same definition is given for both a partial hospital and partial hospitalization. Admittedly the former tends to indicate more a structure and the latter more a process or field of study. Nonetheless, the definition uses the word "program," which includes both these aspects.

To understand this definition it is important to remember that it is the *combination* of all the above-mentioned factors that create the unique treatment, partial hospitalization. Out of the combined individual factors that alone may be features of other psychiatric modalities, a new entity is created. Each of the factors will now be explained in greater detail and contrast between partial hospitalization and similar modalities will be made.

The word "hospital" is used in the generic term "partial hospitalization" because of tradition and because PHPs can provide an essentially equivalent variety of treatment modalities as a psychiatric hospital ward, except for 24-hour care.

The word "designed," admittedly redundant, is added to emphasize that *additional* thought must go into setting up a quality program of partial hospitalization compared to the "traditional outpatient clinic" (or "care"), which entails less than eight hours per week of therapy and, typically, less than three hours per week. Also, an outpatient clinic can offer a variety of services, but it is without the added thought and effort required to achieve and maintain a therapeutic milieu and carefully combined interconnected services that are characteristic of partial hospitalization.

The word "treatment" (see following section) is added to eliminate the misunderstanding of some people that partial hospitalization is just baby-sitting or custodial, instead of active therapeutic intervention.

The word "program" is used rather than "facility" or "modality" because program denotes a system and/or a combination of several services plus a plan oriented to a goal (Woolf, 1975). In addition, partial hospitalization is not inpatient or outpatient but a separate identifiable organizational unit of ambulatory care somewhere in between that may serve both, but never just inpatients.

The phrase "for improvement of" is used broadly, and optimally it indicates observable behavior. The latter would include more positive behavior shown or positive feelings reported or less dysfunctional behavior or dysphoria per time period.

The word "group" is added to bring out the point that partial hospitalization typically uses group psychotherapies over individual therapies and that a sense of a cohesive group/community is important.

The figures of six patients and two staff were used only to include beginning and atypical programs. Much more typical are 15-30 patients and five to eight staff over 20-35 hours per week. Six patients is about the smallest number that still allows full group process. More than one staff are needed for coverage and to give the necessary multidisciplinary effort.

The words "psychiatric," "treatment," and "patients" are added to indicate that a psychiatrist must take ultimate legal and clinical responsibility, and that the individuals admitted are not simply seeking growth experiences or relief from dissatisfaction with everyday living. Rather, these are people with formal diagnosis of mental disorders and, usually, with only fair (often poorer) overall adaptive functioning.

In addition, readers should be aware that the terms "day hospital" and "day care" are used for programs for people with physical disorders, and should distinguish these from psychiatric programs. Day care has also been used for custodial and educational care for children.

The definition gives considerable detail about time periods because it was felt necessary to provide some guideline to help differentiate partial hospitalization from other ambulatory services, by specifying an estimate of a minimum amount of time required for creating a therapeutic milieu. However, other equivalent ways of arranging time periods are possible. For example, the authors are familiar with one patient achieving a very satisfactory outcome after attending a PHP for 30 hours during just one week. Patient needs must be the number one determinant of treatment given. Nonetheless, most PHPs provide three to six hours daily, three to five times per week. Also, sometimes PHP staff provide clinical services to patients admitted to the program, though not receiving formal partial hospitalization. Such often occurs on a patient-by-patient basis by a planned stage of transition into and/or out of the regular formal partial hospitalization program.

CONTRASTING PHP WITH OTHER PROGRAMS

PHPs have a number of features in common with other entities; thus, there is a need to delineate PHP from others. Some of the latter will be differentiated by highlighting the differences, even though there are similarities. All of these other programs and techniques are felt by many to be important, helpful, and effective; they can complement and supplement PHPs.

Sheltered workshops have many similarities to partial hospitalization. However, in the sheltered workshop all activities revolve around the vocation issue with no requisite diagnosis or ultimate responsibility taken by a psychiatrist. And usually clients are given regular individual monetary compensation for their productive efforts in a way similar to that which would occur in the job situation. In partial hospitalization programs, the focus is on the complete range of dysfunctional thoughts, feelings and behavior. In addition, payment is rarely made to the individual patient.

Training-educational programs would come under educational-classroom auspices with teachers instead of psychiatrists. In addition to this organizational structure, a training center would use an education model.

Residential programs in the community (such as halfway houses) may offer a partial hospital program on the premises, but this is neither usual nor necessary. Also, residences do not necessarily have to provide a therapeutic milieu, and partial hospitalization does not include a home available 24 hours a day as does the residential program.

The classic therapeutic community refers to an inpatient ward, harking back to the type of mental hospital of Maxwell Jones that especially encourages normal functioning (Werner et al., 1980).

Partial hospitalization uses types of interconnected group psychotherapies very extensively, but it almost always consists of other psychotherapies too. In addition, partial hospitalization offers the unique complex combination of all the features outlined in the above definition, in contrast to other more fundamental "groups" (encounter group, marathon group, sensitivity group forms, and other group psychotherapy, etc.) which do not encompass a therapeutic milieu and interconnected psychotherapies. Partial hospitalization also offers, to a perceptibly greater degree, several therapeutically tightly integrated staff and clearly defined, regularly scheduled periods of therapy.

In addition, there are separate independent "Lounges," "Ex-patient Clubs," "Day Training Programs," "Drop-in groups," certain British "Day Centers," and "Psycho-social Rehabilitation Services Agencies" (PRSAs) The prime example of the latter is Fountain House in New York City, which has served as a model for all PRSAs (Brown, 1977; Dincin and Vaillancourt, 1980). PRSAs tend to bring to mind a picture somewhat resembling PHPs. However, PHPs have the following features as integral aspects, which are lacking in the above-mentioned programs:

1) Comprehensive detailed written admitting and continuation criteria. Instead, for example, Fountain House staff indicate that to be an active member an individual has only to fill out an application and attend a minimum of one time every three months, and self-referrals are accepted (Glasscote, 1971, p. 51). It also has "no written rules about membership" (Glasscote, 1971, p. 53).

2) A treatment therapeutic milieu model. Instead, for example, Fountain House refers repeatedly to itself as a "clubhouse" for "members of a club" with "clubhouse activities" (Fountain House, 1980).

3) Diagnosing as important and required for admission. Instead, for example, in PRSAs "diagnostic categories of the various mental illnesses are not considered important" (Brown, 1977, p. 3), and these programs commonly believe in an educational model without "clinicians" and with "almost a denial that the client is or has been sick" (Glasscote et al., 1971, p. 18).

4) Emphasis on complete and regular attendance for all members. Instead, members can come and go as they please.

5) A planned integrated schedule of therapies and periods of treatment. Instead, for example, at Fountain House the schedule is "structured around those activities which clearly reflect essential clubhouse activities" (Beard, 1976, p. 395), and Fountain House's "living room is a place to sit by oneself or to chat with others" (Beard, 1976, p. 402).

Any of the above non-PHP programs could be modified so as to be a part of a PHP. For example, a sheltered workshop type of program could be one of the components within a larger PHP supra-system.

DISCUSSION OF TREATMENT AND RELATED TERMS

There is a lack of clarity in terms having to do with treatment. Because "treatment" is so crucial and integral a concept to PHP, this section will discuss "treatment" and related terms.

Treatment is a type of clinically and medically oriented service done in the presence of and with a diagnosed patient and approved and supervised by a physician in order to prevent deterioration and/or to decrease distress and/or dysfunction of the patient (and those involved with the patient). Psychiatric treatment is that type of treatment done with a patient with a mental disorder, and it is supervised by a psychiatrist. Six additional crucial aspects of treatment include the following:

1) An integral part of treatment is a formal or informal treatment plan which includes goals of treatment and anticipated problems. This plan should be revised when appropriate and indicated.
2) Treatment should be based on principles that can be explained and communicated during review by one's peers.
3) Appropriate clinical action always revolves around concern and benefit for the patients; thus, "treatment may begin prior to the establishment of final diagnosis." The processes of evaluation and other preliminary services are acts of treatment (Council, 1979).
4) "Active" treatment simply refers to ongoing treatment after the physician has made a working diagnosis. A face-to-face contact is required at least every 90 days, for a patient to be in active treatment.
5) In the context of partial hospitalization, psychiatric treatment includes several clinical-oriented services; these include transitory, diagnostic, psychiatric rehabilitation, milieu therapy, and psychotherapy services. And, in the partial hospital, all nonmedical (not given by a physician) psychotherapy should be a type of treatment.
6) In the PHP secondary and tertiary prevention are components of treatment.

To *rehabilitate* is to attempt "to restore to a former capacity" (Woolf, 1975). Psychiatric rehabilitation is the process of trying to restore mental health and capacity for behavioral functioning as much as reasonably possible. Also, rehabilitation is "sometimes termed tertiary prevention" (Werner et al., 1980). All PHP rehabilitation (psychiatry tertiary prevention) is a form of psychiatric treatment, with certain goals and premises.

To *habilitate* is "to make capable" (Woolf, 1975), as to put in a condition of "useful and constructive activity." It implies the previous lack of this desired condition.

Therapy is loosely used to mean psychotherapy. Although it is often viewed as synonymous with "treatment," it is different because it does not have to be prescribed and supervised by a physician. Therapy is also anything provided to a patient by a trained person to promote health and healing.

Psychotherapy is a clinical-oriented service rendered through interaction planned and guided by a psychotherapeutically trained professional who inter-relates with one or more recipients to alleviate their mental-emotional-behavioral problems. All contacts between staff and patients within the partial hospital pro-gram are counted as episodes of psychotherapy or part of the milieu therapy. Some types of psychotherapy include:

1) Activity psychotherapy, which is a form of psychotherapy during which the pa-tient is using the body more than usually done during communication primarily by words (doing versus verbalizing). Activity psychotherapies are commonly called "activities."
2) Verbal psychotherapy, which is a form of psychotherapy during which interac-tion is essentially limited to communication by words (or word symbols), and accompanying adjunctive movements of conversation.

Clearly, during any one 30-90-minute session of psychotherapy, there may be considerable alternation between segments of verbal or activity psychotherapy. Usually, the whole session is characterized overall as an activity psychotherapy session if at least 40 percent of the session is activity psychotherapy.

MODELS

All treatment is guided implicitly or explicitly by models, not just by simple at-titudes, knowledge, and skills. If optimal coordinated treatment is to be given by a collaborating multidisciplinary team (as necessary in partial hospitalization), staff must also be unified on clearly understood and commonly shared models underly-ing their clinical work. The authors have given emphasis to the eclectic and medical models to indicate our belief that these are the preferred models to always include in comprehensive assessment of all individuals. Other models can be still included, and any of a number of specific models might be preferable for any one individual's subsequent treatment plan.

The Medical Model

The medical model is a very complex term with *no* single meaning (Bursten, 1979; Engel, 1979). Unfortunately, most professionals use it as if it did mean one thing, with resulting confusion for all. Likewise, it has become fashionable for some to use the term "medical model" in such an outdated, restricted, pejorative way that it conveys something negative (for example, that medical model only means a paternalistic, biomedical model), and such use has occurred despite considerable work in the '70s (APA, 1979; Bursten, 1979; Engel, 1979), which has clarified what an appropriate medical model should be.

In this book the term "medical model" means the flexible, appropriately used biopsychosocial-medical model. This guides the clinical staff to be systems-oriented and to consider the multidimensional factors (ranging from molecular to educational to cultural/international) that always impinge on every recipient of mental health professional services. In addition, this medical model guides clinical staff as to the proper stance (role model) to take toward any patient, which is that, optimally, staff consider themselves compassionate experts, yet without being authoritarian or paternalistic know-it-alls, which tends to stunt resourceful, healthy independence. Also, the staff should enter into a relationship with a patient (including family as patient) with an exquisite sensitivity and readiness to respond to the patient's needs in order to end up with the patient's maximum well-being and with the maximum opportunity for the patient's genuine growth and improved functioning. To induce growth and collaboration, negotiation and patient responsibility are encouraged as much as appropriate within the patient's capacities, yet it is realized that at times staff must be ready and able to act in a benevolently authoritative way in which the patient is given no choice at the moment. This taking of complete command does not usually occur unless there is danger to self or others. For example, staff will prevent an acutely psychotic patient from plunging a knife into her chest. Thus, it is recognized that different patients at different times may need staff to act toward them as if the patients were essentially infants and yet the next moment as if they were mature adults! Finally, the medical model implies that in multidisciplinary work a physician takes ultimate clinical responsibility.

Other Theoretical Models in Partial Hospitalization

This section will briefly explore the other main variations of models used by PHPs. Many additional variations are possible—see Kanter (1980, pp. 28-39), or Memmott and Rees (1980, pp. 132-145) for recent ones. Probably any one of the nearly 150 (Pardes and Pincus, 1980) forms of "psychotherapy" could be used as a model.

Educational model. Inherent in the educational model is the belief that behavior is learned and can be unlearned. Lamb (1976a,b) has recommended this model to decrease the stigma of mental illness, suggesting that locating these programs in mental health settings promotes dependence instead of independence. While the course of content is similar to other programs, there remains a danger of oversimplification in using the patient-as-student model, i.e., equating severe mental illness with ignorance instead of appreciating the complexity and severity of patient problems. Lamb is correct that patients frequently and understandably resent their roles and the stigma attached to mental illness, and the educational approach may be encouraging to patients and help to raise their expectations. However, what is lacking is an alternative way of handling, rather than denying, the problems so clear to patients, staff, and families. Offering education in basic skills is vital, but so is a simultaneous exploration of patients' feelings about themselves and their experiences. An exclusively educational approach can ignore this opportunity, and excludes the external factors influencing the patients.

Social model. Other programs do not restrict themselves to an individual focus, but include dealing with the social context of patient problems. This model focuses on overt behavior and tends to exclude intrapsychic examination. In this model, changes must include single and multiple family involvement and some environmental manipulation, to include the "social context."

Behavioral model. This model emphasizes forms of behavior therapy, one form of which is the "token economy." Use of a token economy raises some strong criticisms and concerns. For example, the model seems to oversimplify an understanding of the complexity of behavior and to limit transferability to similar situations outside the PHP. Instead, these programs can encourage adaptation to the program. What behaviors are the patients learning? How to earn tokens? Or how to modify and change negative or deviant behaviors? Do patients learn new skills, or do they, instead, learn how to "beat the system" while remaining a part of it? Perhaps token economies are convenient motivating techniques for staff rather than significant therapeutic techniques for patients (Luber, 1979). Goals of self-satisfaction, self-evaluation, and self-recognition are downplayed in this model. On the other hand, some research has indicated unusual effectiveness of behavioral methods with chronic patients and others (Eckman, 1979; Paul and Lentz, 1977). The usefulness of this model is increased if one uses a more encompassing definition, i.e., one that includes conscious thoughts and feelings within the purview of behavior therapy.

Rehabilitation model. Historically, rehabilitation dealt initially with permanent, physical-deficit handicaps, e.g., a missing leg. Later, especially with the community psychiatry and deinstitutionalization movements, the term "rehabilitation" has come to be applied in psychiatry but the connotation of a permanent deficiency remains. Thus, staff may be giving a message by calling treatment "rehabilitation," namely, "You are permanently diseased and never going to be cured." On one hand, this would tend to reduce hope and increase depression. On the other hand, this may help staff and patients face reality, develop actual ways to cope, and plan for possibly lifelong (even if intermittent) treatment for the permanent loss of functioning. Lang (1979) suggested seven target areas included in the rehabilitative model: 1) interdependence, i.e., not treating areas with exclusivity; 2) responsibility, encouraging patients to assume as much personal responsibility as possible to determine and implement their own increased functioning; 3) adaptation to the disability rather than cure; 4) focus on and utilization of strengths and self-confidence to overcome difficulties and weaknesses; 5) determining recoverable functions and means to achieve them; 6) goal-directedness and active treatment; and 7) activity psychotherapies resulting in actual skill acquisition (activities of daily living, personal care, and other skills). (See also Chapter 12.) This focus on *skills* is a new one compared to traditional psychoanalytically oriented psychotherapy.

Eclectic or generalist model. Eclectic programs provide both verbal and activity treatments, and they are based on a synthesis of intrapsychic and educational-behavioral techniques and understanding underlying issues, while concurrently offering practical alternatives for basic skill deficits and for increasing behavioral resources. A program focusing only on one or another approach can deny the importance of the complex constellation of problems and conflicts faced by PHP patients.

As long as PHPs treat a variety of patient groups and diagnostic populations, treatment approaches should include a flexible range of therapies to accommodate the range of patient needs.

3

Issues of Efficiency
and Effectiveness

This chapter critically reviews the existing research done on PHPs with particular reference to issues of treatment effectiveness and cost efficiency. It examines the strengths and shortcomings of the studies followed by recommendations for future research standards and measurement tools. The research is reviewed in an attempt to answer, as clearly as possible, the current questions facing PHPs:

1) Which patient populations can be treated by PHPs?
2) How do PHPs help?
3) How do PHPs compare with inpatient and outpatient services?
4) How do PHPs compare with each other?

Requests, even demands, are being made to show how and to what extent PHPs are providing treatment. These requests are frequently made by third-party reimbursement agents who are expected to pay for treatment, and are often focused on cost efficiency factors, the best treatment incurring the least costs. In fact, programs are frequently asked to justify their continued existence before considering requests for added funding.

The care and the cost of treating mental patients, chronic and acute, have also become political issues; more "outsiders" to the mental health professions are looking for answers for treatment for psychiatric patients. It behooves the mental health professions to work toward solutions themselves rather than having answers, policies, and decisions imposed upon them. (See Chapter 16 on Standards.)

ISSUES IN METHODOLOGY

Few empirical studies have been undertaken to measure PHP efficiency and effectiveness. Rather, the literature abounds in impressive descriptions of individual clinical programs.

Problems in conducting this kind of research are many and varied. Control groups are often difficult to establish as are matching of populations, random sampling, and valid and reliable measurements studying such issues as attitudes, behaviors, roles, and psychopathology. Other reasons, including staff resistance and possible staff bias, are discussed in Chapter 22.

It is important to recognize here the difficulties in categorizing the studies according to the differences in study goals as well as the goals of treatment. Penk et al. (1978) raised an important question of whether studies should focus on general treatment goals or individual progress toward goals. Both are vital to measure desired results, but each probably requires a separate research design, thus changing the focus for study. General goals encourage the development of a widely applicable tool of measurement, while individual goals encourage a single case approach, limiting generalizability.

Astrachan et al. (1970) recommended that each PHP choose a single *primary task*, the "one task it must perform in order to survive" (p. 550), then do the task very well. When PHPs have a variety of different primary tasks, comparison of programs and primary tasks is difficult.

Guy and Gross (1968) have outlined a variety of problems in PHP research. "Success rates reported by one author cannot be compared with another, as neither the population, the treatment program, nor the methods of assessment are defined with adequate precision" (p.113). Among other issues, they were also concerned about studies conducted by treatment personnel rather than by researchers; such attempts may encourage "bias and tenuous conclusion" (p.113). Finally, they raised the question of assessment tools, suggesting that several be used since no single tool can measure various treatments.

It is all too easy to disparage the quality of the existing research. While the research done thus far has many shortcomings, it is still important to examine it carefully. While studies seem imprecise and not always statistically valid or reliable, they are beginnings and valuable data can be gleaned from them. Studies included here are not to be considered the total research done in PHP. They are a sample of the research which is most applicable to the goals of this review, to examine PHP research in regard to patient populations, comparison of PHP with inpatient and outpatient care, and comparison of PHPs with one another.

PATIENT POPULATIONS

1) Studies have shown that probably patients in all diagnostic categories can improve after PHP treatment. For example, Beigel and Feder (1970) showed PHP was able to achieve results with depressed patients. Kris (1959, 1962) worked with chronic patients, as did Dzhagarov (1937). Zwerling and Wilder (1964) and Wilder et al. (1966) achieved good results with acute patients, 60 percent of whom had never before been hospitalized. Smith and Cross (1957) worked with neurotics. Hersen and Luber (1977) treated primarily schizophrenics, depressives and schizo-affectives.

Most studies focused on patients over 18 years of age, who were not imminently suicidal, violent, or without night supervision of family or significant other (Herz et al., 1971; Michaux, 1973; Erickson and Backus, 1973; Guy et al., 1969). Other patients excluded from study were those who exhibited antisocial behaviors, were addicted to alcohol or drugs, were severely mentally retarded, or were suffering from organic brain syndrome.*

2) Decisions on who is appropriate for or who benefits most from PHP treatment remain a controversial issue. The literature describes programs including children, adolescents, and adults; programs for homogeneous and heterogeneous psychiatric patients and patients with medical illnesses such as diabetes, epilepsy, or obesity; for geriatric patients, the retarded and brain-damaged; and for those with or without cooperative families. Which patients may benefit most from a particular program is also an issue as yet unresolved. "However, to date, very little hard data exist identifying those variables that will predict success or failure of treatment" (Luber, 1979, p.188). The development of definitive criteria for selecting suitable PHP patients will be extremely useful in maximizing treatment effectiveness.

3) Socioeconomic factors also influence populations served. As described in Chapter 4, Glaser (1969) suggested that some clinicians and some patients view PHP as a luxury for lower socioeconomic class patients rather than as a treatment necessity especially when used as a transition from inpatient care. Some consider it to be regressive since it may delay vocational or educational plans. Accordingly, the lack of third-party reimbursement and consequent family economic pressures can restrict usage.

In contrast, however, Ruiz and Saiger (1972) studied the use of a PHP in an urban poverty area (South Bronx, New York). Two-thirds of the population were Puerto Rican and the rest were primarily Black. Over a two-year period, 343 patients were admitted first to an "overnight" inpatient unit, with an average stay of 3.3 days, and later transferred to the PHP. The only other treatment alternative available was transfer to a state hospital. Two-thirds of the sample were maintained in the community, in PHP, or later in outpatient care, while only 31 percent required longer-term inpatient treatment.

4) The opportunity for overnight guesting also influences patients served. Guesting, a temporary inpatient admission, is not available to all PHPs. Washburn et al. (1976a), Zwerling and Wilder (1964), Wilder et al. (1966), Salzman et al. (1969), Chasin (1967) and McDonough and Downing (1965) were able to treat a selection of patients in PHPs with guesting options, rather than by full inpatient care.

---

* Patients excluded here are usually treated in partial hospitalization programs specifically designed to handle special needs of these populations.

5) External factors including stable living arrangements and adequate transportation also influence patients served. McDonough and Downing's (1965) research pointed to some limitations to the attempt to use PHP as an alternative to inpatient care. Of 100 patients screened for admission, only 23 were accepted to the PHP, 12 were rejected solely for living alone, and another 17 for lack of transportation. Thus, had better living and transportation arrangements been available, the authors estimate that 29 patients might have been accommodated rather than admitted to full-time inpatient care.

Summary

Studies discussed here illustrate the use of PHP as alternative treatment to inpatient care for a wide variety of patient populations. General diagnostic category seems not in itself a basis for exclusion from PHP. Yet no study has defined which group or groups are best served by PHPs. The patient imminently dangerous to himself or others can be treated by PHP when guesting is available. It is generally acknowledged that alcohol or drug abusers, the retarded, and patients with organic brain syndrome are best served in specialized facilities.

Patients with families are preferred, but guesting can help with night supervision. Guesting can also serve patients in crisis. Increased third-party reimbursement and improved transportation can include more patients also.

COMPARISON BETWEEN PHP AND INPATIENT SERVICES

This section reviews studies comparing PHP with inpatient care with reference to the following areas:

1) patients treated;
2) decrease in psychopathology;
3) family and social role functioning;
4) length of stay;
5) rehospitalization rates;
6) cost effectiveness; and
7) treatment modalities used.*

Each PHP, without guesting options, seems to exclude the imminently suicidal, homicidal, and certain acting-out patients or those without families or stable living situations. The PHP has rightfully placed them in inpatient care. PHPs recognize that these problems outweigh the positive aspects of PHP. Nonetheless, there are certain patients who could conceivably be treated by PHP or by inpatient care.

---

* Not all studies considered each indicator.

Hogarty et al. (1968) studied this question and concluded that perhaps the patients using PHP instead of full hospitalization are those potentially hospitalizable, but still not representative of either the traditional inpatient or the outpatient populations, but who seem to be patients with a mid-range of moderate to severe disorders. Erickson and Backus (1973) found corroboration from the referring physicians in their study who rated PHP as moderate in handling the most serious symptoms and as the treatment option midway between inpatient care and traditional outpatient treatment. Other studies seem to agree with this proposal since many used inpatient services during the initial period of admission for screening, evaluation, and stabilization of acute symptoms prior to referral to PHP.

Zwerling and Wilder (1964) studied 189 patients who were acute, florid, often "first-break" patients who had arrived at the city hospital emergency room. After the admitting physician determined that the patients *required* inpatient admission, patients were randomly assigned to inpatient care or to PHP. Some patients (34 percent) were judged not to be able to retain enough control of impulses and these most floridly psychotic and impulsive patients were sent to inpatient care. The remaining 66 percent were managed in PHP. Even more significantly, 80 percent of the nonorganic patients were accepted by the PHP, since they had families and adequate transportation. Twenty-seven percent of the 189 assigned to PHP were maintained with very brief periods of guesting.

Post-treatment evaluations are particularly important in supporting the case for PHP as an alternative to inpatient care. Wilder et al. (1966) analyzed the two-year outcome of their earlier study and found that, at 24 months, there was little difference between inpatient or PHP groups regarding symptom exacerbation, family burden, and aftercare compliance. Readmission rates had some differences, i.e., the inpatient group had shorter stays but earlier and more frequent readmissions than the day group. In general, the findings support the PHP as an alternative to inpatient care for many patients.

Michaux et al. (1973) studied adjustment of day- and full-time patients at two and twelve months post-discharge. Of the 50 day patients and 56 inpatients who completed prescribed treatment, 45 day patients and 52 inpatients were counted in the sample. On the average, the day patients spent 82 days in treatment while the mean for inpatient care was 67 days. Both groups were considered suitable for PHP, but the inpatient group was ineligible because of catchment area boundaries. Several instruments measured efficacy of treatment and were administered by an independent assessment team. At discharge, the inpatient group showed more "symptom" improvement while the day group showed more "social recovery." However, there was no discussion of the amounts of medications used by either group during this time.

Testing continued at two- and 12-month intervals. Aftercare contacts, medications and relapse rates were similar. Differences in symptom relief between the two groups seemed to disappear, with day patients experiencing a mild decrease in symptoms, while inpatients experienced a mild increase. However, the day patients made significant improvement in social functioning. This study suggests that full-time hospitalization may be best for quick relief of symptoms and PHP best for substantial and lasting social adjustment gains and eventual symptom relief.

Herz et al. (1971) evaluated 424 patients, newly admitted inpatients with families, excluding 334 as too psychiatrically ill, or too healthy, without family supports or with major physical problems. The remaining 90 patients were assigned randomly to remain in inpatient care or to attend day treatment. Both groups received the same treatment, in the form of individual, group, family, milieu, and somatic therapies, and vocational rehabilitation, from the same day staff. Matching was attempted, but the inpatient group was younger, of higher social class, and had a greater proportion of schizophrenics. Guesting was once again available and was used by 22 percent of the day patients. Including guesting, average day hospital stay was 48.5 days while inpatient stay averaged 138.8 days.*

Follow-up evaluations were made at two and four weeks after admission to the study and again later at two years. At each point, inpatients had a higher readmission rate, at three and nine months the rate was nearly double that of day patients. "Thus the shorter initial hospital stay associated with the day hospital care was followed by a reduced likelihood of readmission" (Herz, 1980).

Both groups improved in all measures of psychopathology. At the four-week follow-up, day patients showed significantly greater improvement on five out of 19 scales on the Psychiatric Evaluation Form, used for testing. At long-term follow-up, day patients made significantly superior improvement on Daily Routine-Leisure Time Impairment Scales and in Housekeeper-Role Impairment Scales.

Summary

Studies focused primarily on recidivism, reduction of psychopathology, length of stay, and role functioning. Using these measures, the studies show that PHP can be employed as an alternative for many patients. Missing from these studies were measurements of family burden, and comparisons of medications used. No study determined that PHP should be used in place of inpatient treatment for acutely disturbed patients without families. More precise studies are needed before definitive statements can be made.

PHP AS A TRANSITION TO OUTPATIENT CARE

1) *To decrease full-time hospitalization, PHPs have been used successfully as*

---

* Day patients usually spent eight hours per day five days a week in treatment, while inpatient stays reflect 24-hour care.

transitional facilities, bridging the gap to community care. Washburn et al.'s study (1976a) compared treatment of patients following a two- to six-week inpatient assessment. Following the assessment, 30 females remained in inpatient care, 29 others were assigned to day hospital. In addition, 34 females already in the PHP served as the control group. Over a two-year period, using various evaluation tools, the PHP patients were significantly improved at 6-, 12-, and 18-month follow-up on five dimensions: subjective stress, community functioning, family burden, and days of attachment to treatment. At the two-year follow-up, the advantages of PHP patients decreased and the inpatients "caught up" to the day group.

Herz et al. (1975) randomly assigned 175 patients, who had families, to three groups: a *standard group* who would remain in inpatient care as long as the therapist felt necessary; a *brief-day* group who were expected to stay in full-time care for one week with PHP later available; and a *brief-out* group who were to be discharged outright to community care, which was expected within one week.

Average inpatient stays for brief-day and brief-out groups were 11 days, while the standard group's average was 60 days. All groups made substantial and equal improvement in psychopathology. However, at three and 12 weeks post-treatment, the standard group showed more role impairment.

While the standard group's rate of rehospitalization was lowest, their average length of stay per readmission was 42 days, as compared to 13 days for the brief-day group. Alternately, the brief groups received significantly less psychotropic medication and returned to vocational and family roles more quickly than did the standard group.

2) *PHP has been successful without increasing family burden.* In a follow-up report, Herz et al. (1976) studied the effect of brief hospitalization on the patients' families and studied their views of the patients' treatment. Researchers used the Family Evaluation Form to conduct interviews. The study revealed no significant differences among groups as to family burden and satisfaction with treatment programs. However, an important factor in this study was the level of expectations of the patients and families in the brief day group (Herz, 1980). Families and patients were told to expect to leave the hospital in one week. Unfortunately, the effects of these expectations were not specifically studied.

Despite the rise in awareness and application of family therapy, many clinicians still prefer to separate the patient from his family in an attempt to relieve patient's and family's burden on one another and to learn more about the patient. There is no clinical evidence that more information is obtained about him through an inpatient study, even though a substantial investment in time and energy may be made to help the inpatient. Indeed, other family burdens may be increased as a result of the full-time hospitalization, such as increased financial burdens and added household responsibilities for remaining family members.

COST-EFFECTIVENESS

Cost per stay varied in Fink et al.'s (1978) study from $3,243 for inpatients to $1,347 for PHP patients. Guidry et al.'s (1979) PHP patients were charged $8 per day while inpatients paid $152 per day. Washburn et al.'s (1976a) patients—inpatients and day patients—paid $11,525 and $8,670 respectively. Penk et al.'s groups (1978) paid $12 per day for PHP and $117 per day for inpatient care.

It is obvious that cost for eight-hour, five-day-per-week care will be less expensive than 24-hour, seven-day-per-week care. The above listing of dollar amounts may be misleading. There is wide disparity among figures, in favor of PHP use. However, other costs which inpatient services bear must be counted, namely the obvious residential costs, three shifts of staff, and non-psychiatric medical costs. In addition, there are the factors of reimbursement. Generally, third-party reimbursement rates for 24-hour care far exceed those available for day treatment. Guillette et al. (1978) suggest that "most group health insurance policies equate day hospitalization with outpatient or office care; therefore, if day hospital treatment is provided for at all, it is almost always at a lower rate than is inpatient care" (p.525). This may also account in part for the wide disparity in charges for both services.

Programs are frequently categorized in various ways for purposes of funding and fee collection. For example, those PHPs that are closely associated with hospitals and may offer some extra services, otherwise available only to inpatient care, may be included in one group. Another category may be free-standing PHPs; a third may offer less than a full day, and/or a narrower range of services, more closely resembling a vocational or recreational program rather than a PHP (see Chapter 2). Comparisons then become even more complicated.

In simply using total cost figures, the PHP is less expensive than inpatient care, but without equivalent reimbursement rates, figures are misleading. Guillette et al.'s (1978) study, under the sponsorship of the Aetna Insurance Company, compared costs of two free-standing PHPs with costs of inpatient units handling similar patient populations. Reimbursement rates were equivalent for all groups. Cost per inpatient day was estimated conservatively at $150 per day; day treatment was estimated at one-third of that rate, $50-55 per day.

Thirty-one patients, 15 in one group and 16 in the second, were included in the study. Detailed treatment criteria were applied to ensure high quality intensive care, rather than custodial or primarily recreational service. The average length of stay was 88.5 days and average cost per stay was $5,020, or $55 per day. Assuming that these patients would otherwise have been admitted to 24-hour treatment, the total cost for these patients would have been $411,150. The cost of PHP was $155,611, an estimated savings of $255,839.

The authors admit that the study was not controlled and that measures were crude. They conclude that even a smaller saving would be significant and would illustrate cost effectiveness. Accordingly, they suggest stringent criteria for reimbursement and guidelines and standards for PHP treatment. Similarly, Binner (1977) has suggested that focus just on cost per day would lead one to choose the least expensive; thus, this could encourage custodial care rather than the more expensive active treatment. While his study referred to inpatient care, it behooves PHPs to consider a cost-effective model (accounting for fiscal *and* treatment efficiency), to measure costs of an individual's progress toward goals and outcomes similar to Binner's model of costs per live discharges. For PHPs, an additional area for study could be cost of progress toward financial independence, of lessening financial burdens on family and on public assistance agencies, as Endicott et al. (1978) suggest.

Summary

Despite problems with research designs, sample sizes, differing areas of focus, and various research instruments, proponents can be encouraged by the research studies which point to the following:

1) For patients with families or other stable living situations, PHP can offer a viable alternative to inpatient hospitalization, with less stigma and often with less family burden.
2) PHP patients fare as well as or better than their inpatient counterparts.
3) Even the most acute patients can be treated in PHP when guesting is available.
4) Social and familial roles can more easily be maintained.
5) PHP is helpful in reducing length and expense of full-time hospitalization, when it is used as a transition to more traditional outpatient treatment and full community living, without leading to increased readmission rates or other signs of pathology.
6) Although all inpatients may not be suitable for PHP as an alternative to or transition from inpatient care, the studies show that the numbers of those who are suitable are large enough to endorse more complete utilization of PHPs.

COMPARISON OF PHP WITH TRADITIONAL OUTPATIENT SERVICES

Few studies exist comparing the PHP with traditional outpatient services, usually defined as single, weekly, individual, or group sessions, and/or regular monthly or bi-weekly chemotherapy sessions. PHPs are usually considered as midway on a continuum from 24-hour care to once-weekly clinic visits, and usually not as an alternative to weekly sessions. This section will review two studies comparing PHP with outpatient treatment.

Treatment goals for PHP and for outpatient groups may vary. Both are often interested in low rehospitalization rates and in maintenance of patients in the community. However, almost by definition, PHPs offer a variety of intensive treatments daily. As a result, one might expect higher results in both areas for PHP patients.

Meltzoff and Blumenthal (1966) studied 69 male veterans' post-hospital adjustment. This group of patients was assigned to PHP or to traditional outpatient treatment. During the 18-month study, 64 percent of outpatients required hospitalization, while only 30 percent of the PHP patients were readmitted to full-time care. In addition, 51 percent of the PHP patients were involved in vocational rehabilitation, compared with only 22 percent of the outpatients.

Weldon and Frances (1977) studied the comparative effectiveness of PHP and outpatient care for 30 newly discharged schizophrenics. Patients were placed randomly in either form of treatment and results were measured at the start and at the end of a three-month period. Outpatients received group treatment, or group and medication, or individual, or a combination of individual and group treatments. After three months, all patients in PHP were involved in work or job training. Only 30 percent of the outpatients were so involved. No one was rehospitalized in the three-month study from either group. Patients were rated as similar in decreased pathology, family involvement, and community adjustment.

These studies seem to point toward the use of PHP as a treatment modality offering more effective and more rapid return of patients to community living, to work and vocational training, than is provided in traditional outpatient care.

COMPARISONS OF PHPS TO ONE ANOTHER AND SINGLE PROGRAM DESCRIPTIONS

PHP programs discussed in the literature are largely single descriptions of administrative, physical plant, and program issues. They often include brief treatment vignettes illustrating how this particular treatment philosophy can be applied and how it can be effective with various patient populations. The approaches encompassed under the umbrella of PHP vary widely, including numerous program models, such as workshops, educational models, therapeutic community approaches, behavioral models and "eclectic" programs, among others (Austin et al., 1976; Davis et al., 1978; Eckman, 1979; Hersen and Luber, 1977; Lamb, 1967; Linn et al., 1979; Silverman and Val, 1975). While an expanded discussion of these approaches is to be found in Chapter 14, a mention of the variety of program types is made here.

Empirical evidence as to the comparative effectiveness of these models is sorely lacking. Many have tried to describe and justify their own philosophies and programs. For example, Guidry et al.'s (1979) study used five types of activities for chronic psychiatric patients: psychotherapy groups, discussion groups, recreational groups, behavioral groups, and informal and spontaneous groups. Lamb (1967) used occupational, informal, and spontaneous groups to effect goals of "preventing rehospitalization, improving quality of life and returning patients to full effective community living" (p. 221), all highly laudable goals. Lamb (1967) used occupational therapy, recreational therapy, and specific activities as compared with Wilder et al.'s (1966) use of individual, group, and family treatment. Silverman and Val (1975) presented a strong argument in favor of moving the treatment away from the more traditional insight-oriented group and individual treatment to activity-oriented groups in order to provide basic skills to clients to foster home and community functioning. Hersen and Luber (1977) believe that planned activity is critical in a PHP.

Linn et al. (1979) studied schizophrenic patients in PHPs and compared programs in ten hospitals, with good and poor results. A good result center had an average relapse rate of 50 percent while poor result centers had an average of 69 percent. In their attempts to identify variables associated with good or poor outcomes, the study looked at programming as an important factor influencing outcome. Good result centers were those providing recreational and occupational therapies while the poor result centers primarily offered group psychotherapy and family counseling. While no randomization of patients was attempted, this study pointed to what has been a trend among PHPs, that of using more activity-oriented treatment. Further research, including clear definition and description of the programs offered, randomization of samples treated and systematic measurement of outcomes, is needed to draw conclusions as to the value of treatment offered. Linn et al.'s (1979) study attempted to examine factors in PHPs designed for chronic schizophrenics. Their results may not be maintained when applied to other patient groups.

Authors disagree about how much of a variety of patients can be treated together in a single program (see Chapter 14). No empirical research as yet exists as to the comparative value of homogeneous or heterogeneous patient groups within a PHP. Work, however, has been done to make services available to those in need by the levels of care systems, i.e., by offering a variety of groups, higher and lower functioning groups within the same program, and even having a two- or three-track program for the chronic, intermediate, and acute patients. Here the primary variables are staff allocations and patient needs (see Chapter 15).

As yet, only one study done by Austin et al. (1976) has attempted to compare the differential effects of a behaviorally structured program with those of an eclectic program based on therapeutic community concepts. This study was conducted using 56 patients—Oxnard's program had 30 patients and DTC II (as the study terms it) had 26 patients. Every third patient admitted in a 14-month period was accepted in the study. Treatment outcomes were compared at three, six, and 24 months after admission to the programs. Both the Oxnard Day Treatment Center and the DTC II had staffs of ten members each, with similar professional credentials and similar staff/patient ratios. Both programs accepted similar types of patients recently released from hospitals—patients in acute crisis (i.e., needing more than outpatient clinic treatments) and patients with supportive families who might without a PHP need admission to a hospital.

The differences occurred in the program content of each PHP. Oxnard's program consisted of behaviorally based programs of daily education workshops in which coping skills with daily life activities were taught, of groups to improve social skills, of individual patient sessions, and of conferences, recreational activities, and occupational therapy. The program also used a token economy system based on credit cards. The DTC II's program consisted of community meetings, individual and group therapy, occupational therapy, recreational therapy, relaxation music therapy, and exercise.

Both groups were similar in diagnosis, sex, age, marital status, and income. Oxnard patients and DTC II patients had Impairment Quotients (Glaser, 1972) of 54 and 58 respectively. The largest differences between groups were on questions of previous hospitalizations; the DTC II patients had more history of previous hospitalizations—73 percent to Oxnard's 53.3 percent. Also, median attendance at Oxnard was 38 treatment days while it was 27.5 days at DTC II.

Treatment problems were basically the same for both groups; the main problems included socialization, inappropriate behaviors and speech, anxiety/depression, and interpersonal relationships. Goal Attainment Scaling (GAS) was employed to tailor goals to each individual's problems; goals were finalized after patient, therapist, and significant others agreed to them. The Oxnard population scored higher on the GAS than DTC II, from intake through 24-month follow-up. Replication of this study is needed with greater control over the types of treatment offered by PHPs, including careful monitoring of therapist behavior to insure that the stated or expected treatment matches the actual treatment. Austin et al. recognized this problem with the research design—to monitor therapist behavior would be a monumental task.

Beneficial in this study is the message given by the use of Goal Attainment Scaling. GAS is a stimulus for both patients and staff to set concrete and realistic goals and to monitor the patient's progress toward the goals; these activities have only recently begun and are a great improvement over impressionistic reporting of single patient and program goals, found throughout the literature.

TREATMENT MODALITIES

If we are ever going to be able to answer the question of what exactly is producing the benefit in PHP and to whom, an exploration of treatment modalities employed is needed. With the exception of Herz et al.'s (1971) study, where both inpatients and PHP patients were seen by the same day staff using the same treatments, most other studies involved separate staffs and treatment approaches. For example, along with medication and milieu, Wilder et al.'s (1966) inpatients received occupational therapy and recreational therapy, while the PHP patients received individual, family, and group treatment. Silverman and Val's (1975) study illustrated the shift from insight-oriented individual and group treatment to occupational, recreational, and activity therapy being central to the PHP. Beigel and Feder (1970) used group, family, individual, and activity therapies in their PHP.

While each research group seemed to applaud the use of activity-oriented groups and of family therapy, they do not explain why, although seemingly effective in PHPs, these modalities were not widely used in inpatient care. One wonders about the organization of the various services, their sequencing and treatment philosophies. If PHP *is* more effective than inpatient care, what makes it so? Just the fact of being out of a 24-hour total institutional enviroment? The superior use of milieu therapy? The "family prosthesis" aspects? The group emphasis? Frequently, the studies fail to define the specifics of treatment offered in either or both services. If there are differences, little or no explanation is given for them. One is left to speculate about differences in treatment goals, staff biases, and so forth.

DISCUSSION AND RECOMMENDATIONS

Partial hospitalization programs are acceptable alternatives to full-time inpatient hospitalization. They are particularly more cost effective for patients requiring acute care, when overnight guesting options are available, and will be so when reimbursements by third-party payers are more equal to inpatient care.

As a transition from inpatient care to full community living, the PHP has been shown to be an effective treatment, and thus links the patient to the next, less intensive services. The PHP maintains and even augments the progress which the patient made during the inpatient stay, and reduces the number of days spent in full-time care.

In comparison to outpatient treatment, PHPs can provide a more rapid and effective treatment to maintain patients in the community and to encourage vocational goals.

Comparative studies of PHP treatment and cost effectiveness have been reviewed in this chapter. Research into PHP has only recently begun. As with any new studies, much refinement in design is needed for reliable and valid testing. There are obvious deficiencies in the systematizing of data collection and analysis. Measurement tools vary widely. Samples may continue to be small and difficult to randomize if treatment needs always take priority over research. Replication of studies is needed.

Continued research should focus in two areas: 1) comparative study as to PHP's role(s) in the mental health service network; and 2) ongoing individual program evaluation. Both are vital to PHP survival.

However, there are some foundations to be laid, which will later facilitate research. Before more systematic research can be undertaken, PHPs will do well to focus on some definitions and standards. Common definitions and terms will provide a basis for comparison of program goals, treatment approaches, patient populations served, program structures and functions. Without them, research will remain problematic, if not impossible.

Astrachan et al. (1970) recommended that each PHP choose a single *primary task*, the "one task it must perform in order to survive" (p. 550), then do the task very well. When PHPs have a variety of different primary tasks, comparison of programs and primary tasks is difficult.

Clarity of goals using standardized terms is also needed for clearer comparison of programs. Austin et al.'s (1976) study of behavioral versus eclectic approaches represents a valiant first attempt at comparison between PHPs.

Ongoing evaluation of individual programs will be facilitated by standardization. Davenport (1979) offered a three-pronged approach to client care criteria, examining the appropriateness, adequacy, and effectiveness of treatment. The criterion for appropriateness refers to the standards for determination of which patients are compatible to PHP treatment and which patients are not. Adequacy refers to the extent to which treatment plans are implemented. Effectiveness measures the success of the PHP and the magnitude and direction of changes. Assessments of these three areas are measured by a series of rating scales.

To conclude, several questions remain unanswered and, therefore, are areas for further study. Which patient groups are best served by which type of PHP? Are schizophrenics better PHP candidates than depressives? Which are the most effective treatments offered in PHPs? Can PHPs handle heterogeneous or homogeneous patient groups more effectively? Proponents of PHP have many tasks ahead.

4

The Position of Partial Hospitals in the Mental Health System: Current Issues

This chapter discusses issues and current perspectives on how, where, and why partial hospitalization fits into the total picture of mental health services.

BENEFITS AND ADVANTAGES OF PHPS

What does partial hospitalization have to offer? Why would anyone refer a patient to a partial hospital? We agree with Cameron (1947) and Glasscote et al. (1969) that PHPs can essentially treat all types of patients except those few who either are incapacitated *and* without life support services, or are imminently dangerous. PHPs have many advantages over other forms of care and some of these advantages are mentioned below, with some indication of which chapter contains further discussion.

PHP Compared to All Other Programs

1) PHP provides a unique level of treatment intensity, which falls between traditional inpatient and outpatient clinic care. Thus, the patient has more rational and optimal amounts of his *waking* time distributed between a therapeutic milieu (often 35 hours per week) *and* his own natural environment (77 hours per week). This arrangement is also normalizing, since it more resembles usual work, training, or educational schedules.
2) The patient has substantial daily opportunity to actually practice new behavior in real life situations yet also to receive considerable daily treatment with evaluation, feedback, support, structure, etc.

PHP Compared to Inpatient Care

1) PHP results in less stigma than hospitalization.
2) PHP treatment is less costly than inpatient care, yet it yields at least comparable, if not superior, results (see Chapter 3).
3) PHP decreases the risk of regression, institutionalization, and extreme dependency stemming from 24-hour care.

34

4) PHP maintains the social network (including any family unit) and it avoids the social breakdown syndrome.
5) PHP treatment is less restrictive.
6) PHP supports and maintains community functioning (work, school, or home activities) while building on patients' strengths.
7) When PHP treatment is available, it helps avoid "too easy" hospitalization for patients with histories of hospitalizations (Petyk, 1977).
8) PHP treatment can decrease the sexual frustration found in 24-hour supervision and control (Petyk, 1977).

PHP Compared to Outpatient Care

1) PHPs are unique among ambulatory programs (and probably among most inpatient programs) in offering a truly therapeutic milieu or "prosthetic family."
2) A PHP offers a larger variety of interconnected therapeutic experiences within each week. Thus, the PHP gives the patient's entire functioning the opportunity to be observed, exercised, and enhanced. Similarly, the PHP has a greater chance to involve every patient, by providing a variety of treatment approaches.
3) PHPs offer more extensive crisis intervention treatment to avoid hospitalization.
4) PHPs share responsibility for patient care among a team of patients and staff, thus removing the burden from and dependence on one or two clinicians.
5) PHPs provide a larger (community) group process that is brought to bear on problems, besides small group, individual, and family therapy.

NEEDS ASSESSMENT

Is there a need for more PHPs? If so, how is this need determined? The most extensive mental health planning guidelines for PHP come from Great Britain (DHSS, 1975). Even without children, adolescents, and substance abusers, the adult non-florid, stabilized mentally ill are estimated to need at least 125 PHP places per 100,000 population. If a proportional number of places were provided in the U.S.A., there would be about 275,000 places in PHPs. Thus, with an average caseload of 30 in each PHP, there would be a need for about 9,100 PHPs. This is five to six times the existing number.

Some excellent research indicates that 66 percent of patients arriving at an emergency room during the day and needing psychiatric inpatient care could be served almost completely outside the hospital by a PHP (Zwerling and Wilder, 1964; Wilder et al., 1966). In 1977 there were over 1.8 million psychiatric admissions into hospitals each year in the U.S.A. (Klerman, 1979). Sixty-six percent of this yields about 1.2 million possible admissions to PHPs. Since in one year an average PHP could handle 130 of these possible admissions, then over 9,200 more PHPs are needed just to handle acute/florid, hospitalizable patients. Thus, a total of 18,300 partial hospitals could be used in the U.S.A. alone. This figure is more than a tenfold increase over the 1,600 PHPs currently existing in the U.S.A. Clearly, more PHPs are needed (DiBella, 1980).

OBSTACLES TO PHP DEVELOPMENT

Why then are there not more PHPs? There are at least five interrelated retardants to PHP proliferation.

1) Any new program takes time to become established and accepted, and PHP is the newest psychiatric program (DiBella, in press).
2) The PHP is one of the most difficult types of psychiatric programs to effectuate successfully. The patients treated are often among the most challenging, the most severely mentally ill, and the least attractive among outpatients. At the same time, as a general rule PHP workers do not initially have a feeling of pseudo-security and safety that tends to derive from bars, locked doors, seclusion rooms, etc. of 24-hour inpatient care. PHP staff cannot leave their tour of duty knowing the patient is being turned over to another professional staff. In addition, they need to contact and work with the family, which is stressful (see Chapter 9).
3) Much is mentioned of the clinical team and the therapeutic milieu in psychiatry but nowhere is it required more than in the PHP setting, and such intense work requires considerable time and effort.
4) PHPs can use every form of psychiatric treatment. Indeed, a good PHP might be characterized as the program that expresses the height of eclectic pluralism. However, few clinicians have the ability and/or training in milieu, individual, group, and family therapies, etc., or the background to integrate these. There are still only a few programs offering training in PHP work. Thus, each PHP has to struggle through most concepts, techniques and programming in relative isolation.
5) Finally, and perhaps most important of all, funds to pay for PHPs are few in comparison to funds for other programs.

These five problems are not insurmountable, but they do represent pressing obstacles to PHP development and must all be addressed for optimum PHP growth and progress.

ISSUES OF UNDERUTILIZATION

Partial hospital program survival and proliferation are dependent on utilization of its services. Existing PHPs are underutilized (Fink et al., 1978b). This situation exists despite the fact that the therapeutic effectiveness of PHP as an alternative to inpatient care has been well documented.

A variety of factors are involved in any choice of a particular clinical treatment, including PHP. Clinicians' understanding of patients' needs are paramount. Theoretical and practical considerations are also part of planning service delivery. In addition, an understanding of the family is involved, as is an understanding of institutional, administrative, and fiscal issues and constraints. Fink and Heckerman (1979) and Washburn et al. (1976b) have suggested that clinicians' subjective biases are also factors in PHP use.

ADMINISTRATIVE-CLINICAL ISSUES

Despite the increasing numbers of programs begun in the 1960s, PHPs were slow to gain acceptance and use in the U.S.A. Unfortunately, many programs existed in name only; too many mental health centers included PHPs in their service delivery networks to qualify for funding, rather than out of a real appreciation for PHP treatment.

Financial considerations remain a factor for PHPs. Third-party insurance reimbursements are not readily available, thus denying to many the services of PHPs, and clinicians tend to refer patients to extremely expensive treatments. In addition, hospitals are usually under fiscal pressure to keep a high rate of inpatient bed use (Fink et al., 1978b). This issue particularly affects those PHPs associated with hospitals. When wards are overcrowded, PHP use may increase, but when a ward's census decreases, PHPs can lose referrals.

Finally, poor publicity of PHP and of the research showing its clinical and fiscal efficiency has hindered wider use. Perhaps in anticipation of social stigma and community fears, PHPs have not made themselves widely known in communities. Often, administrators have paid inadequate attention to the locating of PHPs, which are not always accessible by public transportation or may require extraordinary travel time (McDonough and Downing, 1965).

PROFESSIONAL-CLINICAL ISSUES

PHPs are still considered a new service offering something between inpatient and outpatient treatment. Partial hospitalization can encompass a number of forms and functions. However this may have been a drawback since ". . . any new notion that wishes to intrude itself into a well-established system ought to have some degree of unity of form or function or both . . . . They serve vastly diverse populations in a bewildering variety of ways" (Glaser, 1972, p. 236). Research is inadequate and referral criteria remain unclear. Criteria are often influenced by administrative factors and by clinicians' biases, as a result of real pressures or lack of objective standards. Thus, each case is often decided on an idiosyncratic rather than a systematic basis. As a solution, Erickson and Backus (1973) recommend that PHP staff join admitting teams in hospitals to encourage referrals. Herz (1980) suggests also a close liaison with outpatient clinics. In short, PHPs remain ill-defined and are still considered new and questionable by the well-established mental health system.

PHPs offer a variety of nontraditional treatment situations of which many clinicians may be ignorant or by which they may feel threatened. Team treatment and therapeutic milieu approaches are felt to result in role-blurring for mental health staff. The physician, in particular, may be dissatisfied by the distancing from full responsibility for treatment. The "here and now" approach of PHPs is still not widely taught. Group therapy is still considered by many as adjunct therapy; activity therapy is held in even less esteem. Washburn et al. (1976b) and Fink et al. (1978b) suggest that underutilization may also be a function of professionals' ignorance of PHPs' availability, since referrals to PHPs most often come from those professionals who have had experience with PHPs and from the patients themselves.

Additionally, there remains the belief that exacerbation of a patient's illness may be a result of a family crisis or added family stress. Thus, a "moratorium" from the family can be considered best, and full-time hospitalization is then the treatment of choice. Yet, studies show that family problems are understood and treated with more success when dealt with in family settings (Fink et al., 1978b; Washburn et al., 1976b; Wilder et al., 1966). Alternatively, clinicians are reluctant to refer patients without families or without stable living situations to PHPs.

Clinicians tend toward needing the total control of 24-hour hospitalization. PHPs offer intensive treatment without demanding total control. In addition, Fink and Heckerman (1979) report that patients referred by private psychiatrists tend to have a higher rate of treatment failure. The private psychiatrists seem often to be less committed to the PHP philosophy, and more readily transfer their patients to inpatient care.

PATIENT-FAMILY ISSUES

Families have difficulties in dealing with a severely disturbed family member. While families want the best treatment, they are often unclear as to the factors resulting in it.

Some families and patients may favor the moratorium approach. Some may fear voluntary treatment of PHP, rather than the control offered in hospitalization. The multidisciplinary team used in PHP may be unfamiliar to families who are accustomed to a model of individual treatment by a psychiatrist. Location of PHPs may have disturbing connotations. Close connection to hospitals may remind them of the institution, whereas distance may arouse concern that care received will be less than needed. Even the term "partial hospital" may arouse fears, namely, that a hospital involves crazy people who need extraordinary care. "Partial" may connote less care than is needed. The term chosen for a program may have its own impact on utilization rates (see Chapter 2). Mistrust about innovative group therapies and therapeutic milieus, as well as treatment by nonmedical personnel, is also a concern.

Glaser (1969) proposed that the PHP movement tends to incorporate middle class values and does not attract lower socioeconomic class, at-risk populations. This patient group, already struggling with failure, apathy, and hopelessness in today's society, may strongly feel the necessity to return quickly to household and job responsibilities, following an acute illness. They may not have families sharing tasks, easing their burdens, or the necessary insurance coverage to pay for this type of treatment. Thus, their involvement in PHPs might be considered by them or by families as indulgence or resistance to responsibility. This raises the question of class and culture bias in PHPs, which also has an effect on utilization. Further examination of these biases in treatment should be included in further research.

In conclusion, despite the substantial benefits and services offered by PHPs for patients and staff, there remains significant underutilization. The factors resulting in underutilization are varied and complex. They suggest directions for the future energies of PHPs. The thrust now is to communicate our techniques, ideas, plans, successes, and strengths to the larger mental health field and to the general society.

5

Establishing a Partial Hospitalization Program

The focus of this chapter is establishing a PHP—to offer assistance to those considering beginning a PHP as well as to those interested in reviewing or revising existing programs.

FACTORS LEADING TO THE CREATION OF PHPS AND RELATED PROBLEMS

There are numerous reasons why PHPs are created. Among these are the clinical benefits derived from partial hospitalization over other types of programs (Preface and Chapters 2, 3 and 4). Indications for utilizing partial hospitals are found in Chapter 16. Also, adequate finances (Chapter 23) are essential for planning a successful PHP.

In addition to the factors cited above, others may be operating which will affect the direction and outcome of a new PHP. Among the less obvious factors in creating a PHP are the following:

1) There is a tendency on the part of professional organizations to keep up with trends. Thus PHPs may be established not because of their clinical value, but primarily because it is "the thing to do." To follow this line of thinking, it is possible, when trends change, that PHPs might be phased out to make way for the "latest" treatment technique. If this is the case, consistent time and effort will need to be expended to illustrate the real value of PHPs to those in positions of authority.

2) PHPs may be started with inadequate or shaky funding. This can result in early pressures to recruit and maintain a full patient census. Aside from the emotional and physical energy involved in this pressure, inadequate funding often precludes sufficient staff to work on developing sources of referral. Similarly, a goal for the PHP may be selected (e.g., providing a crisis/stabilization program),

---

We are thankful to the following colleagues with whom we consulted on the writing of this chapter: E. Cohen, O.T.R.; R. Cutick, Ph.D.; R. Johnson, R.N., M.S.; N. Kushner, M.A.; B. Russek, M.A.; M. Thrash, M.D.; and Y. VonCort, O.T.R.

but with resources adequate to provide only a long-term, maintenance program (see Chapter 14). Rather than consenting to try to begin a quality PHP with such poor planning and provisions, it would be wise to spend time with the controller of funding before starting the program, in order to insure allocation of more adequate and appropriate resources. Other alternatives to this problem include revising program goals, thereby making them consistent with available resources, or devising ways of increasing resources to meet program goals (see Chapter 23).

3) Many additional and related problems arise because the people overseeing and/or funding PHPs lack the clinical expertise to enable them to have realistic expectations of programs. For example, a governing board (or equivalent) may expect a well-functioning PHP in two weeks, whereas it takes many (six to 12) months for this to occur. Full patient census may not be reached or maintained for a number of months. These time frames indicate an appreciation of the complexities and developmental processes which accompany the creation of a PHP even with the hiring of an experienced, well-trained staff.

NEEDS ASSESSMENT AND TARGET POPULATIONS

Assessment of patient, community, and agency needs should precede establishment of a service such as a PHP. When doing a needs assessment, the following are points to keep in mind:

1) Are there groups of patients (e.g., those with acute or chronic emotional problems, alcoholics, adolescents, and the elderly) for whom there are no available or appropriate services?
2) What are the specific needs of these patients, e.g., all-day, evening, or weekend programs, only certain forms of psychotherapy?
3) Does the organization have a commitment to provide services to these patients?
4) Would provision of services to these patients relieve some of the stress felt in other parts of the organization (emergency rooms, medical, outpatient clinics, inpatient services, etc.), thereby increasing the likelihood of organizational support for the new service?
5) Would the provision of these services be cost-effective, and therefore a potential financial asset to the organization?

It is crucial that a PHP be clear about the needs which exist, those which it has agreed to fulfill, and the target population it is to be serving. It is helpful to have these clearly spelled out in program proposals and descriptions, which should be required before final approval for funds is granted and before the program can formally begin (Stemple and DeStefane, 1978). Following this process, a clear rationale and realistic goals are developed for the PHP, based on the needs assessment.

Despite the specific type of program that is finally chosen, many look upon PHPs as cure-alls, where the most difficult ambulatory problems are referred, often as the last resort. Some may consider a PHP as meeting a community's need to clear the streets of "homeless undesirables," many of whom are inaccessible to traditional outpatient treatment but who are also not necessarily appropriate candidates for a PHP. Decisions not to admit patients with certain problems (and neglecting the necessary public relations work) can result in referring sources questioning a PHP's "selectivity" and feeling a program is not responsive to the needs of patients who desperately require help. One answer to this problem is to do adequate work with referral sources. To assume professional responsibility for treating patients with special or specific problems which staff are not adequately prepared to handle is not responsible, and can ultimately be damaging to both the patient and the program. If there is a distinct need for certain other types of services, a program should be designed to meet such needs, possibly sharing PHP space, utilizing different hours, and either training PHP staff in the treatment of the special problems or hiring additional staff with expertise in the specialized area. Exceptions to this occur; for example, PHPs located in a rural area, or in areas where other specialized services are not available, may be forced to accept an extremely heterogeneous patient population.

STAFF SELECTION AND OTHER ISSUES

Once a PHP has been given official sanction for program initiation, it is faced with the tasks of selecting staff members and obtaining other resources. It is recommended that at least two staff be involved in interviewing all potential staff. Also, involving patients in some aspect of the process can be productive.

Formal professional qualification is difficult to determine at best. Nonetheless, there should be a review of credentials and several professional references, as well as the way an applicant verbally integrates knowledge into valid, coherent clinical approaches. The discussion of a sample case, group or family, from an applicant's work experience may be used, or a mock or actual case may be given to the applicant by the interviewer.

In the following section, consideration will be given to the general traits to be looked for in any potential staff member for PHP work, leadership qualities to be sought in the director of the program, and, finally, the use of volunteers. After each quality is mentioned, there will be a discussion and some suggestions for evaluating the interviewee for this trait.

Desirable general traits are the following:

1) Adequate personal adjustment. Is the prospective staff member emotionally stable enough to meet his own needs well enough outside work hours to be able to give the proper amount of physical, emotional, and intellectual energy to the intense work of a PHP? We make no pretense to expound a set of criteria which will allow for completely accurate prediction in this area; however, we do suggest that sound clinical assessment skills need to be brought into full play. Direct questions need to be asked to the prospective employee about personal strengths and weaknesses—has he been in psychotherapy, what has he learned about himself that might affect his PHP work? Concurrently, what are the observations of the interviewer and how do these observations coincide with the statements by the interviewee? Likewise, what are the opinions of reference sources concerning the applicant's level of personal adjustment? A personal call to these sources should be made if at all feasible.

2) Interest and caring for people. Formal professional or paraprofessional training in the helping professions does not guarantee an individual's automatic concern about effective patient treatment. Motivations do vary for entering the helping professions. Information can be gleaned in this area from the affective content of an interviewee's presentation of his work with patients.

3) Intellectual curiosity. In an area of such rapid change as the mental health field, a changing and expanding knowledge base is necessary if a clinician is to be current in his clinical practice. Questions that may relate to this area include a discussion of the partial hospitalization and mental health publications the interviewer usually and currently reads, the nature of his past reading, whether he has a particular area of interest that he would like to pursue, and how he plans to keep abreast of the field.

4) Job management skills. It is important to know how easily and comfortably an individual performs the total range of tasks necessary for his job. If these require excessive time and energy of an individual, he will certainly have little energy left for his work with patients. As to the simpler tasks, it is important to have an understanding of an individual's capacity to chart notes, be accurate and current on other required written material, submit required forms through the right channel at the right time, and so on. At a higher level of job management, it is important to understand issues such as how an individual is able to set priorities for his work, compromise with fellow employees when indicated, keep supervisory personnel informed of problematic areas in his functioning and how he is taking responsibility to correct problems, as well as identifying his own learning needs and how they can be met within the strictures of the setting.

After a general screening, with the above points used as guidelines, focus is needed on an applicant's strengths specifically pertaining to PHP.

Knowledge About and Commitment to PHP Treatment

Does the applicant have at least minimal intellectual, if not experiential, under-standing of the basic structure and process of most PHPs? How does he believe PHPs might be effective in helping patients make changes? Is he willing to invest himself in the successful operation of the PHP system and develop into something more than an independent practitioner?

Role Augmentation

Is the applicant prepared to utilize himself in the varied groups, informal pro-gram interactions and community contacts that are necessary, even though they may not be part of his conceived professional role identification? By participiating in the leadership of a variety of groups, PHP staff (a) gain a more complete evalua-tion of each patient in their program; (b) convey to patients that all the groups are equally important; and (c) are better able to provide for continuity of group leader-ship when other group leaders in the program are away for vacations, illnesses, etc. For these reasons, it is strongly suggested that each PHP staff member be prepared to lead at least one activity and one verbal treatment group in the pro-gram if possible.

Ability to Deal With Ongoing Staff Conflict and Competitiveness

It is important to acknowledge that, even in the most ideal situation, staff members trained in the traditional disciplines, working closely together over an extended period of time each day, are going to get involved in conflict and com-petition over issues such as competency, professional jurisdiction, and treatment approach. The issue then becomes what skills does the applicant possess that will allow him to identify difficulties with collaboration and work them through to resolution, so that staff interactional problems are not channeled into patient treatment and staff conflict and competition do not absorb so much energy that there is little left over to invest in patients or program development?

Community Interphasing

Since PHPs strive to relate their programs to community living, they require an active clinician who can establish and maintain community contacts in such areas as obtaining supplies and acquiring medical, financial, and housing supportive ser-vices. Work is needed with families and vocational rehabilitation services, as well as community planning groups, merchants, and influential political figures. At some level all staff will be involved in community linking; therefore they need to possess leadership skills in being able to establish and maintain relationships with the above types of agencies and individuals.

Leadership Potential

PHP staff members need to provide leadership in terms of identifying problem areas in the PHP of which they are a part and suggesting creative solutions. One director or just a few staff members are not able to do this effectively.

In addition to all the above characteristics, the program director should be considered for his abilities in the following areas:

1) Understanding of how to establish productive relationships with pertinent governing, regulating, and funding figures critical to the survival of the program.
2) Ability to provide reliable, clear, confident leadership without being authoritarian. This will involve being a leader to staff with very different levels and types of training.
3) Appreciation for and understanding of supervision as a motivating and developing process that encourages clinicians to become more effective in their work, thereby attaining maximum job satisfaction and making optimal investment in the PHP.
4) Adequate appreciation of all treatment modalities and the ability to integrate these into a coherent whole.
5) Appreciation for programmatic goals and evaluation besides individual treatment goals, and the ability to manage these effectively.

Lastly, volunteers, students, trainees, and others who give their services essentially without monetary rewards should be considered as valuable potential resources for PHP staffing. They can help in alleviating the staff shortages that face most PHPs because of low funding; they can also add new perspectives to programming and patient care. Their usual vitality and eagerness can be rejuvenating, and they provide extra stimulation in the form of teaching opportunities. However, a major consideration is to avoid the frequently-made error of not making every effort to integrate them, as much as possible, with other PHP staff, thereby causing them to feel that they are not a legitimate and valuable part of the program. A positive attitude toward volunteers, students, etc. can be fostered by treating them as team members from the beginning and carefully planning their assignments and responsibilities. This means that the initial interview(s) should seriously evaluate whether the prospective individual is suited to work in the program, and whether the program will meet his needs.

Finally, and perhaps most importantly, provision must be made for his ongoing supervision. The volunteer or student comes to the PHP expecting to get something for himself, as well as to give something to the program. If he is not given regular input in terms of gaining a fuller understanding of the PHP patients and their behavior, as well as improving his skill levels, it is likely he will soon become frustrated and either reduce his investment in the PHP or withdraw completely and seek a clinical experience elsewhere.

PHYSICAL RESOURCES

A common complaint by PHP staffs is that they are given minimal (or less) amounts of the physical resources needed in order to establish and maintain a program. Further, it is common among administrators of unfunded organizations to wait until the PHP has proved its need, rather than supply and fund the program adequately from its inception. Where will physical resources come from? If a program waited until it had all its needed resources, it would most likely never get off the ground. With this in mind, the following section gives some consideration to the absolute minimal amount of physical resources a program should have before considering opening its doors.

Minimal Requirements

Adequate space. Meeting JCAH, state, local, and perhaps other standards is required; however, rarely are these specific enough, and other considerations need to be made. First, is there a room large enough for the entire community of staff and patients to meet together at the same time? This will be important at times of community meeting, meetings with families, as well as large-scale activities and recreational projects. Second, are there separate rooms available for simultaneously running groups? Since many programs strive to individualize patient needs, they may have two or more groups running concurrently and therefore will need enough separated, private space to do so. A meeting space where there is the constant disruption from outside noises, telephone calls, typewriters, and conversations of secretarial and clerical personnel is inadequate. Third, besides meeting minimal fire and safety requirements, the space must be appropriately heated, cooled, lighted, and ventilated. PHPs normally have art or cooking groups which use pungent substances that can be stifling unless cleared away. Additionally, stagnant, cigarette-smoke-filled rooms can be a real health hazard. Finally, space must also be planned for other functional needs—staff and patient retreats, offices, coat closets, quiet room, waiting room, pharmacy and nursing needs, record keeping, etc. Because of these needs, an architectural consultation before lease signing is wise and well worth the financial investment.

Adequate storage. If supplies and partially completed projects cannot be adequately stored, they soon become misplaced, damaged, or lost. This not only promotes frustration among staff and patients, but more importantly it is counter-therapeutic to the efforts normally being made to promote patients' accepting responsibility and developing organizational skills and self-esteem. Storage equipment does not need to be expensive. Adequate space has been developed from metal stack shelves as well as interlaced bricks and boards. Special provision needs to be made for the storage of valuables such as petty cash and other monies, for potentially dangerous objects like knives, saws, and hammers, and for combustibles such as paints and glue.

Kitchen and bathroom. Because food is such an integral treatment part of a PHP, there needs to be the availability of reliable, safe, sanitary kitchen equipment, utensils and work space. Likewise, there should be suitable restrooms available for both men and women. Hopefully, these would be as spacious as possible as they might be used as part of the personal grooming aspect of some programs.

Adequate furniture. One safely constructed chair for each member of the community is essential. Strange messages are conveyed to patients about their value in the program when there is not at least a safe place for them to sit. Likewise, there should be enough well-constructed small and large tables for cooking projects, recreational activities, and various vocational projects. In addition to the utilitarian furniture described above, it is highly desirable to have a few pieces of lounge furniture available for rest and "escape" periods.

Adequate bulletin board and display space. Because sound communication is so vital in a PHP, there should be some structure available where notices, schedules, plans, announcements, etc. can be placed and altered. Simple bulletin boards can be constructed out of very basic materials. Also, because patient projects and project completion are such an important part of the treatment aspects of a program, there must be locations for these projects to be displayed and recognized. Included here would be adequate wall space that is suitable for individual pictures and group murals (preferably a glossy surface wall), as well as display shelves for craft projects.

Recreational, occupational and vocational supplies and equipment. Minimal amounts and types in this area will vary from program to program. On a general scale, there should be supplies and equipment to allow for a diverse number of indoor and outdoor activities, for large groups or for two or three members. Also, there should be games that lend themselves to various gradations of competition —cards, Monopoly games, volleyball, etc. In the art area, there again should be supplies available for large scale group projects, such as murals which stress social cooperation, to usable individual project materials such as paper flowers, ash trays, and vases, which stress individual accomplishment and self-esteem building. Concurrently, there should be adequate supplies available to complete whatever project is started. It can be extremely frustrating for a patient to start knitting a red scarf and before completion find that only brown skeins of yarn remain to complete the project, and it is likely that the red yarn may never be ordered again. Special plumbing facilities, such as occupational therapy sinks with oversized drains, should be available in order to allow for as wide a range of art activities as possible. Also, pre-vocational testing materials should be readily available.

Clerical supplies.   Valuable PHP time should not be spent looking for an adequate number of pens, pencils, paper, thumb tacks, etc. A regular supply of these items should be assured.

Personal care items.   Combs, safety razors, hair dryers, sewing kits, etc. are essential for teaching personal care skills. Since it might be difficult to have enough of these for every member, there should be facilities and materials available to appropriately maintain and clean personal care items so that they can be used by a number of PHP patients.

Petty cash.   A small amount of ready cash is essential in order to purchase depleted supplies before the next regular order arrives. Other needs for quick money also arise, such as emergency transportation funds for patients, or food and drink expenses for patients who might be in crisis.

Where to Obtain Resources

If the central funding sources do not supply what is needed, the following suggestions are offered as potential areas for obtaining some of these resources. Obviously, these are broad possibilities and the wisdom for using them will depend upon the geographical location and type of PHP.

PHP patients and their families.   It is not unusual for patients and families to respond to simple appeals, at family night meeting, for instance, for cooking utensils and secondhand furniture, as well as foodstuffs and refreshments. Also, families can sometimes give their time to develop neighborhood resource possibilities. Such involvement of families at this level may encourage more investment in the program and patients' progress in the PHP.

Patient fund-raising projects.   Bake sales, craft fairs, coffee canteens, raffles, and many other patient-run projects can be quite effective in fund-raising. Likewise, they encourage the broader therapeutic goals.

Staff donations.   PHP staff are willing to donate a variety of materials if an appeal is made, especially when there is the incentive of income tax deductions. One program made such an appeal and obtained cooking utensils, a piano, a type-writer, lounge furniture, art supplies, food, and pre-vocational testing materials. At times, the problem becomes one of transportation of large items in order to obtain them, but again such facilities may be obtained from families if the PHP is unable to make provision.

Community agencies and merchants. Churches, YMCAs, and community service centers have been known to give low cost or free gymnasium, recreational, or cooking space and materials during slow periods when their facilities are not being used. The key issue in obtaining these is the initial and ongoing liaison work that needs to be done to explain the program and alleviate common fears that PHP patients destroy property, or that others who use the facility may be physically or verbally abused by PHP members. Also, local merchants might provide such items as refreshments, clerical supplies, furniture, or recreational and art supplies.

Charitable organizations. Charitable and fraternal organizations should be approached to consider the entire or part sponsorship of a PHP. An organization may consider making an annual drive for the PHP, or choose a "pet project" such as obtaining lounge furniture or pre-vocational evaluation equipment.

Existing public resources. Parks, beaches, public recreation, and picnic areas, etc. can be integral parts of the activity section of a PHP. Some programs are known to have an entire weekly day's schedule of events outside the PHP agency. In some locations, stores, launderettes, and restaurants are ideally situated for developing activity of daily living skills. Finally, free and low cost events such as concerts, sports events, and boat trips are common to many communities and can be used to further develop socialization skills, as well as help many low income patients become aware of community entertainments resources within their budgets.

Further possibilities for obtaining resources can be found in Chapter 23.

PROGRAM LIAISON AND PROCEDURE FOR ADMISSIONS

Key to the initial phase of a PHP, as well as its continued development, is an adequate supply of appropriate referrals and a clear referral procedure. These do not come with little effort. Referrals can potentially come to a PHP from any number of agencies, clinics, inpatient services, and private practitioners, and each type should be identified. When different levels of care are provided for under the same administrative auspices and continuity of care is emphasized, a patient moves relatively easily from the organization's inpatient service to its PHP or out-patient clinic. Or, a patient can be screened by the setting's central screening services and placed directly in the PHP. The referral sources become more complex and numerous when the PHP is not so closely tied to a network of services of care and is more open to direct referral from the community.

In any case, liaison work would include the same points.

1) There is the educative component for referral sources to understand the PHP's purposes and goals and vice-versa. Inherent in this is a joint effort to see how their treatment efforts can supplement and complement each other and how they can avoid duplicating and subverting one another. For example, it is not unusual for inpatient units and PHP staffs to feel some degree of competition with each other until they more clearly work out their separate and distinct roles in the treatment process. Education can be promoted by staff presentations to one another, as well as visiting each other's programs on a rotation basis. Educative work between staffs is continuous since programs, as well as staffs, change from time to time. For this reason, in addition to staff's general tendency to forget during stress periods, the PHP should have goals, purposes, referral processes, etc. clearly written up and available to referral sources.

2) Liaison work is facilitiated by establishing an identified person from the referral source who keeps abreast of changes and general information about the PHP. He is then able to relate this information to the staff on his unit. He can also facilitate the referral process by discussing questionable referrals with the clinicians in his setting before they make the referral. Finally, if he is kept aware of referral problems by the PHP, he may prevent these in the future by working more closely on the identified areas with his staff. Similarly, one PHP staff should be assigned to each referral source.

3) The referral process is made easier if both staffs have a clear understanding of what the referral procedure is. Below, we suggest a referral process that is effective and efficient. The particular example involves a patient on an inpatient service who is being referred to the PHP before discharge from the hospital.

(a) Inpatient staff determine the need for PHP treatment and conceptualize this in the discharge plan. They may use the regular PHP referral form as a guide for making their decision.
(b) Staff discuss their reasons for PHP with the patient, patient's family and inpatient treatment team.
(c) If agreeable to all concerned, the inpatient worker contacts the PHP intake worker and discusses the appropriateness of the patient for the PHP.
(d) If deemed appropriate from this contact, the inpatient worker fills out a brief referral form and arranges for an intake date for the patient.
(e) Referral forms are sent in advance of the patient to the PHP, and the patient attends an individual and/or group intake. Plans are made for family involvement at this point.

(f) The patient visits the PHP and attends sample groups as well as informal gatherings, such as coffee breaks.
(g) After considering PHP patient input, PHP staff then make a decision as to the suitability of the applicant, and the PHP intake worker discusses the decision with the inpatient worker.
(h) If appropriate, a beginning date is established for the patient.

Inherent in this referral process are a number of understandings, on which the PHP staff should work consistently to help the referring sources. First, when PHP is presented to the patient and his family, as well as the inpatient staff, it is presented as an alternative being considered and not as a final conclusion. This allows the PHP staff to feel more comfortable in rejecting the referral if they feel the patient would not succeed in the program. Also, it allows the patient to feel less of a sense of rejection since this would be only one of several post-hospitalization alternatives being considered. Second, the intake screening process is usually not accomplished in a day—in fact, at least a week may be necessary for some programs—so inpatient staff members will need to consider this time frame in their discharge planning. The time may be longer if there are waiting lists.

Next, because there is an ongoing understanding of each other's programs, rejection of referrals from the inpatient service will be minimal due to their knowledge of how to make appropriate referrals. Referral forms are kept very brief and include only essential clinical information necessary to make a decision regarding admission to PHP. This will allow the inpatient staff not to become overwhelmed with paper work; thus, they can forward the referral information to the PHP staff for evaluation prior to the arrival of the patient. Making inpatient charts available to PHP staff prior to intake is also helpful. Lastly, the purpose of the patient's visit is two-sided. Not only will PHP staff and patients be making a decision about the patient's admission to the program, but the patient will also be deciding if it meets his needs and if he will fit into the program and be comfortable with it.

ESTABLISHING EFFECTIVE CRITERIA FOR PATIENT ADMISSIONS

Once a PHP has arrived at a clear understanding of the needs of the patient population it is to serve, the next task involves establishing admissions criteria which reflect the purpose and goals of the program. It is important for criteria to retain some flexibility, yet it is also important that they are complete and clear enough to minimize inappropriate referrals or admissions. Chapter 15 indicates many different areas for which criteria should be specified. Specificity is often lacking from criteria, which results in time-consuming work around each new situation.

Admissions criteria, while helpful in assessing suitability for PHP admission, are only part of the admissions process in most programs; there is also usually at least one intake interview, with at least one staff member, and whenever possible including PHP patients. The objective written admissions criteria are thereby complemented by a subjective in-person interview, where it is essential for staff to keep their personal biases in check. Patients are occasionally screened out not by objective criteria but due to some countertransferential reactions—for example, "I've never seen such an obese person; she would take up too much space;" "I wouldn't want to be seen in public with him;" "Too many suicide attempts—I couldn't stand it if someone killed themselves while in our program;" or, "I can't stand chain-smokers."

One may argue that such comments, if openly expressed, are unprofessional and that a true professional would be able to assess a patient's suitability for PHP with much greater objectivity. It is our impression that the above examples are very real and common types of reactions, expressed or denied, to which even seasoned, highly qualified professionals are subject. One possible reason for this has to do with the intensive family-like atmosphere in PHPs (see Chapters 9 and 25). It becomes a situation of enforced intimacy, and individuals—staff and patients—must be able to tolerate at least physical closeness, such as sitting together, cooking and eating together, and often sharing bathroom facilities. This adds a dimension of reality to transference and countertransference that is not found in most other therapeutic settings. This can be threatening to individuals (patients and staff) who may try to maintain some sense of control over group composition by excluding deviants from a desired PHP culture. Thus, not everything can be included in the written admissions criteria.

STAFF BEGINNINGS AND RECOMMENDED STAFF MEETINGS

The fact that all staff do not enter a PHP with the same philosophy, information and knowledge base is too often unappreciated (Goldberg, 1977). This can lead, in some instances, to frustration, a heightened sense of mistrust, and inconsistencies in patient care. This problem may not be obvious. Many staff in initial phases of programming are reluctant to share uncertainties and questions, feeling they may appear inexperienced or unsophisticated to their colleagues. Disagreements are often avoided, as staff is working hard on developing a team.

One method which can be effective in assessing and addressing these potential problems is for staff to spend time together (before patient treatment begins, if possible) discussing the following issues:

1) What is partial hospitalization?
2) Which patients are we offering services to and what are some of their problems and needs?
3) What is the purpose of activity groups, and of verbal groups?

4) Why are we developing certain group activities and not others?
5) Why is group therapy the preferred treatment modality?
6) Will we offer individual sessions; if so, what purpose will they serve?
7) How will we involve families or significant others?
8) Who are we, as staff, and what are our roles in the PHP, as individuals and as a team? What is teamwork?
9) Do we understand the funding and standards requirements?
10) Do we understand the place of PHP in the larger system?

Agreeing on meanings of PHP terminology (e.g., "therapeutic milieu," "systems," "team," "chronic," etc.) is a crucial component to implementing an effective program. Numerous other related topics can be discussed which will foster a sense among staff that they are starting at the same place and attempting to function as a team from the outset, in a mutual struggle to comprehend and implement the fundamentals of the PHP.

Since people are people, initial staff development parallels the process of new patient groups. Similarities (parallels) in group process can be utilized by staff to help them better understand what the staff team, the patient group, and the entire community is struggling with.

Recommended Staff Meetings

New PHPs are immediately concerned with the number and focus of staff meetings. Newness creates anxiety in most people, and new programs with new staff often feel the need to meet frequently, to allay anxieties and establish commonalities. Staff may spend hours talking with each other on the telephone about the PHP, after working hours. This behavior usually subsides when staff begin to feel more secure in their working relationships and in their competence as a therapeutic team.

Programs vary considerably in the amount of time allotted for staff meetings. While always considered essential, staff meetings can take time away from direct patient care, particularly if they require excessive time (more than ten hours per week in a full-time, 35-40-hour-per-week PHP). In a new PHP, the time needed for staff meetings may be doubled for the first three months or so. The following types of staff meetings are suggested in order to cover the basic needs of most PHPs.

1) Intake Conference (1-2 hours per week). This meeting is held to discuss PHP applicants, and decide on PHP suitability and initial treatment goals and plans. It may be held once weekly or more or less often, depending on the number and frequency of intake interviews. The entire PHP clinical staff should attend intake conferences, as an introduction to potential new patients and to insure input from all staff in patient screening, admissions and preliminary treatment planning.

2) Treatment Planning Conference (1-1½ hours per week). This meeting focuses on discussing patients in depth for a better understanding of diagnostic and behavioral issues, and formulation of treatment plans, including discharge planning. Staff may prepare recommendations for Patient Evaluation Groups (see Chapter 19) in this meeting also. It is essential, for consistent treatment approaches, for all clinical staff to attend this meeting. Consultants are sometimes helpful here as well.

3) Individual/Group Supervision (1-1½ hours per week). See Chapter 25 for discussion of supervision of PHP staff.

4) Program Evaluation and Planning (2-3 hours every 1-3 months). Programming is reviewed or revised and plans made for improving the program. Administative issues, such as budget, supplies, and vacation schedules, are discussed as well.

5) Daily Summary Group (½ hour per day). At the end or beginning of the program day, this group is held to identify particular patient issues, themes, and so forth, in order to provide treatment continuity. This group can be effectively replaced by open rounds (see Chapter 18).

6) Record Maintenance (1-3 hours per week). This group is often not identified as a formal meeting time; however, it is recommended that it be formalized (see Chapter 22).

IMPLEMENTING EFFECTIVE COMMUNICATION SYSTEMS
IN THE PHP COMMUNITY

PHPs seem chronically plagued by problems of unclear communication. This may appear in regard to announcements ("I forgot to tell the group I wouldn't be in yesterday") and scheduling ("How often must I say I never attend on Fridays?"). The sources of these problems may be varied and complex. They may involve issues of avoidance or withdrawal due to anxiety generated by events in PHP, or resistance to being accountable to a group (see Chapter 7), or, as will be discussed in this section, they may be related to the lack of concrete provision of means for improving communication.

Nonverbal and technical means can be adopted to facilitate clear communication. For example, a PHP might consider utilizing the following:

1) Bulletin boards;
2) "Logs" (community notebooks to record announcements, messages, etc., which are available to all PHP members and can be read by individuals or aloud to the entire community group);

3) Attendance rosters;
4) Time set aside specifically for making announcements (scheduling changes, vacations, appointments and trips);
5) Taking minutes of some meetings as well as reliably taken and posted telephone messages;
6) Clear program schedules which are visible;
7) Daily announcements recorded on blackboards, which are centrally located;
8) Individual or group future events recorded on large-scale calendars, the making of which can be a useful group project.

Providing combinations of such techniques for clarifying communication within the community allows the following to come across: "We are providing clear direction. Now it is up to you to take advantage of the content and direction indicated." Thus, part of improving patient functioning involves being able to adhere to schedules and routines and account for oneself. Providing adequate means for this to be accomplished removes excuses such as, "I didn't know, it wasn't written down," and "No one told me." It also conveys the message that patients and staff are working together toward improving functioning through good communication patterns.

ESTABLISHING A PHP IN RURAL AND OTHER SPECIAL SETTINGS

Most of the points made in this chapter thus far relate to establishing PHPs in general. There are, however, some special concerns to be considered when beginning a PHP in rural or other less typical types of settings. Although recent literature is generally quite limited in this regard, it is recommended that one refer to the Annual Proceedings of the American Association for Partial Hospitalization for, among other topics, relevant recent information on establishing PHPs in a variety of settings.

Many of the points outlined below are presented in greater detail by Stemple and DeStefane (1978) and Kjenaas (1980) and apply to establishing a PHP in a rural American setting.

1) Due to large rural geographic size and an inversely proportional population size, transportation poses considerable problems in terms of availability, distance, and cost.
2) PHP staff recruitment and retention can be problematic since most professional training programs are in metropolitan areas, where most continuing education programs and social and cultural resources are located.
3) Professionals in rural areas can feel isolated and unsatisfied, leading to a reported high incidence of staff turnover.

4) Specialized facilities are scarce; thus, there is an expectation that PHPs treat everyone, including the mentally retarded, adolescents, alcohol and drug abusers, and chronic and acutely ill psychotic patients, simultaneously.
5) Continuity of care after discharge may be more difficult, due to scarcity of community resources.
6) There is generally a greater degree of stigma attached to mental health in rural areas, and entire communities are likely to know who is receiving mental health care, which is often viewed with suspicion, apprehension, and as "outside interference."

Those professionals who reside in rural areas by choice can find these settings challenging and rewarding, particularly if a PHP is part of a primary health care facility. However, recognition of special problems, understanding, generous creativity, and extra expenditures are necessary in order to overcome the obstacles inherent in establishing a PHP in less typical, particularly rural, areas.

II

Theory: The Basic Foundations of Partial Hospital Treatment

6

The Use of Groups in
Partial Hospitalization

At present, PHPs generally utilize milieu therapy and group psychotherapies as the primary treatment modalities. What may be unclear, however, is the reasoning for the use of the group method, in relation to any given single group in a program, and to the system of interconnected groups in an entire program, and as the foundation for the therapeutic milieu.

In order to gain a fuller understanding of the above areas, this chapter will discuss the single group and interconnected groups. Chapter 7 will explore various aspects of the therapeutic milieu. Finally, Chapter 8 will present a hypothetical day in a PHP.

RATIONALE FOR GROUP TREATMENT

PHP by very definition is a group, and the use of the group as a treatment method implies a certain theoretical belief about the origin of psychological problems and how they are best approached in treatment. PHP clinicians stress in one way or another that an individual's psychological problems result from, and/or reflect, a problematic relationship with his social environment. Vinter (1967) states that all alterable behavior is begun and sustained by social interactions. Others in the environment play a highly significant role in whether or not an individual will choose to express a particular type of behavior. Therefore, the implication for change intervention is that the interactions of the whole social network will need to be considered. Cumming and Cumming (1967) indicate ego growth occurring in the individual who moves from states of disequilibrium to reequilibrium as a result of his interactions with those in his environment.

In summary, what counts is the overt behavior of the individual in relationship to the environment. What goes on within the individual intrapsychically is valueless *per se*. Because of this belief in the interactional foundation of psychological problems, it logically follows that therapy should directly approach the interaction with the environment, especially interaction with other people. This is best achieved by a group of people in treatment together. This belief also implies that group treatment is considered valid and complete within itself and, more often than not, does not require the concurrent use of ongoing, regularly scheduled, formalized, individual treatment. Indeed, concurrent individual treatment usually turns out to be countertherapeutic, especially if laborious and continuous extra efforts are not made to coordinate the two treatments. This is so because individual therapy provides the patient with so much opportunity to escape the presentation of problems in group (since they have been previously presented in individual treatment) and to escape the degree of involvement necessary for effective group treatment. Splitting of treatment easily leads to confusion, when a patient presents only partial facts in each treatment situation, and to self-deception that he is working on problems when, in fact, the patient is resisting doing so.

In terms of clinical effectiveness, most PHP therapists contend that when a patient's psychological problems have been approached at the social/interactional level, changes can be brought about in the patient's situation more rapidly in group treatment than in individual treatment. There are a number of studies that could be used to support this position. For example, O'Brien et al. (1972) found that post-state-hospitalized patients treated in outpatient psychiatric clinics improved significantly more when treated by group treatment vis-à-vis individual treatment. May's (1976) study of effective treatment for schizophrenics indicated similar findings.

NINE ADVANTAGES OF THE SINGLE GROUP

Empirically over the years, PHP workers have become increasingly impressed by the special therapeutic powers inherent in groups. These are presented below.

1) The individual has the opportunity to receive support not only from the therapist, but from a number of others as well. The support may be as simple as firsthand knowledge that others in the world also have difficulties. For the newly discharged, long-term hospitalized patient referred to a PHP, a lessening of his sense of isolation may be the single most important factor in his recovery.

2) Groups give greater opportunity to reduce inappropriate dysfunctional interactions (such as shyness, silence, or withdrawal) with real people who are not professional psychotherapists. Peer pressure is present and available for use.

3) The group provides an excellent opportunity for reality testing. Individuals come to the group from varied social and psychological backgrounds and bring with them the results of these experiences. Thus, the individual has the opportunity to test his reality against that of others, making modifications and additions to his views and philosophies.

4) Groups provide an immediate opportunity for individual processing of information that has just been given in the group. Wolf (1975) indicates that the focus

of attention changes from member to member in the group, thus allowing individuals to process what has just been said to them during their nonverbal participation.

5) Groups provide an opportunity for experimentation and practice in the assumption of various roles. The roles are available not only for the individual to experience but also for the examination of others. In groups, skills in listening and conveying feelings are tested with a wider range of people than in individual therapy. In addition, there is occasion for esteem building as the patient gives help to others and receives positive feedback from peers about his concern and/or helpfulness.

6) The group experience provides multiple behavior models with which the group member can identify. Liberman (1972) indicates that our most extensive learning takes place through imitation, modeling, or identification. Further, he stresses that the imitation process is made more effective by having models that have some similarity to the imitator. The implications for group treatment then seem clear. There is a gathering of individuals who share similar, yet also dissimilar, experiences. Their commonality encourages them to trust, share, and be involved with each other, and their dissimilarities provide them with opportunities to learn alternative behaviors, thoughts, and feelings from one another.

7) Reality orientation of the group is strong because transferences are kept in check. This occurs, as Wolf (1975) describes it, because transferences are shared, not only with the authority/parent figure therapist, but also with the sibling-like peers. Gootnick (1975) stresses the importance of decreasing transference to one person in working with schizophrenic patients. Because of intense transference often developed in individual treatment, patients become frightened at the disintegration of ego boundaries and therefore disengage themselves from the therapeutic relationship in order to maintain personality integration.

With a different focus, Alikakos (1965) indicates there is a certain pride among members in a group that prevents them from too extensive a regression so they will not lose face in front of their peers. Similarly, there would be less occasion for the patient to experience the frightening engulfment-abandonment fantasies common in one-to-one treatment. He does not have to suffer the frequently overwhelming fear of the loss of a therapist. It would be logical to conclude that because the patient is not expending so much psychic and physical energy in avoiding treatment, anxiety reactions, or acting out, he is more free to engage himself in a therapeutic dialogue.

8) There is some dilution of countertransferential reactions by the use of the group treatment method. Gootnick (1975) indicates this is a natural counterpart of the reduction of the intense transference feelings. The therapist is not subjected to periods of extreme closeness with the patient, often to the point of dependency, sometimes followed by withdrawal from treatment or some other form of acting out. He also does not have to deal with the extreme splitting com-

mon in individual treatment when the patient attempts to recreate the good parent and bad parent in the therapeutic situation. By the same account, the therapist is more able to direct his psychic energy to facilitating the group process in order to further the progress of treatment, rather than expending himself identifying and working on his own countertransference.

9) Groups permit the conservation of financial resources and greater efficiency of staff time. Per hours of therapy given, more people can be treated by fewer personnel in groups as compared with individual treatment. However, the savings are not nearly as great as would first seem evident. Non-patient contact work, such as charted notes, treatment plans, statistical reports, correspondence, etc., must still be completed on each individual patient group. Group members usually do better if they are prepared individually or in small groups in a number of interviews before they enter a group program, and this does take time. Also, depending on the setting, there are occasional crisis contacts and contacts with family members. Individual sessions with a group member may be necessary for doing individual discharge planning and obtaining life support services (such as S.S.I.).

Finally, most groups require some type of advanced planning or preparation. This may vary from the arrangement of a room for the group to the planning for any indicated media or activities.

Often (particularly in government psychiatric settings, where the pressure is great for service and where resources are limited), the notion of using groups for reasons of economy obscures the idea of using groups for their more valuable attributes.

INTERCONNECTED GROUPS

In a partial hospitalization program, groups follow one upon the other, three to five group meetings daily comprising the usual number. If PHP groups are truly interconnected, their attributes would be an intensification of the attributes of each individual group. However, the whole is also greater than the sum of the parts. New attributes emerge when the groups are linked, resulting in carry-over of the same therapeutic messages throughout the group program.

First, as Glaser (1969) points out, the cumulative attendance at a series of groups causes the individual to be more open to investing himself into the group process. He contrasts this to single weekly group participation where the individual has the opportunity to reactivate defenses between group sessions. In effect, some work must begin again because of the regression between sessions. Interconnected groups, meeting many times weekly, make more possible the confrontation of a patient's problems than would be true in a once-a-week group meeting.

If the setting is warm and supportive, relating to a particular problem is easier. There is ample opportunity to support the patient to receive unpleasant information since he has other group situations that day which will help him with his feeling of isolation or fear of dealing with his identified difficulty.

There is greater probability that more problems can be confronted with patients than in individual therapy group meetings once weekly, with the corresponding possibility of further change by the patient. To illustrate this concept, it might be imagined that patient A was confronted with her overtalkativeness in the morning administrative community meeting and told how it was preventing others in the group from having an opportunity to speak. In the following verbal therapy group, her fears about what might happen if she stopped talking could be explored, and in the summation session at the end of the current events group which follows this, the group might give patient A positive feedback on restraint she may have exercised in order to give others an opportunity to speak.

Next, there is a positive value in experiencing the structured group program. Patients are strongly encouraged to develop enough internal structure by attending the groups so that they will then be well enough equipped to engage themselves in activities after they complete their treatment in the PHP, i.e., a vocational retraining program, employment, household management, or any other task where daily life is experienced in the following of sequences over several hours. This would be most vital, for example, for the chronically handicapped patient who may have spent quite a significant number of years in a psychiatric hospital ward where the only structured activities were meals and medications. Also, the patient may have lived a chaotic community existence of endless welfare hotels, boarding homes or nonstructured home situations. To a greater or lesser extent, such group participation may have a similar value to the more neurotic or borderline personality patient, depending on his ability to structure his time. In addition it is likely that the social skills learned in the intense group participation will have direct application to situations in which the patient will find himself upon termination from the PHP. Maxwell Jones (1952) supports this viewpoint when he speaks of the multiple group experience as being a transition toward other significant groups such as family, employers, or workmates.

To both patients and staff, the interconnected groups should have an evaluative function. Patients attend a variety of types of groups: large groups, medium-sized groups, and small groups; vocational groups, art groups, music groups, trip groups, and game groups. Through such participation there should be some sense developed by the patient with regard to his ability to relate to one or many people verbally, and how he works with others on joint activity projects. Also, he can gain insight into activities from which he may receive self-esteem, as well as knowledge regarding his motor skill developmental level. This information will be helpful not only for his better use of the group program, but also in planning his next step in outside community participation. It will further be useful for vocational planning, recreational planning and even for further therapeutic intervention points that will more than likely follow after his termination from the program.

Lastly, interconnected groups can relate better to the various roles in which an individual will be involved than can an individual group (Glaser, 1969). Groups are provided so that they relate to various needs—vocational, recreational, social, artistic, and so forth. Due to such group specialization, there is more opportunity for effectively addressing the various roles in which the patient is and will be involved. Further, there is less opportunity for the individual to escape or manipulate the therapeutic situation so that he avoids difficult social roles.

7

The Therapeutic Milieu

Interconnected group psychotherapies form the basic structural foundation for the therapeutic milieu, which is essential to any PHP. However, these groups should not be thought of as synonymous with the therapeutic milieu. What is the distinction? Such will be the focus of this chapter.

THERAPEUTIC MILIEU, MILIEU THERAPY, AND THERAPEUTIC COMMUNITY

Cumming and Cumming (1967) indicate that the terms "therapeutic community" and "milieu therapy" have very little real meaning because the terms are used to designate so many different things. For example, at times the term therapeutic community seems to designate the specific treatment technique Maxwell Jones (1952) applied to psychopaths in England in the post-World-War-II period. At other times, it relates to the addition of one or a few group sessions to various programs. Many references indicate that the therapeutic community relates specifically to a hospital setting where the stress is on structuring the treatment framework in order to maximize the opportunities for socioenvironmental influences to become the major agents in the therapeutic process (Wilmer, 1958; Werner et al., 1980; Campbell, 1981). Zietlyn (1967) indicates that therapeutic community has been used confusedly to mean a treatment attitude, a treatment approach that will be used, or a specifically designed unit.

The above are only a few citations from a large body of writings that examine and define the terms therapeutic milieu, milieu therapy and the therapeutic community. Instead of devising yet another term, the phrase "therapeutic milieu" will be used to designate an environment that is therapeutic. This general term seems fairly acceptable throughout the literature and professional practice. Furthermore, it does not seem to suffer from the great number of diverse definitions which have been applied to milieu therapy and therapeutic community. Also, it is not automatically connected to any particular program or patient diagnostic category.

DEFINITION AND ESSENTIAL ELEMENTS
OF A THERAPEUTIC MILIEU

We suggest the following definition: A *therapeutic milieu* is a group treatment environment which is supervised and initially designed by appropriate professionals; it provides a model of the everyday world of reality and maximized opportunities for patients to benefit from their social and physical surroundings.

The following are postulated as necessary and indicated characteristics of a therapeutic milieu, in addition to all the features generally thought to underlie psychiatric treatment:

1) A commitment by the milieu members that milieu therapy is a more important therapeutic process than any individual component therapy.
2) The use of interconnected group psychotherapies that focus on both the intrapsychic and the interpersonal aspects of human functioning.
3) Mutual therapeutic responsibility: maximum patient responsibility for his own behavior, that of his peers, and their mutual destiny in the milieu, including resolving conflicts as they occur.
4) Problem-solving by discussion, negotiation, and consensus, rather than by a few authoritative figures.
5) Community meetings to discuss information and interactions that apply to all staff and patients.
6) Accountability of members for the responsibilities assigned to them by their governing body.
7) Maximum application of milieu events toward success in outside community interactions (with family, friends, employers, etc.).

A therapeutic milieu is not a free-wheeling, completely egalitarian, democratic society which is responsible only to itself for its actions. It is usually responsible and accountable to other authorities outside itself, i.e., hospital boards, administrative policies and mandates, community pressures, etc. Also, there is no implication that staff members should abdicate their professional roles and become patients. Rather, they use their professional expertise to maximize a healthy, responsible therapeutic milieu participation. Similarly, patients do not relinquish their roles as patients, but become more responsible for the actions and feelings of themselves and those who are in the therapeutic milieu.

INTERNAL FORCES ANTAGONISTIC TO A THERAPEUTIC MILIEU

Despite the structures and processes discussed previously that create a therapeutic milieu, there are latent, omnipresent, internal forces that can cause it to be antitherapeutic—frustrating patients' growth or even making them worse.

These forces must be identified. Only then can they be dealt with appropriately so that the milieu does not resemble what Sacks and Carpenter (1974) term a "pseudotherapeutic community."

Main (1946) recognized years ago one of the potentially antitherapeutic forces present in his therapeutic community—the ongoing stress which must be tolerated by staff if they and the patients are to actively struggle with the conflicts and confrontations of their community and attain resolution. The struggle is uncomfortable. It involves fear of loss of patient control, uncertainty, anxiety, and regression. Sacks and Carpenter (1974), in quoting Freud, cite that staff and patients are actively seeking parental figures to help them control impulses, particularly those of a sexual and aggressive nature; therefore they find it far easier and more comfortable for an authority figure staff member to make decisions regarding conflicts. The tendency is always present for one or more staff members to take over decision-making in order to alleviate stress. If staff suddenly find themselves making more decisions than usual or taking the work away from patients in a variety of other ways, they should carefully ascertain that this is not an overreaction to the stress of the milieu at that given moment. By the same token, staff may react to the stress by not providing any type of therapeutic guidance or by expecting patients to do so. The milieu flounders ad infinitum, and the milieu can be said to be antitherapeutic, possibly even physically unsafe for the members. Thus, a proper balance must be found by staff in utilizing their authority. This depends on an assessment of the level of development of the group process as well as the types of patients being treated.

A second antitherapeutic force that is potentially present results from role-blurring (Tulipan and Heyder, 1970). The various types of staff have complex enough conflicts when they are working separately on different issues with the same patients. In the therapeutic milieu, all levels of staff and patients work side by side, and this situation adds another potential area for conflict and uneasiness. The therapeutic milieu is thought to be a system where free-flowing communication of relevant treatment information is crucial and feedback about the effectiveness of clinical interventions is necessary. In order to accomplish this state, a staff member must be able to talk freely with his administrative or supervisory personnel (even if they are doing staff performance evaluations), and with co-workers in different professional disciplines. Evidence of the antitherapeutic aspects of the above includes subtle or overt conflicts between staff members (some of which have no apparent basis), superficial communication between disciplines on treatment issues, no expression of conflict, or subtle or avid competition among staff members for leadership in patient or staff meetings (see Chapter 25).

Third, Sacks and Carpenter (1974) point out that staff and patients can have the same intrapsychic conflicts. When these are discussed in the PHP, this may be more than some staff members can tolerate, especially in consideration of all the other stresses in the milieu. Staff members may handle this poorly by avoidance of the issues raised or retreating into the authority of their professional roles and projecting their own difficulties onto patients. Neither alternative is constructive for treatment. On occasion, these staff tensions can become so great for the vulnerable staff member that he may seek professional help. Some staff, however, who do not have the capacity to do so, may be unable to function or make a suicide attempt (deMare and Kreeger, 1974).

Finally, Skinner (1979) points out a need to be alert to clinicians' misconceptions about the day-to-day appearance of a good therapeutic milieu. If the belief is that the milieu must always be clean and well-organized and that the patients must appear to be behaving, the milieu may be in trouble. Often, such a milieu can only evolve through strong directiveness by staff, which is antitherapeutic for encouragement of individual responsibility. Patients need some independence and opportunity to develop autonomy, even at the expense of some messiness and disorganization for a period of time until they choose to invest in the processes to bring about the changes.

DIFFERENCES BETWEEN A PHP THERAPEUTIC MILIEU AND A THERAPEUTIC MILIEU OF AN INPATIENT HOSPITAL UNIT

While the generic definition for a therapeutic milieu given earlier is equally applicable to an inpatient unit as it is to a PHP, there are a number of differences between the therapeutic milieus of most PHPs and inpatient hospital units. These differences do not imply that they are better or worse.

1) One of the more obvious differences is the greater "outside community" involvement by PHP milieu members as opposed to patients of a hospital milieu. Daily interactions (with family members, friends, landlords, shopkeepers, employers, postmen, bus drivers and policemen, etc.) provide additional material for examination. While the hospital member may have some of these interactions while on passes or leave, he is still a full-time resident of the hospital's therapeutic milieu, and the opportunities are more limited for interaction with the outside community. The treatment implications are obvious. Parallels between difficulties in which the PHP member finds himself in the outside community and difficulties with the PHP can be drawn more quickly and discussed. Such comparing of experiences provides the groundwork for more effective treatment.

2) There is generally a longer stretch of calendar time spent in the therapeutic milieus of PHPs than in those of hospital units. The national trend in the United States is for short periods of psychiatric hospitalization during the acute phase of illness and then a return to the community (Klerman, 1979). PHP therapeutic milieu membership usually covers a period of three to six months, sometimes longer. As Almond (1975) stresses:

The single factor that influences milieu treatment most profoundly is length of stay. In the implementation of a milieu program, this consideration affects every other issue in some way. The role of the milieu in a patient's total experience, and the effect of the individual's stay on the total milieu, determine how intimately these effects can, and should, become interwoven. Specifically, any treatment technique that requires a committed involvement on the part of both patient and staff—including psychotherapy, therapeutic community, token economy—must have time for an interaction to develop. The shorter this time, the more limited will be the involvement and, necessarily, the more one-sided the approach.

Since current inpatient units in general have a short-term, crisis intervention treatment focus, their therapeutic milieus must, by necessity, be oriented more to containment issues such as stabilization and reality testing. Staff must often take a very active, directive role in restraining and limiting patients, particularly those who are actively or potentially assaultive and suicidal. Cohesiveness and leadership roles among patients are more difficult to develop. Individuals are usually self-preoccupied upon entering the hospital, and if they are able to demonstrate leadership skills, they are usually soon thereafter deemed ready for discharge. By contrast, most PHPs have longer periods in which to develop group cohesion, intimacy, and trust and therefore more fully utilize social pressures as change facilitators. Likewise, patient leadership is encouraged and expected. This is not to say that PHPs cannot apply crisis intervention techniques, but these do not generally consume the PHP's attention for long periods of time.

3) The participation of inpatient staffs in joint treatment planning and establishing effective communication is always problematic. It is inordinately difficult and costly to coordinate three shifts of personnel for 24 hours of service, seven days weekly, into a unified treatment effort. Numerous measures, such as change-of-shift logs, informal logs, charted notes, shift reporters, etc., will never be able to be as effective in implementing unified treatment as a single, small, well-coordinated PHP staff. In short, the patients and staff of a therapeutic milieu always benefit from the staff's cohesiveness and suffer when it is disconnected. The chances for staff unity are always greater when the members of a treatment unit can be localized in one place at the same time, resolve their differences and jointly focus their treatment approach.

4) Hospital inpatient wards have long been used as training grounds for psychiatric residents and others. This presents no problem if the trainee is an appropriately participating member of the milieu; however, this is usually not the case. A professional training program often calls for several hours of work with patients on the ward and the remainder of the time spent elsewhere, which has a tendency to weaken the impact of the milieu. In traditional trainee work, the feeling conveyed to the rest of the milieu is that cure results from the therapist's one-

to-one session; the remainder of the activities are, sadly, viewed by patients and staff as time-fillers. All of this, of course, is an anathema to the principles of a therapeutic milieu. Such a tradition of using trainees in this manner in PHP therapeutic milieus is not established on any wide-scale basis.

5) PHP milieus do not normally have the structural elements present in a hospital milieu that convey the messages of patient irresponsibility, lack of control, and sickness. These elements include locked wards, barred windows, seclusion rooms and physical restraint devices. Perhaps most importantly, except for night PHPs, there are usually no, or only one or two, sick beds in PHPs.

6) Patient entrances into and exits from the therapeutic milieu of PHPs tend to be more planned and often involve more patient participation than those of hospital milieus. This is clinically important as an individual's entrance to and exit from a group have much to do with the development of cohesion within the group. Many times discharges from inpatient status are planned quickly due to administrative pressures for keeping the census and length-of-stay figures within acceptable limits. This contributes to members' not making an investment in other members of the milieu because of the constant uncertainty of the composition of the group.

7) The focus of some professional roles is changing somewhat in the milieus of a hospital and a PHP (Epps and Hanes, 1964). The PHP milieu does not have the large number of traditional nursing tasks to attend to, as does the hospital milieu; therefore, nurses are finding themselves being more active as activity and verbal group psychotherapists. Doctors are becoming more involved with families in the PHP. In times past, families turned over the patient to the doctor for his care and treatment in the hospital milieu. Since the PHP milieu only partially cares for the patient's needs, many families look to the doctor for help in how to care for their relative during the many hours when he is not in the PHP.

In summary, historically the term "therapeutic milieu" has been used in such a variety of ways that it has become confusing to the clinician. This should not obscure from us an appropriate consideration of one of the most important elements of a PHP. By using the previously suggested definition of a therapeutic milieu, we are at a better starting point for the goal of establishing a PHP environment that is truly therapeutic.

8

A Day in the Therapeutic Milieu of a Partial Hospitalization Program

To illustrate the therapeutic milieu in operation, four hypothetical members of a partial hospitalization program have been selected, and excerpts from their day in the PHP are described below. It is recognized that the interactions in terms of members' insights and staff interventions have a somewhat idealized quality. Even after a number of months, many days in a therapeutic milieu may not be as productive as the one described.

AN OVERVIEW OF MAJOR THERAPEUTIC MILIEU TECHNIQUES

Special notice should be taken of the following treatment techniques, a number of which are more fully discussed in the chapter.

1) The use of formalized groups to work on problems.
2) The use of informal contacts during unstructured free time for treatment.
3) The constant focusing on members' most prominent conflicts and strengths.
4) The ongoing attempt to engage members into accepting responsibility for their own behavior and for monitoring the behavior of fellow members in the program.
5) The relating of therapeutic milieu life to the outside community life of members.

Informal contacts allow members to relate to one another without the formalized structure and scrutiny of group meetings. Because of their lack of trust in the group, some members may be more likely to reveal concerns in these contacts, where they may feel less guarded. Also, members may use these contacts to "test out," before bringing their problems to groups, i.e., to hear what the concern sounds like when it is spoken, what the initial reaction of others is, etc.

Focusing on a member's most prominent conflicts and strengths is consistent with a rehabilitation philosophy. Because of limited finances and the demand for services, an individual's stay in most PHPs is usually time-limited. Therefore, a refined assessment is done initially and is continuously updated to include the most central conflicts that cause the member to be dysfunctional in the outside community, and how these conflicts can best be approached in the therapeutic milieu. Coping strengths must be constantly identified, as these form the foundation for a member's ability to function and often can be reinforced to maximize coping abilities in the outside community.

The therapeutic milieu only has merit if members can transfer their learning to the broader community. Therefore, connections must consistently be drawn from a member's participation in the therapeutic milieu to his participation in the outside community. One way this is done is by demonstrating or pointing out parallels between PHP behavior and outside community behavior. Also, encouragement is given for bringing in outside family, friendship, acquaintance, and work relationship problems and successes to be shared in the PHP. Not infrequently, homework assignments are given. These are tested in the outside community, and the results are shared with members and staff in the therapeutic milieu. Concurrently, the milieu should foster the members' ownership of their own feelings and behavior and should disallow the projection of ownership to others in the milieu or in the broader community.

In considering the hypothetical day in the PHP, it is helpful to look at a number of specific group techniques that are used to facilitate members' participation in the therapeutic milieu. Rarely are they seen in pure or isolated form. Usually, they appear in combination of two or more of the techniques. They include the following:

1) Letting the group struggle with an issue rather than being rescued by staff members;
2) Focusing tangential group members to the group issues;
3) Retaining role balance—e.g., allowing patients to have leadership responsibility in the group, but not identifying them as additional staff members;
4) Making members responsible for relating to each other rather than through staff members speaking for them;
5) Capitalizing on members' ability to support each other;
6) Therapists disagreeing or asking each other for clarifications in front of the group to promote open communication;
7) Use of humor to decrease tension; and
8) Use of group summation by patients and staff to increase clarity and penetration.

OVERVIEW OF THE SAMPLE PROGRAM, STAFF PATTERNS, AND PATIENTS

The hypothetical therapeutic milieu in this chapter is a half-day program which operates four hours daily, five days per week. There are 20 members and their average stay in the program is four to six months. Members have a variety of diagnoses. Some have had several psychiatric hospitalizations; others have had none. Most are in the lower income brackets. There are both full- and part-time staff members (see Table 1). For the Schedule of Events of the Day, see Table 2.

Table 1
Names and Job Functioning of Staff

Name	Job Function
Elliot	Psychiatrist/half-time
Maxine	Social Worker/full-time
Lynn	Nurse's Aide/full-time
Margaret	Art therapist/full-time
Belle	Receptionist-Secretary/full-time
Bob	Nurse/full-time
Carrie	Vocational Rehabilitation Counselor/half-time

Table 2
Schedule of Events of the Day

Title of Event	Length of Event (minutes)
Administrative Community Meeting	20
Break	5
Open Staff Rounds	25
Break	5
Member Meeting	25
Coffee Break	10
Art Therapy	60
Break	10
Verbal Group Therapy	60
Planning Comittee and Clean-Up	20
Total—	4 hours

Thumbnail Sketches of Four Members

Mary: 35-year-old, single woman whose diagnosis is Major Depressive Disorder, recurrent. Her mother died in an automobile accident when she was two years old. Mary spent many years in foster homes, and she has recently moved to a new independent living arrangement. She has made a number of suicide gestures, but she has never been hospitalized. Almost never has she asked for help beforehand. At times, she presents herself as angry, sarcastic and demanding. At other times, she can be quite warm and giving.

Tom: 22-year-old, single man whose diagnosis is Borderline Retardation and Borderline Personality. Tom has been hospitalized twice in the past four years. He is about to begin a sheltered workshop program, and he will leave the PHP in a few weeks. He is afraid of the workshop program because he thinks he will fail as he has failed at much during his life. He is fearful to bring his concerns to the group because he is not sure if he will be rejected for his anxieties. Further, he has difficulty formulating his feelings and putting these into words.

Susan: 40-year-old, married woman whose diagnosis is Schizophrenic Disorder, chronic undifferentiated type. She has had multiple hospitalizations during the last 15 years. Traditionally, she has not verbalized feelings, particularly angry feelings; rather, she withdraws and becomes silent or delusional. This type of behavior has caused her to be rejected by neighbors, employers, her husband, and her children. Increasingly, she has felt more frightened and abandoned.

Sam: 47-year-old, divorced man whose diagnosis is Generalized Anxiety Disorder and Compulsive Personality. Frequently, he becomes overwhelmed by anxiety to the point that he has been unable to retain a job for more than a month in the past six years. He rarely identifies or demonstrates personal feelings about any issue and intellectualizes much of the time. His intellectualizations come across as condescensions, and he has lost many friends and his wife because of this characteristic. He experiences constant frustration because he has the education, background, and desire to do complex computer programming, yet he has been unable to retain a job in this area. He is fearful that if he succeeds at his vocation, people will expect even more of him, and they will not pay attention to him, as they do when he gives the impression of being inadequate.

THE DAY IN THE THERAPEUTIC MILIEU

Mary is the first to arrive. She is greeted by the receptionist and asked how she likes her new apartment. Mary ignores the question and walks into the large community meeting room. She isolates herself in a corner reading a magazine and does not relate to others who arrive directly after her. Sam and Tom arrive together because Sam is helping Tom learn a new bus route between Tom's home and his new sheltered workshop program. A new member arrives and Tom goes out to the waiting room after he is notified by the receptionist. He is the new member's sponsor and therefore shows him the sign-in roster and begins to introduce him to other members of the community. Mary makes a curt comment to the new member as Tom introduces him to her. Tom's face turns red and he seems speechless for the moment. Everyone else around is silent. At this point, Sam, who is the leader of the community meeting, announces that it is 8:30 A.M. and time to begin the session. Staff and members begin assembling their chairs.

Administrative Community Meeting
(20 minutes)

(The meeting is slow getting started with many long silences.)

Tom: Everything is so gloomy today.
Elliot (psychiatrist): Who else feels as Tom does today?

(There is more silence and then a member states that she is already missing June, a member who is leaving the PHP at the end of the week to enter a vocational rehabilitation program. June is out today because of an intake appointment at her new program. The entire community then begins to talk about missing her because she has been such a strong member of the program, always taking responsibility for many projects and having been a real leader. As the above discussion is taking place, Susan arrives late and starts taking off her coat.)

Susan (anxiously): You will never guess what I cooked for dinner last night. I made Louisiana Gumbo from an old family recipe. It was filled with shrimp and okra. My children just loved it, and let me tell you about how they are doing in school.
Maxine (social worker): I wonder if you are aware, Susan, that the group is discussing an issue now.
Susan: No.

(Susan then begins to listen as others continue to talk about June's coming departure. At that point Mary begins to cry. The group is silent.)

Elliot (psychiatrist): Mary, are you reacting to June's leaving the program shortly?
Mary (sobbing loudly): Everyone is always leaving me—right from the time I was little, and now I'm alone again in a new home.
Sam: This thing about June has really kicked off something in you, Mary.

(Mary nods her head in agreement, glares at Sam, and then looks away.)

Susan: (looking very distant): I don't know whether anybody knows what a world traveler I'm about to become. Very soon my husband and I will go to Alaska, China, and Vietnam.

(The group seems apprehensive after her statements, and there is silence.)

Maxine (social worker): Susan, are you having some strong feelings about June's leaving?
Susan (excitedly): Then, it's onward to India, Russia, and Finland.

(Maxine positions herself purposefully next to Susan, puts her hand firmly on Susan's shoulder and tells her that when she talks this way about a long trip she knows that she has strong feelings she is having trouble dealing with, and she cannot help but feel that they are to do with June's announcement that she is leaving the program. Susan pauses and begins to stare at the floor.)

Maxine (social worker): Susan, I think you are having feelings of being left alone.
Susan (crying): I won't see June any more in our group with Elliot and Maxine. June has been especially nice to me in that group. I even have had thoughts of going away with her.
Tom: It's really tough to think of her going, Susan.
Susan: Yeah.

(Susan seems more relaxed at this point. Most of the members conclude that they are having reactions to June's coming departure.)

Sam: It's time for announcements.
Margaret (art therapist): I suggest that we might continue working on this issue in the art group which will follow open staff rounds. Maybe members will be able to express some feelings in art work that they have not been able to in the community meeting.
Elliot (psychiatrist): People may also want to continue to talk about June's leaving in group therapy after the art group.
Lynn (nurse's aide): I just wanted to remind everyone that our field trip to the vocational center will be next Friday and not this Friday. I will put this on the bulletin board with everyone else's announcements.
Sam: If there are no further announcements, the meeting is over.

Break
(5 minutes)

Open Staff Rounds
(25 minutes)

(Staff members move to the center of the room in a circle and members of the community seat themselves around the staff. Below are the comments made by staff members about the four members identified previously.)

MARY

Belle (receptionist/secretary): Mary doesn't seem to hear me. This morning I made a special effort to ask her about her new apartment, and she walked right past me.
Maxine (social worker): I noticed Mary seems especially angry today. I think people are finding it difficult to say anything nice to her, and in fact they are staying away from her.

SUSAN

Carrie (vocational counselor): Susan still seems overwhelmed. She doesn't seem to be able to get all her housework done and get her children off to school in time to make it to the program.

Elliot (psychiatrist): I think that you're right. Also, the members become frightened when Susan starts talking about trips overseas as she did this this morning. I think we should openly discuss people's feelings when Susan talks this way.

SAM

Margaret (art therapist): Sam is really doing fantastic. In fact, he seems like the leader who will replace June. He really takes charge of the administrative community meeting, and he is helping Tom. He may be ready to leave the program soon.

Maxine (social worker): Margaret, I disagree with you. I think we have to be careful. This is exactly what has happened to Sam on his former jobs and in another program that he was in for a time. He did very well and then he became so anxious about his success he couldn't sleep or eat. Let's check it out with him.

TOM

Elliot (psychiatrist): Tom's problem in getting his feelings into words has come up several times in the past few days, especially this morning when he was trying to introduce the new member to Mary. He didn't know how to respond to her comment.

(Staff now joins members in the circle and the discussion of the information just described begins.)

Sam: Maxine, all you do is put people down. Who says I'm that anxious about success and responsibility?

Maxine (social worker): Are you?

Sam: Of course not.

Elliot (psychiatrist): Do you think Maxine is really off the wall for thinking the way she does?

Sam: I don't know, I'll have to think about it.

Mary: Why don't you shut up. All you do is blabber.

Sam: You old bitch. I think you shouldn't be here.

Elliot (psychiatrist): What do you think is going on?

Margaret (art therapist): Mary is sure doing a good job of scaring people away.

Sam: I think you're right, Margaret. Mary, somehow I think you wanted to fight me a minute ago.

Mary: Drop dead.

Bob (nurse): Do you think we should give into Mary and shut her out when she makes angry comments?

Sam: No, I think Mary is feeling a lot of pain now.

Mary: (Pauses.)

Maxine (social worker): Somehow I think Mary is thinking about what you just said, Sam.

Tom: Elliot, why is Susan staring up at the ceiling again?

Elliot (psychiatrist): Why don't you ask her?

Tom: Ahhhh, I don't know. She, she, she. . . . (Pauses.)

Lynn (nurse's aide): What are you feeling right now, Tom?

Tom: I don't know.

Sam: I think that you are frightened of Susan.

Tom: I am scared. (Silence.) I don't understand her stories and talks about Vietnam and Finland.

Elliot (psychiatrist): Great, Tom, you were able to put together the feelings that are inside you about Susan. What do you think about what Tom said, Susan?

Susan: I don't know. Do I really scare you, Tom?

Tom: Yeah, you sure do, Susan.

Susan: Sometimes I just don't know what's going on inside of me.

Maxine (social worker): Susan, what you just said is crystal clear to me.

Tom: Susan, I think you and I have exactly the same problem. We don't get it together inside.

Margaret (art therapist): I agree with you, Tom. This is something I think that the whole community can be aware of in the future. How can we help you with this problem?

Susan: I don't know.

Margaret (art therapist): What do you think, Tom?

Tom: I don't know. (Silence.) Maybe people can do what Elliot just did. Don't give up on us. Help us to get into words all this mixed up stuff inside.

Susan: Right on, Tom.

Lynn (nurse's aide): It's about time for this meeting to end. I think it might be helpful if some of these same issues we have discussed today could be continued into the member group session without staff that follows, as well as the art group and group therapy. I think June's leaving has stirred up a lot of individual feelings people have about their own situations.

(Staff leave the room and members form a closer circle.)

Break
(5 minutes)

Member Meeting
(25 minutes)

Sam: It's good to know what Susan's and Tom's problems are. I've read about these types of problems in numerous psychiatry textbooks. Perhaps I should tell the group what Freud and Menninger have to say on the issue.
Tom: I don't understand.

(Sam then proceeds on a long oration. There is much restlessness in the room.)

Mary: I can't stand this anymore. Sam, you're full of shit. Who gives a fuck about your theories? What do they have to do with anything. You're talking down to Tom like he is dirt.

(Two members quickly leave the room. Another stares out of the window.)

Sam: Now, Mary, we all understand how angry you are now that June is leaving and you have your own apartment for the first time.
Susan: I don't know what's going on.
Mary: I'm not totally sure either, but am I ever angry at Sam.

(A member of the group looks at Sam and states that she is also annoyed with Sam's orations. Several others agree.)

Tom: I think I—ahh. (Silence.)
Mary: Tell us Tom. I want to hear you.
Tom: I don't know.
Susan: You're, you're, you're like me. You're angry at Sam. Who does he think he is anyway?
Tom: You're right, Susan. I don't like to be picked out by Sam to be in all his theories.
Sam: I don't understand why people are so angry with me.
Mary: That's a big problem with you, Sam. You come across like God-Almighty, and you have as many problems as the rest of us.
Sam: I just don't know.
Tom: It's time for coffee break.

Coffee Break
(10 minutes)

(Several group members and Maxine continue to discuss their feelings about June's coming departure from the program. They decide that one way of dealing with them is to make farewell cards in art therapy. Susan says that she will raise the issue in art therapy.)

Art Therapy
(60 minutes)

(Margaret opens the group by relating to the issue of what the group had decided in yesterday's meeting to do for this session. Susan is able to suggest making the farewell cards that were discussed at the coffee break. At this point in the discussion, Tom responds to Susan's suggestion.)

Tom: I don't think making a card is enough. We should have a party, too.
Sam: No, a card is enough for her.
Margaret: You sound a bit irritated, Sam.
Sam: Why do we have to make a card and have a party? June was good, but she wasn't that good.
Mary: How come you seem so angry all of a sudden about making a card and having a party?
Sam: Seems hard to do all that work now.
Margaret: Sam, how do you feel about June's leaving?
Sam: I'll miss her a lot, but I'm really glad she has a new program to go to.
Margaret: Just nice happy thoughts about her.
Sam: Well, truthfully, I'm a little annoyed with her. She helped us all and now she's leaving us—high and dry.
Margaret: Do others react the same way that Sam does?
Tom: Yeah, but you can't be angry at somebody who's leaving.
Margaret: Why not?
Susan: Are you serious, Margaret?
Mary: I think Margaret's right. Why wouldn't we feel annoyed with June? She's really leaving an empty spot in us.

(Others nod their heads and there is silence for a few moments.)

Margaret: Sounds to me like people are beginning to recognize that they do have glad and angry feelings toward June. This always happens when somebody leaves. Sam, do you think that's why you might not want to have a party and make a card for June?
Sam: Yeah, it's hard to give to somebody when you feel irritated with them.
Tom: What do we do then, Sam—a card, a party, or both?
Sam: Why don't we give June what she really deserves—both the card and the party?

(The group voices agreement with Sam. For the next segment of the group, there is discussion about when to make the cards and when to plan the party. It is decided that the members will make the cards in the remainder of the session, and a committee from the group will meet during the planning and clean-up period which follows verbal group therapy. They will present their plans for the party for June in the administrative community meeting the following day.

As the group members begin their cards, many relate to personal feelings that have been stirred within them. Tom relates to his frightened feelings about going to a workshop. Sam is quite active during this portion of the group.)

Sam: I'm no artist. I can't make cards. I think I'll leave the group now. I want to read the Physician's Desk Reference for a few minutes. There's a new medication I think I want to take.

Margaret (art therapist): How does the group feel about Sam's leaving the card project?

(Several members say that it's OK.)

Margaret (art therapist): I think something strange is going on. People usually don't react so willingly to a member leaving the group. Is there some feeling today about Sam?

Mary: He's been such a bastard today quoting all his theories and now Mr. High and Mighty is going to read the P.D.R. It's almost like he's too good to make a card with the rest of us.

Sam: Why is everybody on my back?

Margaret (art therapist): You know, Sam, I think that you're struggling with some difficult feelings now.

Mary: Sam—feelings? Impossible!

Sam: Don't be so sure.

Margaret (art therapist): Don't leave us hanging, Sam.

Sam: All of you think you're the only ones who have a right to be frightened. I'm scared shitless. It's just like before. Everybody looks to me to be the leader. You were right in the staff rounds this morning. When June leaves, I'll make a mess out of leading the community meetings.

Susan (anxiously): But Sam, you're so smart.

Sam: Bullshit! I know what's going to happen. As soon as I do well as community meeting leader, people will expect me to lead other groups. No one will pay attention to me. Enough of that. I'm leaving this group.

(Sam angrily leaves the room, and there is silence.)

Margaret (art therapist): What do you think is going on?

Susan (anxiously): I don't want to be in this group any more. My husband and I are going to Europe anyway.

Mary: Susan, I think Sam's leaving the room the way he did has caused you to jump away from us.

Tom: I'm scared now. All that talk about trips.

Margaret (art therapist): Tell us what you felt when Sam slammed the door, Susan.

Susan: I felt the world was going to come apart. He was so angry. I was so angry.

Margaret (art therapist): Did the world fall apart?

Susan: No.

Margaret (art therapist): What do you think that means, Susan?

Susan: It's hard to know.

Margaret (art therapist): Can anyone help Susan out?

Mary: Angry feelings are heavy, but they don't kill. They just seem like they're going to kill sometimes.

(Other group members feel the same way and proceed to talk about how they felt when Sam left the room. It is decided that a member will go out and invite Sam to return to the group. Sam refuses to return to the group.

The members proceed to work on their cards for the remainder of the group session. During the last minutes of the group, after the supplies are returned, Margaret assembles the members for a summarizing discussion of the events in the group that day.)

Break
(5 minutes)

(During the break, Tom and Susan talk briefly. Tom seems quite anxious and refers to the possibility of his returning to the hospital. Susan asks him to bring up his fears in the group session which follows, and he agrees to do so.)

Verbal Group Therapy
(60 minutes)
Maxine and Elliot are co-therapists

(The group is silent to begin with for several moments.)

Sam: Well, I suppose everyone wonders why I blew my stack in the art group.

Elliot (psychiatrist): Perhaps you could fill Maxine and me in since we weren't there.

(Sam recounts the events stating that he just didn't know what had overcome him.)

Mary: Does anyone know?

(Several members begin to talk about disjointed subjects including Tom's vocational plans.)

Maxine (social worker): Elliot, I'm getting very confused about what's going on. First of all the group started talking about this event that occurred in art group, and then we moved to Tom's program very quickly.

Elliot (psychiatrist): I think whatever happened is difficult for everyone to talk about.

(Several members begin to talk about how frightening it was when Sam slammed the door and left the room. They couldn't imagine what had made him so upset.)

Elliot (psychiatrist): Sam, maybe that's the real problem; people really don't know how much you hurt inside sometimes.

Sam: It was awful. All I could think about was all those jobs I had when people would expect more and more and more of me, and I was never sure I could handle the jobs. I found a way to muff things up. Then, people like my family would feel sorry for me, and I would quit the job.

Maxine (social worker): What did you get out of people feeling sorry for you?

Sam: Nothing. My wife eventually became angry at me for losing so many jobs and depending on her to work, so she left me. My friends also became very tired of me. They said that they didn't like my whining.

Elliot (psychiatrist): Did it seem like the same thing was happening here today in the art group?

Susan: I think you are right, Elliot. Sam, you really annoyed me at first. I didn't think you could do anything for a minute.

Maxine: Sam, is that the effect you wanted to have on Susan and the others in the group?

Sam: Yeah, I guess so.

Elliot: I wonder if you had ever thought that there might be some alternatives to getting overwhelmed with responsibilities and feeling you have to present yourself as an incompetent person.

Sam: Maybe it's possible. I don't know any other way.

Mary: I was thinking right here in the program. Where is all the pressure coming from that you must take on so much and do all the things June did? Nobody ever asked you to. You did a lot of volunteering as I remember it.

(Several others make similar comments.)

Sam: I guess I plan my failures, then people won't expect so much out of me People don't care about you if you do a good job.

Elliot: What do you think, Tom?

Tom: I don't know what he's talking about. I always get attention when I do a good job at something. I'm not like Sam at all.

Susan: I wish I could do a better job so my husband and children would like me the way they once did when I did all the housework and cooking.

Maxine: Sam, it sounds like Tom's and Susan's experiences have been different from yours.

Sam: Yeah, so I see.

Maxine: Sam, I think you're in a vicious cycle. The way you are using to get attention for yourself isn't working. It sounds like it really never worked for you with family or friends.

Sam: So, what can I do?

Maxine: How do people here in the group think Sam can work on this in the program?

Mary: I think you ought to volunteer for what you know you can handle and leave the rest to somebody else. Believe me, we'll notice you.

(Several others express support for Mary's suggestion.)

Elliot: What do you think, Sam?

Sam: Maybe I could try that. For now all I'll do is lead the community meeting.

Maxine (jokingly): You know, somehow I don't completely believe you, Sam. I have visions of you volunteering two days from now for everything in sight and then saying to us all that we gave you too much to do.

(The group laughs together.)

Maxine: If that becomes a problem Sam, how can we solve it?

Sam: Perhaps people could remind me if they think I'm volunteering for too much.

(Group members think this is a good idea.)

During the remainder of the group session, issues related to Susan, Mary, and Tom are also discussed. It is decided by the group that part of Susan's behavior is related to her being overwhelmed at home and that there should be a joint meeting of Maxine, Susan and her husband to explore how her home responsibilities could be rearranged. Further, it is suggested that Susan should report back to the group about the session with her husband. Tom's fears about the workshop are discussed, and the group is able to relate to strengths he possesses that he did not have in the past when he failed at his previous workshop placement and required hospitalization. Finally, Mary relates to the group her difficulty in asking the group to listen to her communicate her feelings concerning her problems in living alone. She is asked by the group to experiment with them and ask for help, rather than making sharp remarks, thus turning the group members away from her. At the end of the session, Mary discusses the conclusions reached regarding each group member.

Concluding Statements

After group therapy, the planning committee for June's party meets without a staff member. The staff adjourns to have a program planning meeting. They communicate with each other as to what has happened in each group. For example, Margaret reports that a committee will give a report to the administrative community meeting about plans for a party since some staff do not know this. She reports about a revision of the group to focus on making cards for June's farewell party. Other staff members plan their groups for the following day with a focus on termination. They devise ways to maximize opportunities for the members of the therapeutic milieu to have an effective termination with June, as well as relate to the personal issues that June's leaving has activated within each of the community members.

9

The Family and Family Therapy in Partial Hospitalization

This is the first of three chapters involving the more intimate of patients' relationships (specifically families) and the implications of these for partial hospitalization. This emphasis on family indicates the importance of it for PHP work, especially since clinical staff are frequently wanting in the attitudes, knowledge, and skills to comfortably handle social networks, which include families.

The partial hospital program is designed to be a milieu with powerful forces that guide a patient toward mental health. To guide effectively, it is axiomatic that intervention is based on the fullest possible understanding of the patient and his world. This means a careful evaluation of the patient throughout all 168 hours in a week, which reveals that the patient is surrounded by many complicated environments. Significantly, a patient may spend only 35 hours per week in partial hospitalization but 133 hours per week in other systems/environments. Therefore, an examination of these environments follows.

SOME BASIC DEFINITIONS AND HYPOTHESES IN SOCIAL PSYCHIATRY

Systems and Networks

We are all part of and greatly affected by "systems." A system is "a set of units with a relationship among them. The state of each unit is constrained by the state of the other units. . ." (Miller, 1980, p. 99). Indeed, all behavior is the product of intrapsychic processes and the individual's surrounding system. An individual is a system; any therapy situation, such as a partial hospital, is a system. And the individual in his own personal world is yet another system. Although each system is an integral part of another, each is often analyzed separately, to avoid overwhelming complexity.

A social network is the finite group of people socially related to an individual. (Beels, 1981; Pattison et al., 1979; Rueveni, 1979). This group of people impacts on the proband, and the individual has impact back on his network.

The membership and complexity of any social network are overwhelming without some organized ways of analyzing it. Pattison et al. (1975) and Attneave

86

(1976) provide helpful approaches. Visualize a patient surrounded by social network zones (see Figure 1).

Figure 1

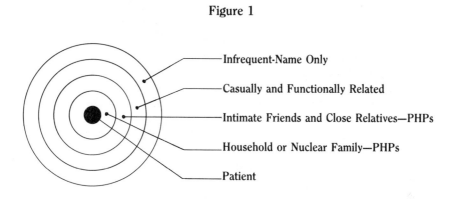

The most emotionally significant subject of the network usually subsumes persons in the same household and/or family of origin (such as parents and the patients' siblings). Next most close are intimate friends (with whom the patient shares worries and hurt feelings and on whom he can rely) and/or close relatives by blood or marriage. PHP contacts and significant others would come under subset one or two. Third are more casual personal contacts and/or functionally related people (from work, organizations, and other instrumental relationships). Finally, there are those infrequent contacts, essentially on a name-only basis.

The members of a patient's network who have the most powerful impact on him will have three characteristics:

1) a high amount of face-to-face interaction;
2) a high level of emotional involvement; and
3) a high degree of instrumental responsibility (Pattison et al., 1979).

If PHP staff explore the patient's network, they will know who are the most likely targets for intervention and involvement in PHP.

It is critically important to evaluate how supportive a network is. Quantitatively, there is research that indicates a healthy adult is associated with 20-30 people in his most intimate network; the "psychotic" type of person has only four to five people (Pattison et al., 1975). Twenty to thirty patients is also felt to be about the right census for a PHP (see Chapter 16). A certain size seems necessary for adequate resiliency and diversity of an individual's social network. Qualitatively, a supportive healthy network provides certain functions. These types and amounts of supportive features are also those that are considered necessary for a good partial hospital, as well as a healthy family!

Families

A family is but one of the subjects in the everwidening spiral of an individual's enmeshing network. It is important to be aware of types of families but in this book we will use "family" to mean a "psychosocial family," i.e. two or more people with considerable emotional involvement and commitment, a high level of interaction, a history together, and unpaid exchanges of concrete aid and service.

THE VALUE OF AND RATIONALE FOR
FAMILY INVOLVEMENT IN PARTIAL HOSPITALS

Family involvement is a vital part of partial hospitalization (Atwood and Williams, 1978; Dincin et al., 1978; Hatfield, 1979; Park, 1978; Pildis, 1978). This conclusion is based on the following:

1) To be most effective partial hospitalization must recognize and use the powerful forces in the environment affecting behavior, including those outside the PHP (Budson and Jolley, 1978).
2) The family is the first and most powerful psychosocial environment for each person, and the influence of the family of origin never disappears even when there is no contact.
3) Family therapy is an effective treatment and it involves the "outside" environment.
4) Families are an important source of objective information, otherwise unobtainable or unreliable (Schless and Mendels, 1978).
5) Families experience considerable distress with a mentally ill member, and they require understanding and support to be maximally therapeutic (Dincin et al., 1978; Lamb and Oliphant 1978; Park, 1978).

The rationale for using family therapy in PHP also evolves from many clinical observations and subsequent conceptualizations:

1) The family behaves like a unique system with a homeostasis principle operating.
2) Since some of the patient's behavior results from his reactions to the family, the patient should be helped to deal with the family more directly by the therapist seeing them all together.
3) Changing one family member really involves changing the whole family system. Why should all the burden be on the patient (Satir, 1967)?

Although there have been countless professional and family testimonials attesting to the positive value and effectiveness of family therapy, careful comprehensive research on effectiveness yields inconclusive results. DeWitt (1978) concluded that conjoint forms of family (two generations) therapy has a similar impact to nonconjoint therapies; nonetheless there is some evidence that the conjoint format is superior. Additional, well-researched evidence continues to accumulate (e.g., Goldstein et al., 1978) that shows a significant, measurable advantage to patients when family therapy is provided.

CLINICAL IMPLICATIONS OF A FAMILY THERAPY
ORIENTATION FOR PARTIAL HOSPITALIZATION

A partial hospital could be conceptualized as a "prosthetic family"; therefore, its therapeutic milieu might best be shaped and evaluated according to features characteristic of healthy families (Caplan, 1976).

Partial hospitalization is strongly recommended for those individuals who do not seem able to develop a healthy social network, e.g., the isolated schizophrenic in an impersonal rooming house. Likewise, PHPs should be used for those enmeshed in a very pathological social network, e.g., a patient in symbiosis within a chaotic family.

Since a "viable social support system is essential to successful coping" (Christmas et al., 1978, p. 186), an overall, long-term goal for a patient is to have him achieve his own adequate social network in the community outside the PHP. Therefore, certain partial hospital groups should be geared to discussing and/or role playing network issues, making and keeping friends, friendship interaction, etc. Special attention might be paid to directing a patient toward setting concrete goals for making gradual additions to his social network. An indication for continuing PHP treatment is the persistent failure of the patient to develop his own outside minimum necessary, sustaining network.

The social network of each patient would be the most acceptable and responsive first choice for the partial hospital's work in consultation and education in the outside community. Similarly, these social networks would be the partial hospital's "natural constituency" and most logical source of support in the community (see Figure 1).

A good working knowledge of the types of processes and dynamics found in families is helpful in understanding certain phenomena in the "partial hospital family." The intensity of the PHP experience tends to recapitulate past and present family experiences, and strong transferences to many members develop in the involved PHP member. For example, in families sexual relations are "permissible" only between "parents" (incest taboo) (Finkelhor, 1978). If staff are aware that this "family rule" might be broken, staff can more easily understand occurrences of seemingly unexplainable anxieties and fantasies among longer-term partial hospital patients. Thus, the partial hospital family must deal with such issues as sex between patients and false fantasies of patients that a staff member's pregnancy resulted from sex with the male co-leader of the partial hospital. To be able to handle such problems, families and partial hospital staff must be able to talk openly about closeness and sexual issues and be able to promote healthy sexual growth and development (see Chapter 11).

OBSTACLES TO THERAPEUTIC INTERACTION
BETWEEN FAMILIES AND THE PARTIAL HOSPITAL

Despite the above advantages and rationale for family involvement in partial hospitalization, PHPs have too little contact with families. For example, out of all partial hospitals, perhaps less than half conduct groups for the relatives of patients (Atwood and Williams, 1978). Very few PHPs achieve a comprehensive program of involvement of families.

Reasons for this lack of interaction have not been formally researched. Nonetheless, some of these reasons seem to be the following:

1) Traditionally, mental health workers have not been trained to be aware of and to work with families.
2) In a new (and potentially threatening) situation there are always "complex resistances that continually operate to counter innovation and changes" (DiBella, 1979).
3) Certain theories of psychopathology tend to prejudice attitudes; thus, staff have tended to view the family negatively (Schless and Mendels, 1978), i.e., as enemies (causing the patient's problems) and impediments to rehabilitation (Dincin et al., 1978), or as nonentities who are simply ignored (Park, 1978). A large part of these anti-family attitudes evolve from unresolved countertransferences against parental figures and overidentification with the "poor helpless miserable patient needing rescue" (see also Chapter 10).
4) Family work is more complex than individual or other group therapy. Exposure to families often subjects the therapist to being the object of the multiple projections from each family member. Without training, staff often feel in chaos trying to cope with the unique intrafamilial culture, with its many complex subsystems.
5) With so much else to cope with, new PHPs feel they cannot handle one more responsibility and neglect to start any planned family involvement.
6) Staff often fail to realize that families, like so many others, are unfamiliar with and do not understand partial hospitalization; thus, they have to be taught about the program in order to appreciate and support it.
7) When staff feel unsupported and insecure, together with their awareness of the family homeostasis principle, they are fearful of "upsetting the apple cart" by

interventions, which they believe might cause even more turmoil, even hospitalization or worse. Framo (1976) and Haley (1975) discuss further difficulties of staff involving families.

Families, themselves, often resist involvement with staff. The family's contact with the therapist results in the family feeling pressure about being "exposed," which is usually uncomfortable emotionally for a variety of reasons. Coming to therapy is so often difficult for an individual alone (Nir and Cutler, 1978); however, when the whole family is to be exposed, unique group resistances are added. Second, "the family" implies the presence of a heightened degree of commitment and responsibility to one another. If one member is symptomatic, it implies that others have failed, often producing guilt, shame, and helplessness. Having others know of this failure can intensify these dysphorias. Since therapists are so frequently seen as authority/superego figures, the family's projection of self condemnation onto the therapist results in further reluctance to come into contact with the therapist. Third, families are so enmeshed in their own interworkings that they have great difficulty seeing their own patterns of interaction. They also have had no training, typically, in understanding how they fit into the puzzling exsistence of dysfunction. Thus, it usually makes little sense and is painful to the patient's family when the therapist says that they should be involved in therapy "because each is contributing to the problem." Fourth, families have usually been turbulently involved with the "identified patient" just before admission to the program. They feel exhausted, worried, and frustrated by the emotional struggle. They usually tend to scapegoat and label the patient as "the diseased one," according to the traditional biomedical model. Thus, they have a tendency to withdraw from engagement with the staff and from further involvement with the patient, and they convey the message: "He is sick. We can't help anymore. Now you do your business and cure him." Finally, families have not infrequently experienced feeling abused by therapists, and they are reluctant to risk being hurt again (Appleton, 1974).

OVERCOMING BARRIERS AND ENGAGING FAMILIES

Some preparation and planning will usually be needed to overcome the above barriers and to engage families. Over time, much can be done by staff within the partial hospital by means of mutual goodwill and support, supervision, regular seminars, and group planning to help make themselves comfortable and familiar with family therapy issues and techniques. Almost all PHP clinical staff can involve families in some meaningful way, without waiting until everybody has become a "good family therapist" or until an outside expert in family therapy is obtained as a consultant.

Above all, staff must reach the point of having the following basic, underlying attitudes and approaches. First, staff will feel a conviction that the family is a vital component of the treatment program and that family involvement is invaluable. Second, staff will expect the family to become involved and will convey this to the family at every opportunity in a supportive, but firm, clear way (Framo, 1976; Satir, 1967; Skynner, 1976; Solomon, 1977). For example, the family should be told, "We feel the family is extremely important and we always hear the views of each member and what he or she feels the needs are," and "Every person has something unique to convey, and no one can be an effective substitute." Staff need to be supportive, empathic, concerned, and willing to teach something of the rationale for family involvement; they should also decrease blame by acknowledging the family's turmoil, perplexity, and good intentions. When there is an organized program to involve the family immediately and to continue flexibly in ways meaningful to each family, most families will come in and become engaged!

A SUGGESTED PROGRAM FOR FAMILY INVOLVEMENT IN PHP

Whatever the ultimate program is for family involvement in a PHP, it is recommended that three overall ideas be kept in mind:

1) Each psychosocial family is different in membership, configuration, needs, readiness to participate, etc. (just like any single patient). Thus, each treatment plan for the family should be unique. At least several different basic approaches in diverse formats should be available (see examples below).
2) There is substantial consensus on what families seem to need (Atwood and Williams, 1978; Dincin et al., 1978; Hatfield, 1979; Lamb and Oliphant, 1978; Luber and Wells, 1977; Park, 1978). Such needs include: (a) concrete respite from feelings of being overwhelmed by the demands of having to cope with a mentally ill member; (b) an opportunity to ventilate concerns and dysphorias in a safe, nonblaming atmosphere; (c) an opportunity to meet with other families in similar circumstances in order to decrease isolation and lack of feedback; (d) concrete suggestions on managing day-to-day practical problems; and (e) basic information that is organized toward increased understanding and skills regarding symptoms, diagnoses, prognoses, optimum communication, healthy family functioning, and their relationship to PHP treatment. Interventions need to be designed toward satisfying these needs.
3) Generally, someone must end up being designated as a patient needing "care agents," and *relatives*, not PHP staff and other members, should be considered the primary care agents. The family is a vital part of the patient's environment and is best approached first as an ally. Thus, strengths of the family should be emphasized and used, and it would seem more constructive to start with viewing the family more as a co-provider of services, rather than as a patient, and as collaborators with staff and patients in a truly therapeutic team effort (Christmas et al., 1978).

Sharing responsibility for improving psychosocial functioning does not mean, of course, that staff ever stop being professional, e.g., independently assessing and deciding judiciously, maintaining standards, and remaining ready to take ultimate responsibility. For instance, if after careful evaluation staff conclude that the patient can be managed at home despite his suicidal ideas and the protestations, even threats, of his family, they will have to make a firm bold stand while still effectively working with the family so they will appreciate and support the staff's plan. It is not easy to strike the right balance between authoritarianism, authoritative capacity, and collaborative problem-solving.

A comprehensive program of intervention in all types of social networks would provide the capacity for:

1) Routine inclusion of the family in intake, discharge, and major changes in treatment plans;
2) Education of the family on the purpose of the PHP and goals for the patient;
3) Family crisis intervention (relatively immediate responsiveness to urgent needs and drop-in visits);
4) Home visit(s) for assessment and/or outreach therapy done by staff and/or patients;
5) Short-term and/or continuing family psychotherapy; and
6) Family night or other forms of multiple family group psychotherapy.

Of practical concern is which of these interventions to offer and when. In order to have adequate emphasis on, assessment of, and connection with the patient's immediate social network, each PHP must routinely carry out the first and second of the above interventions. These two would also allow determination of the family's ability to be involved, which would in turn determine which additional interventions might be best (Solomon, 1977). Then, each PHP should choose a period within which they could work toward a more comprehensive program for family involvement, adding one more modality at a time from numbers 3-6 above. Especially recommended is some form of multiple family group psychotherapy (Framo, 1976 and see Chapter 10). Moss and Moss (1973) provide a good model for a comprehensive program finally developed for families in PHPs.

Finally, although there are powerful resistances in the unconscious, and underlying attitudes which affect behavior, it is not always remembered that these entities do not necessarily require being changed before other, more behavioral, changes can occur. Thus, a pragmatic approach will first provide to all families a short-term educational, supportive psychotherapy experience. For example, this experience would allow exploration and completion of the following ideas: good communication consists of..., schizophrenia is..., healthy families provide..., typical problems with mentally ill members are..., and here are ways of going about solving them..., etc. Afterwards, if this experience does not prove to be adequate, a more ongoing approach (such as insight-promoting) might be used.

10

Family Night

This chapter will describe and discuss family night, a model of family involve-ment developed in one PHP to meet the needs of that program.* The process whereby family night evolved will be discussed, as well as its impact on the pro-gram and its capacity for developing into an effective therapeutic modality within the framework and philosophy of a PHP therapeutic milieu.

IDENTIFYING THE NEED FOR INVOLVING FAMILIES

Family night arose out of an identified need on the part of a newly formed PHP to include families of patients. The recognition of this need, however, did not oc-cur until well into the second year of the program. Until that time energies were put into developing programming and providing care for the identified PHP pa-tients—20 adults with long-standing, severe emotional problems

While many of the patients had been discharged from psychiatric inpatient ser-vices to live with their families (primarily parents), there had been no recognized need for involving family members as part of the regular PHP program. Family problems which arose during the course of an individual patient's participation in the PHP were treated on an individual family basis. It was not until patients had progressed to the point of PHP discharge that staff began to gain a better ap-preciation of the significance and influence of families in the lives of the adult pa-tients.

Families who had been silent during the entire length of a patient's stay in PHP suddenly became vocal, and not always in congruence with PHP planning; discharge planning was affecting not only PHP patients and staff, but also families. While patients and staff worked together almost daily on these problems, families had been left out of this process. Staff, who had previously been praised by families for their good work with patients, were now being told by these same

---

* The PHP under discussion in this chapter is the Flatlands-Flatbush Day Center, an outpatient facility under the auspices of Kingsboro Psychiatric Center, Brooklyn, N.Y.

families that they were making "serious mistakes" and had "done nothing" to help the patients improve.

For example, Daniel R., a 35-year-old man with a lengthy history of numerous hospitalizations and inability to stay with jobs or rehabilitation programs for more than a month, had been attending PHP regularly for 18 months. He had reached such a level of stabilized functioning that discharge planning began, which involved referral to a vocational training program. During this time, efforts were made to elicit Daniel's mother's support through this difficult transition phase. She attended individual weekly family sessions and verbalized support and enthusiasm for her son's progress. Her behavior, however, indicated her own anxieties and fears, aroused by the possibility of her son's success and increased independence, which threatened separation from her after years of living together in a symbiotic dyad.

Examples of Mrs. R.'s ambivalence are illustrative. Following months of preparing breakfast for Daniel before he left home for the PHP, she stopped doing this and remained in bed in the mornings. Daniel had to feed himself or go without breakfast. Also, Mrs. R. no longer gave him money for bus fare, coffee breaks, and lunch. Daniel now walked to the PHP (several blocks) and returned home for lunch, often not returning to the program for afternoon groups. Mrs. R. wrote letters to local politicians demanding an investigation of the PHP which was "forcing" her son to go to work for which he was "not capable." She told staff, in Daniel's presence, that "he tried hard," but "was retarded." (He was not developmentally disabled.) Daniel experienced his mother's withdrawal and hostility as a threat to his very survival and correctly associated it with his progress in PHP. His regression, which followed, succeeded in terms of stopping plans for vocational training so he could remain home with his mother.

It would have been easy to blame this experience on a "destructive paranoid family system" or a "typical schizophrenogenic family, unable to tolerate separation, which subsequently sabotaged all efforts toward this end." This, however, was only part of the picture—Daniel's mother was a strong force in his life and she and Daniel did collude to undo what was seen by staff as a realistic, optimistic treatment plan. To Daniel's mother it meant, quite literally, that "they" were trying to take her son away from her. Had Mrs. R. been involved in supportive services throughout his partial hospitalization (nearly two years), it is possible she could have developed a strong and positive enough relationship with PHP staff and other families to compensate for the loss she would have experienced with Daniel's continued progress. This remained an unknown possibility.

ANXIETIES AND RESISTANCES TO FAMILY INVOLVEMENT

It was through experiencing difficult situations such as the one described above that staff's thinking about improving work with families of the PHP patients was stimulated. The process of exploring means of involving families was done in terms of the following:

1) staff anxieties and resistances;
2) patient anxieties and resistances;
3) family anxieties and resistances; and
4) organizational and structural barriers.

1) *Staff anxieties and resistances* arose from several sources:

(a) *Lack of formal training* in group and/or family methods.
(b) *Staff competitiveness*—the question of which staff would treat which family was a concern, as some families appeared more problematic than others, thus requiring greater clinical expertise.
(c) *Concern over increasing patient rivalry*, which was observed when individual sessions were offered. The idea of involving all families, possibly on an individual basis, magnified this concern.
(d) *Fear of uncovering a whole family of patients*, which would then require ongoing intervention and could overwhelm staff.
(e) *Fear of loss of objectivity*, resulting in blaming families, patients, or staff.
(f) *Unresolved conflicts* around staff's personal family roles.
(g) *Confidentiality*—would staff feel pressured to reveal confidential therapeutic material from PHP groups?
(h) *Stereotyped ideas* of patients' family members being inherently destructive or defective.
(i) *Fear of loss of control*, e.g., staff being confronted by a family group, or a group of families.

2) *Patient anxieties and resistances* were explored in terms of their feelings about including family members or significant others in "their" PHP. The following issues are generalized from material expressed over many weeks in several different PHP groups:

(a) *Fear of being blamed* by their families, who might put on a good front and convince the staff that the patients had indeed caused all the family problems. Underlying this was the fear that staff would identify with the non-patient family members and scapegoat or reject the patient, who had been clearly labeled "problematic" by the need for hospitalization, partial hospitalization, or both.
(b) *Confidentiality*. Betrayal was an expressed worry. Many patients had finally begun to trust staff and other patients enough to reveal feelings (particularly anger and disappointment) about their families and now feared they would be exposed, betrayed, or punished for what they had said.

(c) *Family secrets*, which could be "mistakenly" uncovered in family meetings, were another source of anxiety, and involved issues such as patients' behavior at home, which may be different from that demonstrated in the PHP, incestual (real or fantasized) relationships, and pathology of other family members. Patients feared that exposing family problems would make things worse at home, and felt most of these problems were better left alone.

(d) *Diluted relationships with staff.* Having to share staff with their families, especially their "healthy" siblings, evoked threatening, rivalrous feelings in patients. As one patient directly phrased it, "I think you'll (staff) like my brother a lot better than me; he's better looking, and doesn't have so many problems."

(e) *Fear of confronting family's rejection of patients* was reflected in patients' feelings that their families would not show up and did not care about them; therefore, their families would be less likely to want family therapy.

(f) *Previous negative experiences with family therapy* (see Chapter 9).

(g) *Fears of infantalization* were present as indicated by, "We are adults, after all," and similar fears of family involvement becoming a PHP-PTA, with the patients in the role of children or students.

(h) *Fear of being in the middle*—between famillies and staff—was reflected in concerns like, "My father wants me to quit PHP and see a private doctor. I don't want to because I've already done that. I like it here and know PHP has helped me. But what if he tells me to quit—what should I do? What would you say to him?"

3) *Family anxieties and resistances* were largely of an anticipated nature, since families were not directly involved in the PHP as a group during these exploration stages. Some concerns, however, were expressed to individual staff during the course of individual family work and through the patients:

(a) *Fear of being blamed* by their relative, the patient, and by staff;

(b) *Blaming staff for not doing more* to help their relative improve;

(c) *Fear of being labeled "patients"*;

(d) *Open recognition of having a "sick" relative*, and/or being a "sick" family;

(e) *Demanding answers* and advice while being ambivalent about receiving help.

All of the above real and anticipated concerns and anxieties needed to be recognized, acknowledged, understood, and addressed if family involvement in PHP were to be accepted and productive. Examples of ways to provide a "safe atmosphere" were discussed, e.g., straightforward answering of direct questions, direct handling of fantasy material expressed in groups involving families and with a reality focus, and other means of making all those involved as comfortable as possible, particularly in the initial meetings, until relationships developed that would allow for more difficult material to emerge and be dealt with. It was important, in terms of patients' fears, that they know staff would not let them be put on the spot or humiliated in front of peers or families. This was done by showing them that what they talked about did make sense, if all individuals worked to understand and present their thoughts and feelings as clearly as possible.

4) *Organizational and Structural Barriers*. In addition to emotional and ideational barriers, there were also organizational and structural problems to be confronted. Among these were:

(a) Space was limited and it was not certain where families could be seen, particularly if a multiple family group approach, with as many as 50 people in attendance at one time, was decided upon.
(b) Since the PHP shared space with other staff and programs, administrative sanction was required to bring such large numbers of people into the facility for groups, and to insure cooperation on the part of others in the clinic.
(c) To insure maximum participation by families, it was necessary to offer evening appointments, in order to not interfere with their jobs. This also required obtaining organizational sanction, as it would mean utilizing clinic space in the evening as well as revising schedules of secretarial, maintenance, and PHP staff.
(d) Funds were minimal for additional programming. Depending on the type of family service provided, there had to be consideration of refreshments, paper goods, mailings, etc.

RESOLUTION OF ISSUES INTO FAMILY NIGHT

Crucial to the resolution of the issues identified above was the exploration phase. Through the process of identification of anxieties, fears, concerns, and issues, patients and staff alike were relieved. Energy then became available to begin the work of planning. Many issues persisted, of course, and were to become part of the ongoing process of family meetings.

Discussion of how to best involve families included an examination of the PHP treatment philosophy which utilized group as the primary, and in most cases, the only treatment modality (see Chapter 6). It seemed there must be a way of integrating families into PHP utilizing the therapeutic milieu. Literature reviews supplied ample information on multiple family therapy *small* groups (Laqueur, 1972; Leichter and Schulman, 1968, 1972; Donner and Ganson, 1968), but scant mention of *large* group family work (Wolman, 1976). Nothing was found which related to services provided to families on a similar basis to those of a PHP, e.g., conducting family treatment in a manner similar to other PHP groups and utilizing the therapeutic milieu.

Since very few relatives of the patients in question had expressed a desire or need for family treatment, it was felt that imposing family therapy on them would not help the efforts to elicit their support and cooperation. Based on knowledge of some of the families, it was felt they would be too threatened by this approach since it had been attempted many times in many agencies and they typically withdrew after a few sessions. It was felt that, by offering *equal* services to *all* psychosocial family members of patients which fell somewhere between "social" and "therapy," the best results might be achieved.

Family night was envisioned as an educative experience (with patients and families being mutual educators as much as possible), helping families understand the PHP and how it operated and helping patients and staff understand the families better. Staff were to learn that families rarely understood the intensity of the program or how hard the patients worked on their problems. Many had been under the impression that staff were running a school or adult baby-sitting service. It was also hoped that the meetings would encourage communication and social relationships among families, who were often isloated and lacking therapeutic skills.

Considering and evaluating all the points already mentioned, a family night approach was finally decided upon. It would meet monthly for two hours from 6:30 to 8:30 P.M. All psychosocial family members would be invited, with a flexible upper limit of three or four per patient. Patients decided whom they would invite, but there was a clear expectation that every patient would invite someone. All PHP patients and staff would attend. There was some heated discussion on whether families *and* patients should be seen together, as this might inhibit each group's participation. However, to reflect the PHP policy of open communication through groups, it was decided family night must struggle with the same initial problem, "Can we say what we think in front of the patients?", as the staff and patients had experienced months earlier. Excluding patients from these meetings could only foster feelings that they were being talked about and not capable or adult enough to participate. In addition, the very word "family" indicates *all* members of that system—not all *except* patients.

Preparation for Family Night

Once staff and patients had worked together to identify anxieties about involving families, the actual preparations could begin. Role-playing was an effective means of relieving anxiety.

Role-playing. Staff assumed various patient, staff, and family roles, presenting in the safety of the staff group what they feared would happen—challenging, belligerent, or accusatory questions from parents. For example, "My son has been here for six months and hasn't changed a bit; what are you getting paid for?" Or, "I'm curious about my daughter's diagnosis, which I heard is schizophrenia; if this is so, why don't you have more doctors working here who are *really* qualified to help her—and how will making ashtrays and candles help her get a job?"

Of course, these questions were never asked with much anticipated antagonism. Role playing these situations, however, helped staff think more clearly about how they might respond to difficult questions and avoid defensiveness through preparation.

When staff felt more comfortable and secure with the idea of meeting 20 families face-to-face, patients were encouraged to join in role-playing. They role-played themselves, other patients, staff, and relatives, also switching roles when it would help gain better understanding of another's feelings or situation. For example, John, who feared his father would embarrass him in front of everyone, asked another patient to portray his father making the statement, "I don't know if you all know this, but John paces the floor till all hours of the night." John, who typically would have become angry and walked out, was helped through role-playing to respond to his father. When he was asked to switch roles and become the father, he stated that he, too, might get upset if someone was pacing the floor all night. Another patient spoke up, saying she did the same thing when she was worried. Yet another patient, who was playing the role of a parent, said he also had trouble sleeping and that, instead of pointing fingers at who can't sleep and who paces, the group should talk about why it's hard to sleep sometimes, and what can help with this problem.

In the midst of role-playing, someone commented that they were nervous about family night, but they'd bet the relatives were nervous too—after all, they didn't know anyone here. This comment was important, as it helped place the event in a more realistic perspective. For the first meeting, the aim basically was to meet families and have them meet the staff and patients, to talk about the program and have an enjoyable time in the process. Everyone had to laugh at the "preparations for warfare," and from that point relaxed more, thus enabling staff and patients to move into concrete planning tasks.

Administrative approval was given for family night, although funds remained scarce. In addition to some supplies being furnished by the agency, the PHP members contributed a small amount to purchase supplies for baking cookies. Various committees were formed to handle specific responsibilities, e.g., hosting, refreshments, setup and cleanup.

It was decided that invitations should be mailed to relatives in order to convey the importance of the meeting. Telephone invitations or hand-delivered invitations to the families by patients were considered too informal, and likely to give rise to last-minute ambivalence. Patients wrote and addressed the invitations. Name tags and a sign-in book were made, which, it was felt, would foster an immediate sense of recognition, acceptance and importance.

The actual program was planned largely by the patients, who decided to elect speakers from among themselves to explain various aspects of the program, from which discussion would follow. Hours of hard work went into discussing, preparing, and rehearsing the presentations.

After approximately three months of preparation, the time finally arrived to put all the planning and work into action.

Attendance for the first family night was very high. With the exception of one relative who worked an evening shift and could not take time off, everyone who was invited showed up. There were five staff, 20 patients, and 38 relatives, making a total of 63. The meeting took place in the largest PHP room, which could accommodate approximately 70 chairs, in a double circle arrangement. Refreshments (tea, coffee, punch, cookies, etc.) were served first to provide an informal, relaxing atmosphere. Patients and staff were actively working, making introductions and trying to make everyone feel welcome. It was *not* a party; rather it was a friendly meeting from which, hopefully, would develop strong ties for meaningful, shared family involvement in the PHP.

The more formal program of patient presentations, moderated by one staff member, went very well. Relatives were impressed and felt the presentations were informative. Many said they had very limited knowledge about what went on in the PHP and had often wanted to call or drop by, but felt it was "none of their business." All said they wanted to continue the meetings on a regular basis, and once a month would be suitable.

Predictable issues were raised by relatives, such as, "Wouldn't it be easier for us to talk by ourselves, without the patients here?" Fortunately, prior anticipation of this question and how it should be handled led to a patient answering it, in the form of another question: "Is there really anything we can't talk about together?" This resulted in a lively discussion, mostly among relatives, of this very subject; some felt they could discuss whatever they felt in front of the patients, others felt they could not, at least now. Staff used this opportunity, with the help of patients, to identify some possibly uncomfortable issues, such as coping with anger, suicidal behavior, hallucinations, and the constant fear of breakdowns.

General discussion ensued around only identifying uncomfortable concerns, not examining them. This technique provided permission to discuss these concerns, yet supplied a safety device for preventing "spilling" in the first meeting, which could result in raised anxiety levels and dropping out. By the end of the discussion, there was visible relief on the faces of family members, knowing that they could, in time, not only openly discuss difficult issues, but they also observed that the patients were not overly uncomfortable discussing them. As one patient put it, "This stuff isn't new to us—we talk about it all the time here." There was unanimous agreement to "trying" this—evaluating reactions as they went along.

Another, anticipated question was raised: "Don't you think we could get more out of family meetings if they were smaller, or if we all met with staff separately?" This anxiety was also acknowledged and discussed. Patients, with encouragement from staff, related how they had initially hated groups and wanted individual therapy, which they had had as inpatients. Concerns like, "We won't be heard or noticed," or, "I can't talk up in a group," or, "My feelings are too personal to talk about in a group," or, "I don't even know these other people" were identified. Similar to the discussion around uncomfortable issues, anxiety about the group was handled in terms of identifying it, not reaching for specifics. There would be ample time for this. Patients again explained how groups had been helpful to them. One patient, surprising everyone, since he constantly demanded to be seen alone, said, "You'd be surprised at all the individual attention you can get in a group from a lot of people." Thus, the contract for family night had begun.

The first meeting, by design and necessity, was highly structured and informative—an effort to begin sharing with families in a non-threatening manner the work of the PHP. Everyone left the meeting feeling enthusiastic about continuing it. The hostility and defensiveness which had been dreaded were not expressed; in fact, this was humorously mentioned by the staff moderator in the course of the evening and was responded to by relatives, who agreed they had dreaded the same thing, but from staff and patients! This ground-breaking contributed to the early and continued success of family night.

DEVELOPMENTS AND RECOMMENDATIONS

Family nights have continued (for nearly five years) regularly, on a monthly or six-weekly basis. Attendance remains very high. The focus has become one of bringing relatives up-to-date on pressing issues in the PHP, which often affect the home situation. For example, a social worker had announced she was leaving the PHP and moving to another city. She had been with the program for a few years and everyone was reacting with varied levels of affect—some depressed, some angry, and some feeling glad for her. All patients had carried their feelings home, yet most did not clearly communicate the basis for those feelings to their relatives, who did not understand why the patient was suddenly more depressed, withdrawn, or angry. At family night, the issue was raised and discussed. Relatives were then able to connect the feelings and moods to a particular situation, which was understandable and normal in the circumstances. This understanding relieved parents of anxiety and guilt, some of them believing they had done something wrong. Patients were pleased to hear their families relating to past losses with very similar feelings, and acknowledged they sometimes felt their relatives did not identify with them, so they did not bother telling them how they were feeling. Parallels were drawn to similar types of family situations and reactions. This opened the way for dealing with a major problem for the patients and their families—effectively communicating with each other.

Some family members, once they felt accepted by PHP staff, began requesting more involvement. Some wanted to be seen individually, others wanted individual family therapy. In some cases, individual family sessions were held to handle a crisis or evaluate the need and motivation for ongoing individual family therapy. In the latter case, families were referred elsewhere, with close collaboration by PHP staff. More often, however, these requests were of a testing nature, to see whether the staff were really serious about offering help to families and were serious about the contract for family night—all families and patients in a group, together. Most often, requests for help provided an opportunity for early intervention in situations, thereby avoiding crises. Families were proving they cared and were interested. They were also capable of cooperating with, and significantly contributing to, PHP patient care.

Recent family night developments have included potluck dinners and family leisure outings. These were events which individual families were unable to plan and implement for themselves, and which resulted in increased positive alliances between families, and families and the PHP. Additionally, families have been helpful to the PHP in problem-solving, e.g., donating needed furniture or supplies, searching for community resources (including space), locating potential volunteers and prospective patients, and protesting cutbacks in services.

To reemphasize, it is best that families be invited to participate in PHP from the outset—*invited* because this generally results in lessened power struggles and sets a more respectful tone than *requiring* family participation as a prerequisite to a patient's admission or participation. *Voluntary* family involvement in PHP must by no means result in lack of participation or involvement. Considerable reaching out may be required to overcome some families' resistances to entering the PHP system and risking change.

Offering a model of family involvement that is consistent with the philosophy and structure of a PHP therapeutic milieu and within the limits of manageability by staff is less likely to fall prey to the "it was a good idea, but impossible to implement" phenomenon.

11

Sexuality in Partial Hospitalization

Each individual is a sexual being, and, undoubtedly, the vast majority of PHP patients have had at least one orgasm. Nonetheless, sexuality is typically not adequately dealt with by patients or staff in partial hospitalization (as, indeed, in so many families), yet there is almost nothing in the literature on this area of partial hospitalization to give some guidance. Staff are usually uncomfortable with sexual issues, especially if without specific supports to deal with these. Too often staff conduct "socialization groups" as if they were tea parties for nine-year-olds; too often staff "forget" that the minute they introduce socialization they have introduced the first step toward sex (or having to reject another person's intimations for sex). Both are difficult and scary for many of PHP patients (and sometimes for staff). If the program would allow the material to surface, many overtly sexual concerns are liable to arise. For example, "If she goes out with me, she'll expect me to ask for sex, and I won't be able to get it up."

Out of the restrictive inpatient ward and in the PHP, the patient regains the normal sexual freedom, with concurrent pressures to deal with sex. Successful therapy requires that sexual issues be managed; to do this, the professional must be comfortable with sexuality.

"Sexuality" and "sexual" are broad terms encompassing far more than the term "sex." Sexuality is the quality or state of being that includes: 1) biological sex, 2) gender identity (one's sense of masculinity or femininity (Stoller, 1980), sexual [core gender] identity), and 3) gender role, which includes both sex behavior and the broader gender behavior.

Sexual health is the integration of the somatic, emotional, intellectual, and social aspects of a sexual being in ways that are positively enriching and that enhance personality, communication, and love. Ideally, perfect sexual health includes three components: 1) lack of physical disorders that interfere with sex functioning, 2) lack of psychological factors that inappropriately inhibit the sexual response cycle, and 3) the capacity to enjoy and control genitally focused and reproductive behavior within a moral code. "Fundamental to this concept is the right to information and the right to pleasure" (WHO, 1975).

DETECTING ANTISEXUAL ATTITUDES

How does one know that unhealthy sexuality is being reinforced by a sex-negative atmosphere in a partial hospital? The following are eight indicators shown by staff (although patients show many of these signs too):

1) Staff's assessments "somehow" never quite get around to reviewing details of patients' sexual lives; it is as if the patients had none!

2) An awkwardness on the part of staff around sexuality is evident (even though all people have to cope with the irremovable sexual drives which are always conflicted to some degree [Kaplan, 1974, pp. 145-6]). Planned interventions are not made for sexual issues; instead, these "just happen to emerge."

3) When sexual issues do erupt, staff can be noticed to show various sly smiles (of vicarious pleasure), and/or more tension, and/or more silence, and/or less sophistication and initiative in their formulations and ideas for intervention.

4) In staff conferences, staff might reveal rationalizations for avoiding sexual topics, e.g., "It would be wrong to go into details of sex with patients because it would be intruding into someone's privacy," or, ". . . just professional voyerism," or, ". . . too volatile and upsetting to do in a group format," or, ". . . would cause patients to get angry."

5) Staff have a limited lecture on "family" planning (birth control), and assume that their duty to handle sexual issues has been executed.

6) Around sexual issues, staff show a tendency to retreat from their usual individualizing interventions; instead, they resort to dealing with all the patients according to rigid, unsuitable conceptualization. Some examples of inappropriate misconceptions are as follows:

(a) Schizophrenics should be encouraged to repress sex since sex will result in children and the passing-on of bad genes, and talking about sex will just arouse them to acting out;

(b) The defect in schizophrenia is in the oral stage; thus, Oedipal conflicts and dynamics are not present; and

(c) Sexual issues should not be talked about since the person with severe emotional problems is too unstable to be able to deal with such emotionally arousing material.

These misconceptions may be adhered to despite opposing facts. For example, partial hospital staff have usually learned how to adequately support the severely mentally ill individual in discussing and coping better with other emotionally intense feelings such as anger and fear. Kaplan (1974, pp. 490-500) has indicated that schizophrenics can certainly be treated in sex therapy, and she discusses appropriate modifications of the usual therapeutic techniques.

7) Staff tend not to pick up on early signs of sexuality or to consider interpretations of events in sexual terms. For example, it is very typical of mixed gender

groups to ask for groups limited to one sex, purportedly because certain activities and interests are limited to one gender. More specifically, members request a separate daily sports events group versus a sewing group. Unfortunately, this request is typically accepted by staff with no consideration of it representing sexual issues. Separate men's groups and women's groups should not be formed without attending to how the PHP will help patients deal with such sexual issues, e.g., patients' inabilities to make sexual comments in the presence of the opposite sex, attraction and arousal upon contact with others, and primitive fears of merging into the opposite gender.

8) The specific words used in the partial hospital for sexual issues can also be very revealing. A tip-off that there is a sex-negative atmosphere is when there is avoidance of sexual topics or anxiety manifested by shock or giggling with the use of sexual vernacular (shit, fuck, cunt, mother-fucker, etc.); or, when sexual vernacular more or less only comes out explosively rather than managed as it should be in all good psychotherapy. This does not mean that only sexual vernacular can be used if there is to be a therapeutic milieu. Rather, using vernacular gives the message that it is O.K. to talk about anything and be more truly self-disclosing. This type of permissiveness helps desensitization to and reaching for the more general fears associated with sexual feelings and arousal (Bogen, 1978). Unhandled fears tend to call forth defenses, impairing functioning, especially in relating to others; unhandled sexual problems contribute to a tendency to decompensate and be hospitalized.

In addition, when staff constrict their language to inappropriate, euphemistic, or vague words (e.g., "the curse" for "menses"), they are not following an axiom of good therapy, namely, that therapists should try to use a comfortable, specific, appropriate language understandable to all members. Constricted language also contributes to a subtle distancing from the earthy issues of sex, and maintaining staff in an aloof, superior, overprotective parental role (a type of role generally considered antitherapeutic in a therapeutic milieu). To draw a parallel, parents generally avoid use of vernacular with children, especially in families that are extremely authoritarian, yet these same adults would use this language with their peers (Bogen, 1978).

In summary, too often staff's conflicts and resistances result in their never anticipating sexually related events and providing limits (if needed), never preparing to pick up on early signs of sexual problems and to handle these, never openly supporting one another, and never thinking about a formal, identifiable program on sexuality.

CAUSES OF ANTISEXUAL ATTITUDES

Although professional therapists receive considerable training to be tolerant and accepting, they have to struggle against the powerful earlier and ongoing inculcation of moral condemnation of sex from "the establishment" (DiBella, 1979). Additionally, some programs will be using paraprofessionals, students, and volunteers with little, if any, training in dealing with sexuality. Frequently, it is difficult to bring up sexual matters in a one-to-one situation, and even more so in the more complex group situation. Additional tension usually ocurs when dealing with sexual proclivities which conflict with what society considers normal and proper (e.g., incest, bestiality, adultery, and homosexuality [DiBella, 1979]).

MISCELLANEOUS PROBLEMATIC SEXUAL ISSUES

In partial hospitalization, numerous disquieting sexual themes and events will arise; for example, variants on the theme of members getting pregnant, having sex with another member, worrying about parents finding out about their sex activity (which the parents condemn), being homosexual or transsexual, and exposing themselves. In addition, some staff will have negative sexual countertransferences to patients, while other staff will find one or another patient extremely attractive sexually.

It is helpful if ways to handle these issues are prepared in advance of the events. For example, pregnancy is a very organic, dramatic, visible and earthy situation that will always induce strong reactions in self and others (Butts and Cavenar, 1979). Typically, reactions to pregnancy are concealed by various mental mechanisms; thus, it may not be clear that it is really a pregnancy issue that is underlying various observed emotions. For example, there may be an unusual new focus on a plant and gardening group, or the pregnant member may be patronized, or others may regress with feelings of sibling rivalry or rejection. Clearly, staff cannot be so overwhelmed with unmanaged reactions that they fail to give permission and structure to patients for dealing with these reactions. Many discomforting reactions and pressures arise from internal and external sources concerning the homosexual issue (DiBella, 1979). Homosexuality by definition focuses on the sex act rather than on the larger issue of sexuality in life. This genital focus may be difficult for some to tolerate. Very common is a reaction of moral condemnation toward the frequent pattern of many male homosexuals to have brief relationships/sex contacts ouside the institution of marriage. Partial hospital work is comparably intimate work with much interaction, and this situation may stir up normal latent, homosexual feelings and concerns among all members. Thus, lesbians are often more threatening in this way to other females, as are male homosexuals to other males. Staff still tend to be torn between acceptance versus feeling that acceptance is encouraging more of this "psychopathological enemy," which should be rooted out by change to heterosexuality. Until relatively recently, many felt that homosexual individuals could not be treated in the same group as non-homosexuals, mostly because of intolerance from others in the group (both from staff and patients). This is no longer the general conclusion, and many clinicians have had the experience of seeing homosexuals working out well as PHP members, if there is the appropriate atmosphere of acceptance, openness, support and respect, as should be given to any individual whatever his unique features.

Unfortunately, the homosexual issue, as with all sexuality, tends to be avoided, and total avoidance only intensifies the feeling that there is something wrong that cannot be openly discussed, nor even recognized. This avoidance also fails to give the permission to disclose, which is so helpful for a successful treatment process.

SUGGESTIONS FOR INCORPORATING HEALTHY SEXUALITY INTO PHP

Essentially, no one is completely free of discomfort about dealing openly with some aspects or another of the many possible ways of sexual expression, and resistance can be anticipated in all or part of the staff to introducing a sexuality program. To help overcome resistances, the staff member with the greatest comfort and interest in the area might be the facilitator for a sexuality group or the procurer of an outside change agent (see also Chapter 25). Whoever is chosen as seminar leader would be expected to have less conflicts about sexuality. He should be able to help to motivate and lead discussions in order to inspire a greater conviction in all staff of the value of a sexuality program, a greater sense of what it should include, and an adequate comfort with sexuality, before staff try to guide patients toward healthy sexual attitudes and behavior. To this end, it would be advisable to have four to eight sessions on sexuality for staff alone. Ultimately, sexuality should be considered just another integral part of normal, healthy life, toward which staff are helping partial hospital clients.

Treatment plans and program goals must be established for the area of sexuality, as in other areas. Some reasonable goals to work towards are as follows:

1) Basic sexuality will be examined, explained, and understood forthrightly.
2) A partial hospital participant will become as self-accepting, comfortable, and functional in his sexuality as is feasible within the scope of his unique potentialities and personality. Specific changes in a person's ways of expressing sex are usually secondary in importance, perhaps unnecessary. There certainly should be no kind of dictum that requires any single method of sexual expression, e.g., only sexual intercourse between a male and a female.

Guidelines for sexual expression must consider the following:

1) Many variations in sex activities are normal and healthy.
2) Many individuals have neither the capacity nor the inclination to change their sexual preferences.

3) Individuals should not be discriminatingly refused all treatment just because they cannot or do not wish to change everything.
4) Perhaps most important, treatment focus should be on helping individuals to develop basic abilities to participate in affectionate sexual activity and, preferably, sustained affectionate relationships without exploiting or damaging self and others, or suffering.

Upon the initial introduction of patients to the partial hospital it may be helpful to allay patients' fear of being swept away emotionally by the group. This could be done by providing clarification of the type of social experience they are entering. Thus, one could explain that the PHP is not simply a social club to meet people, as if for a date or such; rather, it is a place to learn about and work with other people, doing a wide range of satisfying, beneficial activities that are to be applied to the real outside world. Consequently, it would seem that romantic/sex activity would be ruled inappropriate between members. As with other powerful emotions (see Chapter 21), a PHP should have well-thought-out structured viewpoints and guidelines about sex between members which would be inculcated on all. There are no perfect or easy answers about rules for sex. Perhaps the process of finding answers is even more important, namely, discussing the issue together at length, agreeing on a coherent rationale, and sharing this repeatedly, with readiness to consider the issues again.

The following are some questions or statements that may arise when contemplating rules on sex for the PHP.

1) If sex between staff and patient is forbidden, why shouldn't this be so between all members (since patients are encouraged to take as much responsibility as staff whenever possible)?
2) The PHP is an artificially created intimacy with members exposing vulnerabilities and urges, and trusting that these will not be exploited, to provide sexual relief or otherwise.
3) Most societies have prohibitions against incest. The PHP shares many similarities with a family. Doesn't that mean a prohibition on sex between the "PHP family" members, if they are not married?
4) Special attachments/liaisons would tend to divert commitment to the entire community and leave the sex-participating members more isolated.
5) Sexual issues are very emotionally laden. Is it wise to bring sex actions so close, by two members being sexually active together, when so many members have such difficulties with sex?

Whatever a PHP chooses, most PHPs discourage sex between patients, and all prohibit sex between staff and patients. Another common rule is that any outside romantic or sex liaison must be reported back immediately to the entire community.

In contrast to dealing with neurotics, staff will work with many partial hospital members in a more structured, concrete, and gradual way with a readiness to reduce stress (not to forever give up on sexuality), if anxiety levels indicate beginning decompensation toward psychosis. Staff are aware that sexual feelings are powerful ones; however, they often forget that open appreciation of this awareness is often enough to be attuned to signs from patients that they need a slower, more concrete and supportive (versus "uncovering") approach.

In addition, the partial hospital has unusual potential, as compared to other ambulatory treatments, to intervene early with decompensating patients. In PHPs, there are so many more opportunities to be with the patient. The patient is not "stirred up" and then dropped for a week or more; rather, in the same day there are multiple opportunities to integrate, stabilize, and work through (see Chapters 7 and 8). Actually, all potentially strong conflicted feelings must be tackled and handled appropriately; any of these feelings that are not sublimated or integrated appropriately into life are more dangerous when left alone. In the latter circumstance there is no predicting what will penetrate defenses and set off an explosion. It is much better to approach a "tiger" in daylight, well prepared, and in a well-thought-out, appropriate way than to stumble into it unexpectedly at night.

Staff need to repeatedly help members appreciate and use rules of thumb to evaluate life and to make decisions. Thus, staff could introduce a guideline definition of sexual health (see above), then bring this up from time to time accompanied by discussion. Ways of exploring sexual health could be arranged through a variety of verbal and nonverbal groups, perhaps with some structuring instrument (for example, the Derogatis Multidimensional Measure of Sexual Functioning, 1979). A topic for a group discussion about love, relationships, and family life might be how a person makes decisions regarding his relationship with others; this topic would include the fact that the sexual issue arises whenever intimacy (mental or physical) increases. An example of an important decision is, "Should I have sexual intercourse?" It might be helpful to keep the material more structured by using a questionnaire made up of factors that influence people in sexual decisions (for example, the questionnaire of McCreary-Jahasz and Kavanagh, 1978).

Patients need to be able to limit relationships, besides initiating and maintaining them; it is important to know how to prevent unwanted sex politely but firmly. Role-playing is often helpful and provides actual practice in relationship/social skills, e.g., handling fears of rejection (and acceptance!), getting to know people (without feeling trapped or pushed too fast), setting limits and expressing sexual interests. Using a male/female co-therapist team may be best. The leaders can support one another in difficult areas, and patients like to be able to identify with a model of the same sex in matters of sexuality.

Rooney (1977) presents a thoughtfully organized "human sexuality program in a day treatment center." She recommends a well-planned outline with structure which is delivered in a calm, confident manner, and suggests the program be done in two stages. The first is dissemination of factual information in a concrete way and without assuming that *anything* is known of the basic facts of sexuality. Topics suggested are sex language, anatomy, birth control, rape, venereal disease, homosexuality and ways of making love. The second stage involves a more personal, abstract, sharing discussion, which would include moral issues, relationships, alternate life styles, sexual myths, sexual fantasies, loss of a sexual outlet, and orgasm.

To conclude, sexuality is an important part of life, but there are strong resistances to and difficulties in dealing with this. By facing these facts, *and supporting one another*, staff and patients can make significant steps toward healthy sexuality. Staff will be surprised that the majority of patients will say how relieved or glad they are after being asked in a supportive, accepting way about details of their physical sexuality, and having had a chance to share their worry about sexual concerns.

12

Variations of Basic
Treatment Modalities

PHPs often vary in their uses of theoretical models. However, despite their general theoretical differences, most programs use groups and task-oriented activities in their treatment approaches to reach similar goals, i.e., patients' successful community living. These goals require abilities to handle the myriad of tasks of daily living, socialization, vocational rehabilitation, recreation and self-expression. This chapter will explore and describe the variety of PHP group approaches beyond the more traditional and primarily verbal group and individual psychotherapies, and also give an overview of the broad range of treatments offered by PHPs.

The modalities discussed here do not indicate a secondary or adjunctive status when compared with verbal psychotherapy. Nor do they imply, as some may believe, "busy work." They are planned therapeutic activities whose goals include dealing with a patient's problems, and enhancing his strengths and "skills," thus raising his level of functioning. Indeed, these activities may be the major and primary treatment focus.

Unfortunately, these activities are considered by many mental health professionals as "secondary treatment." This is so, perhaps, because these professionals still carry biases conveyed, albeit indirectly and subtly, in professional schools that a treatment hierachy exists, namely, that long-term individual psychoanalysis or insight-oriented psychotherapies hold the highest value, while certain groups, particularly task and activity groups, frequently hold the lowest place. Alternatively, the latter may be relegated to a so-called "adjunct" or "auxiliary" staff, such as occupational, recreational and creative arts therapists.

Patients often join PHPs after lengthy histories of marginal function. They may or may not have ever learned these basic skills of daily living; nonetheless, they often feel incapable of carrying out these important tasks and may feel inadequate and ashamed of their lack thereof.

A large range of skills is as vital for successful community living as is control of overt psychopathology. Patients need to develop new behavioral resources to build their repertoire of basic skills, while concurrently working on underlying conflicts, often in the same groups. For example, the patient may not have learned basic meal-planning, shopping and cooking. He may be reticent to make new attachments, ill-equipped to deal with community agencies, isolated, etc. Remediation of these deficits is attempted concurrently in groups along with exploring the causes for these problems.

SKILLS VERSUS THINKING AND FEELING

PHPs work to enhance patients' knowledge and dexterity in physical, social and intellectual tasks. Treatment should reflect this primary goal in a number of ways, most often moving away from the traditional biomedical model of curing a specific ailment, or dealing only with a person's inner inadequacies. Focus is also needed on the social systems on which he depends and which may have previously failed him. "The task is not to cure an ailment inside his skin, but to strengthen him to the point where he can once again participate in the interactions that make up the warp and woof of life" (Smith, 1968).

Although attention is directed at all levels, measurable changes can only be clearly seen in some form of actual behavior. The most desirable goal is not merely a contented patient, but one who can function. Thus, behaviorally oriented approaches should be used. These interventions deal with learning new, positive and transferable behaviors, including verbal, while unlearning the negative behaviors. In addition, staff can see more quickly and directly the effects of their interventions, an obvious advantage.

There exists a reciprocal benefit between verbal and task groups, i.e., each can enhance the use of the other. Task-oriented activities may increase comfort with self-expression. Many an activity has often encouraged social and verbal skills. Conversely, prior verbal discussion of a task may make participation in an activity easier.

IMPLICATIONS FOR SKILL–ORIENTED TREATMENT

In focusing on a skill-oriented approach, PHPs should be organized around the value of promoting translatable skills (Lamb, 1976b; Hersen and Luber, 1977; Carmichael, 1964), i.e., the teaching and learning of skills that will be used in the home and outside community. Lamb (1976b) stated, "A stress on translatable skills emphasizes the ultimate goal of productivity rather than dependency, activity rather than passivity" in the community. This emphasis requires training in treatment approaches beyond the traditional verbal psychotherapies. Thus, specialized staff, such as occupational, recreational and creative arts therapists, are recognized and valued as integral staff members for their emphasis on pragmatic *doing*, not just thinking and feeling, and they are not relegated to an inferior or secondary status within this treatment philosophy.

PHPs employ a variety of personnel of varying backgrounds who generally use a wider variety of integrated treatment approaches when compared to other programs. However, as discussed in Chapter 5, activity groups are also conducted by the more traditional mental health disciplines. Thus, contributions from these specialists are sought and shared to enhance staff roles and program quality, particularly if staffing patterns do not include all these psychotherapists.

In PHPs the program, rather than one or another of its components, is the treatment of choice. Focus may shift back and forth between verbal and activity treatment in order to work towards individual patient treatment goals. Often patients resist activity groups most. These groups encourage patient visibility and thus may seem, to some, more threatening since withdrawal and avoidance are more difficult. This problem of visibility may underlie patients' belittling activities while lauding "talking." Staff must assess this carefully.

Often, previous attempts at learning life-support tasks have engendered impatience, frustration, or even anger in the learner *and* the teacher, causing the skills to be taken over by others rather than encouraging the patient's perseverance. These skills can be taught and practiced in a safe and comfortable atmosphere, in which interfering emotional factors are handled instead of neglected as previously done in non-therapeutic settings. The following sections will detail specific treatment approaches to remediate skill deficits.

DAILY LIVING SKILLS GROUPS

Meal Preparation Groups

These are often arranged to provide daily or weekly lunch for the PHP, providing relatively nutritious and inexpensive meals. These groups also teach basic concepts and practice of nutrition, meal planning, economical shopping, use of shopping lists, food preparation, comfort with cooking utensils and kitchen appliances, and basic rules of sanitation and hygiene. Additionally, these groups offer opportunities to practice social skills, including table manners and mealtime conversation. Without such practice, many patients would take meals alone in restaurants, which they cannot easily afford, or eat less nutritious prepackaged foods at home (Johnson and Flowers, 1977). Patients who live in modestly equipped housing may have access to hot plates only. In a cooking group, creative and wholesome meals can be developed using a minimum of supplies and equipment. Developing menus for such cooking can be a challenging and inviting group task. Learning these new skills offers added opportunities to practice individual and group problem-solving and working with others to learn new and meaningful tasks which can easily be translated into home living.

In addition to the development of specific skills in meal preparation, these groups provide other, often more important, translatable skills, e.g., with meal planning comes the setting of priorities, practice in advance planning and building of self-esteem through task accomplishment.

Health Care, Grooming, and Personal Hygiene Groups

These groups develop skills in clothing care (laundry and sewing), personal hygiene (bathing, shaving, make-up application, and hair care), and health and dental care. All too often, patients use poor personal hygiene to avoid social contacts; institutions or families have acted as if patients were unable to handle their own care, or might be insulted or embarrassed by offers of assistance. These groups can encourage the patients' comfort with themselves, their appearance, and their impression upon others.

Personal Finance Groups

These groups offer assistance in money management, consumerism, and dealings with large bureaucratic systems (welfare, social security, utilities and banks). Role-playing, discussion and practice with pencil and paper can all be helpful techniques. These groups can also offer assertiveness techniques. Patients are often more expert in dealing with bureaucratic systems than staff. Sharing this expertise can improve self-esteem and confidence while promoting communication with others. In one PHP, patients wrote a handbook entitled, "What to Expect When You Apply for Welfare," a factual manual used by new patients and staff alike.

SOCIAL SKILLS GROUPS

These groups can be structured and theme-centered; e.g., having a specific focus such as current events, interpersonal relationships, committees, or sex education. On the other hand, they can be relatively unstructured, such as "coffee breaks." Their goals are similar—to encourage communication skills, interaction with others and development of positive relationships.

Current Events Groups

These groups focus on national, international, and local news. Members can benefit when they read, listen to radio broadcasts, or watch television and they can learn the skills necessary to discuss the information gained. Patients need topics unrelated to their psychiatric illness with which they can relate to others, while increasing their awareness of the world around them. Staff can use other media available, depending on the intellectual levels of group members. These groups lend themselves to a variety of levels and different media can be offered to higher- and lower-functioning patients.

Interpersonal Relations Groups

These groups provide a range of behaviorally oriented techniques for patients. Problems with typical but difficult situations can be reenacted or role played with opportunities to test out new approaches to situations, obtain feedback on problems, and struggle with and work through difficult issues. These groups may also use assertiveness training and emphasize its transfer to real-life situations.

In addition, these groups deal with nonverbal behavior such as eye contact, facial expressions, posture, gestures, voice tone, and quality and loudness (as well as content of) speech. For example, a typical situation is suggested, usually by a patient. Staff and patients role play the scene as it may have occurred, using verbal and nonverbal behavior as described by the patient. Then, the "actors" stop when the patient reports feeling discomfort with himself or the situation. The group's task is to offer alternatives and test or model them in a second role-play. Constructive feedback occurs in discussions which follow, or in segmenting the role-play and practicing each step. Videotape and audiotape equipment may be introduced, with proper preparation, as aids. If patients are able to see and hear themselves as others do, this can reinforce positive behaviors and lessen unsuccessful ones (Wilner et al., 1979).

Interpersonal relations groups may focus on specific problems, such as poor conversation skills, by having patients interview each other. This is an effective tool for: 1) helping members to become acquainted with each other; 2) practicing holding conversations; and 3) reinforcing their abilities to discuss "non-illness-related" subjects. Interviews may be brief (five to ten minutes); even in that short time, members can recognize common interests, topics, and hobbies. Finally, many patients have more trouble listening and maintaining interest in conversations than talking; thus, listening is also practiced.

Coffee Breaks

These are held daily in many programs and provide additional opportunities to help build confidence in social skills. Staff can either join in or not, depending on patients' needs. Sometimes, it is interesting to note how spontaneous and verbal patients can be in the absence of staff. At times, also, staff and patients may need a break from each other.

Committees

Various patient committees can also plan events and carry out chores. An *atten-*

dance committee may have responsibility for telephoning absent members and reporting back to the larger group, and for practicing telephone and other skills. *Party committees* may organize and plan special events using techniques learned in other groups.

Sex Education Groups are often components of social skills programming, and staff need to be well-versed and comfortable with conducting these groups (see Chapter 11).

VOCATIONAL SKILLS GROUPS

"There is not, as many have supposed, a clear relationship between work capacity and degree of emotional recovery; that is, the ability to obtain a job and perform it does not require a certain degree of wellness" (Lamb, 1976a, p. 97). Since social skills may or may not be related to a patient's vocational abilities, specific vocational evaluation and assessment are needed. A structured situation with clear guidelines and cues may encourage solid work skills. Accomplishment of work tasks can foster confidence and later success in social skills. These groups are often combinations of verbal and activity forms of treatment.

Work Readiness or Prevocational Groups

These include prevocational evaluation and testing, discussion of vocational plans and goals, and role playing typical and/or difficult work-related situations, e.g., employment interviews, the first day at a job, potential problems and stresses with co-workers or supervisors. Frequently, patients will verbalize interest in vocational goals, without knowing even the basic steps involved in planning for employment (paid or voluntary), job training, or further education. A patient who is verbally confused, even overtly psychotic, may never feel ready for even the simplest work, or staff may be reluctant to encourage the patient, fearing his failure in a regular work situation.

Here, a work readiness group can be effective for both patients and staff, who may otherwise over- or underestimate a patient's abilities. Tasks are assigned by staff who then supervise (students or volunteers may also supervise). Tasks should be related to the patient's stated goals. They can also be related to program needs, i.e., clerical tasks, keeping attendance records, and filing of non-patient-related material such as recipes for the cooking group. A patient interested in manual work may attempt needed wiring repairs, or may complete a woodworking project for the community's use. Another may take inventories of supplies. The list of tasks can be as lengthy and as varied as the patient's needs and goals. Typing, arithmetic, English, and reading tests should be available. Graduated tasks, from the simple to the more complex, will give patients chances to see their progress or their difficulties. Tasks may be shared among members to evaluate cooperativeness and competitiveness. Tasks can also include preparing resumes or employment applications. Since legal issues may arise in regard to the types of tasks permitted, staff should consult administrators and avoid later problems.

Evaluating work readiness involves the following areas: personal appearance, attendance, punctuality, attitudes toward work, supervisor and peers, ability to profit from criticism, response to praise, following written or oral instructions, concentration, accuracy and speed, flexibility, tolerance, care of equipment and work area, physical vitality, motivation, and adjustment to pressure. The evaluation also includes the patient's stated plans, and it is particularly helpful when presented verbally *and* in writing, with opportunities for discussion. Finally, it includes performance ratings and recommendations. Written evaluations, with patient input, are similar to those encountered in actual employment. This tool helps the client to judge his own actual performance, while it can prepare him for future job performance ratings.

Included also in work readiness groups is discussion of work-related issues. Interviews may be role played; work rules and behaviors are discussed. Potential problems can be worked through prior to actual situations.

PHPs may be reluctant to attempt these groups, believing that they may be unnecessarily duplicating work of vocational agencies, who would prefer their own evaluations. However, it has been our experience that patients benefit from this evaluation, conducted in the safe PHP environment where failure is not devastating. In fact, repetition of previously successful tasks can reinforce skills. In addition, difficulties such as the need for eyeglasses and other physical problems can be discovered and dealt with early, without postponing training or work, or goals can be reevaluated to attempt more realistic planning without subjecting the patient to another failure.

Vocational agencies often request recommendations from program staff for realistic planning. These groups can provide necessary data. Prior consultation with and visits to vocational agencies and personnel can help in the organization of programs to obtain these data for appropriate referrals, which, in turn, can enhance inter-agency relationships, leading to successful treatment planning and patient goal achievement.

Small Business Operations

Small business can be alternatives or complements to a work readiness group. These patient-operated services such as *sandwich sales* and *coffee canteens* may combine daily life, social and prevocational skills. Other examples are *craft and plant sales,* and a *thrift shop* may provide useful merchandise at reasonable prices, while achieving vocational goals (Platt and Jones, 1980). In addition, these services make meaningful contributions to the PHP.

While such businesses do not necessarily translate into jobs for patients, they can test patients' abilities and work readiness. For example, a *coffee canteen* can be organized to sell beverages, breakfast or lunches to staff and patients. Group members operate the business, prepare food, serve customers, and care for the work area and equipment. Staff, or students and volunteers, or experienced patients can supervise. Experienced patients can train new personnel. Work is evaluated daily in writing by the supervisor. Weekly "worker meetings" handle bookkeeping, ordering, planning and discussion of work rules, procedures and problems. Patients can work individually, in pairs, or in small groups.

Other groups, such as plant and craft sales or thrift shops, can be organized similarly. While profits are not always enough for minimum wage, the group can plan special events or buy supplemental program supplies not otherwise available. Clients' favorites are often luncheons, theater parties, special equipment such as phonographs, or hobby tools. Money-making activities should always carry administrative approval to insure that they are not violating any agency regulations or patients' rights.

Staff need to be aware of possible negative biases toward these work groups and should try to avoid transmitting these biases to patients. Work, which may be viewed by staff as repetitive and monotonous, may be providing valuable experiences for clients. The feelings of being productive, useful, and needed may outweigh the tedium; or the so-called tedium may provide needed consistency leading to mastery of tasks. Patients may not necessarily see these tasks requiring fewer cognitive skills as demeaning.

Further, some staff may be concerned that an overemphasis on these groups may detract from the traditional attention to intrapsychic issues. While these groups can de-emphasize the more traditional approaches, they are in keeping with the translatable skills emphasis of PHPs.

RECREATION AND LEISURE GROUPS

Having fun is not a usual goal of psychotherapy. Enjoyment is a nice side benefit, but often not a major treatment objective. PHPs, however, have recognized the importance of learning to have fun and enjoying leisure time; they incorporate recreation and leisure groups into programming. These groups also include practical tasks of exploring resources in the community (Jones and Mowrey, 1980) and learning new skills such as appropriate social conversation and other behaviors, and negotiating travel for other activities. While sounding enjoyable, these groups may be particularly difficult for some patients. For example, a patient may be uncomfortable on a trip with other "mental patients," feeling exposed, or a patient who has difficulty with distorted or otherwise negative body image will be reluctant to join a sports group or beach party. Care should be taken to deal with patient resistances to these activities.

Trip Groups

These include use of community resources such as parks, beaches, movies, plays, concerts, museums, bowling lanes, sporting events and libraries. Members discuss and plan trips, keeping in mind the cost, travel time and accessibility to public transportation. This last factor is especially important so that these trips may be repeated during patients' own leisure time. Funds can be saved for more expensive outings and scheduling can be handled for lengthy trips, but primarily, outings should be those which patients can later enjoy themselves without staff assistance.

Recreation Groups

These groups may also sponsor parties and other celebrations for birthdays, holidays, member and staff farewells, etc. Here members can practice a variety of skills including social and daily life skills (cooking, planning and shopping) while also trying to "have fun." Social dancing, conversing, table and card games, and listening to music provide opportunities for relationship-building, relaxation, and stress relief.

Sports Groups

These can also be multipurpose—for recreation, tension and aggression management, body awareness, and mastery of an activity. Patients are taught rules and scoring for various social games, which they can play in their own leisure time. This group can be particularly useful for younger males who may have difficulties with more verbal and more sedentary groups.

Hobby Art and Woodworking Groups

These groups are designed also to provide alternatives for leisure. Crafts which can be done at home are taught and practiced. Also, crafts can provide successful experiences in making attractive and useful objects. While stimulating interest in hobbies, crafts aid in developing concentration and perseverance; following directions; planning, executing, and completing tasks—all abilities needed for a variety of skills.

Special Interest Groups

These groups offer other hobbies as interest and needs are presented and can include music or art appreciation, and stamp or coin collecting.

CREATIVE ARTS GROUPS

The goals of creative arts groups are similar to the above, despite the media used, and include:

1) identifying and expressing thoughts and feelings verbally and nonverbally;
2) improving interpersonal communication through structured and theme-centered groups;
3) encouraging assertiveness by eliciting opinions and thoughts about projects;
4) offering alternatives to current life situations; and
5) evaluating intellectual and expressive abilities (Hersen and Luber, 1977).

Movement Therapy Groups

These can include warm-up exercises and relaxation techniques to begin the day, or later to help break the routine of more sedentary groups. Techniques can be used at home and can aid in body awareness, physical vitality, and self-image; in release of tension; and in coordination and perceptual-motor problems. Balance exercises can help to determine whether coordination difficulties are due to medication side effects, physical disabilities, or perceptual-motor problems (Fertig and Howes, 1977).

Music Therapy Groups

These may include singalongs, music appreciation, expanding interest in and knowledge about various types of music, while energizing and freeing emotions and expression both verbally and physically. Talents may be discovered or reinforced; spontaneity is encouraged as is group cohesiveness (Fowler and Dunford, 1977). Music can encourage other recreational and expressive activities; common feelings can be elicited and socialization enhanced.

Art Therapy Groups

These provide still another alternative through individual work and group murals. While providing interesting and attractive decoration, projects also offer opportunities to identify and clarify feelings, issues, and concerns. Paintings and drawings may portray life events or feelings, often more graphically and deeply than words allow. Following the graphic exposition, verbalization may be made easier.

Drama Groups

These offer creative outlets, whether using improvisation, actual plays or psychodrama. Both individual and group themes can be identified here and worked on in other groups. Members can learn more about each other and each other's struggles. Feller (1979) has suggested combining art and psychodrama, with each member drawing or painting a picture, later sharing it with the group and, finally, building a scene around the feeling or situation illustrated.

Staff working with severely disturbed paitents should be aware of the need to keep down abstraction and fantasy in order to prevent a flood of feelings or severe regression. Focus on a play or actual story is advisable. Reading lines and practicing stage directions can provide a reality base for expression. Finally, the group may be modeled after the interpersonal relations groups, using real or typical situations.

Poetry Groups

These provide a variety of functions. Luber (1977) has enumerated four basic therapeutic functions: 1) identification with feelings and emotions, using poems that can demonstrate the universality of loneliness, depression, uncertainty, alienation, joy, satisfaction, and meaning; 2) expression of these feelings in a socially acceptable and concrete way, even offering catharsis; 3) creativity in producing individual work or in providing a dramatic reading of another's work; and 4) evaluation of intellectual and interactional functioning, focusing thought and attention on a single topic or feeling expressed in poetry, since it requires "intellectual discipline and organization of thought" (p.71). Interaction is encouraged by sharing opinions, feelings and interpretations of the poetry. Poems can portray feelings, thoughts and even situations faced by patients. Also, song lyrics may be seen as poetry, and music may be incorporated.

Writing Groups

These provide similar benefits to poetry groups. These groups also have a practical function in that members can also be helped in specific areas, such as handwriting, vocabulary, and letter-writing. Groups may construct a PHP newsletter, including reports of events, issues, and creative work. Interviews with new patients or staff may be entries. Members also utilize clerical skills of typing, xeroxing, proofreading, and collating; they may work in collaboration with the work readiness groups.

SPECIALIZED GROUPS

In addition to the five general types of groups described above, some PHPs offer specialized groups such as weight control, reinforcing of ideas and issues of meal planning, and offering low-calorie menus and exercise techniques. Self-management groups provide techniques in "controlling undesirable thoughts and feelings by increasing productive thinking and decreasing anxiety" (Eckman, 1979, p. 37). The "ethnic exchange" groups can identify and deal with overt and covert forms of racism, while also sharing information and experiences regarding the various cultures of PHP members.

Although this list of groups is common to PHPs, other types of groups can be offered. Media may change with patient needs and staff skills, provided that groups continue to offer translatable skills. Patients in PHP have a range of problems and, thus, are in need of an assortment of task and verbal approaches, along with medication and other somatic therapies, to improve the quality of their lives. The expertise of a multidisciplinary staff is needed to provide this variety. Activity treatment approaches may vary to some degree but all need to be based on the concepts of remediation of basic skills deficits and their translatability to successful community living. Further development of these types of resources for PHPs should be encouraged in order to handle even more effectively the problems and needs of PHP patients.

III

Program Types and Standards

13

Toward a Comprehensive, Systematized Description and Assessment of Partial Hospitals

Science only exists if there is valid and accurate knowledge; this results from using a systematized, standardized descriptive method. Unfortunately, no such method has been applied to the infinitely variable partial hospitals, and descriptions of the content and function of partial hospitals are confusing and inadequate. Following discussion of these issues, this chapter makes suggestions for alleviating the problem.

THE CURRENT DILEMMA AND ITS SIGNIFICANCE

Given the great complexity inherent in any partial hospital, no one program is identical to another. A potential asset in diversity is a richness, flexibility, and room for creativity to better meet the needs of potential patients. However, the diversity and complexity can appear as totally idiosyncratic and without underlying commonality, and this situation results in an excess of information which is bewildering and disconcerting (Miller, 1980; Hammersley, 1979).

A scrutiny was made of recently published detailed descriptions of day hospitals in reputable journals (Blume et al., 1979; Fink et al., 1978b; Guillette et al., 1978; Penk et al., 1978; Vannicelli et al., 1978; Watts and Bennett, 1978). None of these six articles presented the same data about their programs or patients! For example, out of 17 reported patient characteristics not one was reported on by all six. Only one program reported on the physical milieu. The six programs gave 23 different ways of measuring outcome! Only two programs shared even one method in common. They called themselves "day hospital," "partial hospital," "day treatment," and "day center," but none presented enough data about themselves for the reader to determine their specific nature and method of operation. None presented enough data to indicate that they met the criteria for a partial hospital as defined in this book. These six incompletely descriptive articles are typical of the articles that make up about one-third of the entire PHP literature of about 475 articles, chapters and books appearing prior to January 1980 (author's analysis of Maxey, 1980). Certainly one could not generalize to other situations or duplicate the work (and a sine qua non of scientific fact is replicability [Garfield and Bergin, 1978]).

Thus, there is still no scientific, organizing framework being applied to the partial hospital entity, and the resulting confusion has contributed significantly to at least five unsatisfactory drawbacks:

1) Essentially no one can feel secure and in control.
2) Good communication is nearly impossible.
3) It is very difficult to share experiences, support, learn from one another, and develop a cohesive association of partial hospitals that can fight for important goals for the partial hospital movement.
4) PHPs fail to explain their programs to outsiders and to win their support, e.g., third-party payers still cannot distinguish a PHP from traditional outpatient care; therefore, they do not reimburse for day hospital, or do so at unrealistically low rates (Guillette et al., 1978).
5) It is nearly impossible to amass a body of good research and evaluation on partial hospitalization.

DEVELOPMENT OF THE PROBLEM AND DIRECTIONS FOR THE FUTURE

Partial hospitals proliferated with a youthful, enthusiastic, creative zeal. Dynamic great leaps forward are generally antithetical to self-questioning timidity. The doctrinal slogan seemed to be "Let a hundred flowers bloom, let a hundred schools of thought contend," made famous by Chairman Mao Tse Tung. Cautious organization and regulation were too stultifying; creation and survival were the top priority (see also Chapter 1). However, continued too long, such a situation ends up with identity diffusion, a very shaky foundation, cynicism, disillusionment, and a susceptibility to attack (Borus, 1978).

The direction for PHPs in the 1980s needs to be one of change from the restless chaos. Repeatedly, important literature trumpets the critical necessity for scientific rigor with systematic assessment and evaluation methods (Endicott and Spitzer, 1979; Report of the Task Panel on Research, 1978; Moos, 1974; Test and Stein, 1978). The central question is whether those in the partial hospitalization movement are ready to accept what is demanded of them and are willing to establish a uniform set of guidelines, standards, and methodology. Some suggested guidelines will be offered here toward a systematized way of describing a program (see also Chapters 2 and 3).

TOWARD A FORMAT FOR UNIFORM AND SYSTEMATIC PROGRAM DESCRIPTION

There must be at least certain basic data reported by all programs to give an adequate comprehsension of the program. Much of this is a part of the evaluation-management information system each program should have for smooth operating (see Chapter 22). The data should accurately cover all vital areas of the program and patients. Although the research has not yet been done which will tell us definitively which measurement instrument is preferable, or which aspects of the program or patients are the ones most determining outcome, this situation does not negate the gathering of data. On the contrary, any adequate program is based on theory and concepts, which delineate essential characteristics. For example, there is a belief that behavior is a function of both the individual and his environment; thus, the treatment environment is a key element in the therapeutic process. Therefore, program descriptions must provide information about all six of the essential dimensions of a therapeutic milieu (see below), especially detailed discussions of the program philosophy and patient-staff interaction (Moos, 1974). What is offered below borrows heavily from unsurpassed surveys of many partial hospital programs by Glasscote et al. (1969) in the U.S.A., Farndale (1961) in Great Britain, plus the prize-winning book by Moos (1974) on evaluating therapeutic milieus. Inevitably, the six major categories are interrelated and somewhat overlapping, and some characteristics could fall into more than one category. They include: organizational structure and procedures, environment surrounding the PHP, dimensions of the program members (patients and staff), psychotherapeutic modalities, characteristics of the therapeutic milieu, and methods of behavior reinforcement.

A PROGRAM DESCRIPTION INSTRUMENT FOR PARTIAL HOSPITALS

Organizational Structure and Procedures

1) List the overall objectives, purposes, and functions of the PHP.
2) Mention when the PHP began accepting patients.
3) The physical plant and equiment: detail the total square footage of available space for clinical activities. State the total number of separate rooms, and describe these, mentioning if these are used solely by the PHP or are shared.
4) Discuss provisions for transportation.
5) For the preceding four-month period describe:
   (a) The average number of patients on the active caseload that would actually attend in a week.
   (b) The average attendance at any one time.
   (c) The lowest and highest attendance during the four-month period.
   (d) The average percentage of expected patients who actually attended.
6) Describe the referral sources for the PHP, and from each source detail the number of patients given appointments, interviewed, and admitted each month.
7) Mention the number of additional patients who were screened by telephone and not given an intake appointment.

8) Screening, selection, and admission processes:
   (a) Mention the hours and days spent on screening each patient.
   (b) Describe the screening process and the structured psychiatric evaluation instruments used.
   (c) Describe in specific extensive detail the staff criteria for admission and exclusion. Criteria are needed in regards to the patient's age; diagnoses (physical and mental); level of adaptive functioning; ability to sit quietly for a period of time in a group; control over impulsivity; ability to plan, commit self to and carry through a task; ability to follow directions and/or respond to requests; ability to respond verbally without digressing; symptoms regarding imminent* suicide or homicide, and history of suicide or homicide; motivition and ability to come reliably to the entire program; living situation (stability, degree of family supports, etc.); travel time from home to program; lack of responsiveness to more traditional outpatient care; lack of clarity of diagnosis under Outpatient Department (OPD) workup; and monetary resources for paying fees and basic living costs.
   (d) Describe any type of patient who staff feel benefits most from this program.
   (e) If staff feel that the PHP is better than traditional outpatient or inpatient care for certain conditions, describe these.
   (f) Describe the initial workup after the admission decision has been made.
   (g) If staff are dubious about a patient's potential success in the program, describe any procedures used.
9) Medical Records: If record procedures differ from standards mentioned herein, specify these differences. State whether or not a patient is encouraged to read his chart. Mention if the problem-oriented medical record system is used.
10) Describe the system of ongoing patient reevaluation and which structured measuring instruments are used.
11) Describe criteria for a patient's continuation or discharge.
12) Mention the average number of admissions per month (over past four months) and what percentage were readmissions.
13) Length of Stay: Give the average, median, and range of length of stay of those discharged in the preceding four months. Give these numbers for both the number of calendar days and actual treatment days. Then give numbers for each of the two subgroups of discharges, i.e., those who completed an entire course in the PHP, and those who dropped out or had their course of treatment interrupted for more than three days in an inpatient service. Describe any strong efforts to limit treatment and mention if there is an absolute maximum number of days that the patient can continue in the program.
14) Discharges: Describe, for the preceding four months, the average number

---

* Likely to occur in 48 hours.

discharged per month. Mention the average number per month that were discharged before completing the planned length of stay (various types of dropouts).

15) Mention the number of PHP patients admitted each month to inpatient care for more than three days and those for less than three days, and returned to the PHP.

16) Describe for final* discharges over the past four months the number falling into each type of a disposition made for patients, e.g., transferred to psychiatric inpatient care, discharged without provision for further treatment, etc.

17) Describe any provision for patients to have a continuing contact with the PHP of fewer than eight hours per week.

18) Outcome Measurements:

   (a) Describe what structured psychiatric measurements (MMPI, etc.) are used to gauge patient's symptoms, satisfactions, instrumental role performance, burden to family, social functioning, and others.

   (b) Mention efforts made to measure patient functioning at 6, 12, and 24 months after final discharge.

   (c) State the percentage of patients at final discharge, and 6, 12, and 24 months thereafter, that achieve at least part-time work, go on to a vocational rehabilitation program, or are hospitalized. Mention the average length of inpatient stay for those hospitalized. In each category, indicate the percentage of patients followed up.

19) Costs and Financing:

   (a) Describe the annual budget, including all expenses (direct and indirect costs), as if the PHP were a completely self-supporting entity, and indicate the percentage of this budget that is for staff salaries and fringe benefits.

   (b) Mention the sources of monies to pay for expenses, according to each type and amounts in each type.

   (c) State the annual budget divided by the number of annual visits to give a cost per average patient visit. Add more details as appropriate, e.g., per three-hour or per five-hour visit. Mention any additional service charges, e.g., meals, transportation, drugs, individual therapy. Indicate any other pertinent fee rules, e.g., sliding scales, obligatory fee for all patients, etc.

   (d) Mention any initial capital costs.

20) Other; e.g., arranged furloughs, etc.

The Environment Surrounding the PHP

1) Describe ownership and any lines of authority extending from the PHP and any formal relationships with outside entities.

---

* Final, here, means readmission is not expected soon.

2) Licensing and accreditation: Describe any outsiders who have some control over the PHP by right of laws or power of funding. Mention if the PHP is accredited by the Joint Commission on the Accreditation of Hospitals.

3) Describe the location and catchment area. Include inpatient services and other PHPs within one hour's transportation.

4) Describe transportation facilities (problems, accessibility, etc.).

5) Community contacts: Describe activities of staff that are spent in contact with others outside the PHP and not related to the immediate referral of, or matters directly related to, a patient. Specify which staff are engaged in this.

Dimensions of the Members of the Program

1) Describe characteristics of the patients on the caseload in the past four months. Include information on:

   (a) The total number of different patients that have been on the active caseload in the past four months;

   (b) Age (average, median, range, and percentage under 21 and over 65);

   (c) The five most frequent general categories of DSM III Axis I diagnoses; and the percentage of patients in each diagnostic category (e.g., schizophrenia 50%). Give similar information on the patient population for Axis II (personality and specific developmental disorders), Axis III (physical disorders), IV (psychosocial stressors) and V (highest level of adaptive functioning in the past year);

   (d) Marital status and percentage of patients in each category;

   (e) Information revealed by structured measuring instruments;

   (f) Sex;

   (g) Number that have had previous psychiatric treatment: average age at first hospitalization, percentage of patients admitted that had had previous hospitalizations, number of days this hospitalized group spent as psychiatric inpatients in the last 24 months (average and range), and the percentage of patients admitted who had fewer than six mental health treatment sessions or visits prior to admission;

   (h) Average and range of educational grade completed;

   (i) Percentage of total patients with history of suicidal actions;

   (j) Percentage of total with history of violence to others;

   (k) Percentage with a history of being in jail;

   (l) Full- and part-time occupational status on admission (employed, student, housewife, odd jobs, other);

   (m) Income level (take-home pay, after taxes, per week);

   (n) Race;

   (o) Living situation (alone, with others, in special setting, etc.).

2) Staff over the past four months. Include information on:

(a) The average number of different paid staff and the total number of hours that they put into the program per week, e.g., "We have ten different staff who put in 200 hours per week." Define "full-time" (see Appendix). Divide the staff into functional groups (social workers, secretaries, etc.), and provide the following data for each group: number of full-time and part-time, total number of full-time equivalents, sex, average number of years of mental health work experience after last degree, average years of schooling post high school, average years in PHPs, how each group spends their employed time (include what percentage of the time is in contact with patients).

(b) Non-salaried staff: Divide this staff into students and non-students. Also specify details about these groups during the school-year and non-school-year periods. Specify the following over the period of a week: average number and age range, the average length of stay (months?), and the average number of hours spent per week by each group and range. Indicate the PHP's purpose in using student and non-student volunteers in their activities.

(c) Miscellaneous aspects of staff functioning.

Psychotherapeutic Modalities

1) Provide a day-by-day schedule of the therapies each hour of the week. For each session give the title/focus, whether verbal or activity, number of patients attending, and the number of staff planned.

2) Indicate the maximum and minimum number of hours per week that a patient can attend.

3) Summarize for the week: hours of free time for patients during the day; hours of psychotherapies (and percentage of time divided between acitvity and verbal types); number of hours and types of staff conferences without patients (staff supervision, treatment and program planning, etc.); and hours with all staff and patients together.

4) If there are different schedules for patients, explain these, e.g., 20 attend five days per week from 9 A.M.-4 P.M.; 10 attend Mondays, Wednesdays, and Fridays from 9 A.M.-1 P.M. with the other 20, etc.

5) Indicate the various therapeutic modalities available and the percentage of the total patients planned to have each type.

6) Indicate provisions for 24-hour emergency and guesting services.

7) Describe procedures and policies regarding concurrent treatments elsewhere.

Characteristics of the Therapeutic Milieu

1) Describe the treatment philosophy and model used to guide the PHP, e.g., eclectic, therapeutic community, or token economy.

2) Indicate the way the PHP conceptualizes the needs of the patients served and the factors thought to promote improvement.

3) Describe the characteristics of the PHP in regard to the following: active involvement of patients; supportiveness to one another; encouragement of patients' self-expression; encouragement of autonomy; practical preparation for leaving the program; concern with and understanding of patients' personal problems; allowing and encouraging expression of anger; emphasis on order and organization in both patients and program; clarity of rules and expectations; and the degree of staff tendency to control.

4) Indicate what is done by staff to systematically assess and assure that the milieu is therapeutic (see also Kopolow and Cohen, 1976).

Methods of Behavior Reinforcement

1) List PHP policies and rules governing behavior.

2) List the reinforcements used by the PHP to both increase appropriate and decrease inappropriate behavior, ranked according to degree of use.

14

Program Classification and
Some Models of Programs in
Partial Hospitalization

This chapter discusses some of the issues regarding classification and models applied to partial hospitalization.

CLASSIFICATION OF PHPS

Despite the ultimate uniqueness of each partial hospital, there are common basic features among them, beyond the criteria for partial hospital as defined in Chapter 2. This commonality allows for classification of partial hospitals into various categories for the purposes of communication, control, experimentation, and comprehension; the specific terms identifying the categories make up a nomenclature (Spitzer and Williams, 1980), further advancing scientific work.

Ultimately there can be any number of classification schemata. Each one can be useful for solving a different problem or satisfying some need. For example, if a decision were made that a heroin-dependent patient needed partial hospitalization, it would be helpful to have a list of partial hospitals classified according to diagnosis of population served.

As a word of caution, although pigeon-holing (classification) can be helpful, it has some drawbacks; e.g., it tends to force any entity into a mold that does not quite fit. A given classification scheme may typically show just four or five categories in the continuum, while in reality there is an infinite number possible in any one dimension. Most programs are mixtures, and they tend to take a position in the central part of any hypothetical continuum.

The following are eight categories of a basic classification scheme and standard nomenclature for types of PHPs.

1) Time Period

The most common and obvious classification designates five periods of the week in which the program operates. Thus, day treatment indicates partial hospitalization occurring essentially sometime between 9 A.M. and 5 P.M.; evening PHPs operate within the 5 P.M. to 10 P.M. time period; night programs fall within any period between 10 P.M. and 9 A.M. All three types run from two to seven days a week. Weekend PHPs operate mostly during Saturday and/or Sunday. If a partial hospital operates during more than one time period, it usually has separately organized "tracks" or subprograms for each time period; thus, it is a mixed time period PHP.

2) Length of Stay

Partial hospitals tend to set up their programs for one of five different lengths of stay, i.e., short-term (3-10 weeks), intermediate-term (2½-10 months), long-term (10-24 months), and indefinite-term (24-60 months). Finally, some programs design their program to be varied-term; thus, there would be a heterogeneous mix of patients in regard to their levels of functioning and ability to improve, and according to lengths of stay. Such varied-term programs would also have mechanisms to be responsive to the differences in the patients served.

3) Five Levels of Intensity of PHP Services

Intensity is basically determined by staff/patient ratio and hours of service offered (not by whether probing of the unconscious or extensive confrontation is done). At one end of the spectrum would be the maximum intensity program with a staff/patient ratio of at least one-to-one and patients attending ten hours per day seven days per week. The minimum intensity program would have a staff/patient ratio of one to eight, with patients attending only eight hours per week. Between these two extremes would be high, medium, and low intensity programs. For example, medium intensity might mean five hours a day, for twice a week, with a staff/patient ratio of one to four.

4) PHP Treatment Philosophy or Model

Although many programs may be eclectic, most of the programs that do adopt a more specific model develop their therapeutic milieu according to variants on an ill-defined concept of the therapeutic community (see Chapter 7). A second model extensively used is an educational-behavioral-learning construct to guide the therapeutic milieu. The third and least frequent type used is a traditional biomedical-psychoanalytic model with definite regular individual psychotherapy and the tendency to stress psychodynamic insight, resolution of internal conflicts, prescription of treatments, and a firm hierarchy. (For other models, see Chapter 2.)

5) Number of Different Patient Schedules Offered

A number of partial hospitals have tried to increase their responsiveness to a single patient by increasing the number of possible schedules that any one patient could have. A different schedule could offer another treatment modality or a different slant, according to staff's judgment of any one patient's capacity to respond, level of functioning, and other special features. Sometimes, under the umbrella of "the partial hospitalization service," there are, in fact, two or more *separate* partial hospitals, each with a single track, e.g., one partial hospital program of ten members with acute florid symptomatology and a completely separate program of 20 chronic patients. "Tracks," "levels," and "stratifications" are the commonly used words for the variations in treatment schedules of groups of patients, while keeping most of the overall program uniform for all.

At the other end of the spectrum from the unitary track program would be a program with so many possible alternative schedules as to fall outside the parameters of the partial hospital designation. Then it would be simply an outpatient clinic, training center, or psychosocial rehabilitation services agency that offers an unusual number of possible treatments (or sessions) each week.

In order that a program retain focus, meaning, and a therapeutic milieu, a patient would have to stay with a group of the same six to ten patients at least 55 percent of his time per week in partial hospitalization. In addition, the number of patients with which any one patient should be expected to interact extensively needs to be limited; an optimum number is 20 (with a minimum around ten and a maximum around 35). Research is needed to evaluate and establish these points.

It would seem highly desirable for every program to offer *some* tracks. This could be done quite simply. For example, the program described in Chapter 15 is two-track. If a program offers two different group treatments in each of four time slots, in a typical week of 25 slots, theoretically, there could be 16 possible program variants.

6) Characteristics of the Patients Served

Programs may be homogeneous or heterogeneous, according to any one characteristic of the patients served. One patient feature is diagnosis. Often, patients with certain primary diagnoses are treated, as a group, separately. For example, physical disorders and significant organic mental disorders are treated separately from psychiatric disorders. Recall that the terms "day hospital" and "day care" (and others) are being used also by programs that are treating patients with *physical* disorders as the primary problems (Weissert, 1976; Hamill, 1981).

If there are enough resources, there are usually separate programs for each of the five following primary psychiatric diagnoses: (a) alcohol use disorders, (b) other substance use disorders, and (c) mild (and more severe) mental retardation. The minimally impaired organic mental disorders and other mental disorders are generally separated into (d) the most acute-phase patients with florid symptoms and (e) stabilized chronically and severely impaired patients.

Another typical classification is according to age group. Programs for children are usually separated from others, as are programs organized for adolescents and the elderly.

7) Location

Three additional terms might designate the locale of the PHP. "Hospital" (as "day hospital") would indicate a PHP that uses the same space (and often essentially the same staff) as does an ongoing inpatient service. "Unit" (as in "day unit") is a PHP located inside a hospital but using primarily different space from the inpatient service. The word "program" (as in "day program") designates a PHP located outside a hospital building. A specific designation of locale may be important because of current reimbursement formulae, which often give considerably higher reimbursement for hospital-based programs. The use of the word "hospital" is minimized in the above terminology because of its connotation of sickness, dependency, low responsibility, and institutionalization.

8) Treatment Functions

In addition to all partial hospitals having a general purpose of striving toward the patients being improved, programs are also organized for a more specific treatment (versus training or research) function. Typically, partial hospitals are classified into types according to which patient needs are served, and these needs are primarily based on current functional status and prognosis (versus diagnosis, etc.). In reality, there is an infinite variety of types.*

(a) A *crisis-support program* has the function of treating patients with "acute phase disability." The patients could be either chronic (with significant exacerbation) or acute (with a relatively rapid onset, short course, etc.) patients, but all would be experiencing florid symptomatology and deficits of functioning to such a degree that strong considerations for hospitalization would arise. The main goal is to have patients return to a pre-florid state and be ready for further improvement by the *stabilization* services provided. This program provides a primary treatment program (instead of the alternative, more restrictive, 24-hour hospitalization) with the goal of preventing hospitalization or decreasing the length of stay in the hospital.

The period after discharge from a hospital is typically a transitional period of continuing recuperation, readjustment to community living, and functioning at a lower level than the patient's potential. Thus, these stabilization services would also be used as *transitional* programs for those individuals who are still quite symptomatic and who might decompensate readily without intensive support upon

---

* The terms "crisis," "support," "growth" and "sustenance" used in the scheme come from the glossary of JCAH (1979, pp. 135-43).

discharge from the hospital. (At other times during the transitional period a patient is less symptomatic and might best profit from entering one of the other programs listed below.)

(b) *A growth treatment program* has the function of serving relatively stabilized patients with residual dysfunction by providing an enhancing *habilitation/rehabilitation* treatment program, for achievement of the best possible functioning. Not infrequently this category of programs is divided into two types:

i) One type (*extensive growth* treatment) would serve patients in a transitional period (or functioning similarly to these types of patients), who were judged likely to respond relatively rapidly (in 3-12 months) and to such a degree as to probably achieve independent living with satisfactory interpersonal and vocational functioning (having friends, holding a job, and managing basic self-care);
ii) A *growth-support* treatment program would serve patients with long-standing disorders including only marginal past functioning, at best, in one or more significant areas of role performance. These patients would be judged able to raise functioning levels significantly (though perhaps not up to full functioning in society), although relatively slowly (about 10-24 months); Weldon and Frances (1977, pp. 339-340) discuss these two types further.

(c) A *maintenance-support treatment program* has the function of supporting stabilized chronic patients by providing a sustenance treatment program. A chronic patient is "a person who is in need of long-term continuing care and rehabilitation" (Talbott, 1978). Thus, he is a person who has persistent marginal functioning and a high risk for hospitalization. This type of program may be required indefinitely because some patients have a permanently unstable extra-hospital adjustment. Thus, the primary goal of this type of program (even though the patients might improve in other ways) is achieving a better record of maintaining skills/functioning and preventing the need for more intensive crisis care of hospitalization than was true for the patient before partial hospitalization. The primary focus is on preventing depths of deterioration, rather than achieving new peaks.

A final category for partial hospitals sometimes listed (see, for example, Glasscote et al., 1969) is that of *diagnosis*; however, no known program is designed to provide *only* diagnostic services. Nonetheless, there are patients whose symptom/functional picture is so confusing and complex that satisfactory understanding and diagnosis are not attainable through traditional outpatient programs. In these cases, the partial hospital is invaluable for providing the necessary, extensive direct observation, identification of problem areas, and formulation of a treatment plan; at the same time, the disadvantages of hospitalization are avoided.

To conclude, PHP clinicians are strongly urged to use a standard nomenclature and classification scheme accurately and consistently; to do so would considerably advance the science of PHP work.

OUTLINES OF THREE BASIC FUNCTIONAL TYPES OF PROGRAMS

Table 1 gives the main distinguishing features typically associated with three different partial hospitals, classified according to the three basic types of treatment uses mentioned above. In reality, a partial hospital often provides a combination of these functions; thus, it also has a combination of features and mixed patient populations.

A SELECTION OF PROGRAMS

There is a myriad of programs written up in the literature. Unfortunately, most have been done so incompletely that they are ultimately confusing and unsatisfying for obtaining good appreciation of the whole program. Presented below (Table 2) are a variety of types of programs. These could serve as a reference source for ideas either to compare with an existing PHP or to plan for a future PHP.

INTERESTING PROGRAM VARIANTS

The adoption of behavioral psychotherapy techniques is common. As an example, Liberman et al. (1977) present a partial hospital heavily utilizing principles of a token economy. Their program involved a regular five-day week with a median two-month stay for 25 patients with eight staff. The patients were generally considerably impaired and half had been previously hospitalized with a diagnosis of psychosis. Liberman et al.'s aims were to reintegrate the patient into the community by teaching skills. Immediate rewards included social recognition and attention from staff, which were found to be very important. Their research found that the careful delivery of reward increased participation and attendance, and decreased dropout rate.

Another program (Spiegler and Agigian, 1977) carried out an educational-behavioral-social systems model to an unusually great degree. Under the aegis of the VA psychiatric day treatment center, this growth-support program was provided for about 43 (29-67) chronic patients (called "trainees") by four staff and a raft of volunteers. The year was divided into 11-week "quarters" with "classes" in the "training center." They wove in very creatively a school model and educational technology (e.g. courses called: "*Basic* Social Communication" and "*Advanced* Social Communication"). Although they were not able to compare patients *randomly* assigned to a regular VA day treatment center with the community training center, their evaluation showed one-sixth the rehospitalization rate for the training center dischargees ("graduates") compared to the regular day treatment center patients (p. 295).

Geriatric day care is a program for the elderly with mental disorders and/or physical disorders. There are recent overviews of geriatric day care programs in the U.S.A. (Rathbone-McCuan and Elliot, 1976-77) and the United Kingdom (Brocklehurst, 1979). Rathbone-McCuan and Elliott (1976-77) also provide a description of their specific day care program to prevent institutionalization. About 30 patients attend five times a week for a year. Socialization needs take a high priority. Requisites for *these* programs are usually provision of transportation, consulting geriatricians, and physiotherapy.

A number of specialized programs for people with physical illness have been written about: cancer, diabetes, epilepsy and obesity day care centers, to name a few. There is a recognition that many severe and/or chronic physical disorders can best be met in a format similar to psychiatric partial hospitals.

Vernallis and Reinert (1963) present a weekend hospital, which is rarely written about.

Any degree of homogeneity can be designed into a partial hospital. Harrington and Mayer-Gross (1959) provide an account of an unusual day hospital in that most patients had non-psychiatric diagnoses (76 percent were neurotics and 9 percent had personality disorders), with a three-month maximum length of stay. Patients attended 9:30 A.M. - 5 P.M. five times a week, with therapeutic community concepts used. They felt the maximum number of patients should be 16 and the maximum percentage of patients with "psychotic" diagnoses should be 30 percent, if group process was to proceed adequately. Quesnell and Martin (1971) present a program in which 88 percent of the patients had personality disorders. Schulte and Blume (1979) highlight programs for alcoholics. Kromberg and Proctor (1970) provide mention of a day program for hard drug abusers, rarely written about.

Many programs have been developed for children. Halpern et al. (1978) present a researched and much written-about program in a community mental health center for children ages 3-13. Classroom models and actual teachers are necessities. They list which types of children might be appropriate. Lifshin (1980, pp. 50-56) adds that family intervention is stressed, optimal staffing is one-to-one, and provision of transportation and two meals is advisable.

Novello (1979) and Linnihan (1977) have described PHPs for adolescents.

The largest collations of PHP programmatic and thematic varients can be found in a series of published proceedings. The latest of these have been edited by Maxey, Luber, and Lefkovitz (1981) and Schippits (1981).

To generalize from the above, partial hospitalization types have proliferated in many ways in terms of the variety of patients served and use of diverse treatment philosophies and techniques, and different treatment settings.

Table 1
Partial Hospital Types

Features	Crisis-Support Treatment	Growth Treatment	Maintenance-Support Treatment
1. Patient characteristics	Patients undergoing severe crisis, with acute states of much lower functioning than usual; they are headed toward hospitalization or are still unstable after hospitalization	Stabilized patients, considerably dysfunctional but judged to have substantial capacity for improvement. Many have not improved sufficiently with just traditional outpatient therapies	Stabilized chronic patients judged to have low capacity for early and/or substantial improvements; e.g., a very withdrawn patient with mild mental retardation and many years of hospitalization
2. Number of patients attending at any one time (most programs have 12-25)	10-15	15-35	15-35
3. Objective	Rapid reduction of florid symptoms, improvement of conditions leading to imminent hospitalization, and maximization of growth opportunities in the crisis	Patients habilitated and rehabilitated to maximum degree in as many areas as feasible	Patients maintained in community and hospitalization prevented; other improvement not impossible.
4. Amount of attendance: a. Length of stay	3-10 weeks	2 1/2-12 months (extensive-growth) or 10-24 months (growth-support)	24 months to indefinite (intermittent leaves of absence may be advisable; see Althoff (1980) for example.
b. Days per week	5-7	3-6	2-5
c. Hours per day	5-15 (usually 6-7)	4-7	3-7

Table 1 (continued)

Features	Crisis-Support Treatment	Growth Treatment	Maintenance-Support Treatment
5. Staffing:			
a. Staff: patient ratio	1:1 to 1:4	1:4 to 1:6	1:5 to 1:8
	(Mean number of full-time staff hired to mean number of actual patient attendees)		
b. Type of staff (special considerations)	Physician or nurse coverage at all times; social worker highly desirable	Vocational rehabilitation counselor highly desirable	Activities therapist highly desirable; a behavior-modification therapist likely
6. Location	Very rapid and easy access to an inpatient service	In the community	In the community
7. Other features			
a. Special facilities and supplies	Medications (oral and injectable) needed on the premises; one "quiet room" with cot/mattress; restraints available	(Medications, a cot, and restraints may be helpful here. All programs have occasional flare-ups of disruptive, florid symptoms, and preparations must be made to handle such.)	
b. Treatment activities	Individual sessions needed. 24-hour emergency coverage required. Patients often walk out or do not show up; outreach and home visits needed. Program overall: high on support, structure, and especially containment.	Extensive-growth group may very well benefit from more verbal psychotherapies. Program overall: high on involvement, negotiation, information sharing, and validation (Growth-support with more structure and support than extensive growth).	Low-key program over-all; high on support, structure, and validation, and more concrete and practical, rather than abstract, matters.

Table 2
Comprehensive Overview Descriptions

Program: Yurmark, J. (See Chapter 15)

Basic Use and Objectives	Growth support; transition from inpatient; prevention of hospitalization	
Patient Characteristics	DX	95% with psychotic diagnosis
	Age	17-53: average age = 29
	Other	Chronic patients: 90% with a previous hospitalization; 85% currently not married
Different Schedules and Tracks	Basically 1 track, but in 4 of 27 slots program divides patients into 2 tracks, *plus* gives 4 extra hrs. per week to the higher functioning patients.	
Philosophy of Treatment	Eclectic	
# of patients attending daily	18-20	
Total clinical staff (full-time equivalents)	4 1/7 (often with 2 or 3 part-time volunteers)	
Hours of programs per week	20-24	
# of days per week program occurs	5	
Length of stay	9-12 months (maximum = 2 years)	
Time period	Mon-Fri. 9:30 A.M.-1 P.M. (till 3 P.M. on 2 days)	

Table 2 (continued)

Program: Glasscote et al. (1969, pp. 105-17) and Glaser (1969 and 1972, pp. 221-50)

Basic Use and Objectives	Intensive Growth/Rehabilitation. Goal is "to have patients give up the sick role."	
Patient Characteristics	DX	40% schizophrenic
	Age	21-65
	Other	70% previously hospitalized, 82% not married, 70% unemployed
Different Schedules and Tracks	Basically 1 track, but 4-6 hrs. per week are quite different for two very different groups.	
Philosophy of Treatment	Therapeutic community	
# of patients attending daily	20-25	
Total clinical staff (full-time equivalents)	5-6 (few volunteers)	
Hours of programs per week	37 hours	
# of days per week program occurs	5 days	
Length of stay	3 weeks (and up to 3 months)	
Time period	Day, Mon-Fri, 9:30 A.M.-5 P.M.	

Table 2 (continued)

Program: Zwerling & Wilder (1964) and Wilder et al. (1966)

Basic Use and Objectives	Crisis support/alternative to hospitalization. (They tried to take all that were to be hospitalized; were able to accept only 66%, *including* organic patients.)	
Patient Characteristics	DX	40% schizophrenic; 23% with non-psychotic diagnoses
	Age	Over 18 years of age
	Other	52% previously hospitalized
Different Schedules and Tracks	Generally each patient stays with 1 group of 8-10; otherwise 1 track	
Philosophy of Treatment	Eclectic	
# of patients attending daily	25-30	
Total clinical staff (full-time equivalents)	14 1/2	
Hours of programs per week	35	
# of days per week program occurs	5	
Length of stay	8 weeks is the median	
Time period	Mon-Fri; 9 A.M.-4 P.M.	

Table 2 (continued)

Program: Linnihan, 1977

	Both A.M. & P.M.		A.M.	P.M.
Basic Use and Objectives	Alternative to hospitalization		Growth Support	Crisis and/or intensive growth
Patient Characteristics	DX	66% Schizophrenic		
	Age	10-18		
	Other			
Different Schedules and Tracks			8 nonverbal regressed	10 "street-wise, acting out"
Philosophy of Treatment	Eclectic; "family therapy in the home is crucial"; staff work closely with schools and encourage attendance			
# of patients attending daily	8-10 in each half-day program			
Total clinical staff (full-time equivalents)	6 or 7 (plus volunteers)			
Hours of programs per week	15 each			
# of days per week program occurs	5 each			
Length of stay	Overall 6 months, but with a wide range, e.g., adjust. react. patients stayed 1-3 months while chronic schizophrenics stayed a year or more			
Time period	Mon-Fri.		3 hours each day	3 hours each day

Table 2 (continued)

Program: Glasscote et al. (1969; pp. 150-61) and Beigel and Feder (1970)

		Day	Eve	Night
Basic Use and Objectives		Crisis Support	Same	Same
Patient Characteristics	DX	64% schizo- phrenic	Similar to night	58% schizo- phrenic
	Age	Mean = 35	Similar to night	Mean = 26
	Other	Av. # of pre- vious hospita- lizations per patient = 1+	Similar to night	Av. # of pre- vious hospita- lizations per patient = 0.6; all occupied during day
Different Schedules and Tracks		3 separate programs, but eve. and night patients are in the same program 5:30-10:30 P.M. Occasionally a patient from one program is also assigned to stay up to 3 days in one of the other programs.		
Philosophy of Treatment		Eclectic; + at least one time per week ind. therapy	Eclectic	Eclectic
# of patients attending daily		17-32	3-6 (+ the 15 night patients)	15-21
Total clinical staff (full-time equivalents)		16	6-7	2 (+1 from 10:30 P.M.- 8 A.M.)
Hours of programs per week		20-45	35	95-100
# of days per week program occurs		7	7	6-7
Length of stay		36% stay 1 month 95% stay < 3 months	Similar to night	31% stay < 1 month 96% stay < 3 months
Time period		9-3:30 for 3-7 times per week (most 5 times)	5:30-10:30P.M. for 3-7 times per week	5:30P.M.-8A.M. for 6-7 times per week

Table 3
Advantages and Disadvantages of Different Degrees of Mixtures of Patient

	Homogeneous	Heterogeneous
A D V A N T A G E S	1) There is a greater commonality and mutual identification. These may promote an earlier and greater cohesiveness and trust. 2) There are more aspects of the program that can be specifically designed to meet the particular needs and goals of the entire group being served by the program; thus, therapeutic experiences have the potential to be more meaningful, appropriate, and tolerable. 3) Similarly, staff may appreciate specializing to meet the needs of a more homogeneous sub-group of patients.	1) Patients can learn to accept and tolerate differences in others that occur in the real world. 2) Chronic patients improve faster and to a greater extent (when they have higher functioning patients to model themselves after?). Acute patients have been reported to show a similar improvement (Ellsworth et al., 1979). 3) Flexibility must be more highly developed. This may promote a greater adaptability to the real world. 4) Continuity of care can be promoted in a program that accepts greater diversity and growth to new levels. 5) Greater financial and administrative feasibility when there are only one staff, one location, and one facility for all. 6) Inclusivity fosters more referrals and acceptances to keep up census.
D I S A D V A N T A G E S	1) The number of patients eligible to enter program is decreased. 2) Referrals may not be abundant enough to support two separate programs. 3) Staffing and other resources must be greater to set up and maintain separate programs. 4) More effort may be required to help staff deal with the special features, difficulties, and limited treatment expectations when dealing with a homogeneous group of chronic patients. 5) Staff may become discouraged and/or bored dealing with only one type of patient.	1) Different levels of patients may form cliques and disrupt formation and maintenance of a cohesive therapeutic milieu. 2) Acute patients may feel held back or demeaned by the chronic patients; thus, there may be a high percentage of dropouts. 3) Chronic patients may feel discouraged by their lack of progress compared to acutes; the higher levels of functioning (verbalization, insights, activity, etc.) of the acute patient may be too threatening for the chronic patients. Increased dropouts here may occur (Linn et al., 1979) 4) Staff exhaustion may result from efforts to accommodate everyone. Similarly, if subprograms or tracks are used, more time is required for organization and planning, and prevention of staff confusion and drain. 5) Intake is more complex and unclear to others.

CONTROVERSIES IN PROGRAMMING

The main controversy concerning which guiding model to use is between advocates of a strict learning theory/behavioral psychotherapy model and those of a
therapeutic community model. For example, behavioral therapy advocates state
that their model should be used particularly for the chronic patient, e.g., only
their model provides for teaching specific skills in an organized enough way.
However, there is no definitive answer to this debate since no research has yet
been carried out with a random assignment of patients to two partial hospitals that
are equal except for the treatment model being used. Nonetheless, some work has
been done in this regard with two different inpatient programs (e.g., Paul and
Lentz [1977] and Mishara [1978]).

Homogeneous Versus Heterogeneous Patient Groups

Since no program is without selection criteria, a more extremely heterogeneous
program (in which *every* patient who might benefit from partial hospitalization is
accepted) does not exist. Nonetheless, there still remains a great diversity of types
of patients that have been treated by and benefited from partial hospitals.
Although it is most unlikely that a *single*, uniform program could adequately serve
all of these patients together, a program was found that boasts serving "the
chronic and nonchronic, the psychiatric and the physically disabled . . . within
one overall program" (Simon and Bronsky, 1977). Currently, separate partial
hospitals have usually been provided for each of the previously mentioned groups
on an empirical basis (see classification method #6, this chapter).

Lefkovitz (1979, pp. 151-170) and Weldon and Frances (1977) provide reviews
of the issue of whether treating patients in an acute phase and "chronic patients"
should be done separately or together. Overall, relative homogeneity for each
PHP would seem to make the best sense clinically; in addition, it is improbable
that the *most* acute, florid patients can be treated side by side with the *most*
chronic, intractable patients. Table 3 provides an overview of advantages and
disadvantages of a separate, homogeneous program versus an intermixed,
heterogeneous program, with regard to the mixing of acute and chronic patients.

15

A Sample Program

Previous chapters have discussed theoretical issues in the multitude of approaches encompassing partial hospitalization treatment. The purpose of this chapter is not to provide a "model" for PHPs but rather to illustrate the application of these modalities and theoretical perspectives within an *existing* PHP.[*] What follows is a description of a PHP in which concurrent verbal and activity psychotherapy groups are applied in treatment with primarily chronic, adult psychiatric patients.

PATIENT POPULATION

The program is geared to serve 18–20 patients at a time by a core of four full-time staff and other part-time staff, students and volunteers. (Staffing specifics will be discussed later.) Actual attendance is usually 80 percent of the total census, or 15–16 patients per day with some patients scheduled to attend less than five days per week.

The nature of the patient population designated for service is the primary, but not only, determinant of the form and content of the programs offered by a PHP. Eighty percent of the patients treated within this PHP carry a diagnosis of schizophrenia, 90 percent are unemployed, and 85 percent are unmarried or separated. Ninety percent have had a number of previous hospitalizations. According to Glaser's (1972) "Impairment Quotient," the highest quotient reported in a day program is 80; in this program, it is 84. According to DSM III, on the Axis V categorization, the average patient functions at poor to grossly impaired levels (American Psychiatric Association, 1980).

The mean age of the patients has changed over the years in favor of younger patients, because of changes in community demographics and a better recognition and appreciation of PHP by clinical staff. Prior to 1977, the mean age was 35, with the range from 17–57. Since 1977 the average age has dropped to 29, while

---

[*] The PHP described here is part of Kingsboro Psychiatric Center, Brooklyn, New York, a state hospital under the auspices of the New York State Office of Mental Health.

the range is similar, 17–53. In addition, the racial and ethnic composition of the population has changed, with more Black and Hispanic patients entering the program. This, too, is a result of both demographic changes and positive changes in staff attitudes regarding referrals.

These chronic patients usually suffer from deficits in interpersonal relationships and in daily life management skills. The patient may have a few friends, but typically lacks the social skills to increase the number of or gratification from his relationships. He may have some solid work skills but also severe difficulties precluding substantial, gainful employment. Patients served here may have good verbal skills, yet may be disorganized in their daily activities, or they may be overtly psychotic but can perform nonverbal tasks well. A population with this range of dysfunction needs a comprehensive program of verbal and activity treatment to provide for the variety of individual needs.

GOALS OF THE PROGRAM

The partial hospital program is designed to achieve the following: 1) reduction of the length of hospitalization, by providing a transition from inpatient hospitalization to a reintegration into community living; 2) avoidance of hospitalization for those in acute crisis, where there is a stable and supportive living situation; 3) improvement of an individual's daily skills, so that problems can be managed later through less intensive outpatient services; 4) preparation for future work or training, returning to a prior position or beginning a new venture; 5) assessment, diagnosis and treatment planning, which PHPs can often provide more effectively than usual outpatient services (for examples, see Chapter 12, Vocational Skills Groups and Chapter 21, Management of Selected Problems); and 6) adjustment of each patient's self-expectations to accurate and realistic levels through education and reeducation, encouraging a sense of accomplishment, and helping patients to achieve, rather than to fail again, and then to build on their successes.

Goals for the program are necessarily broad and generalized to encompass the needs arising from the variety of problems faced by chronic patients. Individual patients goals are general at the start, but quickly become as specific as possible, while retaining flexibility. They are negotiated and set with the patient to guide him to become actively involved in the treatment process (see Chapter 20).

ADMISSION CRITERIA

1) The program is primarily designed for the poorly functioning chronic patients. These patients are given preference, but the program also accepts acute patients and those with nonpsychotic diagnoses.

2) Patients are accepted when less intensive outpatient services seem inadequate to meet patients' needs.

3) There should be some indication that patients will be able to tolerate a structured group situation and become involved in group as the primary treatment modality. For this initial information, the program usually uses three sources: reports from the inpatient or outpatient service concerning patients' use of and ease in groups, discussions with prospective patients regarding group treatment, and trial pre-PHP groups and visits to the program. On occasion, prospective candidates for PHP are referred to outpatient activity groups as a beginning step and may later be re-referred after a positive experience.

4) Patients suffering from an acute crisis may be accepted, provided that they are not imminently suicidal or homicidal, or extremely agitated (requiring restraints, etc.), since the staff and the setting are not equipped to manage the latter patients. (The program has no nursing staff, only a part-time psychiatrist, and is housed in the community, separate from both the clinic and inpatient service.)

5) Patients must be ambulatory and able to use public transportation because the program involves traveling. In addition, the physical setting does not allow for patients using wheelchairs, walkers, etc.

6) Patients must have the capacity to travel independently or make their own arrangements to get to and from the program to meet schedules. They must show physical ability plus definite interest for doing so on their own later. Initially, travel training can be provided to aid in a patient's adjustment to the program.

7) Patients with primary diagnoses of active alcohol or other substance abuse or any but very mild nonpsychotic organic mental disorder are referred elsewhere, since similar programs with special services for these patients exist. The program does accept patients with secondary drug problems, but it is not equipped to provide needed special services such as detoxification, Antabuse and methadone.

8) Patients with primary diagnoses of borderline mental retardation are admitted on an individual basis. An individualized schedule can be arranged, excluding groups too demanding of these patients. While highly structured and task-oriented, the program requires an ability to comprehend its verbal components. Some ability for abstract thinking is important for success in most groups.

9) Clients between the ages of 16 and 65 are acceptable. A client below 16 is referred to the Youth Service; a client over 65 is referred to the Geriatric Service.

10) A physical examination performed within the last three months is required to help ensure patients have good enough health to participate in activities, to protect others from communicable diseases, and to rule out any physical causes for patients' symptoms or dysfunctions.

REFERRALS

The program exists as one part of a large service delivery system. Included in the system are an inpatient service and an outpatient clinic, of which the PHP is one component. The program's mandate is to serve patients from particular geographic areas, which is consistent with the policies of the larger hospital center.

Most referrals are made by in- and outpatient staff, five to seven per month. Referrals are also made by private practitioners and by other agencies without their own PHPs, and amount to another one or two per month. Acceptance rate varies with available space, usually four to six per month.

A close working relationship with referral sources is vital for clear communication and workable planning. The staff has used three particularly effective methods: 1) visits by referral sources to the PHP, with opportunities to observe a full program day including attendance at a staff meeting; 2) periodic meetings between the PHP and in- and outpatient staff to share ideas regarding patient and program planning; and 3) a PHP staff liaison with other staff for rapid assessment, screening, and treatment planning.

Finally, some of the most successful referrals have come via current or former PHP patients. The patients are the best source for public relations, showing others how the PHP treatment is effective.

Optimum efficiency and therapeutic coordination and consistency dictate that clients may not be seen for primary psychiatric treatment by two agencies or in two distinct psychiatric treatment modalities usually considered complete within themselves. For example, a client seen privately or by another agency may be accepted if the other treatment is terminated, or at least suspended, during the stay in the program. However, three to four weeks are given, while the patient is beginning the program, to help the client to separate from the prior worker and treatment process, since the importance of the termination process is recognized. The attempt to maintain two primary modes of treatment tends to lend itself to a variety of problems (see Chapter 7). Further, case management policy dictates that medications are to be prescribed and monitored by the program's psychiatrist. This does not preclude needed treatment unavailable at the facility (e.g., ongoing medical treatment and AA). However, this outside treatment system must understand that it will defer basic decisions to the PHP and that all important material should be submitted to the program.

ADMISSION PROCESS

Patients are screened individually or in groups. A group intake is preferable, since it is helpful in starting the assessment of a patient's tolerance for groups, as well as perhaps decreasing a patient's initial anxiety. Group intakes are also helpful administratively, when staff are faced with waiting lists. However, individual interviews may be scheduled for patients in acute crisis or when there are no waiting lists.

The screening interview is conducted by one or two staff members,* depending

---

* Plans now include current patients' involvement at intakes.

on availability, and includes a discussion with the patient of his current status, problems, living situation, family and vocational background. Staff present the program to the patient and offer a description of various groups and an overview of the program's use to the patient. Family members are encouraged to attend part of the session so that the treatment alliance can include the significant others who have great influence on the patient and a stake in the patient's success or failure in the program. About 50 percent of families attend the interview. The family's cooperation is vital to the patient's participation in the program (see Chapters 9 and 10).

Following the intake, a first program visit is scheduled (usually a full program day), if the patient seems comfortable and motivated to begin the program. If not, a coffee break visit (an informal half-hour socialization group) is scheduled at which the patient simply meets other staff and members and chats with them. Later, a full-day visit can be scheduled for the patient to begin to see the program.

For this initial visit, a current member handles the orientation of the new member, makes introductions to other members and staff, and is available as a "buddy." This plan helps both current and prospective members to feel comfortable with each other, and certainly decreases a new member's isolation. Whenever possible, several new clients join together, as another way to reduce isolation and strangeness.

Following a successful visit, which means that the client has attended and felt fairly comfortable, two more whole-day visits are arranged, usually within a week. During this time the prospective client, or member, as they prefer to call themselves,* makes his own decisions about joining the partial hospitalization program. At the orientation group initial treatment goals are set, and the program is explained and discussed with staff and current members. During this pre-group phase, the prospective member meets with the worker who had conducted the intake, and can also meet with the "buddy" to discuss issues, questions, and concerns. This group can meet weekly for several sessions to deal with the issues facing the new members.

This beginning process, while appearing somewhat complex, is important to ensure a positive, initial adjustment to the program. A patient in crisis can be moved more swiftly through the steps, but these steps are designed to encourage the patient to believe in his own abilities and rights to make decisions. The program is voluntary, thus patients cannot be coerced to attend. Therefore, staff must "sell" the program and emphasize to the patient his right to join or to reject it. The least successful treatment occurs when others push the patient to join, or when a patient joins primarily to please others, or to end battles. However, while the patient can refuse, methods such as strong recommendations by therapists, using PHP as

---

* The patients in PHP prefer to view themselves as members of a program, rather than as "sick" people in a hospital. They consider the term "member" to be more hopeful, without the stigma of illness.

a condition of discharge by hospital and/or family can be very persuasive to a prospective member. Once accepted, the dropout rate is low—10–15 percent.

Each member is also assigned to an individual staff member. While most issues are handled in groups, other problems arise needing extra attention. This is provided by individual staff, as is individual family therapy. The program does not include ongoing individual sessions, but workers are available to handle crises, give concrete services, and can and do offer some individual sessions.

PROGRAM STRUCTURE

The PHP operates five days per week (Monday through Friday, usually from 9:30 A.M. to 1 P.M.), but there is considerable variability in possible schedules. For those preparing for vocational goals, two program days end at 3 P.M., more closely resembling a work day. While a full day, 9 A.M. to 5 P.M., is preferable, the PHP staff have other responsibilities in the outpatient clinic, which precludes a full day. If needed, special outpatient lounge groups or a sheltered workshop can be made available to fill the afternoon. While most members attend five days per week, shorter three- or four-day schedules can be arranged. Often, new members begin with less than five days and then increase to a full schedule within a month. In planning schedules, the main consideration is a patient's current abilities, rather than some rigid standard. Often, patients are referred having had little or no structured daily activity, and/or having little group experience. Plunging into an intensive five-day program may foster failure rather than success. In addition, schedules are planned not to disrupt ongoing, successful activity outside the PHP. A patient who is attending school or has a part-time job will be encouraged to build a weekly schedule which would not disrupt this, but would enable him to work on other areas of difficulty or on needs experienced by the patient. Finally, some patients close to discharge may attend a shortened schedule to make a transition to the new program.

VERBAL AND ACTIVITY PSYCHOTHERAPY GROUPS

The PHP offers a variety of groups to develop new or revitalize former attitudes, knowledge, and especially skills. For purposes of clarification, the groups are categorized in the following manner: 1) verbal groups, including community meeting, orientation, small group therapy, and medication groups and evaluations; 2) creative arts and self-expression groups; 3) activities of daily living; 4) socialization; 5) leisure and recreation; and 6) pre-vocational activities. (For full description, see Chapter 12.)

A TWO-TRACK PROGRAM

Within the overall program, there is an attempt to individualize treatment for each member. The program combines both chronic and acute patients within the PHP. This design originated out of a lack of staff, supplies, equipment, and space for acute and chronic facilities. Nonetheless, acute and chronic patients have been treated successfully. The PHP offers a two-track program where lower and higher functioning patients are separated into more homogeneous groups (see activity schedule). For example, everyone is assigned to one of two current events groups whose goals are similar, but whose form and content differ. Goals of both groups include discussing issues to extend the patients' restricted worlds, and discussing non-illness topics to share with others in social situations.

The nature of the adjunctive media sets the tone for the differences. Current events I uses newspapers and news magazines. Current events II uses simpler newspapers, magazines, school texts, and radio broadcasts, since patients' abilities in reading, verbalizing, and abstracting may be less .developed. Both groups employ tasks with the expectation that patients can handle them, thus encouraging a member's ability to master tasks.

When mastery in the lower functioning group (II) is achieved, the client will usually move to the higher group, to further enhance his skills. Should the opposite occur and the patient regresses or becomes otherwise disorganized, the client will be eased from I to II, to return later if and when appropriate. Some patients may remain in the same groups throughout their stay, with mastery of those groups as the objective. "Promotions" and "demotions" are handled by discussion between patient and group leader. These discussions include a member's ease with and interest in the group, a member's ability to handle demands of the group, as well as the role that this group plays in achieving a member's program goals. Patient resistances to these groups are also explored and solutions are sought. For example, a patient may be interested in the news, but may have great difficulty in reading newspapers and in understanding the content of articles. He is encouraged to try to read less sophisticated magazines or newspapers, so as to reduce frustration, and he is also encourged to test out the current events II group, along with help in remedial reading. Alternatively, another patient, who may appear to be bored in the task group, may have solid verbal skills but may fear failure in a higher group or fear the loss of special status gained in the lower functioning group. A patient may fear the underlying meaning of joining a higher functioning group (i.e., he may be on the road to recovery), and may resist the group on these grounds. Indeed, such discussions of patient reactions to these changes can be invaluable to encourage patients to make realistic plans and explore basic underlying conflicts.

The track system is applied to most task groups such as current events, writing, movement and interpersonal relations. All patients are included in larger verbal groups.

As noted in Table 1, specific groups may be divided by group size, rather than by functioning levels, i.e. small groups, A and B, each include one-half of the larger group. The cooking group is similarly divided: groups alternate activity with half the community cooking and preparing the meal each week, while the other half plans for the following week.

The philosophy and treatment models most closely resemble those of an eclectic model (as described in Chapter 2), including the skill-oriented treatments described in Chapter 12. As the schedule reflects, the program is comprehensive. Program evaluation and program revisions occur several times each year to accommodate patient needs. The PHP also tries to offer special interest groups when staff and patient skills and equipment are available. Groups are interconnected in objective and activity. Suggestions for revisions of the program are elicited from staff and patients, being implemented within time and space limitations.

PROGRAM RULES AND POLICIES

1) Patients are expected to attend daily according to their schedules. Medical appointments or other outside meetings are arranged during non-program hours whenever possible. Should a member need to be absent for an appointment or other legitimate reason, it is expected that the member notify the group in advance. Should illness or other unscheduled issues arise, the patient is to telephone. This rule exists to demonstrate a variety of issues:

(a) to show the patient that staff and other members feel that his attendance is important to the group;
(b) to encourage individual responsibility; and
(c) to simulate the rules of a job situation.

If the patient does not notify the PHP for two days within a week, he is temporarily suspended, pending an interview with the assigned worker to discuss the attendance problem and to help with issues complicating program participation.

2) No physical violence is allowed. People can disagree, even yell, but may not strike anyone. Violators are suspended from the program and treatment is reevaluated and arranged as indicated. Alternative treatment is based on an assessment of the patient's condition by staff with input from the other patients. Treatment issues are discussed with all patients since they, too, are affected and need assurance that workers are handling the situation to reestablish safety in the group.

Treatment alternatives may vary from hospitalization, if controls are severely impaired, to brief suspension with individual and/or family sessions with an assigned worker, in the interim, to understand and deal with the precipitant of the behavior and to work toward alternative behaviors, including controls. Finally, patients may return to the program when they have achieved better control over impulses. Upon return, they are expected and helped to discuss their behavior with the community, thereby giving other patients an opportunity to share their own feelings and concerns (see Chapter 21).

3) No alcohol or non-prescription drug use is allowed on the premises of the program. The same policy of suspension will be enforced. While drug use cannot be prevented outside the program, efforts are made to help educate the patients

Table 1
Program Schedule*

Monday	Tuesday	Wednesday[1]	Wednesday[2]	Thursday	Friday
9 - 9:30 a.m. Daily Staff Review Meeting					
9:30-10:30	9:30-10:00	9:30-10:30	9:30-11:00	9:30-10:00	9:30-10:00
Small Groups A & B (All patients)	Community Meeting (All patients and staff)	Interpersonal Relations I or Movement II	Medication Group (All patients)	Community Meeting	Community Meeting
10:30-12:00	10:00-11:00	10:30-11:00	11:00-11:30	10:00-11:00	10:00-11:00
Hobby Art (All patients)	Writing I and Interpersonal Relations II	Coffee Break	Coffee Break	Small Groups A & B (All patients)	Cooking and Planning A & B
12:00-12:30	11:00-11:30	11:00-12:45	11:30-12:30	11:00-11:30	11:00-11:30
Coffee Break	Coffee Break	Group Evaluations (All patients and staff)	Interpersonal Relations I or Movement II	Coffee Break	Coffee Break
12:30-1:00	11:30-12:30	12:45-1:15	12:30-1:00	11:30-12:30	11:30-12:00
Community Meeting	Writing II and Movement I	Community Meeting	Community Meeting	Orientation or Canteen	Leisure Planning
1:30-3:00	2:00-3:30			1:30-3:00	12:00-1:00
Work Skills (5-7 selected patients)	Staff Meeting (Patient Review and Treatment Planning)			Work Skills	Lunch and Cleaning
3:30-5:00		6:00-8:00		4:30-6:00	2:30-4:00
Staff Meeting (Program)		Family Night (All patients and staff, once every 4-6 weeks)		Alumni Group	Staff Meeting (Group Supervision)

*In this schedule, "I" denotes higher and "II" lower functioning. Groups and media used are flexible and can be changed or revised according to patient and program needs.

about the problems inherent in alcohol or other drug use, particularly while taking prescribed psychotropic medications. The same plans for assessment, treatment alternative, and reentry are employed here as for nonattendance. In addition, the extent of drug usage is explored with staff. If the drug usage has become the major issue, the patient is helped to utilize other services for this primary problem, although, if indicated at a future time, the patient may return to the program.

4) All patients have the right to refuse medication. However, the policy is that patients engage in a comprehensive treatment. Medication is usually an important component of the treatment program, and there is strong emphasis on participating in *all* aspects of treatment. Staff also remind patients that the function of medication is to help people to be calm, less fearful, suspicious, etc., and to support them to use the programs offered; patients are expected and encouraged to discuss concerns about medications. If a patient remains adamant in his refusal to take medication, suspension may have to be discussed, or the patient's risk of rehospitalization as a result of stopping medication. Usually, a discussion convinces the patient to follow the full, prescribed plan. If not, alternative treatment may be arranged through other clinic services.

On occasion, the staff, including the psychiatrist, may concur with the patient's refusal, even to the point of encouraging a drug holiday. However, some clear conditions are made, including daily attendance and an agreement to take medication if appropriate when a significant negative change in his behavior is observed, such as extreme withdrawal, aggression, exacerbation of hallucinations, delusions, and homicidal ideation. This plan has met with some success using the cooperation of staff and patients to note and discuss resulting behavioral changes or attendance problems, and to work with the patient to avoid crisis and/or hospitalization. The plan has worked best with patients who have a solid connection to the PHP. If inpatient hospitalization does occur, readmission is possible, provided that there has been satisfactory resolution of the medication issue.

These rules and policies are explained to patients upon entry into the program in the orientation group and are raised regularly in meetings with the entire community. When a violation occurs, members will discuss the issue and will have input into decision-making regarding plans, i.e., length of suspension, sharing their own concerns and feelings, and even exerting peer pressure on the violator(s).

PATIENT PROGRESS AND LENGTH OF STAY

A patient makes measurable progress when he achieves one or more of his stated objectives. The formal discussions of patient progress occur regularly, usually every two months, in the evaluation group. Here, a patient's goals are shared with the entire community and reviewed by the patient with input from staff and patients in the form of comments and recommendations (see Chapter 19). Patients are included for their support as well as for their keen observations. Their input is often more direct and incisive than that of the staff, and may help the patient to view goals and plans more realistically. Their recommendations often carry more weight because "they have been there." Here, new problems and new plans are discussed and decided upon, for later review.

Progress may be realizing a five-day instead of a three-day schedule, moving from lower to higher groups, beginning the canteen or work skills group, or attaining other interim objectives, bringing the patient closer to his overall goals.

Occasionally, staff and patients disagree on goals or recommendations. Some decisions may not be amendable, such as length of stay, but the patients have the opportunity to share reactions and to question staff for the reasoning behind decisions. Some decisions, such as interim goals or plans, can and have been changed when patients raise issues missed by staff.

The average length of stay is 9-12 months, although some patients have shorter or longer stays. Stays can be extended if patients continue to work on goals and make solid progress. Patients with more severe impairments need prolonged stays to make progress. Second PHP admissions are also possible, as the need arises, but are usually brief.

Discharge usually occurs upon attainment of patients' stated goals and discharge dates are usually set by patients themselves in consultation with the community. However, if patients have difficulty terminating, the staff aid in setting the final date (see Chapter 21 for more on termination).

Continuity of service is important for weaning patients from the PHP. Whenever possible, a transition period is established to ease the patient into a new program or treatment by tapering off attendance. On the average, reducing stays from five to two or three days over a two-month period, while beginning the new program, allows for adequate discussion of feelings and issues provoked by the changes.

Patients may move on to jobs, vocational training, education, household management, child care, volunteer work, etc. To aid in the transition, continuing treatment usually includes alumni groups, which often last from six to eight months after discharge. They are usually held in late afternoon or early evening, in order not to interfere with work or training schedules. Once a month the patients meet with the PHP psychiatrist in a group similar to the PHP medication group.

Alumni are invited to family nights for several months after leaving, to maintain their good relationships with members and to help families to make the transition. They also serve as models for newer patients and encourage hopefulness for families by showing the potential for progress and significant changes.

The employed clinical staff includes one MSW, who directs the program, two BA-level social work assistants, and one registered occupational therapist. This complement of staff is partly determined by clinic staffing patterns and is far less than optimal. Each of these four staff gives approximately 30 hours a week (of a 40-hour work week) to the PHP, including direct service, staff meetings, and recording. A clinic psychiatrist gives the PHP five hours a week, and is available for crises as needed. Thus, the ratio of staff to actual attendees is close to 1:4.

The four main program staff are each responsible for running a variety of groups as well as for case management. Assignments are based on program needs and staff expertise, but the staff are flexible and open to trying new approaches. The co-therapy model is often used in groups to help staff learn new techniques and develop new skills. Individual expertise is recognized and applauded, and is also shared for everyone's enrichment. This is also true of work with families, still a new area for many staff.

The participation of the psychiatrist in this PHP is less than optimal (see Chapter 16). The psychiatrist is available for the medication group and individual sessions (as needed), while also having responsibility for treatment planning approval, diagnosis, etc. However, his limited time precludes a more extended role in programming and in planning meetings with other staff, both significant areas needing input from the psychiatrist.

Volunteers and students are important adjuncts to the program. While offering services to patients, they also offer new perspectives to staff, stimulate ideas, and carry out original and innovative work. They are closely trained and supervised by program staff. Two or three volunteers are usually involved in three or four hours of program and at least one staff meeting each week. In addition, one or two students using the PHP for their field placements are usually involved for one or two program days and also attend staff meetings.

Nursing, vocational rehabilitation, and psychology personnel are available as consultants and, intermittently, as service providers, usually two or three hours a week. Although this arrangement is not the ideal complement of staff, budget and time constraints preclude more involvement.

Support services such as clerical and janitorial services are provided by the general outpatient staff, and this work represents approximately eight to 12 hours a week.

STAFF MEETINGS

Work in a PHP requires much planning and review, necessitating staff meetings as shown in the schedule. The *staff daily review* meetings are brief, usually half an hour, to plan the day's focus, to discuss special patient issues and/or daily themes, and, as in all meetings, to share information. There are, in addition, three longer weekly meetings, each lasting one-and-a-half hours. The *Monday program planning* meeting includes a weekly review of group themes and foci, a review of individual patient participation, and planning for new groups, special events, or modification of the existing program. The *Tuesday treatment planning* meeting with the psychiatrist covers discussion of individual patients and presentation of new intakes. In addition, staff recommendations for patient evaluations are devised here. The *Friday group supervision* sessions cover a combination of issues including staff functioning, dealing with particularly difficult patients and/or treatment situations, and studying new techniques with regard to patients and planning.

In addition to these meetings, the staff meet for a *program evaluation day* once every four to six months to review the full program, to assess whether program goals have been reached, and to make major changes in group schedules as patients' needs change. The staff then present their recommendations to the patients for their input, resulting in new schedules, and clarification of goals and objectives.

The coordinator of the PHP conducts staff meetings and individual staff supervision as needed, while also serving as liaison to the general clinic by participation in case presentation and intake meetings and attendance at inpatient team treatment meetings. In both meetings, the PHP coordinator's role is to offer current information regarding the program and its patients, in order to offer treatment planning recommendations for outpatients or inpatients. At times, involvement with outside community groups also occurs, taking two or three hours a month, and can include various service agencies, neighborhood groups, and planning councils.

PHYSICAL FACILITIES

The PHP is located within an outpatient clinic and space is less than optimal. Presently, it comprises two large, multipurpose group rooms (each 18′ by 18′), and four staff offices (each 9′ by 12′), which can also serve as group space when needed. A separate room (9′ by 12′) houses the canteen. A full kitchen is also available once a week. Gymnasium facilities are not available, but in good weather local parks and other recreational facilities are used. Storage, bathrooms, and secretarial space are shared with the outpatient clinic.

Furniture and equipment are provided by the clinic and donations from agencies and private individuals. Often, special equipment can be purchased through the proceeds from special fund-raising efforts, such as raffles, and bake, craft and plant sales. Fund-raising provides patients with special experiences otherwise not readily available.

FINANCES/COSTS

Specific figures are unavailable for this PHP, since it is not a freestanding program. Staff, facilities, and supplies, including medication, are allotted to the general clinic and are used by the PHP and clinic—few supplies belong solely to the PHP. However, for an estimate of basic costs, the guidelines in Chapter 23 (Cost Finding) were applied to the program. The total program cost is estimated at $122,000 per year, with a daily attendance of 15-16 patients. Costs approximate $31-$33 per day. Figures are based on 1979 rates.

The PHP, as in the case of the clinic, is funded through patients' medicaid payments and sliding scale fees. As expected, these funds do not pay for all expenses. Medicaid reimburses at a 50 percent rate, or $16 per day, and patients' fees contribute 10-15 percent, or $3-$5 per day. The state government underwrites the balance of the expense, $12 per day.

16

Standards for Partial Hospitalization

Professionals cannot comprehensively exercise all of their skills without standards and models; implicitly or explicitly, these are used as background guides for clinical judgments. These then help assure the necessity and appropriateness of treatment. This chapter will present some historical background, overview of current issues, and the concept of peer review. In the Appendix there is a comprehensive set of specific standards for quality treatment and utilization reviews in partial hospitalization. (For models, see Chapters 2 and 14.)

HISTORICAL BACKGROUND

Historically, most mental health standards have been inadequately defined for several, often overlapping, reasons. For instance:

1) It has been very difficult to establish what to measure and to develop measuring instruments. Human behavior—what motivates it and how to change it—is enormously complex; much remains unknown. For example, still unknown are the effectiveness, efficiency, and also risks, as compared to benefits, of most treatments (see Chapter 3). Thus, without a logical, completely scientific basis, professionals are cautious about devising rigid restrictive standards.

2) Rarely does the education of clinicians include methods of evaluation and establishment of standards.

3) Staff who enjoy working with people usually do not enjoy the "dry" paperwork involved in evaluation and research. These processes seem boring and time-wasting.

4) Making clinical decisions in the face of so few proven facts, while carrying responsibility for human lives, requires a great deal of courage, self-confidence, and conviction of one's clinical righteousness. Thus, each practitioner feels the need for flexibility to set his own standards, realizing that each situation or person is ultimately unique. When "outsiders" start imposing standards, they are eroding the practitioner's confidence and status as an autonomous competent professional. Understandably, therefore, colleagues have been reluctant to impose standards on one another.

5) Dealing with slowly changing conditions (as with many mental disorders) in the face of so many unknowns, together with the need for empathic working-through, requires steadfast faith and hope. Faith (religious or otherwise) often necessitates an inattention to certain facts that might undermine this staunch belief. Thus, the clinician would have a tendency to avoid an evaluation that might indicate that he is wrong or useless.

Over the last ten years there have been mounting demands for establishment and clarification of mental health standards. For example, the 1972 Federal Professional Standards Review Organization legislation (Public Law 92-603) in the U.S.A. requires three types of review: concurrent admission certification and continued-care review, medical care evaluation, and profile analysis (Nelson, 1977).

In the 1980s, the mental health field is still adjusting to the arrival of the seven alarming As in the 1970s. These are:

1) Abdication by the practitioner of his supremacy in setting standards, while others, who are distant from the real need of patients, increase their role (Elpers, 1978);
2) Attack from without;
3) Accountability;
4) Astriction (constraining costs and quality care while regulating the practitioner's ability to choose treatments used);
5) Auditing;
6) Authentication (demanding ever more documentation);
7) Automation (depersonalizing and threatening confidentiality).

There is no indication that the future will entail a decrease in these alarming facts; the "seven As" can annihilate our position, or we can use these with leadership and authority.

AN OVERVIEW OF MENTAL HEALTH STANDARDS

Categorization and Specification of Standards

Standards could be categorized in many ways. For example, Nelson (1979) specifies clinical, practitioner, program and facility, and payment standards. Or, one could use systems concepts (Nelson, 1977). Thus, in the treatment program system, standards are categorized into three stages of the treatment process and their subdivisions. An advantage of the systems model is the facilitation of focus on the long-neglected outcomes (outputs) which standards should emphasize (see Figure 1).

Figure 1

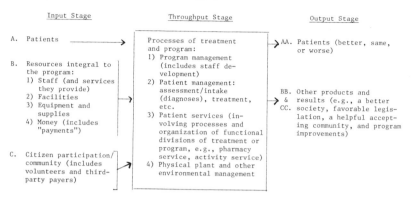

Reference Sources for Standards

There are certain basic published materials on standards to which each partial hospital must have immediate access. In the U.S.A., there are three basic sources of standards: 1) The American Psychiatric Association was one of the earliest specialty organizations to become involved with peer review, and it has many helpful materials (for example, Dorsey et al., 1979; Gibson, 1977; Peer Review Committee, 1981). 2) The Joint Commission on the Accreditation of Hospitals also has some crucial material (JCAH, 1977, 1979, 1980, 1981). 3) There are the federal Community Mental Health Center standards legislated between 1963 and 1978, with guidelines to those published by NIMH (1979).

There are in addition a multitude of diverse standards set and employed by local governments, judicial bodies and local branches of third-party payers. The latter include private insurance companies, Medicare, Medicaid, and the Civilian Health and Medical Program of the Uniformed Services (CHAMPUS). Frequently these different groups interdigitate by referring to one another. For example, JCAH requires accredited programs to be licensed by meeting state standards; Medicare, and often other third-party payers, require JCAH accreditation.

Implications of Inadequate Standards

Eventually the treatment modality that will be utilized and will survive will depend on the payer of such treatments. Thus, there is great power inherent in the payment standards. Third-party payers' main goal is to satisfy their subscriber contracts as cheaply as possible through application of a variety of standards, which do not necessarily conform to professional ones (Nelson, 1979)! For example, under many third-party standards, partial hospitalization is not even considered a reimbursable psychiatric service, sometimes because of arbitrary determination that it is an unnecessary treatment or even "baby-sitting." Indeed, forces exist which, if yielded to, *would* result in PHP's becoming more like a baby-sitting service. For example, in 1980 the New York State executive branch proposed that sufficient staffing is one direct treatment staff per 10-15 patients in day hospitals (NYCRR, 1980, p. 21).

Our task is clear. It is crucial that all clinically active practitioners set standards. This matter cannot be left up to "the other guy," and realistic standards for all mental health service programs must be evolved now (Report of the Task Panel on Planning and Review, 1978). Standards should be clear, operationalized, flexible, complete, integrated, appropriate and commonly accepted. If professionals do "take a hard look at what they do, establish standards, set goals, and measure results against goals, they will clarify what they really do. This is the best way to convince the public, including third-party payers, that [partial hospitalization] is a measurable service, and that this treatment is a reimbursable service" (Gibson, 1977). Reimbursement to PHPs will be dependent upon the ability to document the appropriateness and the medical necessity for services, as well as the efficiency and effectiveness (Peer Review Committee, APA, 1981). (See also Chapter 23 on Finances.)

PSYCHIATRIC PEER REVIEW

Peer review has a tradition as long as medicine itself, but only in the 1970s did it become so extensive and formalized, especially since the passage of the Federal Public Law 92-603 in 1972 on Professional Standards Review Organizations (PSROs). This latter mandates a comprehensive peer review by physicians. If it does not occur satisfactorily, the legislation provides for non-physicians to conduct the reviews.

Although by definition Professional Standards Review Organizations have a mandate for very broad and diverse types of reviews, in effect they have been involved primarily in utilization review of inpatient services (and short-stay facilities). In 1979 they turned toward the development of criteria for utilization review of ambulatory services, including partial hospitalization. Clinicians must assume more leadership in developing these criteria.

It is essential to know certain basic definitions in psychiatric peer review. These include: Psychiatric Peer Review, itself; PSROs, Psychiatric Peer Review Committee, Screening Criteria, Concurrent Review, Claims Review, Quality Review, Utilization (cost) Control (Gibson, 1977), and Utilization Review (JCAH, 1981).

The objectives of psychiatric peer review are 1) to maintain professional self-determination, and 2) to provide professional monitoring of the utilization, quality, and cost of psychiatric care (Gibson, 1977). These goals are necessary concerns for all staff.

IV

*Clinical Techniques
and Issues*

17

Community Meetings

Community meetings are typically among the most difficult PHP groups to study (Rubin, 1979), lead or participate in. They are often a source of frustration to staff and patients. Nonetheless, most authors do not dispute their value. Community meetings, more than any other PHP group (due to size, composition, complex group processes, and varying agendas), exemplify a PHP's philosophy while also mirroring and magnifying a program's strengths and weaknesses.

Community meetings tend to be viewed and described in vague, stereotyped ways, as *one* type of meeting, which contributes to their being experienced as overly complex and frustrating. This chapter attempts to clarify what community meetings are and offers suggestions for structuring.

DEFINITION

Jones (1976) defines a community meeting in a therapeutic community as, ". . . a meeting of the entire patient and staff population who are working together in a single geographical area" (p. 91). Gross and Kisch (1980) describe a psychiatric day hospital community meeting, as, ". . . a window into the functioning of a unit and a practical demonstration of the unit's therapeutic philosophy" (p.15). Rubin (1979) compares the community meeting to "the old town meeting," which "is an excellent place to establish a sense of engagement . . ." (p. 711).

A definition which combines the elements mentioned above would apply to community meetings in all PHPs:

A community meeting is a meeting composed of all PHP staff and patients who work together in the same unit regularly. Its purposes include maintaining awareness of PHP group process and content and, with this knowledge, working on issues reflecting program objectives and other concerns relevant to all members of the unit.

The phrase "all patients and staff" attending community meetings varies between programs. Some community meetings include only clinical staff; some may include clerical and maintenance personnel. The question of which staff should attend this meeting would depend on the *type* of community meeting being held (see section on Suggestions for Structuring).

The above definition of a community meeting is general and flexible enough to apply to a number of variant treatment objectives and approaches, and it assumes the existence of a functioning therapeutic milieu (see Chapter 7).

HISTORICAL DEVELOPMENT AND LITERATURE REVIEW

Community meetings were the focus of considerable interest and some research during the early 1950s through the late 1960s (Gross and Kisch, 1980; Rubin, 1979). This period coincides with the popularization of the therapeutic milieu (see Chapter 1 and 7), and application of this approach to psychiatric hospitals (Jones, 1953; Rubin, 1979; Gross and Kisch, 1980). While holding community meetings is not automatically synonymous with having developed a therapeutic milieu, they are considered by many to be an important, if not essential, element in the therapeutic milieu (Jones, 1953 and 1976; Vitale, 1964; MacDonald, 1964). Wilmer (1958) considered them a requisite for therapeutic milieus, as well as an evaluative measure for the milieu.

Community meetings are difficult to study (Rubin, 1979). Some relevant studies will be briefly reviewed here, which provide interesting data relating to a wide range of issues common to PHP community meetings. (For other studies, see Rapoport, 1960; Fairweather, 1964 and 1967; Crossan, 1977; Gross and Kisch, 1980; Maratos and Kennedy, 1974; Kellam and Chassam, 1962; Roberts, 1960; Sacks and Carpenter, 1974.)

Rubin (1979) presents a comparative study of two types of adult psychiatric inpatient community meetings—one highly structured and open-ended (lasting 30-168 minutes), the other an "open meeting" (lasting 24-40 minutes). In the highly structured meeting, he found that a greater proportion of patients participated, actively and vicariously, than in the open meetings. He also hypothesized that with a patient population deficient in "executive ego functions," a less structured meeting results in greater personal disorganization and less lucid communications than a highly structured meeting.

Mardikian and Glick (1969) reported differing opinions between staff and patients on the value of events discussed in community meetings. For example, events raised by patients were often not discussed by staff and vice versa. Although they reported general consensus regarding the importance of the morale issue, staff tended to rate the level of morale higher by one standard than the patients. They also found that patients with lower IQs spoke more frequently in community meetings than brighter patients. This latter finding supports the findings of Daniels and Rubin (1968) and Fairweather (1964).

Daniels and Rubin (1968) offer a method for measuring verbal interactions in large groups. They found that in community meetings staff tend to scrutinize patient comments for unclarity, which often results in inhibited patient participation. They also noted that staff rarely talk to one another in community meetings. In addition, this study noted that patients addressed clinical issues more frequently than staff, who spoke more about procedural and unit maintenance topics.

The literature on community meetings is predominantly based on inpatient studies, with the exception of Gross and Kisch (1980). They are also generally discussed as if they represent the same thing to everyone. Upon close examination, however, it is apparent that they vary a great deal from program to program in terms of frequency, length, focus, structure, purpose, and goals.

RATIONALE

With all the difficulties inherent in large group community meetings (20-60 people often in attendance), why are they held? The value of these meetings stems from their offering an encapsulated view of the workings of the entire PHP, and thus having great potential for treatment and for learning. As Jones (1976) states, ". . . no community meeting is likely to be very effective until such time as the unit personnel really believe that it has value, not only for the patients, but for themselves" (p. 91).

Gross and Kisch (1980) offer some sound, general reasons for holding community meetings: for example,

1) developing community cooperation and rapport;
2) establishing a norm of frankness, openness, and honesty;
3) providing an emotional outlet for patients' feelings about their environment;
4) practicing communication skills;
5) confronting problem patients; and
6) system maintenance.

In addition to the above reasons, two others are important to include:

1) Community meetings offer an opportunity for regularly updating observations of ongoing group processes and content, as well as individual participation; and
2) Patient's identification with the PHP as a large group and as part of a larger organizational structure can be fostered and evaluated in the community meeting.

Through such organizational identification, patients feel less isolated and helpless. Community meetings provide an opportunity for all patients and staff to see one another assembled in the same space, dealing with common issues. A sense of power, effectiveness, pride, and heightened self-esteem can be achieved through participation in a large (formal) group with personally shared, unified goals.

COMMON PROBLEMS

Attendance. Community meetings are frequently spoken of with dread, or as an unpleasant and sometimes boring necessity. They are typically unattended or attended late by both patients and staff as if they are saying, "There are so many there already; surely I won't be missed." It is not unusual for absent members to be unmentioned or seemingly unnoticed as energies are needed for numerous other matters demanding attention (Gootnick, 1975). This gives the message that community meetings are not important. In addition, the idea which many patients have of being unimportant or unnoticed appears as reality.

Community meeting attendance patterns consistently reflect group process within the PHP community. If pertinent issues are not dealt with directly, promptly and adequately in the community meeting, the resulting anxiety and tension may manifest itself in "resistant" behavior in all groups throughout the treatment day. Resistance takes such forms of behavior as lateness, disruption, silence, and absence.

Procedures, process, and content. Lack of a clear, consistent and meaningful purpose for community meetings contributes to anxiety, frustration, and a multitude of consequent ramifications. Most authors describe community meetings as the *one* opportunity to bring the entire therapeutic milieu population together. This one opportunity may be daily or only weekly. Thus, community meetings are subject to pressures to deal with any number of issues affecting the members and/or program at a given time.

Community meetings are often among the groups most easily reduced in frequency when staff schedules become tight, or when new programming is introduced. This is important to keep in mind when evaluating the effectiveness of a therapeutic milieu—can the milieu function well together as a whole (as illustrated by their community meetings), or only in segments? At least one community meeting per day is recommended.

Some authors describe a hodgepodge quality which these meetings often assume, being seemingly subject to uncontrollable fluctuations reflecting events within the therapeutic milieu (Daniels and Rubin, 1968; Kraft, 1966). How is it determined what will be discussed, and how, in community meetings? How is it determined how often they should be held, or for how long? What are staff roles? What are patient roles? Is there clearly designated leadership? What happens when opposing agendas are presented? Are all issues raised in this meeting to be dealt with in the meeting, and who decides content priorities? These are but a few of the questions to keep in mind when evaluating or planning for community meetings.

Multiple leadership. In addition to reflecting many of the issues and problems within a PHP at a given time, community meetings can have five to ten or more interdisciplinary staff and any number of patients available as potential leaders at one time. This further complicates matters. One staff member may strive to promote group interaction using an active approach; another may pursue individual problems within the group; still others may believe patients need directive leadership. Some staff may adhere to analytic group treatment principles, others to behaviorist or existential orientations.

These differences need not necessarily interfere with effective treatment if they are recognized, respected and, most importantly, consistent with the therapeutic needs of the community. If, however, strong proponents of different orientations are competing for group leadership simultaneously, the results can be confusing and deleterious to effective group treatment.

SUGGESTIONS FOR STRUCTURING

Staff and patients often struggle with ways to ameliorate the difficulties encountered in community meetings. In some instances, a need to make these meetings orderly and predictable results in weary, boring, and sluggish meetings. At other times they may become what Sacks and Carpenter (1974) describe as the "showpiece" community meeting, i.e., with no real value or substance—just there for show.

Other measures for handling the stresses of community meetings include electing patient leaders, minute taking, reducing the frequency or length of the meeting, rotating staff leadership, silent staff leadership, trying to make community meetings into (very large) small group therapy sessions, or making them a forum for organizational matters, e.g., taking attendance, making announcements, and planning trips.

Attempts at improving community meetings are important and in many cases constitute valuable program modifications. Yet they often fail to keep in mind the basic program objectives and how these can be conveyed through community meetings, utilizing the special aspect of total PHP attendance. The community as a group should periodically discuss the value of these meetings, and look for ways to structure them to meet current individual, group, and program needs. A common complaint is that they are boring. This stems from two sources: 1) Pertinent therapeutic material is not discussed, but rather more superficial topics; and 2) the meetings may be so large that many individuals, unable to have a central or active role, withdraw in silence or absence. In one PHP an open evaluation of community meetings led to the development of open rounds (see Chapter 18).

A major problem in structuring community meetings is the tendency to keep them as a single entity—as one type of group, albeit with multiple agendas and directions. Most view them as the first meeting of each day, with members often arriving late (and tired). The meetings often have numerous interruptions, and generally either an air of aimlessness or turbulence prevails, depending on factors affecting the program at any given time.

PHPs need not adhere to a tradition of *one* type of community meeting. There may be a need for several types, e.g.:

1) open rounds, which provides a consistent clinical focus;
2) administrative community meetings, which handle announcements, planning special activities, etc.;
3) program evaluation meetings;
4) patient evaluation groups (see Chapter 19);
5) medical health community meetings (see Chapter 20); and
6) multimedia groups (see Chapter 19), which could be further developed to include the entire staff, focusing on communication skills.

A PHP may utilize a variety of community meeting structures. Figure 1 gives an example of a community meeting schedule.

Figure 1
Community Meeting Schedule for One Week

Mon.	Tues.	Wed.	Thurs.	Fri.
9–9:20 Administration meeting 9:30–10:30 Open rounds	10–11 Open rounds 2–4 Patient evaluation group	9–10:15 Open rounds 10:30–11:30 Medical health community meeting 2–3 Program evaluation meeting	9–9:20 Administration meeting 9:30–10:30 Open rounds 1–3 Multimedia group	9–10:30 Open rounds Weekly sum-up Weekend planning

A community meeting program schedule utilizing this variety of community meeting structures would constitute ten community meetings per week, and would probably feel less time-consuming or draining than one "anything goes" community meeting lasting one hour per day.

By providing a variety of highly structured community meetings while maintaining flexibility to handle special situations (e.g., calling a community meeting to deal with a community crisis, etc.), staff and patients spend a much greater amount of time together as a community and can use the time therapeutically and efficiently. Increasing community meetings should also reduce the time needed for staff meetings, since more information is gained firsthand.

Leadership for various community meetings can be handled by any of the existing means; however, with diffferent types of meetings, different levels of expertise are utilized and leadership skills are thereby distributed more evenly. Using some staff as silent observers can also provide meaningful material during supervision.

PHP community meetings are among the most difficult groups to handle, due to their size, variety of problems requiring attention, diversification of staff training and orientation, plus a number of resistant forces which often result in a multitude of counteractive behaviors indicative of underlying problems within the community.

Through planning and structuring community meetings as carefully as other groups, they can be equally relevant, interesting, and challenging. Organizing these meetings to deal with issues more individually, clearly, and in greater depth can result in greater achievement of patient and program goals. In addition, through constructively increasing personal contact among all PHP members, the therapeutic milieu is strengthened, thereby increasing the therapeutic impact on individuals and on the PHP as a community.

18

Open Rounds: A Type of
Community Meeting

PHPs struggle to develop and maintain consistent focus on pertinent treatment issues. Keeping all staff and patients aware of the numerous daily events in a PHP consumes a great deal of time and energy (see Chapter 22). Open rounds, a type of community meeting (for which there is no known literature), effectively disseminates important clinical information to the entire PHP community on a daily basis. This chapter will examine traditional (closed) staff rounds; description and open rounds; advantages of staff preparation and implementation; and the effect of open rounds on other partial hospital programming.

TRADITIONAL (CLOSED) STAFF ROUNDS

Before moving into a discussion of open rounds, it is helpful to look at the traditional method of disseminating patient information to staff, and on which open rounds is based.

Traditional staff rounds is a meeting of staff, often held daily, where patients are discussed in terms of observed behavior and psychodynamic understanding, with an emphasis on formulating treatment goals and plans. All staff involved in working with the patients participate in these staff rounds in order to maximize therapeutic understanding, cooperation and consistency. The format usually consists of a brief discussion of each patient on a rotating schedule, including patients in crisis. Occasionally staff rounds are used to discuss one or two patients in depth (individual case conferences). These rounds tend to include only those patients viewed by staff as most perplexing or difficult, particularly in short-term or intermediate-term programs (see Chapter 14). It is typical for those patients who adjust "well" to hospital or PHP life to get little attention during staff rounds. These are the patients, however, who may have the most difficulty adjusting to life outside the institution; they can require even more careful treatment and discharge planning than those patients who present more overt problems.

Staff members typically feel it essential to discuss patients privately, to reveal only to other staff (and even then with initial apprehension) honest and frank impressions, feelings or questions regarding psychological or behavioral dynamics.

178

In addition, where closed staff rounds are the only type of regular formal staff meeting, they may be used by staff to ventilate feelings (particularly negative ones) about the program or patients. If these discussions are not worked through to effect quality patient care, they can become a type of resistance to the clinical work and an inefficient use of staff rounds. To suggest sharing information and observations more openly, in the presence of patients, often results in exclamations of, "I wouldn't know what to say," or "That's unprofessional," or "The patients couldn't handle it."

CONSIDERATIONS FOR IMPLEMENTING AND
ADVANTAGES OF OPEN ROUNDS

There is a commonly heard plea for secrecy from patients around touchy matters, particularly those pertaining to other PHP patients or intense transference feelings toward staff—for example, "Please don't mention this to anyone. It must be kept just between us. I can trust only you." Patients may threaten regressive symptomatology or withdrawal from the program if their requests for secrecy are not met. This kind of withholding communication places a burden on any person agreeing to it, since it would prevent him from discussing it in supervision or consultation (or even informal staff "gossip"), and magnifies the possibility of the secret being accidentally spilled.

Difficult situations result when a patient reveals to another PHP member suicidal or homicidal feelings, sexual involvement with another patient, use of illicit drugs, or the presence of psychotic thinking or behavior. There is a tendency to avoid bringing such issues into the open, thereby warding off accompanying anxiety and an intense range of often conflicted feelings that these issues juxtapose on an already highly emotionally charged environment. Open rounds is suggested as a solution to these difficult situations.

Another reason for utilizing open rounds is that it formalizes and openly uses the existing "paralleling" of staff and patient issues (see Chapter 5). Staff frequently gather in a closed meeting, work laboriously to reach some resolution of a community issue, and emerge to discover the patients had been struggling with the same issue—and had arrived at a remarkably similar solution.

Another reason for considering implementing open rounds is the need for PHPs to be flexible, i.e., changing from one format to another (depending on the number of active versus passive patients, philosophical orientation of staff, community size, etc.). The factors of change can lead to feelings of fragmentation and inconsistency. Open rounds can "tie things together."

Open rounds provides an unusually good method of formalizing important communication which is otherwise incomplete, e.g., discussions over lunch, over the telephone, or in hurried half-exchanges betweeen groups. This is particularly relevant as it pertains to the workings of multiple staff teams. For example, a patient problem raised in one group may not be clearly raised in other groups; staff leaders, if aware of the problem through that day's open rounds, can pick up on the problem more easily in their groups. Open rounds affords no staff or group permanent access to more crucial clinical information than any other staff or group. In addition, all patients have access to the same information. Open rounds clearly illustrates the intimate integration of treatment issues in all PHP groups (see also Chapter 6).

Integrating new patients with their uniquely specific individual problems and strengths can be difficult. Patients typically attend the PHP for a number of sessions or even weeks before the community becomes really aware of and interested in them as community members. This awareness may be gained through the new member's increased activity or, unfortunately, when a crisis erupts or the new patient begins showing signs of withdrawing from the program. By that time, valuable ground is lost in engaging the individual in treatment. Open rounds is one way of insuring new patients equal recognition, providing a means of specifically identifying new members and their contributions to the milieu at the outset, thereby lessening the problem of delayed integration.

Open rounds forces staff to give up the safety and power of closed rounds. This is anxiety-provoking, but over time staff relax and become more observant, sensitive, and factual in their reporting. Perhaps the greatest advantage of open rounds is that everyone is openly and promptly made aware of what is happening in the PHP in a more accurate and complete manner, with all the positive treatment ramifications this implies. Most PHP members are at least partially aware of most issues anyway and experience a sense of relief when they are openly discussed.

Patients and staff who have participated in open rounds over a period of time overwhelmingly agree they find the open policy preferable to closed rounds. Patients eventually feel positive about not being closed out of discussions concerning them and their lives. They do not like it if they later participate in a setting where this policy is not practiced.

Some observed and reported results of utilizing open rounds are: greater group cohesion; increased trust of staff; a diminished need and request for private, individual sessions; and decreased narcissistic preoccupation. Patients also tend to work harder to resolve their difficulties when they know the entire community is aware of their problems, accepting of each individual, and willing to help. Patients' sense of self-esteem, confidence, and effectiveness is heightened as they are not only made to feel—but are—an integral part of all PHP activities.

One might also think the technique of open rounds would be most effective with verbal, relatively high-functioning patients. However, experience with many levels of patient functioning suggests it can, with appropriate focus, be equally effective with chronic schizophrenic patients as it is for those with personality disorders or neuroses. Factors of skill, commitment to the philosophy underlying open rounds, and staff comfort in using the techniques are determinants of the successful implementation of open rounds.

There is one note of caution to keep in mind when considering open rounds: Open rounds makes a PHP less tranquil, more active, and potentially more volatile. Staff should make careful assessment of their patient population before beginning open rounds. Although it can be used with divergent diagnostic groups, staff should consider its impact on certain acute care PHPs, treating patients who are floridly psychotic. Open rounds may also be more difficult to implement when the PHP's treatment time frame is so short-term (1-4 weeks) that the therapeutic bonds between patients are not strong enough to withstand the intensity which open rounds promotes.

OPEN ROUNDS: DEFINITION AND DESCRIPTION

Open rounds is a meeting where the work of traditional staff rounds is open to all PHP clinical staff and patients. Open rounds clearly emphasizes the basic concept of a therapeutic milieu (see Chapter 7): When an individual shares any information considered a community issue (anything which might help with a patient's problems and strengths), the individual will be encouraged to bring it up in an appropriate group, reminding him that it will be mentioned in open rounds. If the individual is a staff member, it is assumed that, with training, he will use sensitivity in sharing often delicate and painful information. This policy occasionally angers patients and raises staff anxiety. However, if the policy is clearly stated and consistently adhered to, then issue must be taken with a patient's attempts to engage others in breaking a policy rule. In fact, such anger and confrontation can be therapeutic when handled properly, i.e., when through the exchange a greater understanding is gained of the issue in question.

Open rounds does not mean that staff are abrogating their role as professionals ultimately responsible for the delivery of quality patient care. Nor does it strive to encourage a pseudo-democratic community, where it appears that staff and patients have equal responsibility and authority in making clinical decisions. Rather, it is a means of strengthening the working alliance by fostering an accepting atmosphere where patients have a formalized, integral, and respected role in the resolution of treatment issues, while never losing sight of the fact that they are attending the PHP to work on their own personal problems.

It is important to schedule open rounds in the early part of the program day in order to allow ample time in following groups to work on the material raised therein (Jones, 1976).

If there are 20 full-time patients in the PHP, the staff's reporting would constitute approximately the first 20-30 minutes of open rounds. Those staff involved in direct or full-time patient care are seated in a circle within the larger circle of patients, a kind of "fishbowling." Of course, seating arrangements and staffing are flexible matters (see example in Chapter 8).

Patients are asked to hold comments until staff complete their reporting. Open rounds begins on time and latecomers seat themselves with as little disruption as possible. One staff member has a complete list of all patients, and each patient's name is read from the list, whether present or absent. Staff make observations on each patient (1-2 minutes each) in terms of significant data, usually pertaining to events of the previous PHP day. Patients may comment here, particularly if staff is unaware of some important issue, or reports an erroneous fact. The objective is to strive for concise, relevant reporting. The data may appear at first glance to warrant an entire community meeting's attention for exploration. However, in time both patients and staff come to terms with the fact that little is actually resolved in open rounds; rather, it lays the groundwork for the other groups, and brings everyone up-to-date on the preceding day's work. It is important to keep in mind that *all* issues that are considered therapeutically relevant can be raised in open rounds.

The following is a brief exerpt from a typical open rounds meeting.*

WALTER A.

Occupational Therapist: In OT shop Walter said he was feeling suicidal over the weekend and didn't feel he could call on anyone from the community.

Nurse Clinician: Walter was hospitalized at this time last year. I wonder if we can figure out with him what it is about this time of the year that makes it so difficult for him to cope.

DIANE K.

Recreational Therapist: In dance group Diane said she is thinking of getting a job soon and leaving the PHP.

Vocational Counselor: That's interesting—in vocational group she said she feels she'll need to be here for a long time before she's ready to work.

Occupational Therapist: I wonder why she's giving different staff different messages.

DAVID R.

Social Worker: David asked for an individual session with me and said he and Diane are having an affair. He didn't want me to bring it up in group as he said it would ruin things for them. I suggested he bring it up himself, but he hadn't as of yesterday. I told him that, since he knows the policy against keeping

---

* This hypothetical session reflects those which took place at the Roosevelt Hospital PHP, New York.

secrets, he must really want the community to know and needs help talking about it.

Recreational Therapist: I wonder if that's why Diane is talking of quitting.

JANIS S.

Psychiatrist: Jan looks preoccupied most of the time lately and looked yesterday like she was having hallucinations, but she denied it.

Nurse Clinician: I agree; I'm concerned. She also didn't pick up her prescription for medication yesterday, and in small group said she's worried about having "strange" thoughts lately.

BRUCE W.

Nurse Clinician: Bruce had another "explosion" in small group therapy yesterday. He stormed out, leaving everyone quite upset—and I notice he's not here yet.

Vocational Counselor: It really seems that Bruce sets up crises to get attention off the talk about his moving on to a training program. I'm personally getting tired of it, even though I know he's nervous about leaving here and starting something new.

Lois R. (patient): I saw Bruce this morning in a restaurant. He's OK. I think he thinks if he has enough tantrums and acts sick enough he can stay here forever.

Staff reporting continues until all patients are mentioned—for some patients, staff may report, "Nothing new." After the staff report, staff move their chairs back into the larger circle and discussion opens. It is common for only a small number of issues raised in the open rounds staff report to be followed up in the open rounds community discussion, owing to time limitations. Usually, the "hottest" issues are immediately continued. Patients are encouraged to react to, add to, or correct what they have heard, and to raise new issues if any have been omitted. The following are examples of responses to an open rounds meeting.

David R. (patient): I think it's really crummy you people have to blab everything to everyone. It's nobody's damn business what Diane and I do after we leave this place.

Lois R. (patient): Why are you getting so mad? We all know about it anyway. Besides, it *is* our business if Diane quits—and you know we've talked about how it's not a good idea to have an affair with someone you're in therapy with.

Nurse Clinician: Since Diane's part of this, I wonder what she's feeling about it.

Diane K. (patient): It's embarrassing. I can't talk about it right now—maybe later.

Nurse Clinician: OK, but it's important that you do talk about it, so you won't feel so tempted to run away.

Ross L. (patient): David's been mad at (social worker) ever since she went on vacation. I think that's why he's so angry about her bringing up about him and Diane.

David: That's bullshit.

Diane: David, I think we should both talk about it in small group today.

Psychiatrist: You're right, Diane. You both need to talk about this situation. It's in the open to talk about now, and although we can't go into it in depth in this meeting, there will be time later today and the rest of the week—and as long as it takes.

Margaret L. (patient): After what you guys said about Jan, I'm worried she's not here.

Occupational Therapist: Does anyone know what's going on with her?

Silence.

Mary K. (patient): I feel bad about saying this, but I think I should. Jan told me not to tell anyone. But she's been smoking a lot of grass lately—that's why she looks so spaced out. She's afraid if she talks about it she'll get kicked out.

Linda R. (patient): I think she's in bad shape. She told me this was the time her father died ten years ago and she always gets depressed. I think I'll phone her if she's not here soon.

Psychiatrist: Thank you, Linda. Will someone in the group also tell Jan about this conversation?

Discussion continues.

Vocational Counselor: It's nearly time to end the meeting and I wonder why no one has mentioned Walter's saying he was feeling suicidal and why he hasn't brought it up here?

Larry M. (patient): I've never heard him talk that way before. I guess I don't know him very well.

Recreational Therapist: Why does everyone always talk about and around Walter and not to him?

Larry M. (patient): I guess because he never talks for himself—at least in groups. Why are you feeling like hurting yourself, Walter?

Walter A. (patient): I don't know. I guess I think I'm not getting any better.

Social Worker: Even though it's time to end for today, we're left with some very important issues. There's still lots more time today—and Walter, why don't you try to bring this up in group yourself? How about in patient meeting, which is next?

Coffee break follows (15 minutes) where open rounds issues are typically discussed in smaller groupings; then staff leave for staff group supervision (see Chapter 25) and patients assemble for patient meeting (see Chapter 19).

Groups throughout the day will focus on the issues raised in open rounds, often bringing them up the following day or days. These examples were selected to indicate the nature of open rounds. They strive to deal with *observable* data which the patients have presented, verbally or behaviorally, which helps to eliminate the use of assumptions, jargon, or premature interpretations.

STAFF PREPARATION AND IMPLEMENTATION

Implementing open rounds can be difficult. If not initiated at the beginning of a program, it may be met with tremendous resistance. Actual boycotting by patients may be an early—and painful—experience. However, if there is a firm belief that this treatment technique will be beneficial, these initial fears and resistances on the part of both staff and patients can be closely examined and resolved, promoting a greater understanding of the dynamics of group process.

Initiating open rounds involves a number of risks for both staff and patients. Patients fear being exposed and initially feel vulnerable. At first, staff react with, "How can I say what I really think in front of the patients?" Open rounds does not give staff license to say *any*thing or *every*thing they think about patients. A rule of thumb regarding open rounds is that it is a therapeutic group, as are all other PHP groups. Staff must examine their personal reactions to patients to insure that countertransference issues are not interfering with their ability to be objective (see Chapter 25). This concern provides excellent material for staff supervision as well as for direct treatment interventions.

Staff are frequently concerned with the relevance of their observations and impressions and whether they measure up to other staff. Competition does not end with open rounds, but the issues are usually more obvious and the feeling that staff are participating in a mutual group effort helps the competition develop a more positive nature.

Expert, ongoing group supervision of staff is essential in preparing for open rounds and for their successful integration into a program. Exploration of staff's reactions, together with training in how to "read" an observation and report on it concisely, accurately and with therapeutic impact, is important and may require several weeks' preparation.

Two essential issues to explore during the preparation phase are: 1) how to avoid the tempting trap of reporting only positive, complimentary, nonconfrontive material; and 2) how to avoid doing the work for the patients, e.g., reporting and evaluating incidents or issues so thoroughly that the patients need not do their part of the work. Role-playing possible situations for reporting can be helpful and through this training method greater empathy is gained for both patient and staff positions.

EFFECTS ON OTHER PARTIAL HOSPITAL PROGRAMMING

When used meaningfully, with commitment, open rounds ultimately affects all groups within the milieu. Groups become more clearly focused on individual and group needs, and the specific groups become vehicles for dealing with clearly defined problems rather than ends in themsevles.

Other possibilities for open rounds may include extending them to allow more in-depth examination of problems—a type of "open" case conference. Another may be the implementation of a similar group where patients discuss staff, groups, and program, which could lead to valuable program modifications.

19

Group Techniques for Maximizing Patient Involvement and Mutual Therapeutic Responsibility

This chapter will describe and discuss specific group techniques which promote patient involvement and growth. Such techniques include patient meetings without staff, patient evaluation groups, multimedia (communications) groups, and implications for other programming.

Partial hospitalization program staff are often concerned with the lack of apparent motivation or enthusiasm on the part of their patients. Recurring struggles take place over helping patients speak up, punctuality and attendance problems, and "boring" meetings where staff feel they must take over in order for anything to be accomplished. These are but a few of the numerous, complex processes which staff and patients in PHPs face. The energy involved in trying to resolve problems such as these is great, and at times can leave an entire PHP community feeling helplessly and hopelessly exhausted and exasperated, wondering whether it is all worthwhile.

Certain types of groups yield a greater degree of patient and staff involvement. When patients and staff are working equally hard together in a mutual, therapeutically responsible way to resolve intrapsychic, interpersonal, programmatic, or almost any shared concern, there prevails in the program a dynamic, exciting, therapeutic force which can overcome the most difficult of situations. When there is this kind of shared working atmosphere, attendance or attention is rarely a problem.

PATIENT MEETINGS

Patient meetings are composed of all PHP patients and are led by PHP patients. They are held at specific times within the PHP program schedule and are on specified PHP premises. Staff are not in attendance. Therapists who perceive patients as capable of behaving in a rational, responsible, and mostly healthy way are those who would be likely to support the use of patient meetings. This practice reveals to patients their need for one another, which can extend beyond the hours spent together in PHPs, and to family and friends.

Patient meetings are not new. They are more commonly referred to as "patient government" and "alternate sessions," although these two types of patient meetings connote different meanings. Patient government groups proliferate in psychiatric group settings. However, their degree of impact and effectiveness is questionable. Unfortunately, they often have an outward appearance of providing patients with some control over their course of treatment, but are frequently carried out under existing covert staff attitudes that patients are not really capable of positively participating to a *major* and *active* degree in their own, or especially in fellow patients', treatment. Issues discussed in government groups tend to be of a concrete nature, e.g., obtaining privileges and passes. In addition, at least one staff member is usually present.

Alternate sessions were originally defined and designed by Wolf (1949, 1950) and later discussed by Mullen and Rosenbaum (1962): "The alternate group meeting is established by the therapist, though he does not attend it, occurring between . . . regular meetings and held for the purpose of forwarding the group psychotherapeutic process. And, although the therapist suggests the meeting, he neither controls it nor prescribes how the patients are to act at these times" (p.267).

Alternate group sessions have their proponents (Kadis, 1956), and those who object strongly to them (Slavson, 1956). In PHPs those in favor of utilizing patient meetings would agree that they must be considered in the context of the whole therapeutic milieu and not merely as ends in themselves. In patient meetings, patients experience peers in a new way and learn to separate themselves from staff (parental) dependency. This leads to increased freedom of expression, peer intimacy, responsibility and growth (Kadis, 1956).

Those opposing meetings without staff fear the results of the lack of professional input and control. They believe the meetings will become an arena for patients to act out their transference feelings (affections, hostilities, etc.) toward peers and staff. They fear damage can be done by patients' confusing themselves and other patients with unsophisticated interpretation or suggestion, or, at best, bypassing important latent material to deal with superficial issues (Slavson, 1956).

These strongly opposing views reflect more than just technical differences in group function; rather, they point to basic treatment philosophies which are at tremendous variance with one another. If both of these philosophies are operating simultaneously in a PHP, the results could be confusing, with serious implications regarding patient expectations.

Staff usually have mixed feelings about whether or not to institute patient meetings. Staff feel an enormous responsibility for PHP treatment, which can result in a tendency to control the treatment process. Patient-led patient meetings mean staff giving up some control. There may be unrecognized competition between staff (trained) and patients (untrained) with regard to who are the "best" therapeutic agents. Staff and patients may collude to maintain staff authoritarianism. Patients claim, "You're the staff—don't you get paid for leading?" This can be threatening to staff on at least two levels: 1) Leadership ability and seeming passivity are challenged; and 2) anxiety is involved in giving up some of their control over the program and patients.

Most observations and interpretations offered by staff can, with sufficient time, encouragement, and practice, be offered by patients; this is beneficial to their emotional and social growth. Such a situation can place staff in a superficially less important position, and may play a part in reluctance to formally acknowledge patients' potential for self-reliance and leadership.

History and Description of Patient Meetings in a PHP*

The idea of patients meeting with no staff in attendance arose out of a reality situation: The director was part-time and the staff needed to meet together for supervision, case conferences, intake conferences, etc., in a limited time period, during program hours. There was extensive discussion regarding this dilemma—could patients meet on their own without in some way behaving irresponsibly? Was staff merely rationalizing the use of patient meetings to allow themselves what they needed, over and apart from the needs of the patients? Probably the greatest concern was around safety: Would suicidal risk patients use the unsupervised time to leave the premises and engage in self-destructive activity, and would other patients perhaps lose control and fight—physically—with one another? In addition to concern over treatment issues, legal issues were also at stake. These concerns led eventually to closer examination by staff of their expectations of patients and of the effectiveness of the therapeutic environment in the program—was it self-sustaining or did it require constant monitoring by staff? The expression of staff's fears of certain patients, particularly those prone to aggressive, impulsive outbursts, shed more light on what expectations staff were communicating, mostly nonverbally, to patients, who might then act on those expectations in the manner in which they perceived them.

For example, Bruce entered the PHP with a history of antisocial behavior—stealing, soft drug abuse, violent and vulgar verbal attacks, and occasional threats of physical attack. He reported "losing control" on a few occasions and hitting his parents. (There was a clearly stated rule in the PHP which prohibited physical abuse—"one hit and you're out"—which was stated as firmly and as frequently as necessary, and with the commitment that it would be strictly and promptly carried out.) Staff soon also viewed him as a negative, disruptive force and questioned whether he should be terminated from the program. By expecting him (and cer-

---

* The PHP under discussion here (Roosevelt Hospital, NYC) had 20 adult patients, ages 18-60, who attended from 9 A.M. to 4 P.M., five days per week, Mon.-Fri. Diagnostic categories served were approximately as follows: 43% chronic schizophrenic; 30% borderline; 13% personality disorders; 13% neurotic; 1% other. Approximately 41% had a recent history of suicide attempts. None had been dangerously homicidal.

tainly not without good reason) to behave in what had become a stereotypical "tough guy" role, the entire community really believed he could not and would not change (although they verbalized feelings to the contrary). This was conveyed to Bruce in numerous, mostly nonverbal, subtle communications (which he was able to see through), and he acted on the underlying negative expectations.

Only through painful recognition by staff of their part in the perpetuation of this patient's dysfunctional behavior, and close examination of their feelings about him were they able to begin to understand the dynamics of his behavior and to help him begin the long struggle toward change. Although the inclination was to remove Bruce from patient meetings or have staff present, this was viewed as another way of reinforcing his own—and everyone else's—fears that he was irresponsible and uncontrollable. It was a difficult testing period, during which staff made it very clear they would be immediately available (two doors away) should an emergency arise.

The patient meeting was finally begun, with some trepidation, on a trial basis. There were several weeks of strong resistance on the part of the patients regarding the meeting. They feared (or reflected staff's fears) that they could indeed *not* hold a meeting without staff; they tried to convey that they were both unpredictable and irresponsible. Initially, some patients literally left the meeting—and the program—to go across the street for coffee, or to the cafeteria for breakfast, perhaps symbolic of their not feeling "fed" by staff's presence. This behavior, in addition to the individual problems presented by Bruce and others, nearly convinced the entire community it was time to end such nonsense, i.e., expecting "psychiatric patients" to meet in a group by themselves. However, during this period of approximately four months, staff was called on to intervene in the patient meeting only twice—once when a physical fight was threatening (involving Bruce) and a second time when another patient, identified as a possible suicidal risk, left the meeting unannounced.

Throughout this testing phase, and in both of the situations mentioned above, the events which took place in the patient meeting were taken to other groups in the PHP for discussion and examination. In spite of continuing reservations on the efficacy of this group on the part of some staff and patients, there was sufficient, consistent support for its continuing and working into a viable, productive group.

With painstaking examination of the underlying dynamics involved, there was a gradual resolution of problems and the patient meeting evolved into a well-functioning therapeutic group, which patients enjoyed being part of. The problems experienced in the early phase of patient meeting were frequently raised in open rounds (Chapter 18) and discussed in other groups, as a means of encouraging the patients to continue struggling with the problems encountered by them in their work together as a self-help group.

Some of the issues involved in examining the problems in patient meeting were:

1) The expectation that patients could function adequately in group only with a staff leader. These expectations came from staff, the patients, their families, the hospital system, and previous hospital experiences.
2) The fear of increased vulnerability when staff withdrew their "protective" presence.
3) Fear of regression without staff-imposed and supervised structure.
4) Fear of anger stirred up by being "abandoned" by staff/parents, and subsequent fear of self- or other-harm.
5) Anxiety that material brought up in patient group would not be transferred to other PHP groups for staff knowledge, which would place a greater burden on patients to deal with therapeutic material, as well as the responsibility of keeping staff informed of appropriate information.
6) Fear of potential emotional intimacy with fellow patients and its consequent responsibility and anxiety.

Over the course of approximately four months, the patient meeting developed into a cohesive group, and several simultaneous marked changes occurred. Patients demonstrated greater leadership skills, were less reluctant to risk speaking up to offer their own opinions, were more secure in their place within the PHP, and reported being less withdrawn socially and at home.

Patience and the belief that this group could work and have positive benefits paid off, not only in terms of the patient meeting, but also in the greater degree of involvement patients exhibited in the program, which in turn led to the development and improvement of other PHP groups.

PATIENT EVALUATION GROUPS

When patients enter a PHP, there are usually fairly specific reasons for the referral, although those reasons are often unknown to the patient. This can occur for several reasons: Staff assumes the patient already knows why partial hospitalization is required; reasons for referral are explained in an abstract manner; or the patient is too overwhelmed, too highly defended or psychotic to fully comprehend the explanation. Patients often feel they need help in addition to that which they have been receiving, but are just as often unclear about what PHPs have to offer, what their specific problems are, or what can be done about them.

Example

The idea of regularly scheduled progress evaluations evolved several months after the opening of a new PHP. Although intake meetings provided an initial assessment and general treatment goals, this seemed mainly to be helpful to staff.

Patients were frequently vague and uncertain about the reasons why they were there, what they were doing to help themselves, and whether they were being helped at all.

Individual progress evaluations were implemented to resolve some of these issues. They began by having each patient, on different days, meet with the entire staff. These generally went well, but occasionally patients "forgot" to show up or refused; later they hinted that the odds of all five staff with just one patient were too unbalanced. After that the evaluations were revised to include one patient and one or two staff. However, this method had very similar results to the first approach, plus another problem—staff not included in the actual evaluation meeting did not feel thoroughly informed of treatment plans or goals, in spite of their being discussed in staff meetings and recorded in the patient's medical chart. Another limitation of this technique was the lack of involvement of all other patients in the treatment planning process. Therefore, even if a patient became clearly aware of his treatment goals through the evaluation meeting, no other patients knew of them unless they were specifically informed by the patient who had been evaluated.

The idea of groups for patient evaluation was not fully conceived until a resistant, paranoid patient, openly frightened of being evaluated in the presence of even one staff member, consistently refused to attend any evaluation conference set up for him. He finally announced that he would attend only if he could bring another patient along with him to the meeting, to "represent" him. This request was granted, and the patient attended his first evaluation session, accompanied by another patient, an "ally." His fears of being harshly criticized or kicked out of the program (which had been experienced as reality on previous efforts at jobs) were dispelled during the meeting, and the idea of including more than one patient in the evaluations began to gel.

With this incident, greater thought was invested in the purpose of evaluations in general and what they might mean to patients; perhaps their value as therapeutic tools was being underestimated. After much thought and discussion by staff and patients, the first group evaluation meeting was planned. Five patients volunteered to "be first"; several others attended as "audience." It was an immediate and lasting success.

In order to steamline the process, a questionnaire was drawn up and presented to the patients a week before the evaluation group, with staff comments and recommendations recorded on it, to help organize thinking and stimulate reactions (see condensed example of questionnaire, Figure 1).

Within a short period of time the questionnaire became merely a guide, and patients became actively involved in honestly dealing with one another around problem areas, progress, and even areas of resistance such as attendance or lateness. When patients confronted patients, there was little resultant rebellion against staff as authority figures, previously acted out after the meetings.

Figure 1
Example of Patient Evaluation Group Questionnaire

Member's Name: *Date:*
Staff present: *Evaluation #:* (1st, 2nd, etc.)
Other members attending:

---

1. How long have you been in PHP?
2. What were your original goals (reasons) for coming to PHP?
3. Have these goals changed? If yes, how?
4. What are you doing to work on your goals?
5. Have you made progress? If yes, how? If no, discuss why.
6. Have new problems come up that you need help with? If yes, what are they?
7. Staff comments and recommendations:
8. Members' comments and recommendations:
9. Personal comments and recommendations:
10. Do you agree with staff and other members' recommendations? If no, what do you disagree with?
11. Revised recommendations:
12. Additional remarks:
13. Next evaluation date:

After the first group of volunteers had participated in the evaluation groups and had survived, a schedule was developed which would allow each patient a monthly evaluation. The program had 20 full-time participants, so five patients were scheduled each week. Other PHP members sat in on a voluntary basis. For larger programs, the groups could be held more than once a week (approximately one-and-a-half hours was needed to evaluate five patients), or patients could be scheduled less often than once a month. Where the evaluation group serves as the only individually focused evaluation work on a regular basis in a program, it is preferable to see each individual at least once a month in the group.

Completed evaluation questionnaire forms were filed in a notebook following the evaluation groups and were available to the entire community for reading. They were also used on subsequent evaluations to compare goals and help assess progress. The evaluations were verbally taken back and presented to the entire community by the patients. Patient evaluations may also take place with the entire PHP community in attendance, which, if manageable, could avoid duplicating summarizing sessions.

The resulting increase in patients' involvement in their own and others' treatment process is most impressive. If staff exercise control over their own verbalizations, it is not unusual for patient evaluation groups to be almost totally managed by patients. It would be a mistake to consider these group meetings as "adjunct" groups to be squeezed in after program hours, during lunch, etc. To assign them the relevance they deserve, they must be scheduled into the regular program.

MULTIMEDIA GROUPS

The purpose of the multimedia group is to improve communication skills through a variety of media with emphasis on nonverbal techniques. Also, it encourages professionals to use activities therapies and to see them as valuable. The multimedia group was designed as a bridge between the extremes of verbal groups and activities groups.

Example

The entire patient community (20) was present for the group, which met once weekly for 90 minutes. One staff member led the group, with intermittent involvement of one other staff member. The goal of increasing patient involvement, responsibility, and independence again had to be handled carefully, as initially the patients were not at all sure they shared those goals.

The multimedia group began with a structured, "safe" level of group process. In the initial contracting, the leader made it clear she would offer suggestions and techniques for working on issues involving communication skills. The leader also conveyed a strong belief in the importance of such a group and sufficient skill in nonverbal techniques, thus promoting a sense of security and interest. However, since it was really the patients' group, it would also be up to the patients to plan how they wanted to use it.

The group decided unanimously that they wanted a current events group, using newspapers (a familiar medium) and talking (another familiar medium) about news events. It was a safe place to start, i.e., concrete and familiar enough to be nonthreatening.

The group met to discuss current events for about six weeks, until it became clear this was not really satisfying all members of the community and interest began to wane. The group then evaluated the purpose of the group. Many stated it should be discontinued altogether, since the idea of really creating their own group was threatening and involved a great deal of investment and work—and many patients were not sure they even needed or wanted "communication skills," improved or otherwise. At this point the leader became more active, offering specific suggestions in an attempt to prevent this potentially valuable group from failing before it got underway. Since it had been specifically made clear it would be "their" group, the leader felt she had to "loan" the group ego strengths and plenty of encouragement for it not to become another failure in their lives—this time a collective one—which could result in negatively influencing their feelings about groups and the entire program.

For several weeks the group leader planned techniques prior to each group, always reflecting some current theme in the program that seemed to warrant clarification or exploration. The leader went to the group with suggestions ready, which were used, modified or shelved, to adopt the spontaneous ideas of the patients. Techniques such as sociodrama, role-playing, mime, group murals, autobiographical sketches, poetry writing, etc. were used.

The anxiety present before each group reflected the unstructured format it had acquired, never knowing quite what technique would fit the mood or the level of group development at any one time. The leader had to be flexible and open to modifying ideas based on what was going on in group at any particular time. For example, Lisa, who was quite nonverbal, had been hospitalized for severe depression and a suicide attempt following the sudden death of her husband. Throughout her inpatient stay she refused to speak of her husband or his death, remaining silent and withdrawn. She maintained this affect for several weeks after referral to the PHP, refusing to speak except in abrupt response to concrete questions. The entire community was concerned about Lisa, as she was likeable and demonstrated her involvement in the program by silently cleaning the lounge area, preparing for coffee breaks, etc.

Two months after Lisa joined the PHP, the multimedia group decided that the major theme of the week had been depression—everyone seemed depressed about something. The technique they decided upon was a group mural, something with which they were by then familiar. They decided to affix the mural paper to the wall and each group member (including the leader) would add something that expressed what they were feeling depressed about. After everyone in the group had added a piece to the mural, each person then explained what it was they had drawn and others in the group were free to comment, question or interpret. Only with coaching was Lisa able to add something to the mural—a simple cross. She said she was unable to talk about it. Other patients who were sensitive to her feelings and problems were firm with her in encouraging her to discuss her part of the mural as they had. She finally said, "It's just a cross, that's all." Silence. Someone said, "We know from open rounds that your husband died and you haven't talked about it—does the cross have anything to do with that?" Lisa began crying, then talking. She had begun the process of mourning her husband. From that point she participated much more openly, became close with several other patients, progressed rapidly and was soon discharged to resume her work.

That incident also seemed to mark a turning point in the multimedia group itself. Patients commented that this wasn't "fooling around"—it was "serious therapy." They began to see more clearly how important it is to be able to communicate feelings, and that the most effective way to get at those feelings is not necessarily confined to talking. The group continued for some time to utilize techniques they had learned from the leader until they reached yet another level of group development. They had reached the point of not really needing a staff leader—at least, not in the same capacity they once had.

The group again evaluated its purpose, examined the original goals and progress, and decided they were by now capable of providing the leadership among themselves. They made it clear they would like the original staff leader to be present—for "moral support." It was felt that they needed a staff member's presence to provide sanction and support for their efforts at creativity and continued moves toward self-sufficiency. The group decided to rotate leadership, with the purpose being that each patient would communicate something he was knowledgeable about. The staff member was needed in the first few sessions to hold them to the new contract and to help them handle their anxiety over this potential achievement. (Attempts were made to force the staff member into her prior role as leader.) The staff member did this primarily by providing full support for the patient leader and serving as the role model of a respectful group participant.

For example, James decided to present a lecture on French literature, a course he had taught years before. Thus, he was actually demonstrating skills rather than merely talking about them. The impulse of the group was to act bored, faking yawns, giggling, etc. Rather than treating the disruptive patients as misbehaving school children and developing a power struggle, the staff member instead chose to devote full attention to James' presentation, which was quite good, and actively to join in the discussion following. When others saw this meeting being treated with the same amount of respect as all other groups, they, too, were better able to focus on the presentation. The result was that the group was sincerely impressed with James' scholarly abilities and had not previously known this about him. The esteem he gained from this group experience helped him assume responsibiilties in other areas such as the newspaper group which he had previously refused, saying he had "nothing to offer." Others presented situations for sociodrama (which they had learned earlier in the group), the value of physical exercise, black families in America, religious groups, philosophy, ethnic dancing, poetry, jokes, games, music, horticulture, and recipes. Cohesion was at a high level in this group, which spread to other groups as well. Patients constantly remarked on being impressed with being shown other patients' "hidden talents" in action. Participation in and attendance at this group were always high.

IMPLICATIONS FOR OTHER PHP PROGRAMMING

Once PHP programming has reached the point of high investment by all participants, and all those involved seem willing and able to progress even further in these directions, patients can be included in group intake of PHP patient applicants. Interviewees often comment they are relieved to be jointly interviewed by staff and patients. Patients often ask more direct, pertinent questions about another patient's problems, goals, etc. than staff. It also allows prospective patients to experience from the beginning: 1) that the PHP is group-oriented; 2) the expectation that they will be a vital part of the program; and 3) firsthand accounts of what the program is all about and what it is like to come in as a new member. Current members become aware of the central problems the new patient is struggling with, so potential "secrets" are in the open at the outset. Also, when new patients enter the program they have already met participating patients in a meaningful, therapeutic exchange, therefore integration into the program is facilitated.

It is important to note here that patients' impressions and opinions of intake interviews are strongly considered by the staff intake team. Final decisions regarding acceptance or rejection of applicants, however, rests with staff. This is made clear to the patients.

Patients can also play an effective role accompanying staff on home visits. Of course, legal issues must first be cleared with the program's administration, e.g., would the home visit be considered "work" or "therapy?" The visits, usually connected with crises, are customarily made by staff, but at times by specialized teams not familiar to the patient in crisis. Having program staff *and* patients conduct home visits, when appropriate, enhances the special PHP therapeutic atmosphere, which includes mutual therapeutic responsibility. Once patients and staff become accustomed to this concept, all kinds of exciting things can happen. For example, patients may initiate the development of staff and program evaluations, results of which can include improved staff/patient communication, leadership skills on the part of both staff and patients, more meaningful relationships, and important program changes or revisions. Another area of patient inclusion would involve assisting in interviewing volunteers, new staff, etc. An interesting issue which arose out of patients' involvement with interviewing potential PHP volunteers was their questioning why volunteers were needed—were the patients not capable of assuming some of those responsibilities? This led to a valuable reevaluation of expectations and roles.

In conclusion, PHPs are frequently beset with continual pressures which make overall functioning at an optimal level difficult. A combination of positive expectations and carefully designed programming can promote a healthy, growth-inducing atmosphere, capable of weathering the numerous demands and stresses encountered.

20

Physical Health Issues, Somatic Therapies, and Group Psychopharmacotherapy

A majority of partial hospital patients have psychopharmacotherapy and/or other somatic therapies prescribed for them at some point in their lifetime; for many, these therapies may be critical requirements for maintaining outpatient status. In addition, the biological structure of the human being is subject to both functional and physical disorders and can be affected by both psychological and organic treatments. People appreciate and benefit from being treated as holistic entities, so that none of their complexly integrated and inseparable biological, psychological, and social aspects are neglected.

Although the above seems obvious, many therapists do not attend to all three aspects. In particular, day hospital (Burke, 1978) and other (Karasu et al., 1980) patients have frequently overlooked physical disorders which could be the cause of the psychiatric symptoms (Hall et al., 1978). The patient may be unnecessarily burdened with a psychiatric diagnosis and/or denied an available physical cure.

The dichotomization between mind and body still contaminates our thinking. Treating people holistically may be too overwhelming and complex a concept since so many act as if attention to only one aspect of biopsychosocial functioning is the way to improve feeling and functioning (Schoenberg et al., 1978). A unity of mind and body is needed, with a combination of simultaneous approaches to both. Treatment considerations should be focused on improving functioning by the most efficient and effective therapies (somatic or psychological). At the same time, each therapy's particular cost/benefit ratio must be acceptable to professional and patient. Therefore, it behooves all partial hospital staff to be familiar and comfortable with somatic therapies and have a lively appreciation of physical health issues (see also Chapter 21).

RATIONALE FOR ORGANIC THERAPIES AND/OR PSYCHOLOGIC THERAPIES

The Value of Medications Alone

Quite simply, drugs have been proven to work. They are effective therapeutic agents for psychiatric symptoms, and they have, perhaps, the lowest cost/benefit ratio of any therapeutic agent (Goldstein et al., 1978; Hollon and Beck, 1978; Davis et al., 1980; Talbott, 1978).

At least for that portion of the population diagnosed as having "functional psychosis," drug maintenance is felt overwhelmingly to be the single treatment most directly contributing to prevention of relapse into psychosis and rehospitalization (Barter, 1978; Hollon and Beck, 1978). However, drug therapy alone does not result in the levels of skills attained in conjunction with PHP treatment (Linn et al., 1979).

Somatic and Psychologic Therapy Combinations

Use of medication should not exclude psychologic treatment. Psychologic and somatic therapies can be used in combination compatibly and may have mutually positive influences if used appropriately (Hollon and Beck, 1978). "Pill-taking" may be the best method for some patients to get enough hope mobilized to want to get better, while reducing symptoms (such as decreasing agitation) may make the patient amenable enough for psychologic therapies (Almond, 1975). Psychotherapy could be used to work through difficulties with adherence to a drug regimen. Hansell (1978) even suggests that the main value of any psychotherapy in schizophrenia may be primarily to keep a person with schizophrenia on medication.

Value of Psychologic Therapies Alone

To date, research makes contradictory, confusing, and inconclusive statements about the value or lack of value of psychosocial treatments (either alone or in combination with organic therapies), and nothing yet tells the clinician what is "the best" treatment for any specific psychiatric diagnosis (Hollon and Beck, 1978; Mosher and Keith, 1980). Hollon and Beck (1978) make the following two additional conclusions:

1) Research seems easier and better when done on cognitive, behavioral, and goal-oriented therapies. Perhaps from this fact alone these therapies seem more effective than nondirective psychotherapies or waiting lists.
2) Present instruments measuring outcome are inadequate, and basically they seem only able to indicate that drugs alone are as good as psychotherapy. With better instruments perhaps more research would indicate that psychotherapies are essential for certain behavioral changes.

Non-drug Organic Therapies

The only non-drug organic therapy currently much in use is electroconvulsive therapy (ECT). This is electrical stimulation applied to the head producing a cerebral seizure. Erroneously ECT has fallen into disrepute, and the myth has grown up that ECT is a treatment of last resort for hopeless patients or psychotherapy rejects. Thus, despite current technical modifications, so that morbidity is very low and the typical bodily manifestations of a convulsion do not occur, the mere contemplation of ECT engenders great alarm in many staff and most patients. Therefore, time must be repeatedly made to deal with these fears, since the issue of ECT being used is bound to arise in PHP. However, education alone is not enough to allay the fears about ECT, since they have a much deeper psychological basis; ECT stirs up fears of loss of control, low self-worth, past transgression and punishment, and awesomely powerful, primitive lightning bolts, among others.

There have been recent judicious overviews of this therapy (APA Task Force, 1978; Weiner, 1979) indicating ECT for certain types of severe manic, depressive and schizophrenic conditions. ECT has been tried in many other disorders, but research is conflicting and inadequate as to its effectiveness.

In regard to memory impairment, the APA Task Force could not conclude that ECT is a cause of persistent memory complaints six to nine months later. Impairment is temporarily caused, but, in the usual treatment course (less than 15 treatments given three times per week) with healthy patients, memory impairment essentially lasts only one to two weeks, and gross impairment usually lasts only an hour or two.

SOME GUIDELINES FOR PSYCHOPHARMACOTHERAPY

A psychiatrist who is an expert in psychopharmacotherapy (and other organic therapies) should be available to teach and prescribe in the partial hospital. A great deal of literature, for example, Appleton and Davis (1980) and, for the nonphysician, Goldsmith (1977), is also available. The Task Force on Psychopharmacological Criteria Development of the American Psychiatric Association (Dorsey et al., 1979) recommends a physical examination within the past six months prior to initiating medications; also, a search for any symptoms of tardive dyskinesia should be conducted at least every three months when an antipsychotic drug is being used.

Common Problems and Issues in Psychopharmacotherapy

1) There are incomplete guidelines for drug use because of incomplete research in psychopharmacotherapy. For example, little research has taken into account that a therapy for chronic patients must be given for approximately six months to be effective and that comprehensively measured follow-up needs to be done for at least two years (Mosher and Keith, 1980) because of the slow changeability of typical chronic patients.

Thus, practitioners must still achieve optimal chemotherapy by "a mixture of intuitive judgment and pragmatic trial and error" (Van Putten et al., 1979).

2) Many patients do not seem to respond to any single, presumably indicated therapy. A solution to this problem of the nonresponsive patient is only possible if the practitioner has the flexibility to change the treatment plan, the awareness of a wide range of possible therapies, and a belief that all patients can improve.

3) Incomplete patient "treatment adherence" (now preferred to the old term "compliance" [Eisenthal et al., 1979]) is an enormous problem. Despite recommendations to the contrary, no more than 25 percent of former mental inpatients continue in regular aftercare, and fewer than one-half of these take medication as prescribed (Minskoff, 1978). Many have tried injectable medication (e.g., prolixen decanoate) to cope with this.

A level of at least 80 percent treatment adherence is desirable. The factors working against achievement of this level are myriad and complex: these can be divided into treatment modality, patient, and treatment interrelationship issues.

As an example of treatment modality issues, Van Putten et al. (1979, 1981) report on poor adherence arising from physical side effects of medications. Some staff fail to appreciate the mental turbulence in patients due to side effects; other staff overreact and add to the patient's worries. Van Putten et al. (1979) emphasize the importance of staff's recognizing side effects and working continuously with the patient for an exquisite balance that maximizes desired effects and minimizes undesired effects.

As an example of the staff-patient interrelationship issue, Minskoff (1978) mentions the lack of meaningful, supportive treatment experiences in much outpatient treatment of the chronic patient. Many staff experience such a degree of frustration when a patient does not comply that they frequently exhibit impatience and anger, and conceptualize the patient as simply no good and purposefully rebellious. This occurs despite poor adherence having unconscious causes like any other issue (Nir and Cutler, 1978).

4) There is no simple answer to what, when, and how to tell the patient before treatment begins, i.e., informed consent. The trend is toward telling ever more, written consent, and contractual, consensually negotiated (rather than authoritarian prescriptive) therapy (Schwarz, 1980; Deveaugh-Geiss, 1979).

INTEGRATING ORGANIC THERAPIES INTO PHP

One problem is antitherapeutic use of the traditional biomedical model. For example, a number of programs based on this biomedical model may have psychiatrist time that is barely sufficient for initial intake, diagnosis, discharge, approval of treatment plans, and medications. The psychiatrist has little time for staff development conferences, is rather isolated, and unilaterally prescribes medication. In this situation, one person has a monopoly on knowledge and power over vital areas (organic therapies and others); hence, resentment and power struggles follow, resulting in weakening of one of the unique therapeutic forces inherent in a good partial hospital, i.e., that derived from a mass of nonhospitalized people united to a uniquely high degree in goals and methods. Consider the following dialogue:

Patient: Why do I have to take this medication? My menstrual period stopped, and I think the pills are making me worse.
Nonmedical primary therapist: Well, I don't know, but it sounds terrible. Wait till you see the doctor next week; then he can stop them.

The situation results in the doctor being considered a pill-pusher, the patients poorly complying, and other staff complaining of possible negative effects of medicine, thereby undermining treatment adherence.

A second problem concerns the need for role augmentation in PHPs (see Chapter 5) and the accompanying discomfort. Change is ubiquitous, as is resistance to it. In addition, other factors involved in change are capabilities, values, information, circumstances, timing, motivation, and yield (Davis, 1978). Some staff will have little or no training in psychopharmacotherapy. Rarely do psychiatrists have training in evaluation of and prescribing medications in a group setting, and many have not had any training in group psychotherapies. Frequently, the psychiatrist will find it difficult to believe that the group setting can be equally or more effective than an individual session, especially when diagnosing and prescribing.

During a transition to becoming knowledgeable and skilled about medications, staff will have discomfort and self-doubting questions. For general pointers concerning a solution of these problems, see Chapter 5 about developing necessary mutual staff support for healthy PHP growth and maintenance. In addition, it would be helpful to design a treatment modality, such as the following, to address these issues.

GROUP PSYCHOPHARMACOTHERAPY AND PSYCHOSOMATICS

One recommended mechanism for tackling these issues is group psychotherapy and psychosomatics ("medical/health group") using co-therapists. This is a supportive (versus psychoanalytically oriented) group psychotherapeutic method with the following specific goals (in addition to more general group goals):

1) reliable, appropriate medication-taking to reduce those symptoms interfering with improved mental health;
2) a high level of participation of patients (Barter, 1978; Hansell, 1978; Schwarz, 1980) and all staff (Van Putten et al., 1979) toward optimal evaluating, diagnosing, prescribing, and monitoring (Working Group of JAMA, 1979);

3) an appreciation by participants of the theory and practice of psychosomatics and good health care;
4) evaluation of the patient and prescription writing done during the ongoing group therapy; and
5) appropriate knowledge, attitudes, and skills of staff and patients necessary for the above.

There is relatively little literature on this form of group psychotherapy. To our knowledge, none has been published on this modality used in a partial hospital. Similar forms are often referred to informally as medication groups (Levine and Dang, 1979; Powell et al., 1977) and more formally as group pharmacotherapy (Payn, 1974). However, these articles neither mention the use of these groups as a technique for education of staff in psychopharmacology, nor develop the idea of using them to discuss the entire range of biological aspects of health and disease.

Advantages of This Group Method

The rationale for using group therapy is partially based on the advantages of using groups in general in PHPs (see Chapter 6). Group peer pressure and support provide unique and powerful tools for molding behavior around the critical issues of medications, physical health, and diagnoses. The group method is specifically needed to counteract the detrimental aspects of an authoritarian biomedical model which tend to arise when organic therapies are used.

The psychiatrist and other staff and patients can be exposed to one another in a therapy situation longer than could be achieved by one-to-one contacts. For example, ten patients can be seen individually once a month for ten minutes each of therapy-medication evaluation. If the psychiatrist spends the same amount of time in group psychotherapy with these patients, he will be exposed to each patient ten times as much, and the patients will spend ten times as much time in therapy.

It seems helpful, when dealing with complicated technical matters and jargon, to have group participants with many different levels of sophistication and roles. The more sophisticated may be better at bridging the gap in language and training between the psychiatrist and the novice. Testimonials from successful patient medication-takers provide the "old timer" with an opportunity to show an achievement appropriately and to gain satisfaction from a helper role. Testimonials also provide the novice with a unique type of reassurance and guidance for participating in psychosomatic and organic therapy issues.

When staff are members of this form of group psychopharmacotherapy, they have a unique opportunity to observe (and later participate in) the interaction around biological medicine. Lectures, seminars and readings may be helpful, but these will not provide an experience with the more complex task of coping with signs and symptoms of live patients.

Finally, evaluation of disorders can sometimes be extremely difficult. Non-medical patients and staff are often invaluable in the process, if given the training and opportunity.

Advantages also derive from the specific focus in these groups. Powell et al. (1977) found that group treatment which focused on medication produced a high rate of attendance, perhaps because the concreteness of medication was so easy to see as something in common. Thus, group cohesion was fostered. A focus on the workings and needs of the body in health and disease seems to be a particularly intriguing subject to people, and patients attend eagerly. Schwarz's (1980) impression was that, by more sharing and teaching about psychopharmacology, the patient was less alarmed about risks, reported side effects more completely, was more liable to collaborate (rather than battle) with the psychiatrist over medications, and was more reliable.

Techniques and Structures

There are a number of formats that have been used in medication groups. The psychiatrist is always one of the involved staff, and the time of prescription-writing is almost always the last half hour of the therapy period (Levine and Dang, 1979; O'Brian, 1975; Lesser and Friedmann, 1980; Powell et al., 1977). A suggested format for medication groups is 60 minutes each week with 3–4 staff and 10–15 patients, to provide adequate regular emphasis and involvement in this area; however, meeting patient needs is the most important determining factor. One-half of the patients can be prescribed a 1–4 weeks' supply each time. Additional staff might participate on a selected basis if they have some particular concerns.

Time must be reserved before the group to make preparations, including collecting all the charts. Time is needed afterwards for notations in individual charts and "posts" for staff. The "post" discussion will continue the education of staff in psychopharmacotherapy and keep the core leadership group working together smoothly.

Modifications of psychoanalytically oriented techniques are needed, but this does not mean neglecting to use uncovering psychotherapy (Lesser and Friedmann, 1980) approrpiately. O'Brien (1975) mentions the "go-around," structured dialogue, role-playing, and group activities.

Therapeutic contacts of any real length (over ten minutes) by the psychiatrist with only one patient (without other patients) are best reserved for crises that demand individual contacts.

Common Themes and Content

Schwarz (1980) and Working Group of JAMA (1979) provide a good list of material to promote the most comprehensive appropriate knowledge, skills, and attitudes of patients for psychopharmacotherapy.

Much of the symbolic meaning of medications arises in a therapeutic group. For example, in receiving medication the patient is reminded of being labeled "sick." Patients often think that getting sick is a result of being wrong or transgressing. Thus, the reasoning follows, "If I don't take medicine, I am not wrong (sick). Not being wrong, I can accept myself, and society will accept me." Also, medications often symbolize control issues. Patients worry about the ideas of medication changing the body, or being a form of mind control, or otherwise changing fragile identities.

Concern about side effects can consume, at least initially, a great deal of energy of patients and staff. This is especially true if knowledge is minimal and obtained mainly through uninformed rumors rather than detailed teaching, e.g., "Don't take the Mellaril; it will make you sterile," and "Oh no! ECT! You'll never remember things again." Patients often need extra support to talk about certain side effects which are frightening or embarrassing (e.g., constipation, dysuria, etc.) and sexual functioning (impotence, amenorrhea, etc.).

Given the vicissitudes of everyday life, there will be plenty of opportunities to discuss physical health issues, e.g., first aid, obtaining yearly physicals, managing the medical care system (including doctors and hospitals), common diseases (infections, high blood pressure, diabetes), aging, diet, preventive maintenance, smoking, and over-the-counter drugs.

Similarly, many questions come up with diagnosis and organic therapy in mental disorders. Patients need answers to these, and responses will include teaching them about early symptoms of decompensation and what steps to take. For example, patients can be taught to titrate their own medications, within a given range.

Staff Preparation for Group Psychopharmacotherapy

There will have to be a considerable number of preparatory sessions among staff before utilizing psychosomatic group psychopharmacotherapy. Procedures and techniques to be used will be hammered out in detail to avoid surprises, misunderstandings, and lack of coordination. Staff also need to accept and build in mechanisms so that the physician will exercise legally required ultimate responsibility and final sign-off approval, based on his professional medical expertise.

21

Management of Selected
Patient Problems

PHP patients manifest certain behaviors that are sources of stress, difficulty, or crisis. Although there is no *single* correct method of treatment or "cookbook recipe" to deal with these problems, there are a number of techniques that are useful.

This chapter presents and defines the common problematic situations, then deals with the common reactions of staff and patients to them, and offers suggestions for coping with them. In all cases, the assumption is made that physical and psychopharmacological treatment issues have been addressed and resolved as much as possible. The problems are listed by problematic behaviors and/or situations rather than diagnostic categories since any single behavior could be part of an individual at any moment in time regardless of specific diagnosis.* The problematic behaviors and/or situations are not necessarily in mutually exclusive categories; often, patients evidence them in combination. For example, the delusional patient may be both suicidal and in need of life support services.

Common to all the behaviors and situations discussed here are several factors: 1) Individual issues are routinely raised in groups and made community issues; 2) various PHP groups are used to approach the same problem(s) in a variety of ways; and 3) staff's reactions frequently parallel patients' reactions (see Chapter 5).

The problematic behaviors and/or situations that are bound to appear in PHP work are:

1) New arrival
2) Termination
3) Anger, threats, and assaults
4) Withdrawal, depression, and suicide
5) Drug and alcohol abuse
6) Delusions and hallucinations
7) Physical illness
8) Inadequate personal hygiene

---

* See also bibliography for readings related to treatment of specific diagnostic categories.

9) Illegal actions
10) Need for personal care services
11) Borderline mentally retarded and mildly neurologically impaired.

NEW ARRIVAL

Problem

The patient beginning a PHP is anxious about whether he will be accepted, what the new members and program are like, and, often, whether he will be able to tolerate the commitment of so many hours of therapy and closeness, etc. He often demonstrates this anxiety by lateness, absenteeism, dropping out of the program; or he may show the opposite behavior, being overly active in groups. It is not unusual for him to make frequent trips out of the group sessions to go to the rest rooms, make "important" telephone calls, or go to appointments that are "necessary and cannot be changed." If there is a lounge area, he will not infrequently isolate himself behind a magazine or in front of a TV, stereo, or radio. He is most likely to become engaged with persons perceived by him as being the most supportive and least threatening, e.g., a clerical staff member, not uncommonly the receptionist.

Anyone newly arriving in group is initially treated by the group as an outsider and must go through an acceptance process. The new member changes the group structure and the group members need time for adjustment. The adjustment problems of PHP members to a new arrival are compounded by the fact that there is a structural change in a series of interrelated groups not just one isolated group. Often, PHP group members react to a new member with resentment because they will now have to share group leaders (parental figures) with another arrival. Typically, old group members see the new member as a threat to the pre-existing status and roles of the old group members, and this may result in their giving complicated, confusing or vague explanations to a new arrival as to how one participates in a group project or PHP tasks such as record-taking and attendance-keeping. Also, since the new member is probably replacing a patient who has only recently terminated from the PHP, it is not unusual for remaining PHP patients to displace their termination reactions from the previous members to the new member.

While staff have feelings of wanting to accept a new individual, there are also staff anxieties about what types of demands he may make on them. Staff may react by not adequately pursuing the process of preparing the PHP patients for the arrival of the new group member. They may not take the outreach steps necessary for getting a late or nonattending new arrival involved in the program, i.e., by telephone contacts, home visits, etc.

Intervention

There are several ways of handling these behaviors. First, a prospective PHP patient might participate in a PHP orientation group (see Chapter 15)

Second, there should be acknowledgment and discussion by staff and patients before the arrival of the new member that the PHP will have a new member and that, as a result, the group structure will be somewhat altered. Staff may deal with this in staff meetings by discussing the new patient in terms of his strengths and problem areas and how these can be geared into maximum success. For those programs which utilize open staff rounds, the new arrival can be discussed before or at the point of his initial participation.

In these meetings, it is particularly helpful for staff to identify the new arrival's probable anxiety in starting the program so that PHP patients can think more pointedly about how they can make him comfortable. Patients can deal with this issue in community meetings in terms of discussing their positive and negative reactions to the arrival of a new member before he comes. It is important for staff to be accepting of both types of feelings to help convey the message that a mixed reaction is normal. Likewise, it is important for staff to stress the positive abilities or unique attributes that a new member has, recognizing that it will usually require time before the PHP patients are prepared to really hear these. It is also beneficial for PHP members to recount their own experiences in beginning the program as part of this discussion. This may lead to more empathy and identification with the new member.

Concurrently, community members can be involved in the arrival of the new member at a very concrete level by a variety of methods. A patient sponsor may meet with the patient on the first day, introduce him to community members, explain the program to him, and guide him through the first few weeks of the program. If PHP patients are uncomfortable with this job, it might be role played in community meeting or other PHP groups. A formalized group, the "greeters committee," can perform the same function.

Staff need to be alert to whether the arrival of the new patient is going smoothly. Staff should note whether patient sponsors are doing their jobs and intervene where necessary. Finally, staff need to be sensitive to the new arrival's needs for individual sessions and/or family supports at the beginning of PHP attendance.

TERMINATION

Problem

Ideally, all terminations would be planned and occur at the conclusion of a successful treatment period; however, this is not always the case. Other ways involve discharge "against medical advice" (AMA), inability of a patient to meet or adhere to minimal PHP standards and requirements, psychiatric hospitalizations, and physical illness or death.

A terminating patient and the remainder of the PHP community have an extensive range of intense feelings in response to terminations. After all, for many PHP patients, the intense community life they have experienced in the PHP is the only stability and consistency they have experienced for many years, if ever.

If the patient's termination is planned following improvement, usually he and the remainder of the PHP community initially express overall happiness and pride. While this is often supportive to patients, it may also be threatening and encourage regression if staff praise is too strong. When the patient is confronted with his own success, he may feel undeserving of the success or unable to fulfill the expectations of others. Strong staff praise that is not evaluated carefully may also discourage the expression of the above insecurities and prohibit them from being resolved in the termination process.

In addition to the positive feelings, all will feel sadness over the upcoming separation. This reaction is followed by envy in the nonterminating patients because of their own desires to be healthier and going on to something "better." Patients try to defend against the psychic termination discomfort by the partial or complete denial of reactions to termination.

It is not unusual for the terminating member to demonstrate more symptomatic behavior. This might evidence itself in sudden poor attendance patterns, hostility toward staff and peers, inability to perform as well, and other physical or psychological symptoms. Other PHP patients commonly react to this behavior with fear and/or rejection of the terminating member, particularly if the reasons for the behavior are not explored in PHP groups.

If the termination of a member is AMA or for failure to meet the standards of the program, it is common for patients to experience the same feelings described above, but some reactions are more pronounced. Patients may indicate little concern for the departing member, especially if he has been attending the program sporadically and/or has devalued the importance of the program to himself or others. Beneath this facade, however, there is usually some anger toward the terminating member.

This type of termination also stirs up patients' own ambivalence about being in the program; therefore, they may have feelings of envy that they are also not terminating. If the AMA-discharged patient was disruptive or demanding, it is usual for patients to experience relief. Not to be ignored, however, is the guilt patients feel when a member leaves under these circumstances. Members frequently have the fantasy that they are to blame for the departure, and they should have helped the member more. Concurrently, they may project and feel angry that staff have "kicked" the member out, that they are powerless in the face of staff authority, and that they, in fact, may be the next to leave.

If a member leaves for reasons of serious physical illness, psychiatric hospitalization, or death, the PHP departure may be sudden. Members frequently experience shock and disbelief. In addition, they may feel that the same may occur to them because they are already in a vulnerable position. In cases of physical illness and death, they may generalize these to psychiatric problems and have fantasies that they are decompensating and will have to be hospitalized. Discussing and dealing with death is particularly difficult for most people to face and PHP patients are no exception. They are more inclined to express their feelings by being absent, silent, or hostile. In cases of psychiatric hospitalization, PHP members usually express not only concern for the involved patient, but also promulgate general societal attitudes that psychiatric hospitalization is bad and to be avoided at all costs.

Staff may have some responses that are not shared by the patient community. Termination dysphoria is evidenced by staff not introducing and dealing adequately with the issue in the PHP community. Also, because PHPs must usually maintain a certain census, the staff will soon be working with a new unkown patient, who may be more problematic and difficult. It is much simpler for PHP staff to keep a "good" patient who has given them little grief.

In response to AMA discharges or patients being terminated because they could not meet the standards of the program, it is common for staff to experience relief, anger and guilt.

Statements such as, "What did we do wrong?" and "We should have never accepted the person into the program in the first place" are common. This is especially true if the PHP patient suddenly drops out of the program, refuses to return, develops his own plan, or is unable to be located.

When there is a psychiatric hospitalization of a PHP patient, staff at times feel that this is a result of their own failure to do effective treatment instead of seeing its positive aspects, e.g., gaining support, controls and safety for self or others. A negative or uncomfortable staff attitude toward the psychiatric hospitalization may lead to missing valuable treatment issues. If a patient can recount the circumstances of his own past hospitalization(s) or discuss his fears of future ones, he may resolve his conflicts. Further, he is able to evaluate his own strengths and the circumstances that may prevent a future hospitalization.

Intervention

Treatment interventions in dealing with termination begin at the point of the PHP patient's entry into the program. At that point, PHP goals and a time frame for the achievement of these goals should be established. For some programs, the time frame for PHP participation is set by administrative policy. Other programs allow enormous latitude, almost a completely open-ended time contract of several years. Whatever the administrative policy, the time for a PHP member's participation should be set, as much as possible, for clinical reasons which reflect consideration for treatment goals and length of time to achieve them. The time frame can always be revised, if indicated, but whatever the period is, it and the treatment goals should be understood and referred to consistently throughout the PHP member's treatment, in open staff rounds, patient evaluation groups, community meetings, etc. By doing this, several things are accomplished. First, patients are not allowed to relax working on problematic areas as they might if their time in PHP seemed unlimited. Second, the foundation is laid for dealing with termination feelings. Third, the feelings of being rejected by staff at termination are decreased. Fourth, the opportunities for "will struggles" with the terminating patient and/or the patient community over the appropriateness and timeliness of a patient's discharge are minimized.

In order to make appropriate treatment interventions at the time of termination, all PHP staff, even experienced staff, need to be constantly aware of and work on their discomforting reactions to a patient's termination. Adequate time should be allotted for termination discussions. For example, in nine-to-12-month programs, four to six weeks should be allowed for the termination process. Some patients may need an even longer period of time.

While termination is discussed from the beginning, the emotional impact of termination does not usually evidence itself in the community until there is a known termination date. At this point, it is important for staff to "give permission" to the patient community and the terminating patient to discuss not only their "nice" feelings about the termination, but also their angry, envious, anxious and hurt feelings.

Because the PHP community may have great difficulty at various points in the termination in verbalizing their comfortable feelings about the termination, the activity segment of the program should also be geared toward resolution of these feelings. For example, a writing group might write a group essay on an experience they have had with the terminating member, the drama group might do a skit on the member's first day in his new vocational training program, or the art group might plan a farewell party and make "good-bye" cards. To allow for the release of the physical energy that is present at these times, it is wise to consider focusing the recreational group toward an activity requiring stress such as volleyball, rather than an activity requiring tedious waiting such as checkers or cards.

In all terminations the overall treatment interventions in a PHP are always focused on helping the individual patient consolidate his gains. If staff have stability, they can in unified fashion use the PHP community as an ally in the process, thus providing the terminating patient with constant, intense reinforcement and support throughout several hours of the day for one of the most difficult and growth-producing experiences of his life.

Finally, an important part of the PHP termination process is to effectively connect the patient to his next level of care or support system, e.g., volunteer work or vocational training. Ideally, patients would begin their post-PHP involvements a considerable time before their termination date. They are then able to share their reactions to their new programs, jobs, etc. with the PHP community. By such a process, they are not only supported to make new investments, but also they are aided in their separation from the PHP. Another mechanism to ease the transition process is having formalized times for former members to return. This may take place in meetings of alumni groups or some participation by former patients in regular PHP groups such as community meetings or family nights.

ANGER, THREATS, AND ASSAULTS

Problem

Provoking arguments, storming out of groups, remaining sullenly silent, complaining chronically and rejecting activity groups as childish are all typical behaviors of an angry patient in the PHP. He may scapegoat another patient, shun new members, refuse to cooperate with plans made, and be critical of everyone and everything. The patient may monopolize discussions and encourage others to be obstructionistic. He is constantly testing, almost begging for rejection. He may try to get people with authority over the PHP to side with him, or he may initiate litigation against the PHP.

Threatening behavior is commonly evidenced in the PHP by a patient verbally threatening to harm another or even threatening with a knife or gun. At other times, it is more indirect, e.g., a patient makes reference to violence he has done to others in the outside community. Physical assaults often include hitting, shoving, throwing objects, and fist fights. Patients and staff frequently respond to angry behavior with fear followed by further maneuvers, such as over-solicitousness, giving in to the angry patient, or engaging in power struggles. By giving in to the patient, they avoid having the angry behavior directed at them. Also, if they have some unresolved anger against others in the program, such concurrence with the angry patient provides them with a channel to vicariously express their anger.

Angry patients frequently provoke fear, anger, frustration and humiliation; as a result, staff frequently avoid and ignore veiled or direct threats. Often, these allow the threatening or assaultive person to become more agitated since he feels there will be inadequate controls on his behavior. If physical assaults—a slap or shove—do occur, staff may be reluctant to restrain the patient for fear of their own safety. Instead they may be inclined only to call for help from outside the PHP; this leads to a delay in response to the situation and the possibility of more dangerous behavior.

Intimacy is a vital issue in the treatment of the angry patient. He is wary, even rejecting, of the closeness of others, continually questioning, while wavering about accepting help. The anger is used almost as an armor to stave off closeness leading to vulnerability, followed by pain and anguish. The patient is fearful but hopeful for rescue, but defends vigorously against the closeness.

Regardless of the type of threat or assault, it is important to keep in mind that neither staff nor PHP patients will be able to invest themselves in treatment as long as there is any potential danger from program members.

Intervention

For treatment of the angry PHP patient, several considerations should be made. First, there should be some understanding of the sources of the behavior. Groups wherein staff openly discuss the patient's underlying pain rather than merely relate to examples of angry behavior will provide a basis for the community to think more effectively about their responses to this type of patient.

Next, staff should try to help the entire community respond appropriately and consistently to the angry patient. For example, when the patient devalues activity groups as being childish, the PHP therapist can help the community to at least give him the respect of listening seriously to his criticism. Sometimes, the criticisms might even be used as an opportunity to solicit everybody's ideas about why the activity groups are important.

Staff should also encourage others to accept that everybody has a right to feelings. This may help them be less likely to talk a patient out of these feelings or discount them because of the seeming lack of a reality basis, as in the case of paranoid ideation.

Evaluation of the potential for this type of behavior should occur before the individual is accepted into the program. Information may be obtained from clinical summaries, contacts with previous treatment personnel and family members, as well as direct interviewing with the PHP applicant.

An initial contract is made clear from the outset, stating that: 1) He will be prevented from hurting himself or others as much as possible; and 2) he will be immediately suspended from the PHP if he threatens or shows violent behaviors and an alternate treatment plan will be made. If a potential member will not agree with these rules, he should not be allowed to begin the program. Although this contract is no guarantee against assaultive behavior, it does establish a behavioral expectancy, helping the member recognize mounting anger and deal with it appropriately.

If there is an actual threat or assaultive act by a PHP member toward another patient or staff member, staff must be prepared to act decisively. Threats are always taken seriously. After a short suspension and discussion, if the individual is still unable to see anything wrong with his threats, he should not be allowed to return to the PHP community. If there is recognition of the problem by the patient and a strong possibility for behavioral control, he might be returned to the community, and a decision should be made by both staff and patients as to the most appropriate corrective measures. It should be made clear in advance that this is one area where staff judgment will take precedence over that of PHP patients as to the best corrective measures, since staff are ultimately responsible for the physical safety of PHP members. Emergency meetings, which are often needed to deal with these threats, bring the importance of the safety issue more into focus and allow the patients a more responsible role in determining the limits to be established for a peer member's menacing or violent behavior. Concurrently, there should be a new contract initiated with the individual so that he accepts the responsibility to actively identify the reasons leading up to his making threats. The offending patient should agree to express his anger by socially acceptable means, e.g., angry words, asking for a short break to gain control, and physical activity such as walking, running or hammering in the workshop.

Mild assaults such as shoving and pushing may often be handled in a similar way to threats; however, more severe assaults, such as hitting, throwing objects and fist fights, may require physical restraint by staff members. Adequate restraint requires both the psychological and physical preparation of staff members of the PHP. Psychologically, PHP staff—both female and male—must feel this to be part of their role, and they must realize that only with a deep confidence in their ability to handle assaultiveness will there actually be minimal violence and maximal safety for the whole PHP community. Staff can learn proper restraint techniques to be used in PHPs by conducting appropriate inservice training programs.

One important aspect of the restraint techniques is that the training should allow the staff enough time to practice on each other. All staff should also be competent in the procedures which may follow physical restraint, e.g., placing the patient in a camisole, and enlisting outside help.

Staff must encourage the rest of the group to express reactions to the violent situation that has just occurred. These usually include fear, gratitude, and/or anger toward the therapists for taking action, as well as impulses to make their own threats and assaults toward patients or staff. Several group sessions are usually required before there is any sense of resolution. Open staff rounds can be used constructively here, as staff may discuss their own reactions and decisions regarding the threatening or violent incident. Viewing these sessions often frees PHP patients to continue discussions among themselves and in other groups of the PHP.

WITHDRAWAL, DEPRESSION, AND SUICIDE

Problem

Patients showing withdrawal, overt depression and/or suicidal feelings and behavior occur in all PHPs. Suicidal behavior can arise in any type of patient. Withdrawn and acutely depressed patients often appear similar in terms of their behavior. Patients who are both withdrawn and acutely depressed tend to isolate themselves from the rest of the PHP community. Frequently, they are absent from the program, resulting many times in discharge from PHPs because of poor attendance. Although the depressive picture referred to here is classical and typical, there are also many types of masked depression that are expressed in other ways, such as hyperactivity, hypochondriasis and social effervescence. Withdrawal is dissimilar from acute depression in that the former may have been an essentially lifelong condition. Withdrawn patients rarely complain of or seem motivated to change their behavior in treatment. Acutely depressed patients are typically more conscious of painful emotion and often demonstrate this in words or actions.

Suicidal ideation by a patient may appear anytime in PHPs, sometimes in direct, clear and vivid detail, though more frequently in a less specific manner. Considerable exploration to obtain a more accurate assessment of suicidal ideation is warranted. For example, a patient may look depressed in community meeting and talk about how hopeless things are, but he may not indicate if he plans on doing something to harm himself until questioned in specific detail for a lengthy period of time.

Suicidal actions in PHPs may vary from overdosing on pills, cutting wrists (particularly in rest room areas), ingesting art supplies such as paint thinner and glue, or injuring oneself with woodworking equipment or kitchen utensils. Suicidal ideations and actions occurring outside the PHP are not uncommonly reported by relatives or friends of the patient to the staff.

Intervention

Effective PHP treatment approaches for both depressed and withdrawn patients require steady and consistent staff and patient outreach and availability without being intrusive. Because it is so exhausting and frustrating for any single person to do this persistently, it is fortunate there is the entire PHP community to share in outreach efforts. For example, if the patient is absent from the program, he should be contacted by staff and patients, taking turns in making the calls by telephone and/or home visits.

The patient is in such need of a boost in self-esteem that rapid success in groups is very important. These normally are the activity groups, because frequently the patient has great difficulty verbalizing. Whatever positive features the patient demonstrates can be rapidly identified in the many varied groups. Then, the patient might be encouraged to try to remember these features as part of his PHP treatment contract. Listing his own problems and faults is an easy task for the withdrawn or depressed patient, but another's praise is difficult to take and involves relearning or new learning. It is important also to consistently assess the depth of depression, since this may involve suicidal ideation.

Common reactions to suicidal behavior include, shock, fear, denial, guilt, and anger. It is not unusual for others to deny or devalue the seriousness of what has been said. Patients may change the subject quickly in group discussions. Staff may become fearful of what they will uncover if they explore further with a patient, or they may feel that a group, especially a large group such as community meeting, cannot handle the information if it is raised there. It may be that both staff and patients feel that they will provoke a suicidal action if it is discussed with a patient who is entertaining suicidal ideation.

Fear is common among patients because the concept of a loss of control leading to death is so difficult to contemplate. For some patients, there is little distinction between suicidal thoughts, feelings, and behavior; therefore, they may be afraid to raise the issue. Also, the suicidal ideation or behavior of one patient may stir up suicidal feelings in other patient. Likewise, there is often anger against the person for having caused these feelings to surface.

Pervasively, others feel that they might have done more to have helped the person who is suicidal, thus preventing the suicidal ideation or behavior; subsequently, they may act out by being absent from the program, displacing anger to other patients, or faulting staff for not stopping the behavior of the suicidal patient.

Interventions for suicidal behavior begin before a prospective patient is admitted to a PHP. Accurate history-taking from varied sources for clues to suicidal features, as well as a current clinical assessment, will be helpful in revealing the level of suicidal risk of each new applicant. If staff determines that the individual is a high risk for imminent suicide, the patient is hospitalized, and will perhaps have future treatment in a PHP.

If a patient is admitted to a PHP and has some suicidal risk in his behavior, it is important that all staff members are clear about this and they all should know his history well enough to identify the circumstances under which suicidal behavior is likely to occur. Part of the initial treatment contract should be a delineation of how the community can work with him on monitoring this suicidal behavior on an ongoing basis. All patients in the PHP should also be aware when suicidal impulses are a problem for any patient.

A final intervention which should take place for a suicidal patient before he is admitted to a PHP is to build a formalized relationship with significant others in his life outside the PHP. They become part of the patient's treatment in the PHP and serve both as support and monitoring agents for the patient.

PHP training for learning the techniques of suicidal assessment and management is an important aspect of dealing with suicidal behavior. First of all, staff need to feel comfortable facing the possibility of suicidal behavior and applying techniques for pursuing assessment of suicidal potential, both individually and in groups. Concurrently, they need to be familiar with the concrete procedures for intensifying the level of patient care and monitoring, e.g., how to hospitalize a patient voluntarily or involuntarily.

If a patient has suicidal ideation inside or outside a group of the PHP or reports that he has had such ideation at home, this should be explored and assessed as far as possible in a group session. Other PHP patients can be helpful in asking a potentially suicidal patient about his intentions to harm himself, if they are given the encouragement to do so. In suicidal assessment, the same questions are asked in group as would be asked individually, i.e., Is there a specific plan? When will the patient attempt suicide? Is there still hopefulness? Patients can also aid in the exploration of alternative behaviors that the suicidal patient may not have considered. Group members could become part of the patient's support system, e.g., making telephone calls and home visits, as well as other supportive measures. Finally, group members can often give support to the suicidal patient by sharing similar feelings and how they have been able to resolve them.

If a PHP patient does make a serious suicidal action or completes the suicidal act, this behavior becomes a community issue and needs to be faced openly. Patients need a structured forum to work through their feelings about the suicidal behavior.

DRUG AND ALCOHOL ABUSE*

Problem

With the widespread availability of drugs, including alcohol, it is not uncommon for some patients in a PHP to indulge in their non-prescribed use while attending the program, even after hearing warnings. In some instances, the drug use may be extensive enough to warrant a secondary diagnosis. These problems may be increasing in programs as within the larger society. PHP patients have greater access to drugs than inpatients. In addition, because of daily attendance in an intense program, chances increase for a patient to attend while intoxicated or "high."

Finally, despite the existence of drug and alcohol programs, patients who carry dual diagnosis may be admitted to a psychiatric PHP, since drug and alcohol programs may not be equipped to handle the psychiatric illness. Often, such programs use confrontation approaches which may be overwhelming for some of these patients with severe emotional problems. Thus, it is important that staff and patients be aware of potential behaviors and other difficulties for the individual member and for the PHP community.

A patient arrives at the program, flaunting a can of beer, appearing giggly and tipsy. He has difficulty sitting in the room and proceeds to interrupt, laughing and talking incessantly, keeping the group's focus on himself. Everyone is made tense;

---

* Patients with clearly defined primary diagnoses of substance abuse are usually referred to PHPs specially designed for these populations.

some staff and patients are angry. On another occasion, a member arrives "stoned" and proceeds to give the staff a hostile analysis of the program and of other patients. On a third occasion, three members disappear during a coffee break. On their return one is drowsy, another is euphoric and the third is quietly grinning from ear to ear. Other patients complain of the odor of marijuana in the rest room. These may all occur in a PHP.

Staff and members may feel angry, betrayed, frustrated, embarrassed, fearful of the member's potential violence, and fearful for his health. They may be unsettled by the behavior, particularly fearing a personal verbal or physical attack. Others may become moralistic and condemn the member. The hostility may stimulate other patients to do their own acting out. They may scapegoat the member, trying to force him out. They may even become protective of the member, anticipating strong staff reactions of rejection and punishment. Other members may withdraw from the group session or from the program, feeling that the security of the group has been violated. In addition, if the program is community-based, perhaps housed in a host agency, staff may feel concerned about administrative consequences for the patient and for the program.

Intervention

Both staff and patients need opportunities to deal with their feelings, and to act after consideration, not out of haste. Often the immediacy of the situation urges dealing swiftly with the patient, and staff may postpone working-through the feelings evoked by the episode; nonetheless, time must be alloted for airing these feelings.

Staff reactions regarding the incident(s) are to be shared in supervision and in staff meetings, to arrive at a unified stance. The most effective stance seems to be a synthesis of varied positions, taking the behavior seriously, as a problem for both member and group, stating that drugs and alcohol on the premises are a violation of the PHP rules, as is appearing at the program "high" or intoxicated. Staff will need to consider their concerns for the member's physical safety and their questions about treatment effectiveness of the PHP for the patient. It is important to recall that staff cannot stop a patient's drug use, but they *are* helping the patient by providing the external controls (exerted through enforcing the program's rules) that the patient shows he lacks.

Treatment interventions are made on a variety of levels:

1) before the situation arises;
2) with the patient and members to end the disruption;
3) with the PHP to resolve the aftermath and determine appropriate consequences;
4) with the family to work around monitoring and prevention; and
5) with the community to help deal with re-entry issues.

At intake, a new patient usually learns several firm rules or policies of the PHP. One such rule usually forbids use of unprescribed drugs. This rule is discussed repeatedly and regularly to provide safety for the group and individual alike. It may also be necessary to require the patient to agree to the possibility of giving blood and urine specimens for drug testing at any time. Should he refuse, he will be denied acceptance into the PHP.

Patients who abuse drugs or alcohol with prescribed medications run a risk of endangering themselves, physically and mentally, exacerbating emotional illness or possibly causing death. Staff should inform the patient of these risks without exaggeration. Consequences of such infractions (suspension or expulsion from the PHP, rehospitalization, etc.) can then be understood as attempts to protect the patient, to reestablish controls over impulses, and to deal more effectively with the problems precipitating the drug use, while protecting the rest of the community.

Concurrently, rules against the bringing and selling of drugs in the PHP should be discussed early and often, since these acts may be illegal and endanger other patients and the safety and survival of the PHP. It may bring in law enforcement agencies, and administrative and community reactions.

In any such situation, the first step is to end the disruption. Some staff calm the patient, perhaps escort him from the group before the patient causes himself or others further pain, embarrassment, anger, or even physical harm, while others deal with the rest of the community. On occasion, with careful consideration, other patients may be enlisted along with staff to deal with the patient, provided an assessment is made that the patient will not cause bodily harm or further upset others. Another patient's presence may sometimes have a calming effect on the member, so that he can then rejoin the group for a discussion of the immediate issue, the causes and results of the disruption.

The next step is to discuss and deal with the group members' reactions. They may be upset and unnerved by the behavior, needing reassurance from staff. Members should be helped to share their feelings about the patient and the integrity of the group being violated, which also helps them to see the consequences to the group of the individual's inappropriate behavior, and the reasons behind the rules.

Concurrently, staff should explain what they are attempting to do with and for the patient, e.g., physical evaluation and assistance, hospitalization, containment, or whatever a patient needs to reestablish control. This can work to relieve group members' anxieties about the patient.

Deciding on consequences is a group task. Some patients may suggest that dealing with the member's behavior is the responsibility solely of the staff, although this should not be so (see Chapter 19). Patients and staff will discuss the range of possibilities, from suspension for one or several days to exclusion from special activities or responsibilities, expulsion, etc. with the patient if possible, so that he can understand the gravity of the episode. Such discussions can occur without the patient if necessary, but at least a summary will be shared later. In helping a patient by peer and staff pressure, the other group members can see their own impact on someone else, reinforcing the belief that they have valuable contributions to make. Staff can also be helpful in preventing extreme patient responses, e.g., suggestions for expulsion, or extreme words of condemnation and rejection.

The decision for suspension or other consequences does not resolve the issue. After the decision, further discussions are held to work through the feelings evoked, to prepare for the patient's possible reentry, and to increase awareness of the problems inherent in drug abuse, both physically and emotionally. This might be discussed within the medication group. Here, the nurse and the psychiatrist can be particularly helpful.

Working with the patient during the suspension, hospitalization, etc. will involve exploring and identifying feelings, problems, or events precipitating the drug use, dealing with other underlying issues leading to the episode, while assessing the extent of the drug abuse. Is he withdrawing from emotional stimuli? Is denial/avoidance operating? Awareness and understanding of the group's reactions will be helpful to the patient, particularly in defusing some of the anger and feelings of rejection experienced by the suspension, which may otherwise be projected only toward the staff who enforce the rules. Reevaluating treatment issues and priorities will also be major themes of individual work during the time away from the PHP. For example, the PHP may not be meeting the patient's treatment needs, or there may be a significant issue or event heretofore unknown which has provoked the behavior. Also, any need to be rejected by the PHP can be dealt with during the suspension, as will reinforcement of the issue of personal harm caused by the drugs.

On some occasions, staff may not have direct knowledge of the drug use. Instead, they may hear from families or friends about such episodes. While staff may prefer the patient to share reports of such behavior, a patient may be reluctant to do so. In these circumstances, the staff should discuss these issues with the patient, while encouraging the family to do the same. Following such discussion, the group can also provide a format for dealing with the problems. Again, evaluation of the drug use, the underlying reasons for the use and reactions by staff and other group members can be handled in similar ways to dealing with the overt behavior. Taking strong action, however, may not be necessary.

While the family and the patient may experience uncomfortable feelings of disloyalty, and while sharing information with the PHP may anger the patient, informing the staff will usually help the patient and, ultimately, the patient may be relieved that he can be helped. Families can be allies in the patient's treatment, as supporters of positive behavior and as monitors of the patient's mood changes. Family nights, as described in Chapter 10, can be a valuable format for educating relatives and significant others to the problems, the behaviors and their ramifications. Here they can also learn and get support for constructive ways of coping with the problems, without shame, disappointment, or undue anger.

Finally, plans for reentry to the PHP or entry into another form of treatment will be made during the absence from the program. These plans should be shared with the community. If reentry is preferred, patients and staff will be able to prepare through group discussion without the patient, so that feelings can be openly expressed without burdening the patient unduly. These feelings will be worked on so that extra stresses surrounding the patient's return can be reduced, without blocking all feedback to the offending patient.

Reentry can be initiated on a trial basis with a clear contract, preferably in writing, with provisions for length of stay, adherence to rules and consequences for a second episode. This type of contract can be reassuring to all. On the patient's return, staff and other members can, hopefully, deal effectively with preventing further episodes for the member and for the rest of the group.

Finally, joint treatment approaches, e.g., using PHP three times per week and individual and/or group sessions in drug or alcohol programs, or concurrent attendance at AA or Pills Anonymous, can be effective alternatives for these patients to handle both major treatment areas.

DELUSIONS AND HALLUCINATIONS

Problem

During a community meeting, one patient sits quietly in a corner. When his opinion is solicited on an issue, he begins to talk about the "devil," who is giving him bad thoughts, and curses God, the group and himself. The other patients and staff become visibly uncomfortable upon hearing this. They grow restless and one leaves the room. Anxiety mounts in the group. The patient continues to answer "voices," disregarding the group's discussion. The leader tries to hush the patient, moving on to another member; thus the patient's painful isolation remains or intensifies. He continues to share the frightening material, or perhaps, withdraws.

Frequently patients and staff are unnerved by this kind of psychotic material and may try to argue against this with the patient. Other patients may ignore this patient or may try to stifle the material. They may leave group sessions, even leave the program, in fear of the patient, or, worse, in fear that the staff is unable to control him. Others may look to staff for model responses.

Staff may get involved in decoding the psychotic material and search for the symbolism in a misguided effort to deal with the patient. Such an attempt further excludes the patient, defining him as different, strange, perhaps someone to be feared, while also conveying the staff's discomfort, and/or inability to deal with this patient's problems. This latter situation can be even more frightening to the other patients who are seeking guidance, limits and controls from the staff.

If staff hear only the psychotic material they will tend to miss the patient's strengths and abilities, and this may happen most in verbal groups. Such "tunnel vision" may lead staff to preclude inappropriately the patient's involvement in groups. Thus the patient would be alienated. This, in turn, can lead to a patient's poor attendance, withdrawal, or exaggerated outbursts.

Intervention

Dealing with these patients may be new and troublesome for less experienced staff, students and volunteers who have significant group roles and responsibilities. Their discomfort and anxiety may cause problems to escalate. Here, the experienced staff or supervisor can offer frank and open discussion of the concerns, difficulties, fears and fantasies evoked, and may model alternative interventions through role play.

Included in the effective handling is an understanding of the treatment goals for the group member. The multitude of groups provides a unique opportunity for assessment and development of the patients' strengths and assessment of weaknesses, instead of discouraging staff and other patients about a member's potential. The delusional patient may participate well in the arts and crafts activity group, or show ability to do clerical work in the prevocational group.

These are but a few examples of how a PHP can help with this particular member and they highlight the need for a clear assessment along with an awareness of a patient's history. The latter will help to understand factors provoking the upset, as well as the form it may take.

Occasionally, the above approaches are insufficient to contain the feelings and their expression within an ongoing group. If so, leaving the situation, the room or the group may help. Leaving the group for ten quiet minutes can help to establish control, while maintaining a less disruptive environment for the remaining members. Often, initially, a staff member's going out with the patient aids in reestablishing control. Occasionally, staff presence may be threatening, and perhaps another group member can assist. An evaluation of each situation is needed. By staff's modeling the handling of these types of situations calmly, the group feels assured, and the session can continue. It is best for the therapist to encourage the patient to rejoin the group as soon as he can take the stress.

Open discussion of the issues with the PHP community is vital to the patient's continued stay. Patients and staff should work together to elicit and to work through the feelings and concerns evoked by this member. As the staff demonstrate their increased comfort with this patient, other patients will feel more at ease with the patient, and will become desensitized and more accepting of the patient. As this process develops, the patient will often become less overtly psychotic and can establish a role for himself—often nonverbally—in the group as secretary, treasurer, dishwasher in a cooking group, or player in a sports group.

The use of these techniques can later be employed elsewhere—at home, at work, or in other potential stress situations. The variety of situations faced in a

PHP's daily schedule will encourage the transferability of the techniques. Group members can be enlisted in the use of any successful approach, which, in turn, may allay the helpers' own anxieties.

Eventually, the therapist tries to identify, with the patient, the primary feelings behind the psychotic productions; the worker "reaches for the feelings," to help the patient identify the disturbing feelings or events setting off the hallucinations or delusions. If this is not immediately productive, the worker may explain what is happening by "translating upward" from primary to secondary process. This helps the patient to resist the voices and focus on the real situation. The worker then tries to support the patient's efforts to follow the discussion and fight off the voices. This technique usually allays anxiety; thus the patient may be calmer for the rest of the session. Its success involves patient and staff trust in each others' abilities to deal with such situations quickly, as well as assurance that staff are not frightened or otherwise "put off" by the delusions or hallucinations.

PHYSICAL ILLNESS

Problem

Physical problems of PHP patients may vary widely, from chronic disabilities such as partial blindness, deafness, paraplegia, seizure disorders, hypertension, and diabetes, to psychosomatic illnesses, to the acute communicable diseases which can spread in an intense environment such as a PHP, increasing attendance problems, and thwarting group process.

Patients with physical problems often have particular difficulties in a PHP, e.g., illness-related absences, exclusion from specific activities, physical reactions to stress and anxiety, and medical emergencies. These clients may exhibit a variety of additional problems. The patient may try to hide behind his illness to avoid an unpleasant task, to use the problems to elicit sympathy and protectiveness from other members or staff, or otherwise obtain the benefits of secondary gain from the illness. He may withdraw, become self-involved, show antagonism to healthier patients, be ashamed of the problem, and feel worthless, helpless or depressed. Alternatively, a patient may risk probable harm by trying to overcompensate for his disability.

Other patients may have reactions including discomfort, denial, even outright fear, causing them to avoid the physically ill patient. Furthermore, the other members may resent the extra attention or concern shown by staff for the physically ill member. This may surface in snide comments, teasing, or competitive behavior. Finally, some patients may fear and believe that physical problems are results of the psychiatric illness and may be contagious; as a result patients may be ostracized.

Staff may react inappropriately to the illness. They may prod the patient to attempt extraordinary tasks, deny illness and resist discussion of the medical problem. They may overprotect the patient and treat him as more disabled than he actually is. These reactions are common to people uncomfortable with patients with various physical illnesses and PHP staff are not immune to this discomfort. Additionally, staff may be uncomfortable about providing first aid or handling medical emergencies.

Intervention

Handling of these issues includes a four-pronged approach, involving: 1) the medical examination prior to full PHP admission, in addition to ongoing treatment as needed; 2) participation of the patient and family in plans and care for special needs; 3) sharing knowledge of the illness and planning with the PHP community; and 4) having good general health care as part of routine procedures.

1) Requirements for a physical examination are noted in Chapters 15 and 20. This examination helps to clearly assess the member's strengths and limitations; it will work toward ending denial and anxiety, and limiting overprotectiveness, while recalling that all problems are not always emotionally based. If the physical examination identifies new problems, staff can assist the patient in obtaining medical treatment. Consultation with medical personnel will enable planning for contingencies with a minimum of anxiety. Other agencies may be enlisted to provide ancillary services such as transportation and medical equipment.

2) Building an alliance with the patient and family is vital for providing full treatment. They can learn to deal with the limitations, while building on the patient's strengths.

3) Sharing the knowledge of the patient's physical problems with other members of the PHP community as early as possible will further reduce the fear, isolation, overprotection and confusion surrounding dealings with the patient. The group will be able to deal more realistically with the patient when he is no longer viewed as frightening or fragile, while also helping the patient to understand how he may use his illness against himself. Other members can encourage the patient to participate as fully as possible, telephoning or visiting when he is absent, sharing their care and concern, and perhaps also helping with alternative activities when the full schedule is precluded. Within the program, groups can be focused on negotiating medical care issues, being assertive and questioning of care, and complying with the treatment regimens. Other patients may be enlisted to accompany the member to medical appointments; they may even help by acting as advocates for the reticent or confused patient.

4) Finally, health groups can be instituted in the program providing patients with basic information about medical care, first aid, nutrition, and other related issues, perhaps preventing some illnesses or encouraging mechanisms for coping

with problems arising among healthier patients. All staff and patients can benefit from learning about the planning for possible physical problems and emergency first aid. For example, staff and patients can learn important techniques such as cardio-pulmonary resuscitation, the Heimlich maneuver, etc. These are vital for PHPs located away from hospitals.

INADEQUATE PERSONAL HYGIENE

Problem

Some PHP patients do not give adequate attention to personal appearance and hygiene. At worst, patients may appear daily with soiled clothing, an unwashed body, unbrushed teeth, unshaven beard, unkempt hair and dirty fingernails. At a more moderate level, a patient may have one or two ongoing problems such as foul breath or body odor. At a more subtle level, a patient may be wearing inappropriate clothing for a training program interview, while still a part of the PHP. Further examples of this include seductive apparel or childish dress.

Most often staff and patients are repelled by the behavior, but they are reluctant to say anything directly to the patient about it, even in the relative intimacy of the PHP community. Both staff and patients may handle their reactions by avoiding the issue and the individual involved. Not infrequently, they mask their anger by being hypercritical of the patient's comments. Or, they may be fault-finding of a patient's project. Concurrently, there may be no positive reinforcement for things well said or well done. In addition, staff or patients may talk among themselves in hallways and behind closed doors about the problematic behavior and their reactions to it. Staff may raise and discuss the issue intensively in a treatment planning meeting but fail to develop plans for coping with it. Lastly, staff may talk about personal hygiene in general terms in meetings and/or encourage patient discussion about it, hoping the problematic patient will identify himself and correct his own behavior.

Intervention

Staff must first be encouraged to express their own difficulty in raising this issue with a problematic patient and with the PHP community. Ideally, the problem will have been noticed at the time of PHP intake. At that point, a determination can be made as to why the problem exists. Questions that might be raised include: Is the inadequate personal hygiene due to lack of knowledge of how to take care of oneself and dress appropriately? Is there a deterioration of good habits? Is the behavior a means of gaining attention or expressing anger? The particular reasons would then influence the planning of the applicant's PHP program. Improvement in personal care habits could be one of the requirements for admission to the program; thus, the individual involved would not be subjected to the rejection he would most certainly get if he arrived as a new member in such an unacceptable state.

A health, hygiene and personal appearances group should be considered as a routine segment of the PHP. By establishing the expectancy that all members could use some help in better or easier methods of self-care and appearance, the foundation is set for relating to the issue. Therefore, when a particularly problematic patient appears, there is less possibility that he will be isolated or scapegoated by the group for his behavior. He is part of a group where everyone's personal care is an issue. By addressing and generalizing the problem constantly, there should be more license for the group members to give aid and criticism to each other.

Advantages of a personal hygiene group include:

1) The problematic behavior may be resolved within the group.
2) A diversified treatment plan may be formulated for the patient who demonstrates particular resistance to self-care or who has multiple problems related to inadequate personal hygiene. He may be given extra help by one or several patient members in and outside the group. This may include regular supervision by patients of shaving, hair grooming, etc. which will initially need overall staff supervision until patient community members become comfortable in doing this with each other.
3) Attentiveness will eventually allow for the identification of psychodynamics for the inadequate personal hygiene, which can then be more fully explored in other PHP groups.

The appearance of PHP staff members is also important. Patients use staff as role models for behavior, which includes dress and appearance. If the staff member dresses inappropriately for work patients will tend to do the same. This is not to say that there should be a unified PHP dress code. PHPs differ from geographic area to geographic area—each with its own dress style. Similarly, PHPs vary in the amount and types of activities they have which require the use of soiling materials such as art supplies and food. The point is that staff should self-critically evaluate their personal appearance and determine if it reflects appropriateness for their particular clinical setting.

ILLEGAL BEHAVIOR

PHPs may serve clients who have legal difficulties including: 1) child abuse or neglect; 2) spouse abuse; 3) crimes against property or persons; and 4) crimes committed while in the program. When these behaviors are secondary to or symptomatic of mental illness, the patient may be referred to a PHP.

The patient who is having legal difficulties may often be overwhelmed, angry, provocative, withholding in groups and suspicious; on the other hand, he may try to overcompensate and work diligently at becoming a model patient. He may try to hide or minimize the details or extent of the legal problem, fearing rejection by patients and staff.

Child Abuse and Neglect—Problem

In cases of child abuse or neglect, staff and other patients frequently deny and avoid the issue altogether. They may try to "understand" the patient and make allowances. They may be oversolicitous and protective of the "bad parent," not wishing to see the problems realistically. They then may offer unrequested advice or unrealistic pep talks about the value of good parenting. Or, they may openly shame or devalue the patient, reinforcing the patient's own anger or guilt feelings. Finally, they may be angry and/or rejecting of the patient, perhaps leading the patient to withdraw or terminate. Others may overidentify with the child or the spouse, rejecting the patient. Members may be extremely harsh and critical of the patient's performance in the program. Finally, staff may feel overwhelmed by the magnitude of the patient's problems and feel inadequate to handle all the emotionally laden issues, along with the legal implications.

Intervention

Approaching these issues is best attempted after full discussion with the entire team and involves four areas: 1) work with the patient; 2) work with outside agencies; 3) work with the family; and 4) work with the PHP community.

1) The PHP staff can help to evaluate the child mistreatment. It can be especially helpful to draw parallels between home behavior and PHP performance. For example, a patient who makes unreasonable demands and is quick to anger in the PHP may show similar behavior at home. These parallels can foster realistic, relatively objective appraisals of the patient and his situation, providing opportunities for direct intervention, while discouraging overidentification or condemnation by PHP members.

2) PHP staff have clinical and legal obligations to act judiciously but swiftly in cases of current allegations of neglect or abuse. The legal obligations involve formal notification of the outside agency legally mandated for child protection; this agency is mandated to conduct its own investigations and take appropriate action. Local laws and notification procedures should be familiar to staff.

In these instances, other agencies such as Parents Anonymous, emergency hot lines, and the Society for the Prevention of Cruelty to Children, and staff with specific expertise can be helpful in providing guidelines for intervention including home assessments.

Dealing with legal notification can create added difficulties among the staff, the patient, and the community. In child abuse or neglect situations, usual rules and rights of confidentiality may no longer apply, and reports of suspected abuse can be made without the client's knowledge or consent. However, sooner or later, the patient may learn of the identity of the informant. Thus, the preferable approach is for staff to clearly explain their concern and responsibilities for parent, child, and family in an individual meeting with the patient. In the end, the patient may be relieved. However, he may see the intervention as a condemnation and withdraw from the PHP. Or, his reaction may lead to an exacerbation of the psychiatric illness, to hospitalization, or to arrest. While this leaves the staff in a difficult position, they must remember their overriding responsibility to the child, to the rest of the family, and the laws requiring reporting (Kempe and Helfer, 1972; Fontana, 1971).

3) Individual and family sessions will be needed to deal with the family. Their reactions might range from relief that the situation is no longer secret, to guilt, shame, and rage, including anger toward the complainant. These sessions should be held with an objective and neutral therapist, if possible from the PHP; however, if the patient or spouse has strong objections, a therapist outside the program should be enlisted. The treatment should include exploration of the psychodynamics of the child abuse, the patient's history, his underlying feelings and events surrounding the abuse.

4) Close collaboration with PHP staff will facilitate unified treatment goals and plans. As soon as possible, the issues surrounding the abuse or neglect should be made a PHP issue so that the community can help the patient plan for his and his child's futures. Due to the power of the issue to arouse strong reactions, preparation of the PHP community is important, probably excluding the patient in question so that there will be opportunities to work on others' discomforts and plan constructive responses to the patient's difficulties. These responses should include reaching-out measures by patients and staff, such as cards, telephone calls and informal talks, since the member may be reluctant, even resistant, to becoming more involved and invested in PHP treatment, and stay home, leave groups early or arrive late.

Finally, since patients hearing that staff have informed legal agencies may fear future staff actions against them, too, the staff must address these issues clearly, explaining the bases for the actions taken, including the requirement to report child abuse or neglect.

Spouse Abuse—Problem

Staff and patients reactions to spouse abuse may parallel reactions to child abuse. The problems of denial, overreaction, fear and/or strong judgemental attitudes and behaviors against the patient in favor of the abused spouse may result in the PHP community.

Intervention

Areas for focus of treatment are also similar, dealing with the patient, the family, outside agencies and the PHP community.

1) The PHP can help to evaluate the abuse, again by parallels between home and PHP behavior. Focus for treatment should include a behavioral assessment, and the teaching of alternative, less destructive responses to difficult situations in which abuse may occur.

2) PHP staff have an obligation to the spouse and to offer controls for the abuser, once the threat or real situation is established. While, as yet, there are no known statutes requiring reporting as in child abuse, staff should be familiar with and be able to offer resouces such as shelters, hot lines, legal services, and medical supports.

3) Individual and family sessions will be needed.

4) Finally, preparation of the PHP community is vital, and the spouse abuse should be made a community issue.

Other Criminal Behavior—Problem

Patients may attend a PHP as a stipulation of their probation or parole, following conviction for a crime. They may react similarly to the patient suspected of child mistreatment. In addition, they may equate treatment with punishment since they may have no choice, or they may flaunt their criminal status as a way of gaining status or maintaining distance from others. These patients may be highly resistant to treatment.

Staff and patients may be fearful of a patient who has committed a crime, fearful of assault or theft. The staff may attempt to hide the circumstances of the crime, while trying to protect the group from future crimes. If they do so, they run the risk of losing the trust of the group, since the truth must eventually be disclosed. Fear may result in ostracism of the patient, encouraging him to withdraw, or later possibly to retaliate, further escalating the difficulties. Staff may also be conflicted about a patient who is "forced" to attend PHP (see Chapter 24).

Intervention

Close collaboration with probation or parole departments can ease the staff's burden of management problems, although it may provoke strong reactions on the part of the patient, particularly regarding confidentiality issues (see Chapter 24). This collaboration should be a condition of admission to the program, particularly since these departments will be making requests for information regarding attendance, behavior and prognosis, which may then be used in determining the probation or parole status of the patient.

As with other special problems, these should be dealt with directly, including the aforementioned issues of sharing information with legal agencies. Explanation of rules and consequences for violations are especially important for these patients.

Open discussion of concerns among staff and in groups, as early as possible, help prepare for the patient's admission. Focus should be on the person having a special problem, rather than on the problem itself. Staff should take care not to overemphasize the crime or share their own biases with the group. Staff members who are comfortable with this patient will reassure the group. Perhaps the patient may be helped to discuss these issues himself, first, to give him some control of the situation.

On occasion, there may be inquiries from formidable legal agencies, such as the police, the FBI, or the Secret Service. Staff must try not to feel intimidated or overwhelmed by such requests, remembering always to secure written permission to discuss treatment with these agencies, preceded by a full discussion with the patient. These requests should be carefully handled, with compliance to program policies and with the knowledge of administrative personnel. Staff should keep in mind how the information may be used, including only facts, and deleting any theories or speculations. Since information may be damaging, outside legal advice should be obtained if staff are requested or subpoenaed to testify, or if medical records are subpoenaed (Spingarn, 1975). (See also Chapter 24.)

Crimes While in the PHP*—Problem

There should be open, clear, repeated rules on safety in PHPs. Violations should be handled quickly but judiciously by staff and patients. A crime or serious threat of harm against another patient, member of staff or outside person, a theft of personal or PHP property, or damage to property is a community issue. Community members may be angry, upset, fearful and rejecting, feeling that they and the program have been violated. On the other hand, they may feel protective of the patient, even vicariously pleased by the act.

Intervention

All must work together to deal with the consequences of the violation. Discussion with or without the patient, depending on the nature of the crime, the patient in question, and the group's abilities to deal with the issues, can prepare the group to handle the issues later openly and directly.

On rare occasions, if the crime or threat is severe, the staff may be required to inform legal authorities and may also inform the potential victim. This latter issue is presently highly controversial (Wexler, 1979). Erring on the side of personal

* See also Section on threatening patients.

safety in making such evaluations is recommended. However, staff may be conflicted about such actions, not wanting to "step outside their roles" to be involved in a legal issue, possibly testifying or pressing charges against a client. But, once again, the protection of others' safety remains the overriding issue. Legal counsel and administrative personnel should be consulted.

If the patient spends time away from the PHP after his criminal act, an assessment of the patient's difficulties is made, while work on underlying issues continues individually. The crime may be symptomatic of a variety of issues, e.g., negative transferences to staff, negative reactions to counter patient improvement, reactions to termination and nonverbal expression of feelings. Working on these issues in depth may lead to valuable insights and changes that would be missed by simply suspending or terminating the patient.

Patients and staff can share their feelings with the problematic member upon his trial reentry. A written contract for trial reentries can be employed with provisions for length of stay and adherence to rules clearly defined, along with consequences for violation. This contract, with input from the patient and community, is shared with the entire community, who can then help to enforce it.

Concrete tasks can be undertaken to reestablish the security of the program. Staff and group members should evaluate the procedures for protection of valuables and of tools or other objects that can be used as weapons. These objects should be locked away with access limited to staff.

NEED FOR PERSONAL CARE SERVICES

Problem

At any point during a PHP patient's treatment, he may have problems involving a need for personal care services, frequently referred to as "concrete services." Such problems may include inadequate money, housing, legal aid, medical care and food, all of which are necessary for basic life support. Patients sometimes focus their discussions and concerns only on these areas. Their attendance may suffer for days or weeks, until they have negotiated the welfare system or fought their battle against an apartment eviction. More urgently, patients may appear at the PHP's doorstep in need of food, an immediate tooth extraction or attention for excruciating stomach pain. To complicate the issue, they may have no funds, no medical insurance, and they may have no general doctor or dentist who is familiar with them.

Staff and patients may initially react to the member with sympathy and concern, offering suggestions for solving the problems or even personal assistance. If the patient seems to frequently evidence problems in the above areas, they may become impatient and even disgusted with the patient's inability to deal with the realities of life. If the personal care service problems are severe and multiple, PHP patients may react with fear, not only for the patient's physical safety, but for their own as well. Finally, patients may focus on endless details of getting the needed assistance and exclude exploring with the patient how he might have been responsible for getting himself into the situation, or more crucial current treatment issues.

Staff upset is based on several factors.

1) Many clinicians simply do not know how to negotiate community support systems themselves, much less help someone else do it. Therefore, they may feel helpless in the eyes of the PHP patients.
2) Many clinicians do not view performing life support service advocacy within their professional role.
3) It may be extremely time-consuming to help the patient resolve these types of problems.
4) It is not unusual for PHP staff to be angered if they feel the patient is in dire life circumstances because he has consciously or unconsciously set the situation up to appear victimized and therefore gain attention from others.

Intervention

Interventions for these PHP patients must involve the PHP community—first the staff, then the patients. Staff may view the obtaining of personal care services as a burdensome assignment that should be delegated to the PHP staff member least resistant to taking on this task. If this view is not changed the PHP patient in need may not receive the required service. Equally as important, the patient may miss learning valuable problem-solving skills. These skills to deal with his concrete needs are as important a part of treatment as the skills he develops to cope with the emotional and interactional problems of his life.

Seeing to personal care services is another area where all staff need to augment their skills and knowledge so they will have a general awareness of community resources and how they are acquired. Social work staff are usually responsible for keeping themselves abreast of community life support services and how they are best utilized. More specifically, staff need to have some idea of where emergency food or lodging can be obtained at 4:30 P.M. on a Friday. Staff must have some appreciation for the conditions and process by which a person receives food stamps, for the legal steps a patient may take if he is evicted from his apartment, etc. Optimally, PHP staff should visit and observe the commonly used agencies for personal care services. Armed with firsthand knowledge, they can better help patients with their needs. Staff resistances to acquiring knowledge about issues related to acquiring personal care services should be handled in PHP staff meetings.

A beneficial aid to staff for familiarizing themselves with community services and how to acquire them is a community resources handbook that is regularly updated. It is usually wise to have one staff member in charge of this project as a legitimate part of his job description. Not only would this individual be expected to maintain the handbook, but he would be expected to update the PHP staff regarding important changes in any commonly used community resource. Many staffs include this update as a regular part of their agendas in administrative staff meetings.

If a PHP patient develops life support service needs after admission to the program, a decision will need to be made by him and the entire community regarding his ability to handle these problems effectively while in the program, or whether he needs to take a formalized partial or complete break from the program. In either case, the community should be involved in helping the individual define his life support service needs, why the needs exist, in what priority they should be approached, and possible solutions. PHP patients are often helpful in aiding a fellow member negotiate a system they have successfully negotiated themselves.

Such community treatment of personal care service problems can result in PHP patients being able to offer one another concrete help such as going with a frightened member to a medical appointment, joining a patient in making a telephone call to the welfare department and filling out welfare or SSI applications from PHP model forms. In addition, with staff support, the community members can be strikingly effective in helping a patient through a difficult period, confronting a patient with his resistances to solving his life support service needs more independently, and pointing out to a patient how he might be undermining his own efforts.

BORDERLINE MENTALLY RETARDED* AND MILDLY
NEUROLOGICALLY IMPAIRED**

Problem

The borderline retarded and neurologically impaired may frequently be referred to PHPs not specifically designed to serve these patients. These patients may enter the PHP in a variety of ways. They may be misdiagnosed initially as schizophrenic, impulse disordered, or depressed, since much of their behavior may closely resemble symptoms observed in other patients. Also, a confusion between primary and secondary diagnoses may further complicate accurate assessment. Patients who carry two or more diagnoses often have difficulties in finding programs willing or able to accept them. Thus, one disorder may be emphasized by referral sources to secure admission. As a result, in part, of the move toward

---

* The borderline mentally retarded patient is one who WAIS IQ scores fall with the 70–84 range, and/or who functions on a retarded level, as shown through functional abilities testing.

** These patients are commonly referred to as "brain damaged," and patients with nonpsychotic organic mental disorders.

deinstitutionalization and normalization, these patients are more frequently being referred to PHPs, when services are otherwise unavailable.

Services are often arranged quickly, particularly when the PHP is used as an alternative to inpatient hospitalization. More careful and in-depth evaluation and differential diagnostic study may be postponed in the interests of crisis intervention. As a result, diagnoses by referral sources are usually accepted and major issues may initially be overlooked.

The mentally retarded or neurologically impaired patient may demand numerous explanations of instructions. The patient may become confused in verbal groups and repeatedly ask the same questions, halting group discussion. The patient may withdraw, leave groups, or fall asleep during discussions. Regular attendance and punctuality may be problems for this patient. Finally, he may suddenly "explode" verbally, or physically, later denying knowledge of the episode or even the precipitant. Other patients and staff may become confused, frustrated, and angry, and interpret these behaviors as provocative and deliberately hostile. The patient's outbursts may arouse fear for personal safety. The patient may become isolated, or worse, the group scapegoat.

Staff may assume that the problem which the patient experiences is based on emotional conflicts, and that, with encouragement, he will be able to verbalize and work to resolve the underlying issues. When the patient does not respond, he may be considered as stubborn or resistant, adding to staff frustrations (Emerson and Fagan, 1977).

Intervention

Outdated beliefs regarding the mentally retarded or neurologically impaired patients may further complicate staff interventions. Staff must examine their own reactions to the clients, their feelings of helplessness invoked by the difficulties exhibited by these patients, as well as working through the erroneous bias that these clients are hopeless. There needs to be a clear assessment of the problems and a realistic appraisal of what can be expected from these patients.

Psychological and neurological testing can be particularly helpful in providing a clear assessment of the client's verbal and nonverbal abilities, such as eye-hand coordination or other perceptual-motor difficulties, and in subsequently designing an appropriate treatment plan. The patient should be informed of testing results and then helped to share them with the family and with the PHP. Families may need extra staff time and understanding while dealing with a variety of feelings and issues. A close relationship with family is needed for a coordinated plan of treatment since they may be called upon for assistance with difficult issues such as helping with medications, helping the patient to attend daily, even waking, or verbalizing for the patient.

Sharing the results with PHP members reduces frustration, antagonism, resistance and fear that the patient's previous behavior may have provoked. Staff and patients can discuss the patient's limitations and the special problems inherent in a full schedule, as they do with the severely disturbed or physically disabled members. These discussions provide guidelines for treatment, a frame of reference for the puzzling or frightening behavior, and should ease tensions while encouraging group acceptance. Other patients may be encouraged to assist these patients, thereby increasing their own self-esteem.

Treatment planning may exclude some of the most abstract verbal groups, particularly those involving sharing of emotional issues, at least initially. Discussion of complex or highly charged issues is carefully monitored to protect the patient from a flood of feelings which may overwhelm him. To maximize the opportunity for a successful PHP experience, staff may want to start with those that can be accomplished quickly, such as simplified art projects which are time-limited with clearly defined steps, social groups with low expectations, and behavior modification approaches. Staff may offer some added individual work to these patients who may have difficulty in grasping the content of discussions, even those of a concrete nature.

Exclusionary planning will reinforce isolation and separateness. Planning should be tempered by suggestions for tasks based on the patient's assets. Taking charge of attendance, keeping the group to time schedules, involvement with regular chores, helping to orient new patients to rules and procedures will offer distinct and positive roles for these patients as well as positive recognition in the PHP.

Finally, these patients often have difficulty in obtaining continuity of care after the PHP. Many PHPs are time-limited and expect and encourage patient movement within specific guidelines. However, problems may arise in placing these patients. Staff need to prepare themselves and the community for the special circumstances faced by these patients. There may be only a limited number of available programs with stiff admission criteria and/or long waiting lists. The patient's stay in the PHP may be lengthened, as a result, and should not be viewed merely as patient or staff resistance to termination.

V

Miscellaneous
Critical Components

22

Communications, Information Systems, Research, and Medical Records

"Unexamined life is not worth living" (Socrates in Plato's Apology, 4th century B.C.). The PHP without adequate communication is meaningless, unmanageable and unbearable. To prevent a deficiency in communication, PHP staff and patients must expend much time and energy daily. In striving toward openness and completeness of communication of accurate inclusive information in a PHP, from time to time partial hospital staff need to step back and take a good hard look at the information that flows in planned and unplanned ways throughout the work with patients and the maintenance a PHP to insure that there is an adequate information system.

The PHP information system should provide a matrix for all activities and provide answers to the ten fundamental questions about what goes on in a partial hospital: Who? Does what? For whom? How? Where? When? How much? At what cost? With what results? (Baxter, 1980, p. 5). An additional question should be: Why?

As indicated in Chapter 16, work in the field of mental health is ever more characterized by accountability, auditing, authentication demands, and automation. Demands for data have continued to escalate over the past 15 years, especially, and there is no indication of a reversal in this trend. This chapter considers how to master data and make them work. First, guidelines toward adoption of a PHP's information system and program evaluation are suggested, followed by a section on research. After consideration of medical records and the problem-oriented record, the chapter finally examines staff motivation to maintain data.

GUIDELINES TOWARD A PHP INFORMATION SYSTEM
AND PROGRAM EVALUATION

There is still no one specific information system or set of procedures for program evaluation that can be adopted in all details identically for all partial hospitals. Nonetheless, these are important and necessary components of a successful PHP; therefore, PHP staff are advised to carry out the following:

239

1) A decision that program evaluation and other information management are vital necessities. Program evaluation is the process of "determining the degree to which the organization is fulfilling its mission, by meeting its prioritized goals and objectives" (Baxter, 1980).
2) Involvement of all staff in the development and maintenance of an adequate information system to gather and deal with information effectively and appropriately.
3) A commitment to answering the fundamental ten questions essential for an adequate information system.
4) A collection of necessary reference materials: The PHP should contact the NIMH to receive free mailings and publications of their Division of Mental Health Service Programs and Division of Biometry and Epidemiology, especially the latter's Series C, D, and E reports. (See also Carter and Newman, 1976, Hargreaves et al., 1977; Werlin, 1976; NIMH, 1976 and 1978)
5) An acceptance that an adequate information system and peer review will require three to five percent of the operating budget. NIMH (1979) guidelines for community mental health centers require that program evaluation and quality assurance alone take two percent of the budget.
6) A decision to collect and analyze the data to be able to answer the ten fundamental questions and do problem-solving.
7) Adoption of an information system in writing, which should help increase clarity, commitment and consistency.
8) The work of maintaining the system, including a yearly update.
9) Usage of the system with timely practical feedback to clinicians. Anthony et al. (1978), Berner (1980), Carrol (1980), Williams (1980) provide examples of evaluation.

RESEARCH NEEDS

As discussed in Chapter 3, existing research is rudimentary up to now. With the rising costs of PHP treatment, third-party payers will demand facts and figures to justify continuance of existing programs as well as to justify increased funding.

Frequently, proponents of PHP still rely on single program descriptions and clinical vignettes to illustrate treatment effectiveness and still use comparison with 24-hour care programs to promote the cost and therapeutic advantages of their own programs. Often the view of PHP superiority is derived from a subjective opinion that less hospitalization, less institutionalization is better than 24-hour care, particularly in light of many negative aspects of full-time care, rather than derived from empirical studies of effectiveness and efficiency.

Areas for Study

Important questions remain. Who is best served by a PHP? Which type of program best serves a particular patient groups? How do PHPs compare in terms of cost and treatment effectiveness with inpatient and outpatient care? Which treatment modalities are best for which patient? What is the optimal size of a PHP? How many staff are needed? Which mental health disciplines are most effective? How much prior training is needed? Which patients need guesting? For what length of time? How can the dropout rate be reduced? Can PHP be used as a measure of progress toward lessening financial burdens on family and on public assistance agencies as Endicott et al. (1978) suggest?

Continued research should focus in two areas: 1) ongoing individual program evaluation, and 2) comparative study as to PHP's role(s) in the mental health service network. Both are vital to PHP survival.

Ongoing Program Evaluation

Ongoing program evaluation should work to provide answers regarding which patients are best served by a particular program and why this is so, as well as which patients are served less effectively. Thus far, a variety of populations have been treated in PHPs, but no single diagnostic group or groups have been designated as best served. PHPs have tried to do the impossible by attempting to be all things to all patients. Doing so confuses referral sources and encourages underutilization. Coordination and clear communication with referral sources will help to identify target populations and current patient needs.

Program effectiveness studies, though few in number, have pointed toward the need for commonly accepted measurement tools and stricter sampling techniques, especially using randomized experimental and control groups. Replication of existing studies can help to delineate valid and reliable studies.

Ongoing evaluation of individual programs will be faciliated by standardization. Davenport (1979) offered a three-pronged approach to client care criteria, examining the appropriateness, adequacy, and effectiveness of treatment. The criterion for appropriateness refers to the standards for determination of which patients are compatible to PHP treatment and which patients are not. Adequacy refers to the extent to which treatment plans are implemented. Effectiveness measures the success of the PHP and the magnitude and direction of changes. Assessments of these three areas are measured by a series of rating scales. Other studies have used different scales, working toward similar results. Regardless of the specific scale used, measurement should include these three areas.

Goal Attainment Scaling (Kiresuk and Sherman, 1968) is one measurement technique for PHPs. It offers a stimulus for staff and patients to set operationalized, concrete, and realistic individual patient goals and a structured measurement of adequacy and effectiveness of treatments offered to a specific patient. Unfortunately, it does not allow easy comparison because GAS is so unique for each patient that one does not know how to quantify results for comparison with other patients. Other tools may be found which can be more amenable to comparison among patients.

Comparing Programs

Comparisons of PHPs with each other and with other services have their own design difficulties to overcome so that they may later provide clear comparisons. Required are clear delineation of the functions of the various units (comparing a short-term acute inpatient service with a long-term PHP would be unfair to both programs), and close examination of each element in programs, such as guesting and family supports.

Comparison of PHPs with more traditional weekly outpatient care requires envisioning the PHP as aftercare treatment following a crisis and/or hospitalization, or as maintenance treatment, rather than intensive care, or as a clearly valid ambulatory treatment in its own right. Certainly, these services could hardly be considered as equivalent (see Chapter 3).

Treatment models vary from program to program. Austin et al.'s (1976) study, comparing a behaviorally oriented program with an eclectic program, is a first attempt at such comparison and should be followed by further examination of the value of specialized PHPs and their abilities to treat specific patient groups. Comparisons of patient populations, treatments offered, staff ratios, etc. are sorely needed for more accurate study.

Finally, for continued existence, particularly in these times of stricter cost analysis, PHPs need clear cost effectiveness criteria to maintain current funding, while encouraging full third-party reimbursement. Both cost per day and length of stay comparisons have shown the PHP to be less expensive than inpatient care, but as Binner (1977) has stated these figures and archaic guidelines do not measure treatment effectiveness. A model including fiscal *and* treatment efficiency and effectiveness is needed for valid comparison.

Implementation

Studies are often avoided by programs which do not have distinct research staffs. Practitioners may resist, claiming they are too busy providing direct services to undertake extensive research. Perhaps they may also be uneasy about critical examination of their work by others, and thus discourage research.

In accordance with the need for ongoing evaluation of programs, Eisen et al. (1979) proposed the following recommendations for implementing evaluation:

1) Research the instruments to find those most suited for use in your system.
2) Meet with staff to discuss the project.
3) Capitalize on staff interest and select two or three staff members to help with the evaluation procedures and data management.
4) Develop a systematized method of data collection and storage.
5) Educate and train staff in proper use of the instruments they are to complete. Problems of instrument reliability must constantly be addressed.
6) Utilize students and volunteers to score instruments completed by clients.
7) When appropriate, give the client feedback on the information given you and how it relates to programming and treatment goals.
8) Do not attempt to interpret results of ongoing studies without the expertise of a trained methodologist (p. 165).

Continued scientific and systematic research based on commonly accepted program standards and guidelines and using similar measurement tools for cost and treatment effectiveness and efficiency will provide PHPs with the generalizable results needed to find answers to the recurring questions faced by PHPs.

MEDICAL RECORDS AND THE PROBLEM-ORIENTED RECORD

If PHPs improve patient functioning, how should it be documented? How should "problems" be defined and quantified? How should priorities for treatment interventions be set? How should what is actually done to help patients be determined and defined? Finally, how should systematic recording of what is being done and plans regarding patient care be effected? In considering these questions, particular focus will be put on issues of quality recording, the salient features of the psychiatric problem-oriented record,* and its suitability for use in PHPs.

Issues of Quality Recording

Recording is a thorn in the side of many mental health professionals. At times, it seems one must choose between direct patient contacts and required recording. This is unfortunate, since effective patient care and quality recording are inseparable. Clinical recording is a valuable tool for putting theory into practice, and putting it in writing helps in mastering complex material.

All PHPs must try to piece together the variety of requirements from agency, departmental, governing, and funding sources and develop their own unique systems of record-keeping. Yet it is important that PHPs develop standardized means for gathering data which will enhance effective treatment and lay the groundwork for much needed research (see Chapters 3 and 13).

---

* Lawrence Weed's Problem-Oriented Medical Record (1971) provides the basis for the problem-oriented record, modified for psychiatric settings (Mazur, 1974; DiBella, 1975).

Records which accompany patients to the PHP from other services can be voluminous, requiring a great deal of time to read through the assortment of valuable information and synthesize it in such a manner that it is useful in PHP. It is not unusual for important information to be neglected due to the time involved in searching for it.

Another problem involved with much record-keeping is the unfortunate yet common split between "medical" and "psychiatric" data (see Chapter 20). PHP records should reflect a comprehensive, individualized, biopsychosocial approach which is understandable to and usable by the entire multidisciplinary PHP team.

The problem-oriented record has the potential for meeting all of these needs. In addition, the principles of the problem-oriented record have been accepted by the Joint Commission on the Accreditation of Hospitals (Mazur, 1974), an important consideration for PHPs. The following outline of the highlights of the problem-oriented record is applicable for use in PHPs (Mazur, 1974; DiBella, 1975).

Highlights of the Problem-Oriented Record

1) The entire chart revolves around the numbered problem list, and the (capital letters of the) assets/resources list.
2) Initial workup and charting.
   (a) Information gathering, which provides the data base.
   (b) Developing the list of problems, ranked in order of importance (or taken from standardized lists).
   (c) List of assets and resources, in reasonable order of strengths and usefulness.
   (d) Initial assessment, for each numbered problem and lettered asset, in a SOAP format.
      i) *S*ubjective assessment: How does the patient view his problems and strengths and need for partial hospitalization? Direct quotes from patients are helpful
      ii) *O*bjective assessment: Staff observations, clinical facts.
      iii) *A*ssessment (combining subjective and objective assessments): Staff's clinical impressions; definition and discussion of the problem, integrating information from the data base. Can the problems be treated in PHP? Is the patient aware of his strengths and able to use them?
      iv) *P*lan: For each identified problem and asset, and based on the assessment, there are short-term and long-term treatment goals and plans developed.
3) Additions to problem and asset lists are made as new information is obtained.
4) Notes: They must always be started with a corresponding numbered problem or asset/resource (with its capital letter). Notes are structured in the format of *S*ubjective, *O*bjective, *A*ssessment and *P*lan (SOAP).

5) Each doctor's order is cross-indexed to the problem or assets list.
6) Discharge summary includes comment on all of the numbered problems and lettered assets/resources.

Data base should provide the information which the clinician needs to prepare the initial problem list, assessment, goals and plans. A specific plan for collecting and recording additional needed information is made at the time of intake.

The problem list is a central focus around which the problem-oriented record revolves. The problem list serves as an index to the entire chart and is located in a permanently visible and easily accessible place within the chart, usually in the front. Some programs prioritize problems, others have standardized lists.

The list of assets/resources gives the "positives" an equal status with problems in the chart, and offers the professional a more complete and positive picture of the patient. The assets/resources include such areas as skills, talents, interests, supportive resources (family, friends, employers) and community resources (Mazur, 1974).

Treatment goals and plans specify operational, measurable goals with time frames and indicate clearly what is to be done about each problem and asset listed and by whom. They can also indicate what are staff goals, patient goals and mutual goals.

Notes reflect the following: 1) the problem or asset and how it is manifested (or not) in PHP activities; 2) an understanding of the problem or asset and what is being done about it; and 3) an ongoing evaluation of the effectiveness of treatment plans, e.g., is the problem reaching resolution, does it need to be redefined, or do the goals and plans need to be reevaluated?

The notes should contain as much observable, objective, (briefly) descriptive material as possible, and are usually written as a team or by specifically assigned staff. PHP patients may also write notes, which could be recorded on separate, colored sheets or in separate PHP folders. Patient teams could be formed for this task also.

The frequency of recording notes is a function of the type of PHP. For example, a program treating chronic patients on a long-term basis may record notes weekly. An acute-care PHP, on the other hand, might record daily.

Discharge summaries summarize a patient's course of treatment. They represent the end product of PHP treatment, including recommendations for continuation of care and use of the problem-oriented record. They are also, therefore, an educational instrument for staff and patients with which to evaluate their therapeutic abilities.

Supervision of the problem-oriented record is usually a responsibility of a physician and/or PHP administrator. In some programs, certain staff are responsible for writing all or parts of the record. All staff who are involved in the formulation of treatment goals and plans, based on the team's assessment of the data base, problem and assets lists, sign their names and titles to the treatment plans. Patients may also be asked to read and sign them. The physician and/or administrator typically sign last, indicating their overall supervision and final approval of the work.

The work involved in implementing or converting to the problem-oriented record may seem overwhelming at first. However, the benefits gained from its use far outweigh the initial effort. The clarity and individuality which the problem-oriented record promotes make the hard work of PHPs easier, in that members struggle together over patient issues which are as clear and focused as possible. In addition, the problem-oriented record does well to insure that specific patient problems and strengths are not lost sight of and that information recorded is not buried amidst the bulk of medical records. It remains visible, intact, active, and easily retrievable for synthesizing and integrating into any ongoing therapy and research.

MOTIVATING STAFF TO MAINTAIN STATISTICAL AND TREATMENT INFORMATION

"Who wants to maintain a daily record of services to patients? Why should I do treatment plans and charted notes—does anyone really read them?" "Why should I help administration gather information for their research projects? My job is to spend time with patients, isn't it?"

These, and numerous other complaints, are common PHP staff responses to meeting paperwork requirements, and this negative attitude is often reflected in late, incomplete or inadequate records. At its worst level, a contest of wills may develop between administrative/supervisory personnel and line PHP staff, concurrent with threats to the latter of disciplinary action, possibly even suspension from employment. These negative attitudes are unfortunate. All psychiatric programs are held increasingly accountable for what they are doing, and funds for all resources are based on documentation of services provided.

Our objective here is not only to suggest alternatives to reducing staff resistance to maintaining records but also to indicate the opportunities for using statistical and treatment information to greater clinical advantage. This in turn will provide greater job satisfaction for PHP staff.

The problem has some origins in the negative attitudes that are conveyed by administrative/supervisory personnel toward staff in the following ways:

1) Giving hurried or inadequate instructions to staff on how to establish and maintain written records.
2) Delegating to the least clinically knowledgeable or skilled person (sometimes clerical staff) the task of instructing staff (particularly new staff) on how to maintain information, while reserving supervisory time for "more important" clinical issues.

3) Not allowing a designated time period in a PHP staff member's schedule for record maintenance and information-gathering.

4) Raising the issue of proper record maintenance and the need for gathering statistics inconsistently or during "crisis periods" such as shortly before an accreditation or a medicaid inspection.

5) Openly ridiculing and/or condemning (either in formal staff meetings or informal contacts with PHP staff) the boredom and time consumption involved in doing paperwork.

In addition to the attitudes discussed above, PHP staff members frequently have their own reasons for resisting such work. They may have difficulty seeing a connection between statistical material and their own job functioning. This is particularly true in some settings which require rather detailed information such as the daily number and length of patient contacts or the weekly frequency of group and family sessions. There is always a tendency to view this work as being done for "administration" or "some clerk up there who needs a job." Too often PHP staff are not included in the process of how this information is used, e.g., to make salary determinations, determine leasing of building space, etc. Staff may also see little relationship between their work and the writing of treatment records, especially when it seems that the only clinicians who read these materials are those who are writing them.

Possible interventions that may be made by administrative/supervisory and line staff to ameliorate this situation are as follows:

1) Each new PHP staff member should have an adequate, positive introduction and follow-up of his maintenance of written information, this being made a regular part of a PHP staff member's work supervisory contract. Initially, complete instructions for acceptable record maintenance should be given by the supervisor to his supervisee. Further evaluation of the adequacy of functioning in this area should be as regular a part of periodic assessment of a PHP staff member's work as are his clinical skills. Any deficiencies should be cited, along with a plan for correction. If there is adequate performance in this area, reference should also be made to this in the employee assessment.

2) Record-keeping and the maintenance of statistical material should be legitimized as part of the overall job functioning. This means that a specific time period or periods are allotted during the program for such work. Also, availability of and proper instruction in the use of dictaphone equipment can aid immeasurably in reducing the time spent doing this part of the job. It may be advisable to have part of the time allotted to a formalized group where staff work together on charted notes, treatment plans, etc. By doing so, PHP staff members could lend support to one another. In addition, since PHP treatment is in essence a joint staff treatment venture, charting together contributes to staff assisting one

another in making joint formulations and writing treatment plans, or clarifying points more specifically for charted notes.

3) Charted notes, treatment plans, and other written medical record materials that are required of PHP staff should be referred to consistently in PHP staff meetings. This is clinically sound because it becomes clearer to the entire treatment team whether or not they are following a treatment plan adequately or if there need to be revisions in the plan or their treatment. Also, they can see a patient's problems and progress more clearly in the charted notes or other written materials. It is self-evident that a staff member will be less likely to become deficient in his written work if he knows it will be regularly consulted by his peers in a group and that it has considerable relevance to the treatment.

4) Clear connections should be established between the maintenance of nonclinical materials (telephone contacts, numbers of various types of patients in the program, etc.), and the PHP's physical survival or its receiving adequate funding for resources to conduct patient treatment. Often, PHP staff are told to submit various statistical material. They comply and this is, unfortunately, the end of the issue. Staff are not always included in how the information submitted by them is used in order to determine the number of staff members the PHP will be allotted or how many telephones will be installed in their building. One method some programs use to facilitate effectiveness in this area is to have representatives from business and statistical offices associated with the PHP periodically review the purpose of statistical forms. Following this, they might give the latest feedback to staff on how their information was used in determining the PHP budget.

5) Written information should be used regularly and clearly for evaluation of the program, patient goal attainment, and the clinical work of staff. No staff or program is perfect; critical self-examination is vital just to maintain standards, and even more so for improvement!

6) There should be a periodic review of administrative/supervisory personnel of the amount, type, and form of written information they are requiring of their staff. This is done to determine that staff are legitimately being asked to do no more in this area than is worthwhile.

23

Finances and Marketing for Partial Hospitals

This chapter first examines management of finances, cost finding, and rate setting. There follows a discussion of the current sources of funding for PHPs and overcoming resistances to money issues. Marketing philosophy and methods and how they can be applied to the planning of PHPs are presented next. Finally, obtaining support and achieving funding through good community relations are considered.

Money is the fuel to power any mental health system. Without it, no amount of talent, caring and goodwill will prevent a treatment system from shriveling up and dying. A related aspect is the need for "fuel" conservation. There is always a greater demand for resources than are actually available. Therefore, utilization of resources must be optimized, and funding should flow, generally, to the system proven to be the most effective and efficient.

Why is it necessary to emphasize these points? First, mental health staff have a strong tendency to neglect monetary issues in their professional work (DiBella, 1980).

Second, the threat of collapse of monetary support is looming so large it can no longer be ignored (Stratas, 1978). For example, in 1978 citizens of California voted for an unusually large cut in taxes (Proposition 13), and what is being axed include, as usual, mental health services (Talbott, 1979). Since about 1974 the mood of the United States citizen is one of rebellion against paying out money for anything (Panel, 1980).

Third, PHPs are most vulnerable in face of the unrelenting demand for proof that every dollar purchases top efficiency and effectiveness. Research has provided less than perfect proof of PHP effectiveness and efficiency (see Chapter 3), and partial hospitalization is the least understood and entrenched of any mental health services, and also the least supported by third-party payers.

Finally, under threats of poor funding and cutbacks, staff tend to become worried and demoralized, with resulting decrements in performance.

MANAGING FINANCES

Failure to manage the financial aspects of PHP will cause it to sink. Management involves the administrative processes (part of intraorganizational-oriented support functions) attempting to insure that the whole organization achieves its goals efficiently and effectively. Financial (fiscal) management is that part of resource management which deals with all organizational components, activities, and outputs expressed in monetary terms, so that money is available over the long term to pay for achieving clinical goals of the partial hospital (Herzlinger, 1977). Thus, financial management touches on all activities. However, there are certain aspects of any organization (as in a PHP) that are traditionally placed within the area of "financial management."

These aspects are:

1) accrual accounting using double entry book keeping;
2) analyzing and reporting with resultant financial statements (the balance sheet and income statement—see Figures 1 and 2), cost finding, and rate setting;
3) budgeting;
4) controlling (the process of assuring that plans are adhered to); and
5) auditing (Baxter, 1980, p. 57-58).

Worthwhile to know are the terms "cost finding," "direct and indirect costs," and "rate setting," etc. (Baxter, 1980). Derivative in part from these are cost benefit analysis and cost effectiveness analysis; Frank (1981) gives a summary of these important areas.

The degree to which PHP staff become involved in details of financial management will depend on the overall organizational structure. For example, staff of a freestanding partial hospital will need to be considerably involved and hire a consulting accountant to help set up accounting records (original documents, jour-

Figure 1

Bestcare Partial Hospital

Balance Sheet as of December 31, 1980

Assets

    Current Assets:

Cash (checking account and petty cash)		8890
Short-term investments (savings account)		1000
Accounts receivable (from patients)	46851	
Less Uncollectable accts.	2000	44851

Inventories		2757	
Prepaid expenses (as taxes or insurance)		818	
Total Current Assets			58,316

Fixed Assets

Land		11,700	
Buildings and equipment (purchase price)	130,000		
Less Accumulated depreciation	13,000	117,000	
Total Fixed Assets			128,700
Total Assets			187,016

Liabilities:

Current Liabilities:

Accounts payable (to suppliers)	4993	
Taxes payable	127	
Salaries payable for past two weeks/staff services	6103	
Current loans (less than 1 year)	400	
Advance payment (for services to be given to X company, etc.)	4000	
Total		15,623

Long-Term Liabilities

Long-term loans (including bonds and mortgages)	136,393	
"Fund" balance (non-debt gifts, grants, etc.)	35,000	
Total:		171,393
Total Liabilities:		187,016

Figure 2

Bestcare Partial Hospital

Income Statement for Jan. 1 to Dec. 31, 1980

Revenues:
    Net patient service revenues   231,100
    Other operating revenues   3,300

Total Income   234,400

Expenses:
    Salaries and benefits   151,200
    Supplies and medicine   33,000
    Depreciation   13,600
    General expenses   13,000
    Interest   14,800
    Miscellaneous   8,000

Total Expenses   233,600

Net Income (Excess of revenues
    over expenses)   800

nals, and ledgers) and to audit (annually at least). On the other hand, a PHP that is part of a general hospital will have much of this financial management dictated. All heads of partial hospitals should be comfortable with and aware of the essentials of financial management (NIMH, 1977b).

BASIC COSTS OF PARTIAL HOSPITAL TREATMENT: COST FINDING

How much money does a partial hospital need? Cost estimates (cost finding) are easy to work up once the planner has decided on the type of partial hospital desired and its staff/patient ratio to match (see types of PHP especially in Chapters 2, 14, 15, and 16). For example, in general, the crisis support/alternative-to-hospitalization PHP will require double the staff/patient ratio (hence it will be more costly) of a long-term PHP dealing only with relatively stable, chronic, low-functioning patients. The following guidelines are useful for determining estimates of cost.

The mental health services industry is a labor intensive type; thus, the largest single cost is the compensations paid for personnel. Estimate that 60-90 percent of operating costs will always result from direct salary and fringe benefits (NIMH, 1977a, p. 19; Seawell, 1975, p. 194). In 1980 average salary of staff members was perhaps $18,000. Fifteen to 20 percent of this amount is the cost of fringe benefits on top of basic salary. Add these two figures together and assume this represents 65 percent of the total budget, divide by 0.65, and this will yield a good estimate of the total program cost (direct and indirect expenses) with a little leeway for miscalculations and contingency. Thus, a partial hospital of seven clinical and nonclinical staff would result in a cost of 7 x (18,000 + 0.20 x 18,000) ÷ 0.65—a partial hospital program that will cost about $232,600 per year to operate. Inflation will add 5-20 percent yearly to these figures.

At any rate, the total program costs should never be more than twice the personnel costs. Keep this "two times" rule in mind. Staff in a PHP that is part of a larger health center which dictates budget will often find themselves greatly pressed to get inappropriately high revenues because the health center has piled on expenses not from the partial hospital but from the rest of the hospital (Berman and Moloney, 1978)! A quick check of the income expense statement (see Figure 2) for the program using the two times rule will indicate if an inappropriate allocation has occurred. Although there are complicated reasons for this state of affairs, such a situation can be avoided if there is good management (Berman and Moloney, 1978; Balachandran and Dittman, 1978). Even if a PHP cannot get immediate relief from inaccurate budgeting, persistent efforts with higher administration may pay off; also, with just a little knowledge about financing the PHP staff may relieve the pressure on the partial hospital to obtain unrealistic amounts of revenues.

RATE SETTING

How much does a partial hospital cost per patient day of treatment? Present programs seem to have a range of $35-210. In order to determine this charge to each patient per day in any program, first find the average daily actual attendance (usually 75-85 percent of the overall census of "active cases"); then multiply this number by the days the program operates (usually 5 days a week for 51 weeks, or 255 days). Use this number as divisor of the total annual program costs. For example, using the costs found above and on actual daily attendance of 20 patients, then 232,600 ÷ (255 X 20) = $46 per day that must be collected from each of 20 daily patients to cover costs of operating this program. Where will this money come from? Few patients can pay out $175-1050 per week from their own pocket.

CURRENT SOURCES OF FUNDING FOR PHPS

Payment for services provided by partial hospitals are made in two basic ways.

The patient, and those legally responsible for him, can pay directly from personal funds, or payment is made by a host of "third parties." The former is rather simple, direct, and easy to understand. The third-party methods are much more varied and complex, although all involve a common denominator, namely, that some third entity (which is not the direct primary recipient of the staff's clinical services) makes payment toward cost of the services to the patient. A comprehensive list of these entities follows, ranked according to direct relationship and obligation to the patient (most to least):

1) Private insurance companies (typical third-party payers).
2) Government public funds (federal, state, city, and local): Medicare and Medicaid, community mental health center grants, special grants for research or demonstration projects, and other miscellaneous sources such as CHAMPUS, the Veterans Administration, and other programs for government workers or children.
3) Private institutions (gifts and grants from foundations, religious, and other charitable institutions, businesses and corporations, etc.).
4) Individual citizens (gifts, donations, bequests, fund-raising events, etc.).

Each of these methods of payment have a differing impact on patient selection, treatment planning, providers, and the treatment relationship, among others (GAP, 1975).

Unfortunately "society" and its third-party component in the USA provide health care payments in an inflationary, prejudiced, shortsighted, and disjointed way (Morrison, 1977). For example, the highest level of funds is provided for the most expensive care; this is inpatient hospital treatment of acute physical illness. Thus, inpatient care is used even though outpatient care would suffice, if the latter were only funded adequately. Payment for mental illness (versus physical illness) is made at lower levels, and payment for PHP is at the very bottom end of a scale of payments made for ambulatory services. Nowhere is there a third party that pays for partial hospitals in all states in the USA. An exception was the federal Community Mental Health Center program begun in 1963, which provides temporary grants declining over eight years. The end of this eight-year period results in severe fiscal crisis and, some say, "extinction" (Sharfstein, 1978). However, since 1978 PHPs are no longer required to be initial services in CMHC's (Hammersley, 1979). Langsley et al. (1964) wrote that it was "almost impossible to obtain insurance that will pay for partial hospitalization." This is essentially still true today! Great Britain, however, is more supportive of PHPs and the USSR has vigorously supported the PHP concept.

On the assumption that costs will be very high, insurance companies seem to react with horror to the idea of insuring psychiatric outpatient or office care, and most companies equate day hospitalization with this type of care (Guillette et al,

1978). Third-party payers complain that there are too many problems concerning the uncertain incidence of mental illness, unclear criteria for starting and stopping treatment, inadequate proof of effectiveness, etc. (Guillette et al., 1978; Langsley et al., 1964; Towery and Perry, 1981). In addition, most PHPs do not have the goal of crisis support and are not truly substituting to the maximum extent for in-patient care (for florid conditions). Thus, it appears PHPs are not really going to save insurance companies the money having to be paid for very expensive inpatient care. If mental health professionals could address the above and similar issues satisfactorily, it is likely that PHPs would be funded by third-party payers.

If partial hospitals are to serve all those needing partial hospitalization, there must be indirect sources of payment (primarily public funds and insurance companies). Their absence results in fewer partial hospitals than needed and an enormous additional burden on staff to spend unusually large amounts of time in obtaining and maintaining sources of funding (rather than direct contact with patients). The alternative is to go bankrupt.

OVERCOMING RESISTANCE TO THE MONEY ISSUE IN PROFESSIONAL WORK

All staff must be active in helping the partial hospital become and remain solvent. However, staff do not traditionally see this role for themselves, and they will not be able to overcome deep resistances to dealing openly with money in their clinical work by just hearing about the fiscal difficulties and being subjected to exhortations to help out (DiBella, 1980).

What can the responsible leader do to reduce interfering conflicts? First, he must accept the existence of the above-mentioned attitudes and realize that implementation of a program to obtain stable funding cannot be consistently carried out without time regularly and persistently spent by all staff to decrease inappropriate feelings toward money.

Second, a specific planned educational program must be set up, which will probably need four to six hours to make significant impact. The following topics should be presented:

1) reviewing the meaning of money in general and the ubiquitious role it plays;
2) helping staff to consider the many ways the money issue is present in therapy and openly to share their reactions to these;
3) devising, practicing, and role playing clinical activities with a view toward overcoming inappropriate countertransference-based behavior around money issues;
4) reviewing the importance of openly dealing with money for the purpose of the solvency of the PHP, continued staff employment, helping the patient deal with money in his life, and preventing money issues from interfering with the therapeutic relationship. Examining some actual program that did go bankrupt could also be helpful; and

5) involving staff in the development of specific systems that will lead toward more complete stable reimbursement. This program together with ongoing reminders and support given in meetings will enable staff to more consistently and reliably participate in financial management and marketing.

MARKETING PHILOSOPHY AND METHODS

Marketing is the organized body of knowledge and methods that focus on the exchange of value between human entities and the influences on this exchange. Convincing others to take value in exchange for giving value is only a small part of marketing; a larger part deals with voluntary types of exchanges. Unfortunately, the term "marketing" brings a mistaken perception to the minds of many in the health field; i.e., it elicits distasteful ideas of shysterism, hard sell of unnecessary, poor-quality merchandise, etc. For these and other reasons, marketing has long been neglected in application to mental health care, compared to its use in other fields. Indeed, the first book specifically on marketing health care appeared in 1977. Nothing has yet been published on marketing partial hospitalization.

Applied marketing of the PHP is needed to overcome those problems mentioned by Fink et al. (1978a) and Washburn et al. (1976b): namely, the resistance of third parties to pay for partial hospitalization and the resistance of family and physicians to utilize partial hospitals. A bit more active promotional effort is required from partial hospitals.

Marketing provides a structured, pragmatic way of taking action on a primary assumption in the community psychiatry movement that programs should be committed, accountable, and responsible to the needs of the entire community and remain responsive to it (Langsley, 1980).

Traditionally, mental health professionals have followed a philosophy that they should give the highest quality services, as judged by themselves to be best. In return, they expect people will be willing to utilize these services and give adequate compensation. This philosophy has resulted in health professionals being unresponsive to realities and changes, disgruntled patients, and lack of adequate monetary support. The marketing philosophy is significantly different, and it is compatible with good treatment orientation. It urges the organization to focus on how the public perceives its own needs, to decide on which of these needs the organization can best serve, and to plan accordingly (Cooper, 1979).

A prime maxim of marketing for PHP is that no planning and evaluation of the partial hospital program can exclude the application of marketing principles. Thus, the first step in planning becomes an analysis of the market (market research). As applied to the PHP, this involves breaking the market down into logical categories. In the broadest sense, "the market" is simply anybody (or group, sometimes called constitutents or consumers) with whom anybody (or an entity, such as a PHP) might have contact and exchange. This amorphous market is made more manageable by "segmentation." This term simply means dividing the market into logical useful categories and specifying the attributes of these groupings. Three helpful and commonly used categorization schemes are as follows:

1) A four-way classification of the market:
   (a) external groups that support, supply or regulate the organization, e.g. the larger hospital reported to by a PHP, Medicaid, staff of the emergency room, JCAH, and the federally backed Health Systems Agencies (HSAs);
   (b) internal groups that run the organization (the partial hospital staff);
   (c) client groups that recieve services; and
   (d) similar organizations in cooperation or competition with the partial hospital (other partial hospitals, inpatient services, etc.)
2) A three-way grouping, based on potential interchange:
   (a) current consumers;
   (b) potential consumers; and
   (c) those who will never or are highly unlikely to enter into exchange.
3) Another three-way grouping is based on location, demographics and, optimally, on actual behavioral-attitudinal features.

Each of these ten overlapping subgroups of the market will require a different approach from the partial hospital. Each market "segment" should be considered every six months so as to remain in touch with what it wants and will give in exchange.

After market analysis, the next basic steps of a marketing planning model are:

1) analysis of the organization's goals, performance abilities, and strong and weak points, and whether these are congruent with the PHP's submarkets;
2) analysis of the other treatment entities competing for the potential patients for your partial hospital; and
3) analysis of "marketing mix" (Simon, 1978). This includes analysis of "the four Ps."
   (a) (Product) services, e.g., Does your partial hospital offer something superior or distinctive to patients? to staff? to referring physicians? Which on your list of services is most praised? most complained about?
   (b) Price, e.g., What is the cost of each partial hospital visit and does reimbursement cover all the costs? Are the PHP's pricing policies viewed favorably by all your different market segments (patient, physicians, third-party payers, etc.)? What nonmonetary price do constituents have to pay? This may include a price in waiting time, loss of a sense of independence by patients and exposure to callous intake and dirty surroundings, etc.
   (c) Promotion, e.g., How do you promote a positive focus to overcome the pa-

tient's negative self-image that accompanies attendance at a mental health program? How do you organize public relations? Are all staff able to talk easily and comprehensively of the positive aspects of partial hospitalization compared to other treatments? What media do you use, and how do you measure their effectiveness? Does promotion search out new markets? Are you well publicized?

(d) Place-accessibility, e.g., How does your location affect the PHP? Can clients arrive within one hour's travel time? What distributors do you use? Is it easy and smooth-going for referring physicians to get an appointment for a patient? Is the referral form short and simple enough? Is the waiting list less than two weeks? These are but a few of the questions that can be asked.

Finally, select goals representing the best opportunities for the PHP, resulting from the above analysis; then, implement these!

The following is a hypothetical situation in which the staff are trying to satisfy all their various constituents. First, the type of health care that all segments of the populace want most is short episodes of compassionate, effective care as soon as they feel an urgent need (Bailey, 1973).

Office therapists most urgently want a program that will effectively treat their nonresponsive decompensating patients. Inpatient professionals want a program that will adequately treat patients they estimate are too mentally fragile to be discharged to the few hours offered by the the the traditional outpatient clinic. Both groups want uncomplicated acceptance of their patients with minimum intrusion on already hectic schedules (see Chapter 5 on admission).

Partial hospital employees want job satisfaction including using their clinical skills with resultant positive patient response without an exhausting schedule and with competitive compensation.

Third-party payers seek adequate care at the lowest cost, e.g., a substitute for inpatient care.

Based on the above it would seem advantageous to initially set up the type of PHP that offers a short-term crisis-support alternative to an inpatient program. For the problem of clinician bias toward nonselection of partial hospitals (Fink et al., 1978b), the head of the Admissions-Intake-Hotline-Walk-in-Unit(s) should at least consult regularly with the head of the partial hospital. The PHP admissions process should be carefully arranged. During hours the partial hospital is open, a caller must always be able to talk to a competent, calm, receptive, verbally clear admissions officer within five minutes, and some answer to the phone must occur by the fifth ring. The partial hospital should be set up so that an appointment can be given within two days. Even better is conveying an attitude embodied in such words as, "Sure, have them come right over." Forms should be streamlined. Duplicate paperwork should be minimized. When not interviewing and responding to calls, the "admission-interface officer" can be calling referral sources to promote the program and review procedures with referrers, etc.

In summary, to market is to comprehensively utilize all current knowledge and techniques that might assure that services given by producers (partial hospital staff) and the return of value (fee payment) given by recipients/consumers will occur efficiently and reliably and be of mutual benefit to all parties over the forseeable future. Marketing does not provide easy answers, but using it as a model does assure a responsive and comprehensive structure for planning for a successful partial hospital.

COMMUNITY RELATIONS—OBTAINING SUPPORT

Marketing concepts and techniques are also helpful in structuring and directing a partial hospital's effort at community relations. Good community relations are based on mutual knowledge, respect, and joint effort, but even more than these, interlocking needs and exchanges must exist for groups to have any real relationship. The goodwill of the community underlies many types of valued support to the partial hospital—namely, volunteer staff, students, advice, money, referrals, favorable laws, space or buildings, supplies, equipment, time, acceptance, and a more therapeutic stance toward patients. A minimal goal for partial hospitals is enough acceptance of the program so that clients will be referred and accepted by the community, despite the frequent negative views of the mentally ill held by the general public (Armstrong, 1976). (See also Chapter 9.)

These valuable items rarely flow into the partial hospital without planned expenditure of time and effort. Optimally, the partial hospital staff will have already done the work of segmenting the overall community. Since the resulting parts are still unwieldy groups, influential accepted leaders in each group should be sought out, and their alliance should be cultivated. By tickler file or check-off lists, one can be sure to maintain contact with them regularly. Some examples of people not to neglect are local politicians, newspaper staff, and members of formal political or planning groups (HSAs, community planning boards, etc.). Religious groups and parent/teacher organizations are also often productive contacts (Armstrong, 1976).

There need to be goals and methods for each community segment. A single person should be assigned the job of being the main coordinating contact person. Sometimes contacts will be made with a very specific goal in mind, e.g., a contribution for a fund-raising raffle. At other times, there is only a broader aim of continuing to create goodwill, exchange information, and move them from awareness of the partial hospital, to its use, to recommendation to others. Optimally, each staff member will see himself as an ambassador of the partial hospital. Thus, he shares information, cultivates understanding, promotes mental health needs, and shows partial hospital staff's trustworthiness, purposefulness, competency, energy, dedication, caring, and congeniality. Many opportunites for productive interchange will present themselves if only staff will remain alert to these and be willing to take advantage of them.

A program of formal and informal consultations is recommended, as it is "probably the single most effective tool for developing a broad base of community support" (Whittington, 1972, p. 138).

COMMUNITY RELATIONS—ACHIEVING FUNDING

There are examples of organizations that have been successful in obtaining financing (Garber, 1977; Guillette et al., 1978; Silber, 1974). Essentially there needs to be initially an attitude, nicely expressed by Eisenberg (1978), that professionals must not passively acquiesce to the politics and prejudice involved in underfunding mental health in the face of continuing conspicuous comsumption; instead, professionals should accept the obligation to act as advocates for patients.

After adopting this appropriate attitude, staff should analyze the problem of low-level revenues and its causes. Next mobilize resources (e.g., join up with other partial hospitals). Establish obtainable goals, e.g.:

1) studies to prove the value of the PHP;
2) medicaid approval of and payment to the partial hospital as a "provider"; and
3) insurance company funding of a pilot study in the PHP to study the value of replacing inpatient treatment with partial hospital treatment.

These are usually long-term goals. The important thing, as with all areas of partial hospital activity, is setting some goals and making some progress towards them.

24

Legal and Ethical Issues

Laws vary considerably in each level and type of government. Laws also vary for different patients. For example, in New York State, different laws apply to records of court-referred patients than to those referred under the more typical clinical circumstances (West, 1978). To interpret the complexities of the existing laws, judges and attorneys are required. Therefore, the purpose of this chapter is not to analyze specific laws, but to identify and heighten awareness of pertinent ethical and legal issues in partial hospitalization, for which legal consultation may be sought.

"VOLUNTARY" STATUS OF PHP PATIENTS
AND EXCEPTIONS TO THIS STATUS

Volumes of literature exist pertaining to involuntarily hospitalized and institutionalized patients; there is less written regarding outpatients; no information was found dealing with legal/ethical issues for partial hospitalization, specifically. Partial hospital patients are in the category of "outpatient" and usually "voluntary." A major reason for this paucity of literature is that, unlike outpatients, inpatients' civil liberties may be interrupted during the course of confinement to a hospital.

The word "voluntary" means, "brought about by one's own free choice; given or done of one's own free will; freely chosen or undertaken" (Guralnik and Friend, 1964). In most cases, PHP patients are legally voluntary. Important aspects of the state of "voluntary" as it pertains to PHP patients include the following:

1) patients rarely *want* to be mental patients (Ennis and Emery, 1978), therefore it seems contradictory that they would want to participate in a program for mental patients which, unfortunately, carries with it a social stigma;
2) patients entering PHPs often feel they have no desirable alternative, knowing they are at the time unable to cope with personal pressures;
3) patients may feel they cannot challenge the recommendations of referring physicians or therapists and accept referral to a PHP without question, often not understanding why they were referred; and

4) patients' families may offer ultimatums such as, "Get help or you cannot live with us."

The above situations, while not resulting in legal involuntary status, can result in patients' experiencing PHP as not really voluntary. It is important for staff to understand patients' feelings about being forced or coerced to attend PHP, and to help them deal with the subtle implications of involuntarism beneath the term "voluntary" by bringing it up for open discussion. Even so, involuntary participation does not necessarily preclude positive treatment results. Exceptions to legally voluntary PHP participation are those patients referred by legal systems, e.g., courts and bureaus of child welfare. (See Chapter 21 for discussion of clinical issues affecting court-referred patients.)

Staff should make a concerted effort to know the rights of PHP patients and the legalities involved in their treatment. For example, does the court-referred parolee have the right to refuse medication while attending the program? Would that refusal indicate a lack of court-ordered compliance and thus jeopardize the parole? The pressure on involuntary patients to "cooperate" can be great, and affords an easy way out of necessary, therapeutic negotiation/collaboration issues. Staff will need to be careful not to abuse their power.

THE RIGHT TO TREATMENT

According to Ennis and Emery (1978) ". . . voluntary patients. . .probably do not have a *constitutional* right to treatment" (p. 153). The constitution offers protection to those persons who have simultaneously been deprived of another constitutional right—in the case of involuntary patients, the right to liberty. It is not clear whether this would apply to involuntary PHP patients, e.g., within a "voluntary" environment.

Some states provide voluntary patients *statutory* rights to treatment (Ennis and Emery, 1978; Golann and Fremouw, 1976). In addition, others feel it is only right and just that every individual has the right to adequate treatment and the best opportunity for health. This is a hazy area; the terms "voluntary," "involuntary," "treatment," and "liberty" are subject to the vicissitudes of changing moral attitudes. PHP staff may be called upon by patients to answer questions pertaining to their rights to treatment, or what "treatment" is. It would be helpful for staff and patients to familiarize themselves with the applicable laws regarding rights to treatment.

THE RIGHT TO REFUSE TREATMENT

PHP patients do have the right to refuse treatment. However, a consequence of that refusal may be discharge or hospitalization, depending on the seriousness of the individual's condition. Such consequences of the refusal of treatment are complex and difficult for staff to carry out; they do reflect a type of bind, e.g., between allowing and developing a patient's free choice versus the responsibility placed on staff to treat and maintain a safe environment. Can staff accept responsibility for a patient's overall treatment when he does not adhere fully to what is clinically indicated? How and when do staff conclude, "We are sorry, but we can no longer treat you because of your lack of cooperation"?* Again, it is important that staff familiarize themselves with their state's statutes governing the right of a patient to refuse certain aspects of PHP (e.g., medication) while insisting on a right to treatment in the form of PHP participation.

Issues of this nature are often seen in PHPs; discharge from the program should not be used every time a patient refuses treatment as offered. Staff must carefully assess each situation, holding in check biases and rigid policies in order to consider the benefits of a patient's freedom to exercise his rights as long as they do not interfere with the rights of others. This includes the subtle rights of others in the PHP "family" to not be unduly worried or preoccupied about any one patient, who may be better helped by an alternative treatment approach.

THE DOCTRINE OF THE LEAST RESTRICTIVE ALTERNATIVE/ENVIRONMENT

The doctrine of the least restrictive alternative or environment (Bachrach, 1980) is a constitutionally based doctrine which prohibits involuntary commitment if a less restrictive alternative would preserve the basic right to liberty, while adequately complying with the purpose of the restriction. Only recently applied to the mental health field (Appelbaum 1980), this doctrine has far-reaching significance for partial hospitalization. Avoiding hospitalization whenever possible and striving for brief hospitalization with discharge to PHPs would help to insure that patients are not unduly deprived of their right to liberty. Exceptions would be during those times they are determined incompetent by due process, are actively in danger of harming themselves or others, or are otherwise unable to handle the most basic, life-sustaining care.

INVOLUNTARY HOSPITALIZATION

Patients may require hospitalization while participating in a PHP. It has become more difficult, in recent years, to hospitalize patients without "just cause," e.g., when they are in imminent danger of harm to self or others (Roth, 1980). However, this varies from state to state and institution to institution. In addition, the criteria for determining the need for hospitalization are inexact, and the expertise of those making the determination varies.

---

* The American Psychiatric Association includes, "Noncompliance with Medical Treatment" (V15.81) in its manual of mental disorders (Task Force, 1980).

PHPs have some advantage in determining the need for hospitalization of a PHP patient. Because of the long, intensive hours of treatment daily and/or weekly, patients are usually known better than is possible with most other forms of outpatient treatment. The patient is in constant contact with other patients and staff during program hours. Very little escapes notice, and when a patient begins to experience symptoms which could result in decompensation or hospitalization, early detection and intervention often prevent the need for hospitalization.

In some cases, the need for hospitalization is strongly evident, and it is unavoidable. For example, the patient has a clear plan of suicide, which he insists on carrying out promptly, and has a history of serious suicide attempts. When people are intimately involved with one another in PHP, the philosophical question of, "Does one have the right to control their death (to commit suicide)?" rarely emerges, at least during a crisis. All efforts are expended to prevent the person from harming himself. Other times, even with careful mandatory assessment, the case is not so clear; then it is better to be "safe than sorry" and hospitalize.

Concurrent with the above, staff must make every effort to preserve the rights and dignity of the patient. Staff tend to worry about the following: Do we have the right to break confidentiality and contact a patient's family or friends? Do we have the right to accompany the police into a suicidal patient's home and to transport him, against his will, to be hospitalized? Do we have the right to involuntarily hospitalize a patient because he is clearly threatening to harm another person—must we wait for "proof"? These pose challenging ethical, and even legal, considerations. It is not known how many people are alive who would not be if threatened suicides and homicides were not handled by prompt, preventive action (see Chapter 21).

Hospitalized patients often return to the PHP after a brief inpatient stay, in which PHP staff and patients have maintained involvement; thus, the PHP provides a high degree of continuity of care.

CONFIDENTIALITY

Will what is discussed in PHP remain in PHP or will it be broadcast to "outsiders," verbally or in writing? Keeping verbal confidentiality is a major and ongoing clinical issue in all forms of therapy. Although in groups it is rare that patients are requested to legally swear not to disclose information to persons outside the group, confidentiality is an important concept to stress in order to develop a greater sense of trust in the PHP's group treatment.

It is useful to keep in mind certain legal terms with respect to confidentiality (as well as other issues): "*Slander* is the utterance or spreading of a false statement or statements, harmful to another's character or reputation; *libel* is any written or printed statement, or any picture, sign or effigy, not made in the public interest, tending to expose a person to public ridicule or contempt, or to injure his reputation in any way" (Guralnik and Friend, 1964, p. 843).

The confidentiality of written material is also important. What rights do patients have for protecting their records? What becomes of records after patients are discharged? What becomes of information disclosed with consent to other parties? Do patients have the right to review their records? What does "consent to permit release of information" look like? What information should be placed in records? These are but a few of the questions that are raised.

Most states have statutes providing for confidentiality of mental hospital records (Ennis and Emery, 1978), and they indicate that states vary in specifications regarding confidentiality—to whom the material may be disclosed. For example, within a particular mental health system, there may be no precautions used to prevent disclosure of patient information between various components of that system.

These statutes vary greatly at different levels, and it is important that PHP staff be well aware of the rules regulating confidentiality in their PHP, city and state. In addition, staff should be aware of specific professional groups' professional standards regarding confidentiality (The American Psychiatric Association, National Association of Social Workers, etc.).

It may become tempting in the course of hard work and tight schedules for PHP staff to "bend the rules"—to consider disclosing information about a patient without a signed, informed consent to release information. This is neither clinically nor legally sound. Staff must take special care to protect these rights. The Joint Commission on the Accreditation of Hospitals (JCAH, 1979) has outlined the content of an appropriate written consent to release of information. It would be worthwhile for PHPs to follow this outline. In addition, it would be wise for staff to consult with their State's Attorney General's office regarding even written consent for information release, particularly if the information may be used as legal evidence against a patient's wishes.

"Open-ended" releases (consent to release of information forms signed by patients for future use) are not recommended. While those for a specified time may be legally valid, it is preferable that written consents for release of information be completed for each specific request, and that the patient is competent to understand and is fully informed of the reason for the release of information, and who the recipient is. There is little difficulty with sharing this information with patients when appropriate, often to the point of their reading the material which is being released. This practice allows the patients to be fully aware of what is going on in their treatment, to proofread for possible factual errors, and to develop a greater sense of trust in the PHP.

The issue of patients having access to their records varies considerably between institutions, cities and states. In some states it is strictly prohibited. In some private institutions it is left to the discretion of the administration or therapist. In other settings, rules are set according to each situation. It is important to establish clear policies around this issue, reflecting both sound clinical and legal practices. Requests to review records arise invariably in PHPs and should be carefully evaluated in each case. Frequently this request masks other concerns, e.g., "Can we trust you (staff) to understand and be objective?" and "What do you (staff) really think—and write—about us?" If the decision is to allow (or as may be their legal right) a patient to read his record, it will be important for staff to consider whether it would be clinically indicated for a PHP clinical staff member to sit with the patient while he reviews the record, to deal with anxiety-laden material which may arise.

LEGAL CONSIDERATIONS FOR STAFF

It is not unusual for PHP staff to rather naively assume responsibilities without being aware of possible legal ramifications. Some questions and examples will be mentioned here, though, undoubtedly, many others are possible:

1) When staff are hired to work in a PHP are they covered for professional malpractice/liability under the umbrella of the PHP? In most cases this is not an issue; occasionally, however, professionals must purchase their own insurance to cover their PHP work. This information can be obtained through the facility's personnel management or through professional group regulatory bodies.
2) Are PHP staff fully covered by insurance when they take PHP patients outside the PHP itself?
3) Are patients insured when they are traveling to and from a PHP and to and from PHP activities located on different premises?
4) If the PHP utilizes community facilities for their program, e.g., gymnasiums or pools, do these facilities meet with the safety standards required for insurance protection by the PHP policy?
5) If staff use their personal automobile to transport patients, are they covered by the facility's insurance or by personal insurance for this purpose?
6) When third party payments are received, are all regulations pertaining to this payment strictly adhered to by the PHP?

THE ROLE OF THE MENTAL HEALTH PROFESSIONAL
AS ADVOCATE OF PATIENT RIGHTS

It is essential for staff to familiarize themselves with the rights of patients. Since there are some complex differences in laws and policies regulating nearly all of the issues mentioned here, it is recommended that each PHP obtain legal assistance in answering questions specific to their program and to draw up a document of patients' rights (such as Allen (1976) offers) and update it regularly. There are several groups which offer such legal services, some free of charge, such as the office of the State Attorney General, and those mentioned by Ennis and Emery (1978, pp. 216–219). In addition, each PHP professional's code of ethics and standards should provide further specific guidelines.

25

Developing and Maintaining Staff Teams

After staff have been hired, how will they function together and obtain job satisfaction? This chapter addresses how staff will operate as a well-integrated unit. Issues to be considered are the stages of staff group development, establishing staff team integration, providing educational input staff, and finally the many problems in maintaining staff teams.

Staff group process must be appreciated, understood and respected from the onset, or effective treatment for patients will never occur. Suppressing staff group process or using sensitivity groups or T-groups to speed up the development of the staff relationships can lead to dismal failure.

Numerous writers have developed a variety of theoretical constructs on the stages of group development. One of the clearest and most usable frameworks is presented by Garland, Jones, and Kolodny (1973). They define five stages of group development, including:

Stage 1: Pre-Affiliation — Approach and Avoidance
Stage 2: Power and Control
Stage 3: Intimacy
Stage 4: Differentiation
Stage 5: Separation

Using the above model, each stage or group development will be discussed, followed by a presentation of typical staff behaviors that occur during each stage.

This knowledge can be used by those in staff and leadership positions in PHPs to gain some insight into where interventions might be made in the staff group process so as to facilitate the staff moving from one stage to the next.

Stage 1: Pre-Affiliation — Approach and Avoidance

Members are getting to know one another. Close bonds among staff have not

268

been established, and the pervasive question, "Is this a safe place?" is being asked by all. Staff are conflicted about, on the one hand, wanting to be members of the group and gaining the potential satisfactions from it, and, on the other hand, wanting to avoid the group because of its unknown present or potential character. Investments in the group are ambivalent and dependency on leadership for direction and meeting needs is high. Members use societal groups they have been familiar with rather than their own families for their frame of reference.

Typical Staff Behaviors in Stage 1

1) Comparisons are made to previous work settings or community groups in which staff are or have been involved.
2) Discussions tend to be superficial with few real differences of opinion.
3) Staff allow themselves to be interrupted in staff meetings or other PHP activities.
4) Staff are late to staff and patient meetings.
5) Staff may discuss plans to remain in the program for only a short period of time because of other job possibilities, dissatisfactions with the present setting, etc.
6) There is great difficulty in defining the purposes and contracts for various staff groups.
7) Staff fluctuates between volunteering readily for assignments, and then sometimes not completing the assignment adequately or not volunteering for any more assignments.

Stage 2: Power and Control

As soon as they have been able to establish a feeling of safety, the staff then begin to struggle with and test each other and the leader to determine status and rank. Competition, subgrouping for support and protections, as well as scapegoating, are not unusual in this transitional stage. The group is unlike other groups the staff member is involved in outside the PHP.

Typical Staff Behaviors in Stage 2

1) There are strong alliances among two or several staff members. There are sometimes more than one set of alliances and they are frequently formed on the basis of sex, age, race and discipline.
2) Disciplines emphasize the distinctness and importance of their professional roles.
3) Members compete with each other and the leader in staff meetings and co-led patient meetings for who has the best or most accurate viewpoint.
4) There is a reluctance to reveal weak areas of work.

5) There is a reluctance to share the content or process of individually led groups.
6) Co-leading groups is often problematic and difficult. For example, in community meetings staff members might talk more with one another, rather than responding to patients.
7) In staff meetings there is a general inability to cover an entire agenda or reach firm conclusions.
8) There are verbal attacks against PHP supervisory/administrative personnel or other such personnel connected with the program. Generally the comments deal with complaints about lack of caring and understanding for the PHP.

Stage 3: Intimacy

If the dust finally settles from the strife of Stage 2, the group members usually move into a more trusting, caring concern for each other and the work. There is an increased ability to carry work projects to completion. The frame of reference is the family and usually not groups in the larger societal structure. In particular, there is a focus on the sibling aspect of familial relationships.

Typical Staff Behaviors in Stage 3

1) Staff members discuss their own family events in staff meetings as well as at informal gatherings. Not infrequently, they compare their own families to various staff members.
2) Friendships and "chum" relationships develop. They are very different from the subgroups formed in Stage 1. Stage 3 relationships are formed out of interest in one another, while Stage 1 relationships are formed for protection and survival.
3) Staff work more smoothly together. They are much more able to complete the discussion of entire agendas, plan changes in program and co-lead groups than they had been able to in earlier stages of group development.
4) There is increased ability to make long-range plans.
5) There is sharing of weaknesses and an increased ability to give and receive criticisms.
6) Countertransferential material is more openly shared.
7) There is more cooperative work in groups and volunteering to cover for one another during absences. There is concern for the health of an absent staff member.

Stage 4: Differentiation

At this stage of group development, staff group members become comfortable enough with each other to respect and appreciate individual strengths and weaknesses. Individuals are appreciated for the unique contributions that they can make to the program. In addition, the leader is looked at more realistically and objectively for his abilities. The staff group is given more credence and value as a means for providing a distinct service for patients as well as fulfilling the needs of staff. The frame of reference is the group itself, as there is a heightened sense of group identity.

Typical Staff Behaviors in Stage 4

1) Staff lead groups on the basis of abilities and not professional degrees. For example, the clinical psychologist asks to organize a cooking group, while the social worker expresses interest in organizing and supervising volunteers in groups.
2) There is stronger interest in each other's professional development. For example, members may tell one another about seminars in their special areas of interest.
3) Co-led groups become less competitive and the amount of activity the leaders take depends on the skill and knowledge of the individual leader at a given moment, rather than his professional status.
4) Staff discussions are focused on objective facts rather than personalities.
5) There is more acceptance of deviance in staff members and less gossiping behind closed doors about a typical characteristics of a staff member or unusual things that he might have done.
6) There is more serious discussion of long-range, complex planning.
7) There is an active examination of other PHP groups to determine what can be learned from them and what can be offered in return.
8) There is more focus on integrating the PHP into other community service groups such as outpatient clinics, hospital services and sheltered workshops.
9) The limitations, strengths, and responsibilities of the PHP leader are more objectively and clearly seen by staff. Staff initiate discussions and problem-solving on patient and program issues without waiting for the "administration" to do so.

Stage 5: Separation

In this stage, members of the group have attained the satisfactions they desire from the PHP, and they are ready to move to other groups for professional gratification. This, of course, does not usually happen to an entire staff of a PHP concurrently, but does occur to one or two members periodically as they acquire positions of advancement, more challenge in other settings, etc. As members separate, they demonstrate the classical symptoms of loss, i.e., denial, anger, regression, recapitulation of the group experience, and, finally, some evaluation and resolution of the group experience.

Typical Staff Behaviors in Stage 5

1) Departing members may be reluctant or unwilling to announce their departure to other staff or patients and need encouragement in doing so. Likewise, they may need help in working through the termination process with patients.
2) There may be regression to some aspects of earlier stages of group development.
3) There is a recounting of past group events and personal involvements.
4) A departing staff member may become overly involved in a treatment situation or in long-range patient or staff-planning process.
5) A staff member may suddenly withdraw from the program by having numerous absences after his announcement of termination, or he may be unresponsive to patients in the PHP when he is present.
6) There may be a pervasive atmosphere of tension and anger among staff and patients.

In conclusion, staff usually move backward and forward through the stages of group development, often making a number of progressive and regressive moves before they make a firm advancement to the next stage. The movement of the group is affected by many factors, not the least of which being the composition of the staff group and how well the members gel together.

Another important factor is the leadership skills and intervention abilities of the staff group leader and his powers to implement the above in moving the group from one stage of group development to the next. Also to be considered are the agency structure and its demands. For example, if a PHP is only a part of the staff member's assignment, it might take him longer to integrate himself into a PHP staff than if he were on the full-time staff of the PHP.

STAFF TEAM INTERRELATIONSHIPS

Given the preceding overview of typical stages of group development and their concurrent range of behaviors, the process of building effective working relationships among PHP staff teams will be discussed. The focus in this section is on formal staff meetings as the arena for developing effective, satisfying working patterns. Obstacles to the development of team relationships and leadership skills required to facilitate high quality teamwork are reviewed. There will also be suggestions for organizing staff meetings which promote adherence to patient-focused work.

The basic task ("contract") of PHP staff is helping patients enter, negotiate, and benefit from a partial hospital system. Staff groups are often faced with obstacles to this work. These obstacles, some indicative of group developmental stages and others illustrative of problems within the PHP, all present valuable material for learning about the group processes in the therapeutic milieu.

1) *Staff Utilization of Staff Group Meetings to Consistently Focus on Their Own Group Processes*

PHP staff groups invariably spend some time examining their own group process as a means of overcoming obstacles to their working together as a team. When this becomes the main focus of staff meetings it is indicative of underlying problems, although some programs develop a staff meeting specifically designed to discuss staff relations.

A major source of the focus on staff group process concerns staff's own reality needs for nurturance. It is acknowledged that mental health professionals frequently subject themselves to mental strain by expending so much effort in their work that there is little energy or time left for their own professional or personal needs (Pines and Kafry, 1978; Resnick, 1979; Scholom and Perlman, 1979). However, staff demands to focus attention on themselves (claiming no energy to attend to the demands of a staff meeting with a patient-focused agenda) can have implications beyond the sincere recognition of staff needs expressed in terms of "getting away" from the PHP. This situation could imply the presence of problems in the entire community which require attention before giving the green light to escape.

Ineffective treatment interventions can be a source of loss of esteem among staff groups, can result in feelings of gloom, anger, and exhaustion, often masked by the expressed need for external solace or nourishment. For example, a patient exhibiting uncontrolled manic behavior which taxes an entire community's tolerance can underlie staff's need for a break. Locating the source(s) of the energy drain and formulating effective treatment interventions can afford relief and reinvigoration.

Yet another source of staff's need to focus on themselves lies in efforts to cope with external change. For example, a dedicated PHP staff, informed of being "phased out" by their funding source, may need to band together in order to defend themselves against the overwhelming sense of helplessness and anxiety accompanying such news.

Suggestions for resolution. PHP leaders need a good understanding of group dynamics. They must be able to determine when work is underway, when obstacles are interfering with the work, and how to effectively intervene. There is a need for a strong mutual support system for staff to withstand the stress involved in their ". . . incessant and chronic search for ways to help troubled people" (Pines and Kafry, 1978, p.499).

The leader must be a source of nurturance to the staff in terms of support, direction, objectivity, availability, knowledge and positive expectations, without giving up the demand for quality work. The effective leader also serves as mediator between PHP staff and the larger organizational structure, thereby relieving staff of some of the external pressures of dealing with administrative problems.

Staff may focus on themselves when they are feeling insecure about their roles or status. These feelings can lead to, or result from, feelings of rivalry, competition, etc. To minimize the possibility of these feelings being acted out, it is important that the leader exhibit equal caring and attention to all staff in the group (Freud, 1955). Favoritism, or even assumed favoritism, can lead to schisms in staff unity and can undermine their ability to function in a secure, mature way. The leader must be able to encourage independence and to hear and work with criticism from the staff. Paradoxically, staff autonomy can result in greater cohesion and harmony.

2) *Inability of Staff to be Clear on Their Main Purpose of Working Together*

If this problem results mostly from an early stage of the staff group's development, it usually ceases to be problematic as the group advances into other developmental stages. If, however, it persists beyond a few weeks, it may be indicative of other problems. It could illustrate insecurity on the part of the leader to insist that the staff examine their purpose and goals and come to grips with the tasks needed to accomplish them. Or, perhaps the more basic purpose or goals of the entire PHP are not clear. Some questions to keep in mind concerning the problem of ambiguity are: (a) What is the parent organization's (hospital or other governing and funding bodies) concept of the PHP? and (b) what are the staff's individual concepts of the purpose of the PHP?

Suggestions for resolution. It is important for PHP staff to be ever cognizant of the purpose and goals of their PHP; therefore, it is useful for staff to have access to and periodically review the formal program proposal. Staff may find themselves at odds with a formally stated program definition, e.g., one which stresses short-term care, when staff believe longer-term treatment is more beneficial to their patients. If there are differences in understanding, it is necessary to establish whether these can be bridged, or changes should be initiated.

If, upon examination, the organizational and staff conceptions of program purpose are similar enough to eliminate the possibility of confusion due to conceptual differences, then attention must be focused on other possibilities. It is important for the staff leader, consultant, or staff members to be able to judge when issues are normal to a particular phase, or problematic.

If the above suggestions do not prove helpful, it is suggested that an objective outsider who is experienced in groups be asked to observe and/or conduct meetings and consult with staff on their difficulties in establishing clear, constructive ways of working together in staff meetings

3) *Staff Lateness to Staff and/or Patient Meetings*

This may be a symptomatic dramatization of an early phase of group development. If so, the wise administrator will continue to express positive expectations regarding punctuality without labeling it as a problem unless there is sufficient evidence to confront it as problematic.

Underlying causes of lateness can be simple or complex. It may be one staff member's nonverbal manner of expressing a desire to be recognized, needed or appreciated. Another staff member may use lateness to express hostility. When staff arrive consistently late to staff meetings, anger is usually being displayed toward administrative personnel, and may involve conflicted feelings about authority figures.

The issue of lateness may be indicative of staff feeling overwhelmed and overworked. If there is a pattern of lateness, time schedules may need examining, as it is a tendency for PHPs and their staff to run nonstop several hours each day.

This pattern may also represent an issue of competitveness regarding which staff are doing the most work, which staff are the most needed by patients, etc. Or, a staff member may feel his status in the community is lacking in importance and that groups can do just as well without him.

Interpersonal differences between staff also contribute to reluctance to attend staff or patient group meetings where other staff are present. Fear of confrontation by fellow staff, verbal expression or exposure of anger, or insecurity can result in staff attempting to avoid uncomfortable situations.

Suggestions for resolution. It is important that administrators know their staff (Hersey and Blanchard, 1972). For some staff this problem can be effectively handled in group; for others, individual exploration may be indicated in order to reach an understanding and resolution. Discussing the problem individually may allow some staff members to raise it in staff group meeting, if, for example, the behavior is significantly affecting patient care or effective teamwork.

It is also important for staff leaders to be positive role models. They convey this through their own appropriate behavior of being consistently on time for meetings, thereby conveying the expectation that the work is important, even when it is fun; lateness is not expected or condoned and meetings begin on time. This situation is often corrected over time by just this kind of role-modeling leadership.

A final suggestion is that the staff leader be well aware of the process in the PHP community: Is lateness an individual staff member's personal problem or is it representative of other problems? Is it a situation of scapegoating, where one or two staff are exhibiting the problems of an entire staff or program? If patients are manifesting an increase in lateness coinciding with staff lateness, this may very well indicate that a problem has developed in the community which everyone is unaware of or feels unable to handle. If so, the issue can be raised in community meetings.

The major obstacles discussed above are typical of PHP staff meetings. Others include—but are certainly not limited to—the following:

1) *Scheduling of staff meetings late in the day or on Friday afternoon.* Staff meetings at these times tend to be "tired," more superficial, blanketly supportive and less productive.

2) *Insufficient time allocation for staff meetings.* This can result in superficially addressing numerous issues which require more time—the dilemma of, "We begin everything and finish nothing."

3) *Anxieties regarding the development of staff intimacy.* Do staff really want to work in the PHP or with one another, or do they feel they have no choice?

4) *Fear of success or failure.* This could reflect individual personal insecurities, or pressures to make the PHP work. Unclear expectations of what a successful PHP is, with no clear-cut guidelines on which to base realistic expectations, contribute to the problem.

5) *Staff's negative expectations of patients or disgruntled professionals.* Attitudes, such as "Nothing is going to make us/these patients better," or "What makes you think this program is any different from any other that hasn't helped?", inhibit the beneficial working of staff groups.

The brief outline of suggestions for organizing staff meetings that follows can facilitate adherence to the patient-focused work while allowing flexibility to recognize and address obstacles as they arise.

Organizing Staff Meetings

1) The entire PHP staff are involved in deciding what types of staff meetings are crucial to their program (see Chapter 5).
2) Purposes (verbal or recorded) are established for each staff meeting. For example, Intake Conference: "In this meeting staff will discuss the referred patient in terms of the formal referral papers, impressions of the intake interviewer, those of patients who participated in the intake, and all other available information (charts, history, letters, etc.). We will then determine if our program is the best one for this patient. If so, we will establish primary treatment goals and plans."
3) Staff meetings are mandatory, with a clear expectation that they are a time for working.
4) Agendas are important for guiding and establishing a sense of importance through formality. They may be developed in a number of ways:
   (a) drawn up at the end of a meeting by the staff, covering issues to be carried forth at the next meeting;
   (b) developed and recorded briefly at the beginning of a staff meeting;
   (c) written and distributed by the PHP director prior to any meeting, with space left for revisions, additions, etc.; and
   (d) developed by various staff for different meetings, following the previous suggestion (c).

There is generally considerable resistance to using agendas. They may be enthusiastically received and later forgotten or considered not necessary or important. This may happen if agendas become too standardized or if they do not accurately reflect the issues in need of discussion. For agendas to prove useful, it is essential that the staff member responsible for them be acutely sensitive to the ongoing process in the PHP community.

Discontinuing the use of agendas can be another obstacle to the work, for it can lead to an overly relaxed or free-floating focus in staff meetings where the least obvious issues—and sometimes the most glaring—are avoided, with sanction.

It is important to identify obstacles to effective staff working relationships, and offer suggestions for recognizing and resolving them. However, too much of this is also a serious obstacle to the potential effectiveness of PHP staff teams, i.e., a pessimism arriving from incessant soul-searching and an inclination to be problem-focused. It is crucial for staff to build in another routine element to their staff meetings: What accomplishments have been made? What can we feel good about in our work together as a team? These convey that staff are basically pulling in the same direction and are capable of effecting positive change through their collective and dedicated efforts. These are too often taken for granted and rarely verbalized, though they can have as much positive impact on the esteem of a staff team as searching for problems and ways to improve the work.

CONTINUING EDUCATION: SUPERVISION, CONSULTATION, INSERVICE TRAINING, AND OUTSIDE CONFERENCES

Questions continually arise concerning what treatment interventions should be made, why staff are reacting so strongly to one or a few patients, why a particular patient is behaving the way he is, to name but a few. Unless there are formalized structure and methods for dealing with the above questions, staff tend to become frustrated and overwhelmed, and feel generally incompetent to handle their jobs. Evidence of this includes listlessness, depression, self-flagellation, increased levels of physical illness with a concurrent increase in absences from work, and discussion about or actual resignations. PHP staff need a constant input into their clinical skills to support their feeling that they can handle their jobs and to experience maximum job satisfaction.

The necessary intellectual/emotional nurturance to PHP staff is basically provided by four different types of input—supervision, consultation, inservice training, and outside conferences. All four types of input are needed and have unique importance. Supervision is of value because PHP staff must be directly accountable to someone for their work. They must also have a framework to identify practice strengths and problems so that they can develop the former and correct the latter. Consultation with experts in particular areas is important because it provides staff with an outside viewpoint that can be more objective and stimulating than they could obtain from their own personnel. Inservice training provides the opportunity for staff to receive formalized didactic, theoretical and experiential material that is difficult to obtain to any large extent in either supervision or consultation. Outside conferences can provide material and experiences which are relevant but unavailable locally.

Supervision

The person who gives supervision varies in PHPs. Some programs are relatively self-contained and supervisors come from within. Others are connected to larger institutions and various members within the PHP identify with a designated professional department and receive their primary supervision from that department. Of the types of supervisory structures used, internal supervisory structure, even though it may cross disciplinary lines, is preferable because information is directed out of the PHP when discussed by a supervisee with his supervisor outside the PHP. The areas identified in the latter arrangement may become largely lost to the rest of the PHP staff and therefore are not worked on as group issues.

The role of the supervisor can be problematic in a PHP. He serves simultaneously as peer, boss, and observer. For example, he may be relatively inactive in an administrative community meeting in the morning and watch several supervisees take prime leadership responsibility in the group. In the activity group which follows community meeting he may co-lead the group with one of his supervisees. Finally, in a supervisory session at the end of the work day, he may hear displaced angry feelings toward a patient from one of his supervisees. All the above suggest that the supervisor and staff need to learn to redefine their traditional authority relationships so that they can be more fluid. This problem is probably never totally resolved and therefore demands attention in staff discussion at various times in the program.

Supervisory structures vary, but one that is strongly suggested is a combination of complementary individual and group supervision within the same PHP. Individual supervision not only provides a forum for PHP clinicians to work on practice areas, but also provides a framework for resolving individual issues such as vacation times, job deficiencies and individual professional evaluation. Group supervision is valuable because it provides group support for staff in dealing with difficult patient issues. It also allows staff to be clearer with each other about the strengths and problems each possesses to offer realistic feedback from their observations of each other's work in the program. It would be ideal if group supervision could develop to the point that individual supervision would no longer be needed regularly and most supervision could occur in the context of the group, including evaluations of each other's work. Typical patient issues that would be discussed in both individual and group supervision include planning strategies for treatment interventions and identifying reactions to patients, concurrent with their origins and effects on treatment.

Consultation

Consultation provides staff with the opportunity of discussing an issue without the consultant being a supervisor. No matter how benignly advisory a supervisory relationship is, there are always the threads of accountability, responsibility, and evaluation involved, which elements do influence what is disclosed in the supervisory relationship. On the other hand, consultation is normally more free from these strictures, even with the supervisor present, and affords to many the opportunity of being more open to disclosing their weaknesses, insecurities, and problems.

Consultants may be obtained from a variety of sources including outside community agencies as well as the treatment suprasystem of which the PHP is a part. Often, there is the feeling in PHPs that only a consultant from an outside agency can offer a truly valid consultation. Additionally, there is sometimes the impression that a consultant must have a reputation. Neither of these premises have much validity and, in addition, such consultants are often beyond the reach of many PHPs due to the very limited financial resources in their budgets. In fact, most often PHPs feel fortunate if they have enough funding to maintain normal operational expenditures.

This leaves PHPs in the position of obtaining low-cost or free consultations from their own treatment system or from the occasional good-willed community consultant who can be persuaded to give his services for minimal or no cost. Unfortunately, there has been a tendency not to use resources within the PHP's system. Helpful, supportive, informative consultants can indeed be found many times in the PHP's own suprasystem. For example, the chief of occupational therapy might consult on the best utilization of space and materials for low-cost activities that could be used for a large number of patients; an experienced social worker might be asked to discuss treatment strategies to be used in a complex family situation; and a staff psychologist might be called in to discuss psychological testing and its use in treatment planning.

Consultations can be used for a broad spectrum of topics, including patient and program planning issues. Two key problems, however, frequently emerge in the process of obtaining consultants. One is that there is a tendency to have experts present material that is quite interesting, but it may not be the most relevant information for the PHP. For example, a relatively new program might get a consultant on family network therapy, when, in fact, what is most needed is a consultant on planning the initial sessions of a family night. A second problem is clarifying with the consultant the focus or expectations of the consultation. For example, staff may ask for a consultation on the general area of adolescence when in fact what they really wanted is help in dealing with some specific problematic acting-out behaviors of a PHP adolescent patient. This latter problem can usually be resolved by PHP staff meeting together, formulating specific questions and issues to be raised, and then sharing these with the consultant in advance.

Inservice Training

Most PHPs are affiliated with systems or institutions which offer lectures, courses, etc. Staff often experience such learning in these settings as direct "feeding." Sometimes the psychological impact of this "feeding" or knowledge that their administrative/supervisory personnel are concerned enough to see that they obtain such an educational experience is as valuable as any specific learning they may receive. If PHP staff are doing their job correctly, they are expending a quantity of emotional and physical energy. A limited time allotted each week by administration/supervisory personnel to PHP staff for the purpose of "recharging" themselves is a valuable part of the staff member's overall work schedule.

One recurring problem with inservice training is keeping abreast of the types of training being offered, where they are being offered, how to apply for them and what gains could be expected by attending a specific lecture, course, etc. This information is usually easily obtained if lines of communication have been established and maintained, but, since this is not always an easy task, it is wise to designate a specific staff member or members as education and training resource persons. This would be an integral part of their job assignment. They would keep staff posted in meetings on the upcoming programs and courses being offered and how to obtain admissions. Also, this staff would maintain a bulletin board in the PHP unit on upcoming inservice training programs.

Outside Conferences

Specialized professional discipline conferences can be stimulating to any PHP staff member and should be encouraged, especially for those PHP staff members who work in rural settings and have little contact with other professionals. This is problematic if the conference is held some distance from the PHP because funds for travel, lodgings, and registration fees are difficult to obtain in most PHP budget requests. However, support to PHP staff at a minimal level can be demonstrated by allowing each staff member three or four days of salaried conference time yearly. This will encourage staff to at least participate locally in conferences. In addition, staff should be given compensatory time for attendance at local partial hospitalization study groups or chapter meetings of the American Association for Partial Hospitalization. Ideally, at least one staff member from each PHP should attend the annual September meeting of the American Association for Partial Hospitalization.

MAINTAINING STAFF TEAMS

When PHP staff have struggled arduously to overcome major obstacles to the development of effective program and teamwork, the work of maintaining them demands immediate, consistent, and ongoing attention. In this section, various aspects of PHP which affect staff morale, effectiveness, and productivity are discussed.

Staff Vacations

When a small number of staff work together in the same limited space, vacations occur frequently and regularly. Staff, partly because they need vacations and want to feel they can depart from the PHP with "good cheer" from patients and other staff, find it difficult, time after time, to recognize or deal with the disruption in the community which their vacations (or other absences) engender. Staff often do not perceive that for many patients separations are synonymous with termination (see Chapter 21). Patient absences tend to increase during staff vacations, as if they were taking their own vacations or abandoning the source of the abandonment experienced. Gootnick (1975) mentions the hostility experienced by schizophrenic patients when faced with staff vacations, staff's negative countertransference reactions to the hostility, and staff's responsibility for dealing with the issue, e.g., by increased staff activity, which dilutes the intense transference and countertransference feelings and allows the issue to be dealt with more positively.

Staff must be aware of the ramifications of their taking vacations and it is essential that they give adequate notice of vacation plans, so the PHP community can have time to react to and plan for the anticipated loss of the staff member as well as to any program changes. Three to four weeks' notice for a lengthy vacation (two to five weeks) is suggested and one to two weeks' notice for shorter absences. It is also important to have adequate coverage during staff vacations. While most staff are willing to distribute and assume much of the vacationing person's work assignment, it is often necessary to consider minor program revision or reduction to avoid the remaining staff being overwhelmed by the responsibilities of running a full program with reduced staff.

The issue of vacations can mask conflicts involving staff relationships. The manner in which vacations are handled reflects the staff's ability to work maturely together. The staff who struggle so long to work out vacation schedules that there is barely time to announce their leaving are experiencing problems around handling the issue of separation and must be helped to examine and deal with the problem appropriately.

Termination

Under this category the major types of staff terminations in PHPs are resignation, involuntary terminations, and death.

Resignation. Not unlike the disruption which results from vacations or other absences, feelings increase in intensity when a staff member announces a permanent, planned departure from the PHP. It is especially difficult if the individual has been with the program for a long time, and/or is "popular," or if he has held a position of leadership.

During the stress of early phases of termination, PHP communities often regress to earlier stages of group development. Some patients or staff may feel the PHP will disintegrate without a particular staff member. This may be the case if the individual leaving is the director, and if the staff group has not reached a mature stage of development. An element of contagion may develop, also, with other staff and patients hinting at or declaring their own resignations, often setting a date close to that given by the original resigner.

Staff should take care to not mistake the typical *denial* of feelings or reactions about a recent announcement of termination (see Chapter 21) for *absence* of feelings or reactions. For example, a staff member seeking reactions to his announced resignation in a community meeting met with general silence and occasional comments from patients such as, "We'll miss you," "Good luck," and "That's too far away to even think about." Staff may accept these responses because they can become so self-involved around their terminations that they either feel they are imposing the importance of their leaving on others, or they are reluctant to deal with their own guilt and others' anger about their decision to leave.

Unresolved conflicts regarding separations and loss on the part of staff can inhibit their ability to deal with the issue effectively. The PHP leader can help by taking an active role in helping staff deal with their own feelings while also helping them understand the impact of the termination on the entire community. We recommend at least four weeks and preferably six weeks be given for work on termination, from the time of the first announcement to the actual departure. This time period is particularly useful if the PHP is of a long-term nature.

Involuntary staff terminations. The issue of "forced resignation" or "firing" of PHP staff is always stressful. The actual termination usually follows a lengthy process of problem identification, measures for resolving problems and, when these prove fruitless, termination. Involvement of unions can also significantly prolong definitive action.

It is imperative that PHP administration utilize precaution in assessing "problematic" staff, e.g., making every effort to rule out scapegoating and displacement. If a staff member has a consistently poor record of attendance and/or dependability, engages in destructive encounters with patients or other staff, and/or has emotional problems which prevent appropriate involvement with patients, he must be provided sufficient supervision and/or other supports to determine whether adequate improvements can be made.

Routine use should be made of staff probationary periods, and problems must be openly recognized and attempts made to work on them during this time. Flagrantly inappropriate behavior, such as striking a patient or engaging in sexual activity with a patient, are normally grounds for immediate dismissal.

Staff who are experiencing problems in their PHP work can rarely conceal this fact from other staff and patients. Skillful and sensitive handling is required to prevent acting out, either on the part of the staff member experiencing difficulty or other staff and patients. If the problematic staff member feels unjustly treated (and he often does), he may attempt to solicit "allies" among other staff as well as among patients, resulting in collusive behavior which can have a lasting negative effect on the PHP community. If a PHP administrator has been consistently open about discussing the individual's problems with him and has demonstrated an appropriate time-limited willingness to help the person with his work-related problem areas to no avail, the next step is to help that person terminate from the program with as much dignity, self-respect, and lack of disruption as possible.

Death of a Staff Member. No other type of separation from PHP carries with it the irrevocable finality of a death. Whatever the cause, the impact of the death of a staff member on the PHP "family" is tremendous. Members must deal with the situation thoroughly and immediately in order to ". . . achieve emancipation from the bondage to the deceased, readjustment to the environment in which the deceased is missing, and the formation of new relationships" (Lindemann, 1965, pp. 10-11).

There may be strong resistance to dealing effectively with death in PHPs. Some staff, fearing patients will regress or become severely depressed, may address the issue briefly and move on to other matters. Some patients, particularly regressed chronic schizophrenics, may manifest no need to deal with their feelings, since their frequent lack of appropriate affect can be mistaken for lack of attachment to or feelings about the deceased.

During the mourning period, staff may find it helpful to educate themselves and patients about various reactions associated with death, as another means of mastering and coping with the situation. In addition to normal grief reactions, staff should be aware of pathological grief reactions, which represent distortions of normal grief. These may include delayed reactions and distorted reactions, as discussed by Lindemann (1965). (See also Chapter 21.)

The length of time needed to work through grief may vary from two weeks to many months, depending on the particular patient population and the staff's skill in dealing with it. Feelings about a deceased staff member which are not worked through to some resolution may have serious implications regarding the prognosis of success for anyone attempting to fill the position. The new person may be the object of stressful, distorted transference reactions, making acceptance as a "replacement" difficult.

New Staff

A new staff member hired to fill a vacancy is often confronted with the need to continue the work of termination from the previous staff member. This is more difficult when patients and staff express predominantly positive feelings about the replaced staff member and pay little attention to or express disappointment in the efforts of the new staff member. It is important, during this phasing-in process, for the new staff member to be aware of his own feelings and the meaning behind some of the attitudes and behaviors displayed toward him. For example, it is likely that a new staff member may experience feelings of anger at being ignored, not readily accepted or compared with previous staff members. Rather than responding to the manifest content of these reactions, it is helpful to keep in mind the various stages of group development to help understand the level of group process which he has moved into. It cannot be expected that a PHP community will accept a newcomer with open arms; indeed, one should wonder about being accepted too quickly and without reservation, as this can be an attempt to cover up more ambivalent feelings. It is wise for new staff to be patient, lonely as it may be, and to let the group process include him in a meaningful way when it is able. Usually within three to five weeks there are beginning signs of real acceptance. However, approximately four to six months is the length of time for a new staff member to become a fully integrated into the team.

Status and Role Changes

Over time, staff members may experience a variety of role and status changes: marriage, promotions, achievement of professional degrees, divorce, pregnancy, parenthood, etc. Patients are usually aware of the effects of these changes, either from their own astute observations, from "grapevine" gossip, or from overhearing staff conversations. The staff member who is happy and excited about her marriage plans may be asked by patients, "What's going on—you seem so happy lately?" Others may guess the news, to the surprise of staff who felt their conversations with other staff in the PHP were truly private. Likewise, the stress and depression surrounding family and marital problems or personal strain are also usually obvious, and may affect not only the individual staff member but his ability to work effectively with the patients.

Staff vary in their feelings about sharing factual information regarding personal status changes. If the change is adversely affecting patient care, it is important that staff consensus be reached on how to best handle the issue, and that it be made clear to patients that it is indeed a staff member's personal issue and not a reaction to the patients. If staff do elect to disclose personal information about themselves concerning marriage, divorce, promotions, advancements, etc., they must then be prepared to deal with patients' feelings about it. Patients may show jealousy, anger, fear, anxiety, pity, seduction, etc. Staff should be able to anticipate possible reactions and prepare themselves to work with the reactions.

Role-change involved in pregnancy is usually more difficult to conceal. Most patients, even those considered severely regressed, are very cognizant of changes in staff; thus, pregnancy is best brought to the community's attention when it begins to be visible, unless the staff member plans to leave the PHP early in the pregnancy.

Pregnancy stimulates considerable feeling in a PHP. Underlying the typical initial expressions of "Congratulations" and "How nice," are feelings of envy ("I'd like to have a baby too, but probably never will"); anger ("We're just a job to you, after all"); rejection ("You'll leave us to take care of someone who's more important to you than us"); and depression ("You're healthy and successful; if I had a baby it would turn out to be sick like me"). There is generally an increase in reference to or direct mention of sexual issues, as the pregnancy visually represents a result of sexual intercourse. There may be a renewed interest in the pregnant staff member's spouse and immediate family. Patients may disclose fantasies about the pregnancy resulting from an imagined affair between staff members. Male patients may reveal their own fantasies or wishes of impregnating the staff member. Some homosexual patients have been observed to exhibit increased anxiety over their sexual identity.

Individual Staff Differences

Among these differences are cultural, racial and ethnic factors, physical disabilities, and sex and age factors. These elements can be tempting to overlook, deny or rationalize away as having no effect on teamwork or on patient treatment; indeed, they may eventually have little effect. However, PHP staff must be able to acknowledge these factors and encourage their discussion, particularly if there are indications that they are interfering with treatment. For example, male patients may exhibit reluctance to discuss sexual concerns with female staff; there may be references made in passing about racial or cultural differences; obvious physical disabilities may seemingly go unnoticed.

PHP staff are usually sensitive to patients' reactions to them. In some instances, staff may find it helpful to identify the difference for patients and reach for feelings about it from the beginning. Often this is met initially with blanket denial of reactions, but it does give patients permission to discuss the issue when they feel more comfortable in doing so. Many (adult) patients feel it is "not nice" to comment on or raise questions about these differences, feeling they will be considered rude or inappropriate; at the same time they may be preoccupied with burning curiosity or concern. It is important for PHP staff with "differences" to have come to some personal resolution and acceptance of their differences, enabling them to openly deal with reactions and not encourage denial or suppression of reactions to them.

Environmental Crisis/Disaster

This topic is included because of the tremendous strain and responsibility on staff to cope with crises such as fire, vandalism, flood, relocation, and tornados. It is crucial for staff to be aware of all safety measures (see Chapter 16). The staff must be able to mobilize themselves quickly and work as a team to insure protection of patients and themselves.

Environmental crises and disasters are frightening. Usually, for a long time following the emergency there is expression of fears of being injured or killed, anger over feeling vulnerable, and increased dependency on staff who are seen as holding the key to safety. These feelings must be worked through in order to free up the community to move on with its work together.

PHP patients can be more than passive participants in preparing for possible emergencies. They can be involved in mapping out suitable exit routes, helping to coordinate evacuation drills, etc. However, this does not mean the patients are then responsible for assuming staff-like tasks or responsibilities during an actual crisis. They are ways of meaningfully involving the patients in their community's functions, including safety.

The above examples of types of chronic stress take a toll on staff. To avoid occupational burnout, it is essential to provide sufficient support to PHP staff teams to insure their survival. Some of these supports would include adequate supervision, staffing, financial remuneration, effective leadership, in-service training and consultation. Without these supports, staff can feel isolated and discouraged. Supports must be relevant, consistent and stable in order to promote a growth-producing atmosphere in which staff are able to deliver high quality service.

Appendix

The following standards are based on:

1) The authors' many years of personal experiences in and involvement with partial hospitalization;
2) The JCAH accreditation manuals (JCAH, 1977, 1979, 1980, 1981),
3) Finally, the work on standards done by G. DiBella with other members and directors of the American Association For Partial Hospitalization Inc. 1978-80 (West et al., 1980).

Basically the sequence and outline of the "Consolidated Standards Manual for Child, Adolescent and Adult Psychiatric, Alcoholism, and Drug Abuse Facilities" (JCAH, 1981) will be used as an outline for this section. Any direct quotes come from JCAH (1981), unless otherwise specified. To enhance substantiality and status, which generates referrals and funding, each program should plan to become accredited by JCAH as soon as possible. A program can be surveyed if it meets all federal, state, and local laws, and has been serving patients for six months. Freestanding partial hospitals (if not primarily serving the developmentally handicapped-disabled) will be surveyed according to the "Consolidated Standards" (JCAH, 1981); other PHPs will be surveyed by this manual or one of the three others (JCAH, 1977, 1979, 1982). Partial hospitals (as of 1981), which are part of a Department of Psychiatry with fewer than 100 psychiatric inpatient beds in a general hospital, are surveyed according to the Accreditation Manual for Hospitals (JCAH, 1982); this manual appears in a new edition each August, to be used for the subsequent calendar year. One or two of these manuals (and other sources of standards) should be used for guidance during the planning stage of every partial hospital (see Chapter 5). It is not unusual for JCAH to make yearly revisions.

One word of caution cannot be overemphasized. All standards in this appendix are not permanent. They represent only a consensus at the current time. These standards will undoubtedly change as more experience is gained and research is completed. There must be enough leeway to allow for experimentation.

There are four main categories of standards: Program Management, Patient Management, Patient Services, and Physical Plant Management; under these are 39 sub-headings. In regard to terminology, "shall" and "must" mean a mandated standard; "should" means the commonly accepted way of compliance; and "may" means an acceptable way for compliance.

A) Program Management

1) Governing body. Bylaws and regulations must be established along with a written description of the administrative organization of the partial hospital, including lines of authority. The partial hospital shall be a separate identifiable organizational unit with staff given sufficient authority and autonomy to carry out its responsibilities in a high quality way. There must be written descriptions of the relationships/lines of authority of staff to one another within the program, to the outside community, and to any supra-system of which the PHP is a part. A pictorial organizational chart is recommended.

The partial hospital shall be able to show evidence of integration with the community in order to: avoid duplication of and gaps in services; help provide a continuum of comprehensive community mental health services; and provide a program that is attuned to the unique characteristics of the community it serves. (See also subsection on Quality Assurance and Program Evaluation.)

It is the responsibility of the governing body through its chief executive officer to provide adequate resources to achieve objectives appropriately and adequately.

2) Chief executive officer. The director has overall responsibility for the operations of the entire partial hospital program, which is delegated to him by the governing body. Thus, he has to be able to skillfully develop and integrate a multidisciplinary, multileveled staff and to be familiar enough with all the different therapies to provide supervision and leadership for effective operation of the program. The director's overall responsibility means that he has all staff reporting to him, including any non-director physicians.

The chief executive officer must be a full-time qualified mental health professional with at least a master's degree. If not a physician, the director (or coordinator) shall have had at least two years of clinical experience (post-master's) plus one year of mental health administrative responsibility; however, it is preferable that the director should have five years of relevant post-master's experience.

3) Professional staff organization. The staff primarily concerned with clinical care will be organized with rules for qualifying, selecting, and reappointing its members and for organizing itself. The rules must indicate that the medical director should be a qualified psychiatrist. Otherwise he/she must be a licensed physician who specializes in the care and treatment of patients with mental disorders. If the physician is not a qualified psychiatrist, then a qualified psychiatrist shall provide at least ten hours in the PHP each month and be available as needed. Typically, however, a psychiatrist is present at least half of the total weekly operational hours of the program. The ultimate responsibility for treatment of all patients rests with the medical director. The physician must evaluate the condition of each patient, physically and mentally, and diagnose all patients on registration into the program, and a physician must approve and review regularly all treatment plans and discharges. A licensed physician shall provide enough hours in the partial hospital to perform these functions in a high quality, comprehensive way, and he shall always be present at least one-fourth of the time.

4) Written plan for professional services and staff composition. All programs shall have sufficient numbers and types of appropriate clinical, administrative, and support staff as delineated in the mandatory written plan. These staff are determined at least by a written description of the following:

a) size of the program;
b) clinical characteristics of the patient population, including their fundamental needs;
c) number of hours and days of program operation;
d) all applicable federal, state and local laws and regulations;
e) specific skills of the staff;
f) therapeutic philosophy, and others (JCAH, 1981, p. 17).

It may be noted that qualification does not denote equivalency in training and/or experience between professionals. The qualified professionals have been listed below in descending order according to decreasing time of training and experience; when there was equal time, an alphabetical order was used.

In attempting to avoid too great rigidity in evaluating clinical staff the phrase "or equivalent training and experience" is used. This should allow consideration and acceptance of credentials slightly different than specified. In the following, it is understood that "or equivalent" holds for all, when judging clinical staff. Often one-and-a-half years of full-time, supervised, paid experience with mental patients is about equivalent to one year of full-time schooling in one of the mental health professions. All degrees must have been from accredited institutions.

With the above in mind, qualified professionals include, but are not limited to, the following:

Qualified Psychiatrist: A licensed physician who is eligible for admission to the certifying exam of the American Board of Psychiatry and Neurology.

Qualified Creative Art (Art, Dance, Music, and Other) Therapist: A therapist with the appropriate master's degree in one of the creative art therapies from an accredited program and two years supervised, paid, full-time work experience dealing with people with mental disorders.

Qualified Psychiatric Social Worker: A person with:

1) a master's level degree from an accredited school of Social Work, and
2) two additional years of supervised full-time paid experience dealing with persons with mental disorders.

Qualified Psychologist: A clinical psychologist with at least a master's degree in clinical/counseling psychology and with at least two years supervised full-time paid experience dealing with people with mental disorders.

Qualified Vocational Rehabilitation Counselor: A person with a master's level degree from an accredited vocational rehabilitation counseling program with at least two years supervised, paid, full-time experience dealing with the mentally ill.

Qualilfied Psychiatric Nurse: A licensed nurse who has a master's degree in clinical psychiatric nursing and who has been certified to practice psychiatric nursing by the voluntary certification process of the American Nurses Association.

Qualified Occupational Therapist: A registered occupational therapist certified by the American Occupational Therapy Association and who has the equivalent of a master's degree in occupational therapy.

Qualified Recreational Therapist: A registered recreational therapist with a master's degree in therapeutic recreation.

Beginning professionals are those individuals who have completed the academic requirements from accredited programs in their disciplines but do not have the service experience required for full qualification.

Mental health workers are all other clinical (salaried and/or volunteer) staff members. While such staff should have at least a high school diploma, their capacity to work appropriately with emotionally disturbed patients is the final critical determinant for their inclusion in a partial hospital.

In addition to the employed staff, there may also be volunteers, including "students" (See below). Essentially all students are also volunteers (unsalaried); however, occasionally they might receive some monetary compensation, such as a token stipend or honorarium. Despite their trainee status psychiatric residents are considered in the category of paid physicians or (perhaps erroneously) "psychiatrists" (non-board eligible or certified).

The ratio of full-time equivalent hired clinical staff to actual attending patient should be at least 1:1 for the most intensive crisis support program to 1:8 for the least intensive maintenance programs (see also Chapter 14 for various model programs). Thus, with an average (over the past two months) actual daily attendance of 20 patients (9 A.M.-4 P.M. and 5 days/week), the number of clinical staff employees would range from 20 to 2 1/2 full-time equivalents. Most programs will have a hired-clinical-staff to average-daily-attendance ratio of 1:4 (Edwards and Carter, 1979, p.43).

In addition to the physician, there must be a multidisciplinary clinical staff, because the need for a range and complexity of services is too great for all services to be provided by any single discipline. There must be an activities therapist who at least plans, supervises, and evaluates activity services, and there should be a qualified social worker, and a qualified activities therapist at least part-time. Often there is a nurse and/or a vocational rehabilitation counselor. When nursing services are given, a registered nurse shall plan, supervise, and evaluate nursing care (JCAH, 1981, p.18). It is almost mandatory that the equivalent of a full-time staff position should be made up of time from an occupational therapist and/or a vocational rehabilitation counselor. Psychological testing will also be needed. (See also Chapters 5 and 14 on further staffing suggestions, including role augmentation.)

A written plan must specify that all clinical activities will be done by staff with competency to do the assigned treatment. Depending on their qualifications, each group of between five and ten of these staff will be supervised by a supervisory staff, who are chosen by the executive and medical directors. Chosen supervisory staff are qualified professionals who have had at least six months full-time PHP experience and have had at least five years relevant full-time training and/or experience beyond a bachelor's degree.

There must be a core staff which consists of full-time qualified clinical professionals. At least 60 percent of total clinical staff work must be composed of core staff hours. Unless the total number of clinical staff is fewer than three, there must be at least three core staff. The work schedules of the PHP's staff must contribute to good communication, consistency, and coordination among staff, e.g., part-time staff should be able to attend at least 75 percent of staff and community meetings.

Others have specified in greater detail standards for staffing. For example, Guillette et al. (1978) indicate that they were able to get an insurance company to pay for a PHP which substituted for inpatient care. They required that a psychiatrist and registered psychiatric nurse, among others, be present all the time the PHP was open. Also, Veil (1965) gives not unreasonable overall recommendations for an average PHP. For every 30 patients attending 9 A.M. to 4 P.M., five days a week, he recommended the following full-time equivalents: 1 psychiatrist, 1 secretary, 1 non-clinical administrative assistant, 1 1/2 cleaning and maintenance staff, 2 activity therapists, plus 3-8 other clinical staff.

The partial hospital's written plan shall also specify the optional, yet reasonable, target for: the number of patients to be on the active census and number of patients who are actual regular attendees. And these figures shall be consistent with the partial hospital's therapeutic philosophies and operating principles, together with goals and objectives. It is doubtful whether the positive therapeutic forces of partial hospitalization (including its group processes) can operate if the percentage of patients who actually attend a scheduled session is less than 75 percent of the active caseload planned to be attendees (the optimum is over 85 percent). In addition, therapeutic value is doubtful is a patient has to cope with intense interaction with more than 30 other partial hospital patients on a regular basis. Optimum would be an average actual attendee group of 20-25 (see Chapter 9 on research on social networks). Partial hospitals that deal with more acute florid symptomatology tend to arrange for a lower number of regular attendees, e.g. 8-13. At any rate, partial hospitals obtaining more than the optimal number of patients should subdivide into small units, and the number of all PHP members (all staff and patients) actually attending should not exceed 50.

Based on therapeutic rationale, the written plan for the partial hospitalization program shall also specify the operational hours and days of the clinical program and a targeted average length of stay. The partial hospital shall specify in writing the services and functions to be provided, through which its goals and objectives can be obtained. To this end, a partial hospital typically provides the following range of clinical-oriented services:

a) psychotherapies (individual and group, including family, in both verbal and activity forms);
b) psychopharmacotherapy;
c) transitory services;
d) diagnostic services;
e) personal care services;
f) adjunctive services;
g) other services that may be required.

All PHP also perform training-oriented functions and intra-organizational support functions. In addition the PHP may provide prevention oriented services, consultation-oriented services and research-oriented functions. (Services and functions terminology is from Baxter [1980, pp. 12-13]).

5) Personnel policies and procedures. These shall prohibit discrimination on the basis of race, creed, age, national origin, sex, or sexual preference (also see JCAH).

6) Volunteer services. See JCAH and appropriate chapters in this book. Many feel that student volunteers should receive at least one hour of supervision for every five hours of treatment services they provide.

7) Fiscal management. See JCAH and Chapter 23 in this book.

8) Facility and program evaluation. See also Chapter 22. Each partial hospital "shall have a written statement of goals and objectives (that) result from a planning process (and there shall be) a written plan for evaluating (the partial hospital's) progress in attaining its goals and objectives" (JCAH, 1981, p. 31).

All partial hospitals have at least the following process-outcome goals in common:

(a) to provide a systematic response to mental health needs of individuals and community;
(b) to provide needed services that will enable patients and others to ameliorate, cope with, and work with mental disorders;
(c) to provide these services built on patient's assets, and in the most natural and least restrictive environment and while maintaining and cultivating social networks; and
(d) to provide "only those services necessary to maintain the maximum level of development and function" (JCAH, 1979, p. 24).

Some samples of objectives are: increased skills of daily living, increased ability to complete tasks, and decreased symptoms.

9) Quality assurance. Quality assurance is a reasonable guaranteeing that there will be superiority or excellence. The quality assurance program shall include at least the following five components: identification of significant and potential problems; evaluation of the cause and scope of the problems; implementation of actions to diminish and remove problems; monitoring to ascertain desired outcomes have been achieved and maintained; and documentation of actual achievement of higher quality of patient care and effort to assure excellence (JCAH, 1981).

10) Utilization review. This shall have its own written plan that provides for every effort to be made to assure appropriate allocation of resources. The utilization review shall also address underutilization and overutilization and support serious endeavors to provide the optimal achievable quality of treatment in the most cost-effective manner. Utilization review shall be done at least monthly by at least three professional staff, one of whom must be a psychiatrist.

11) Patient care monitoring. See JCAH (1981).

12) Staff growth and development. Development programs shall be provided for all staff (see suggestions, Chapter 25).

13) Research. See Chapter 22 for research needs for partial hospitalization.

14) Patient rights. Written policies and procedures shall describe patient's rights and the means by which these rights are protected. These shall be posted in a prominent position in the PHP for patients. See also Chapter 24.

15) Patient records. See JCAH (1981) and Chapters 22 and 24.

B) Patient Management

16) Intake. Written intake procedures shall determine that: (a) the patient requires treatment of the intensity and restrictions of the program; and (b) alternatives for less intensive and restrictive treatment are not available or appropriate. There must be clear written criteria for determining the patient's eligibility for admission. (See utilization review below and Chapter 5.)

17) Assessment. Assessment is part of intake and of ongoing processes; it is the process of evaluating an individual's strengths, weaknesses, problems and needs. The patient's "fundamental needs" shall be clinically evaluated, and these needs shall include (but are not limited to) "physical, emotional, behavioral, social, recreational and . . . legal, vocational, nutritional needs (JCAH, 1981, p. 65). A qualified physician shall be responsible for assessing each patient's physical health. Written procedures shall state the method used for determining the necessity of a physical exam, and this determination shall be done before making the treatment plan. Also, these procedures must provide the following information: date of last physical exam; date last treated by a physician; any present (and pertinent past) physical problems; and medication history including present medications. A basic physical workup shall be done on all patients upon admission (see Chapter 20).

The social assessment shall include information on the family's treatment expectations and their expectations for involvement in treatment. The type and severity of psychosocial stressors significant to each patient should be noted.

The activities assessment shall include information about the patient's current skills, talents, aptitudes, interests, and highest level of adaptive functioning in the area of "use of leisure time" over the past year.

18) Treatment Plan and Progress Notes. There must be an individualized treatment plan based on the patient's fundamental needs and the program's philosophy of treatment. Also, the master treatment plan shall indicate:

a) how the psychosocial family will be involved;
b) goals necessary for the patient's attainment and maintainance of health and maximum growth and capabilities;
c) specific measurable long- and short-term objectives and methods to achieve these and anticipated time to achieve these; and

d) how the patient will participate in development of his treatment plan.

Upon admission there shall be a preliminary treatment plan. Within 72 hours there shall be an initial treatment plan. For programs with lengths of stay averaging over two months, the master treatment plan will be established within two weeks; after this, the treatment plan shall be reviewed and updated in a multidisciplinary case conference once every 30 days for the first three months, and every one to two months thereafter for the first year. After one year, review can occur as little as every three months. For programs with briefer lengths of stays more frequent plans must be prepared.

Progress notes are required at least every other visit for the first two weeks and weekly thereafter. These shall include documentation of all treatment given. When a patient attends less than weekly, a note shall be made at every visit.

19) Special treatment procedures. These include such as electroconvulsive therapy, restraint, seclusion, and others (see JCAH, 1981). Many written procedures are required.

C) Patient Services

20) Anesthesia services. See JCAH (1981).

21) Community education services.

22) Consultation services. These are helpful and require written plans and procedures.

23) Dental service. There shall be a written plan whereby the dental needs of patients are assessed and handled.

24) Dietetic service. There shall be a written plan on the organization and provision of dietetic services.

25) Emergency services. A written plan will indicated how patients can receive these.

26) Outreach services, 27) pastoral services, and 28) pathology services. These shall be available as needed.

29) Pharmacy services. There shall be at least written arrangements by which pharmacy services can be obtained.

30) Professional library services. These shall be made available to meet staff needs.

31) Radiology services. These shall be available as needed.

32) Referrals. The program shall have written policies which assure continuity of care. *Continuity of care* is an uninterrupted succession of the care that the patient requires. There shall be written agreements between the partial hospital and an inpatient service and outside ambulatory programs and services (such as 24-hour emergency care) to ensure speedy access to these programs and services whenever needed by PHP patients. These agreements shall provide, as much as possible, for obligatory intake, communication, and continuation of the patient's treatment plan. The services of "guesting" should be readily available (*guesting* is a simplified process of admission to 24-hour care with no more than a three-day stay).

33) Rehabilitation and other treatment services.

a) *Activity Services.* Activity psychotherapies shall be provided for all patients and shall be organized by a qualified activities therapist, in conjunction with all clinical staff. This activities therapist shall provide adequate supervision of the activities psychotherapies component of the therapeutic program of the partial hospital. There shall be appropriate staff, space, equipment, and facilities for activity services to meet the patients' needs. As for the entire milieu, the activity services shall be carefully planned to specifically provide a consistent, well-structured, yet flexible, framework for daily living and shall be reviewed and revised according to the changing needs of the patients.
b) *Education Services* and
c) *Speech, Language, and Hearing Services.* These shall be available in or outside the facility as needed. See JCAH (1981).
d) *Vocational Rehabilitation Services.* All patients shall be given specific vocational counseling. If the PHP arranges for this by an outside agency, the PHP will at least assign a specific staff member to be a coordinator of vocational rehabilitation. Vocational assessment shall be carried out by each PHP.

D) Physical Plant and Environmental Management

34) Building and grounds safety. There are many regulations that must be followed to ensure the physical safety of users from fire, explosion, and panic (See JCAH, 1981). The space of patient areas must be adequate and will vary between 50-175 square feet per patient, according to the specific features of the program (JCAH, 1979, p. 79).

35) Functional safety and sanitation. Before using any facility, the partial hospital director must first designate a safety director, who chairs a multidisciplinary program safety committee, which meets at least monthly. The safety director must assemble and be familiar with all applicable local, state, federal, National Fire Protection Association and JCAH safety standards.

36) Therapeutic environment. The environment shall enhance the positive self-image of the patient, preserve human dignity, and be responsive to the needs of patients. A written plan shall describe how this responsibility will be carried out, i.e., community meetings and other pertinent meetings should be part of partial hospitalization.

Lighting shall allow clear perception of people and functions. Major patient areas shall have windows or skylights, clocks, calendars, and mirrors. Areas and surfaces shall be free of undesirable odors. Each room shall have acceptable temperature and air, provided by an air conditioning system or operable windows. "Safety windows" are recommended.

The program shall encourage patients to take responsibility for maintenance and other day-to-day housekeeping of the facility. Also, staff should spend time daily over a meal or snacks with patients. Finally, staff shall assist and encourage patients to assume responsibility for self-care with good standards of personal hygiene and grooming.

37) Housekeeping, 38) infection control and 39) sterile supplies and equipment. Written policies and procedures are needed for these.

AN OVERVIEW OF UTILIZATION REVIEW STANDARDS

The psychiatrists who are appointed by the Professional Standards Review Organization (PSRO) (or other agencies) to perform peer review functions on partial hospitalization for the agency should be nominated by the local branch of the American Association for Partial Hospitalization, and standards should be set in conjunction with partial hospital clinicians.

The discussion of standards herein will generally follow the format of the Peer Review Committee's "Manual of Psychiatric Peer Review" (1981). Clinicians must make standards as specific, concrete and operationalized as possible in order to ensure high quality, yet without being inappropriately limiting (on reimbursement or treatment) and stultifying to innovation.

One approach to the above problem is the use of less definitive screening criteria. These allow a reviewer to select certain cases which are "abnormal" for subsequent peer scrutiny.

Whatever criteria are developed, all guidelines and standards need modification to fit local needs.

Factors to Be Considered in Screening Criteria

Using diagnoses alone has been recognized as inadequate to make a determination of when partial hospitalization is indicated. Each official diagnosis can pertain to too large a range of patients. Some of these patients could benefit from partial hospitalization; others would probably become worse (Gibson, 1977, p. 7).

Thus, *exclusionary* (as well as *inclusionary*) criteria are advisable. It is suggested that criteria be based on four factors:

1) Diagnosis;
2) Severity and type of signs and symptoms;
3) Level of adaptive functioning of the patient during the last twelve months;
4) Severity of various types of psychosocial stressors.

The last two are factors mentioned in DSM III of the American Psychiatric Association (APA, 1980), which suggests that evaluation of each patient include description along these two dimensions. Thus, for the third factor, the level of adaptive functioning of the patient during the past 12 months, the clinician determines the highest level of functioning by the patient, and this is a composite of three major areas: social relations, occupational, and use of leisure time. The occupational area includes all productive work of benefit to others and schooling. Use of leisure time will include self-maintenance activities, in addition to recreation. Dimension 3) also reveals deficits in "role performance," which is defined as patterns of "behavior to meet societal and individual needs" (JCAH, 1979, pp. 140-141). Seven levels are possible, ranging from superior to grossly inpaired functioning. Finally, the fourth factor is the severity of various types of psychosocial stressors; e.g. conjugal (with spouse and relatives), parenting, other interpersonal, occupational, living circumstance, financial, legal, developmental, physical illness, and other psychosocial stressors. The APA again gives seven possible overall severity ratings ranging from none to catastrophic (1980, pp. 26-28).

Components of Utilization Review Screening Process

The Peer Review Committee of the APA (1981) lists six components in their recommended screening format for each patient; i.e., admission review (includes reasons for admission and initial length of stay assignment), continued stay review, validation, critical diagnostic and therapeutic services, discharge status, and complications. Validation includes a list of standards stating what documentation must be contained in the medical records to validate an admission and diagnosis. Discharge status is a list of standards stating the conditions under which a patient might be discharged. Complications refer to a list of conditions that frequently arise to complicate and/or prolong treatment, and require a change in the treatment plan.

The review process is concurrent with treatment. The following two procedures are recommended in the screening process for partial hospitalization: 1) By the sixth visit (screening-day visit or full day visit), the concurrent reviewer will examine the patient's chart and complete the processes of admission review, validation, and critical diagnostic and therapeutic services. If the record meets these standards, the reviewer will make an initial length of stay assignment, which is the median length of stay determined by local statistical norms of programs; 2) Before the end of the initial length of assignment, the reviewer will reexamine the chart, completing the processes of continued stay review, critical services, discharge status and complications. If the chart again meets these standards, the reviewer will make an extended length of stay assignment. This period is based on the individual patient's condition, and it is the length of time that is 0.5 to one times the initial stay period. If at any time the chart does not indicate achievement of standards, the reviewer will call an outside psychiatrist reviewer. Following this format on a regular basis will accomplish the utilization review required by JCAH and, undoubtedly, will provide better treatment when also done by the partial hospital staff itself.

Length-of-stay Norms and Percentiles for PHPs

In addition to standards for measuring the appropriateness of type of treatment a patient should receive, there must also be standards on length and frequency of treatment. Frequency should be based on local conditions, meaning that partial hospitals in each city must collect the data to determine median lengths of stay. There is still a nationwide lack of such data, and action is urgently needed. The following tentative median lengths of stay for several types of programs are based on the authors' own experiences, readings, and the JCAH length-of-stay standards (1979, p 86).

Despite the data in Figure 1, lengths of stay should not be approved for longer than 3-6 month periods until further research is completed. Clearly, for short-term programs the continued stay review should be done earlier, e.g., at 6 weeks and extended, perhaps, 3 weeks at a time.

SPECIFIC PHP UTILIZATION REVIEW AND SCREENING STANDARDS

Diagnosis

No diagnosis in the "Diagnostic and Statistical Manual of Mental Disorders" of the American Psychiatric Association (DSM III) by itself mandates or prohibits partial hospitalization; however, there must be an official, accurate, and valid diagnosis of a mental disorder before a patient is formally admitted.

Figure 1

Program Type	Typical Initial Median Length of Stay	Typical Range of the Initial Length of Stay in this Type of Program
Short-term (usually crisis support) treatment	6 weeks	3-10 weeks
Intermediate-term (usually extensive growth) treatment	6 months	2 1/2 - 10 months
Long-term (usually growth-support) treatment	14 months	10-24 months
Indefinite-term (usually maintenance) treatment	3 years	2-7 years

(NOTE: Length of stay terms are not equivalent to intensity type of treatment terms)

Admission Review

In order for the reviewer to approve an admission, he must find certain indications for admission; specifically, the reasons from Group 1 *plus* one reason from Group 2 *or* one reason from Group 3 (see below). In searching for documentation, the reviewer must find more than summary statements of the reasons; he must be able to find supporting details in the patient's record. In addition, firm criteria for exclusion should be absent.

Group 1: Severity and type of signs and symptoms. Signs and symptoms will include those essential for the patient's diagnosis. In addition a psychiatrist judges that a less intensive level of treatment will not produce equal results and that a partial hospital is the optimal treatment and is liable to ameliorate the situation (specifics required). Plus there is at least one of 1-6 below.

1) Symptoms have not responded, or will not respond, or will exacerbate by other ambulatory treatments (specifics required); or
2) Symptoms are such that relief may be possible with other treatments only at excessive personal or social cost; e.g., probable dependency on antianxiety drugs, patient taking a job way below potential to avoid anxiety, undue family burden, etc.; or

3) Chronic symptoms and/or disability will remain even though acute symptoms may be relieved with other treatments; or
4) Symptoms are such that there is need for more intensive or complex levels of skilled observation for diagnostic purposes and/or medication supervision than is available in other ambulatory treatments; or
5) The patient's symptoms need a therapeutic milieu (details required); or
6) The patient meets the PSRO criteria for hospitalization, but a psychiatrist judges that partial hospitalization would produce equivalent (or better) results.

Plus:

Group 2: Impairment in one or more important areas of functioning. These include, in particular, problems in performing socially productive activities (housework, study or training, or employed work), impoverished relationships, marginal daily self-care activities, and poor ability to recognize and avoid danger. Or/and:

Group 3: Psychosocial stressors.

1) Legally mandated partial hospitalization; or
2) Patient's behavior is intolerable to others (at the current levels of interaction); or
3) History reveals that current stressors are similar to those that have precipitated hospitalization in the past (when the patient was not in partial hospitalization); or
4) Psychosocial supports and other ambulatory treatments are inadequate to maintain the patient, or are unavailable.

The Following Reasons for Exclusion Should be Absent

1) Patient's thoughts, actions, or feelings (documented in the record) are judged by a psychiatrist as likely to lead imminently to consequences which are a significant danger to the patient or others (e.g., imminently suicidal or assaultive, severe disorganization or disorientation, or severe acting out, and severe uncontrolled substance abuse). Thus, the patient requires 24-hour treatment or special residence; or
2) There is a physical illness that precludes adequate participation in the partial hospital program; or
3) There is inability to form or maintain the requisite degree of therapeutic alliance, e.g., the patient is unwilling to attend (except when legally mandated) at all or to attend regularly, or the patient gives recent evidence of being unable to tolerate, or benefit from group therapies, or programs similar to partial hospitalization; or

4) The patient and/or others cannot see to it that he arrives at the program relatively reliably and punctually; or

5) Living situation is too precarious and the patient needs more extensive resources than are available from the PHP; or

6) Others, as deemed necessary by each specific partial hospital.

A number of the above criteria are similar to those for simple outpatient group therapy. Frances et al. (1980) provide some concrete elaborations on the above mentioned suggestions that may be helpful in screening and admission review.

Length of Treatment

"Initial length of stay assignment" will be locally established, based on statistical norms for various types of partial hospitals (see suggested medians above). "Extended treatment" will be allowed according to the patient's condition at the end of the initial period of treatment. Reasons for extending the initial period of treatment are:

Referral to a less intensive level of treatment is judged by a psychiatrist to be inappropriate, i.e., will lead to relatively rapid deterioration. Plus, there is one or more of the reasons below:

1) Continuation of above listed reasons for admissions (symptoms, and impaired functioning or psychosocial stressors). When this is the case there should be indication that the PHP has considered the possibility that partial hospitalization or the individual treatment plan is inappropriate, yet has determined the PHP to still be the best treatment;

2) Development of complications (see examples under Complications Section below);

3) Continued treatment at a less intensive level is judged appropriate, but this treatment is not accessible to the patient;

4) Discharge from this partial hospital at this time would be detrimental (substantial explanation required);

5) Patient and/or society give clear indications that symptoms or behavior are intolerable, and recorded clinical evidence justifies continuing this level of care, and no other equal or lower level of care is appropriate.

6) Lack of sufficient progress, which necessitated a significant change in the treatment plan, together with an explanation of why this partial hospital program is still considered able to produce the needed improvement.

Validation

The medical record contains documentation of findings (by history and mental status) to substantiate the diagnosis.

There is also documentation of specific findings to substantiate the summary statements representing reasons for admission and why the patient is judged to be likely to benefit by the program under review. For example, in general, patients are most likely to do in the future as they have done in the past. Thus, if a patient is accepted into an Extensive Growth Treatment program, the record data will indicate that the patient had functioned, for example, at a "fair" level for at least six months sometime within the immediate past five years.

Critical Diagnostic and Therapeutic Services

A reviewer will have to be called if any of the following is absent or present: Review if absent:

1) Treatment plan (including problems, long- and short-term objectives or goals, treatment modalities, discharge and aftercare plan; see JCAH criteria for adequacy of the treatment plan);
2) Physical exam documented as performed within the past six months;
3) Appropriate organic therapy, as indicated;
4) Appropriate documenting progress notes.

Review if present:

1) More than two changes made to different psychotropic medications in any 10-day period;
2) More than one drug of the same class used at the same time for more than five days (e.g., two antipsychotic drugs at one time).

Discharge Status

The patient can be discharged when:

1) Objectives listed in the treatment plan have been achieved:
2) A specific adequate follow-up treatment plan is established.

Complications (events that legitimately prolong treatment).

One or more of the following:

1) Lack of improvement at the halfway point of the program's median length of stay (or at three months, whichever is less).
2) Unexpected relapse;
3) Complication of medication or of other organic therapy;

4) Significant worsening of symptoms or an admission of the patient to inpatient service;

5) Patient's present admission is a readmission within 90 days of last discharge from this or another partial hospital;

6) Treatment interrupted by a discharge against medical advice;

7) Breakdown of socio-environmental support systems;

8) Hospitalized within five months prior to this admission.

In summary, establishing and following standards is vital if PHP patients are to receive the best care as efficiently as possible.

References

Ackerman, N.W. *The Psychodynamics of Family Life*. New York: Basic Books, 1958.

Alikakos, L.C. Analytical group treatment of the post-hospital schizophrenic. *International Journal of Group Psychotherapy*, 1965, *15* (4), 492–504.

Allen, P. A bill of rights for citizens using outpatient mental health services. In: H.R. Lamb (Ed.), *Community Survival for Long-Term Patients*. San Francisco: Jossey-Bass, 1976, pp. 147–170.

Almond, R. Issues in milieu treatment. *Schizophrenia Bulletin*, 1975, *1* (13), 12–26.

Althoff, J. Time limits in and leave from a day treatment program. *Hospital and Community Psychiatry*, 1980, *31* (12), 841–844.

American Psychiatric Association. A.M.A. looks at revising ethics code. *Psychiatric News*, September 1979, *14* (2), 16.

American Psychiatric Association. *Diagnostic and Statistical Manual* (Third Edition). Washington, D.C.: APA, 1980.

Anthony, W., Cohen, M., and Vitale, R. The measurement of rehabilitation outcome. *Schizophrenia Bulletin*, 1978, *4* (3), 365–83.

Appelbaum, S. Feedback: Least restrictive environment: Some comments, modifications. *Hospital & Community Psychiatry*, June 1980, *31* (6), 420.

Appleton, W. Mistreatment of patients' families by psychiatrists. *American Journal of Psychiatry*, 1974, *131* (6), 655-57.

Appleton, W. and Davis, J. *Practical clinical psychopharmacology* (2nd. Ed.). Baltimore: Williams and Wilkins, 1980.

Armstrong, B. Special reports: Preparing the community for the patient's return and gaining community acceptance: Some practical tips. *Hospital & Community Psychiatry*, 1976, *27* (5), 349-356.

Astrachan, B.M., Flynn, H.R., Geller, J.D., and Harvey, H.H. Systems approach to day hospitalization. *Archives of General Psychiatry*, 1970, *22*, 550-559.

Attneave, C. Social networks as the unit of intervention. In: P. Guerin (Ed.), *Family therapy: Theory and Practice*. New York: Gardner Press, 1976.

Atwood, N. and Williams, M. Group support for the families of the mentally ill. *Schizophrenia Bulletin*, 1978, *4* (3), 415-425.

Austin, N., Liberman, R., King, L. and De Risi, W. A comparative evaluation of two day hospitals. *Journal of Nervous and Mental Disease*, 1976, *163* (4), 253-262.

Bachrach, L.L. Is the least restrictive environment always the best? Sociological and semantic implications. *Hospital & Community Psychiatry*, February 1980, *31*, 97-103.

Bailey, R. An economist's view of the health services industry. In: S. Levey & N. Loomba (Eds.), *Health Care Administration*. Philadelphia: J. B. Lippincott, 1973.

Balachandran, V. and Dittman, D. Cost allocation for maximizing hospital reimbursement under third party cost contracts. *Health Care Management Review*, 1978, *3* (2), 61-70.

Barter, J. Successful community programming for the chronic mental patient; Principles and practices; Chapter VII. In: J. Talbott (Ed.), *The Chronic Mental Patient: Problems, Solutions, and Recommendations for a Public Policy*. Washington, D.C.: American Psychiatric Association, 1978.

Baxter, J. (Ed.). *Definitions for Use in Mental Health Information Systems*. Rockville, Md.: National Institute of Mental Health, 1980.

Beard, J. Psychiatric rehabilitation at Fountain House (Chapter 25). In: J. Meislin (Ed.), *Rehabilitation Medicine and Psychiatry.* Springfield, Ill.: Charles C Thomas, 1976.

Beels, C. Social support and schizophrenia. *Schizophrenia Bulletin,* 1981, *7* (1), 58-72.

Beigel, A. and Feder, S. A night hospital program. *Hospital & Community Psychiatry,* 1970, *21* (5), 146-49.

Bennett, D. British day hospitals. In: R. Epps and L. Hanes (Eds.) *Day Care of Psychiatric Patients.* Springfield, Ill.: Charles C Thomas, 1964.

Benningfield, A. Multiple family therapy systems. *Journal of Marriage and Family Counseling,* 1978, *4* (2), 25-34.

Berman, R. and Moloney, T. Are outpatient departments responsible for the fiscal crisis facing teaching hospitals? *Journal of Ambulatory Care Management,* 1978, *1* (1), 37-53.

Berner, J. Tell it like it is: A non-statistical presentation on the use of a program evaluation tool. In: J. Maxey et al. (Eds.). *Proceedings of the Annual Conference on Partial Hospitalization (1979).* Boston: American Association For Partial Hospitalization, 1980.

Bierer, J. The day hospital: Therapy in a guided democracy. *Mental Hospitals,* 1962, *13,* 246-252.

Bierer, J. *Therapeutic Social Clubs.* London: H.K. Lewis, 1948.

Binner, P. Outcome measures and cost analysis. In: W. Nuglier, R. Hammer and G. Landsberg (Eds.), *Emerging Developments in Mental Health Program Evaluation.* New York: Argold Press, 1977.

Blume, R., Kalin M., and Sacks, J. A collaborative day treatment program for chronic patients in adult homes. *Hospital & Community Psychiatry,* 1979, *30* (1), 40-42.

Bogen, I. Logophobia-Some hypotheses and implications. *Journal of Sex Education and Therapy,* 1978, *4* (2), 47-49.

Borus, J. Issues critical to the survival of community mental health. *American Journal of Psychiatry,* 1978, *135* (9), 1029-35.

Brocklehurst, J. The development and present status of day hospitals. *Age and Aging,* 1979, *8,* 76-79. (Supplement)

Brown, B. Responsible community care of former mental hospital patients. *New Dimensions in Mental Health,* Department of Health, Education, and Welfare, Publication number (ADM) 77-428. Rockville, Maryland: National Institute of Mental Health, 1977.

Budson, R. and Jolley, R. A crucial factor in community program success: The extended psychosocial kinship system. *Schizophrenia Bulletin,* 1978, *4* (4), 609-621.

Burke, A. Physical disorders among day hospital patients. *British Journal of Psychiatry,* 1978, *133,* 22-27.

Bursten, B. Psychiatry and the rhetoric of models. *American Journal of Psychiatry,* 1979, *136* (5), 661-66.

Butts, N. and Cavenar, J. Colleagues' responses to the pregnant psychiatric resident. *American Journal of Psychiatry,* 1979, *136* (12), 1587-89.

Cameron, D.E. The day hospital. In: A.E. Bennett, E.A. Hargrove and B. Engle (Eds.), *The Practice of Psychiatry in General Hospitals.* Berkeley, CA: University of California Press, 1956.

Cameron, D.E. The day hospital: Experimental forms of hospitalization for patients. *Modern Hospital,* 1947, *69* (3), 60-62.

Campbell, R.J. *Psychiatric Dictionary (Fifth Edition).* New York: Oxford University Press, 1981.

Caplan, G. The family as a support system. In: G. Caplan and M. Killilea (Eds.), *Support Systems and Mutual Help.* New York: Grune & Stratton, 1976.

Carmichael, D.M. Day hospital program with emphasis on translatable skills. In: R. Epps & L. Hanes (Eds.), *Day Care of Psychiatric Patients.* Springfield, Ill.: Charles C Thomas, 1964.

Carpenter, W., Mc Glashan, T., and Strauss, J. The treatment of acute schizophrenia without drugs: An investigation of some current assumptions. *American Journal of Psychiatry,* 1977, *134* (1), 14-20.

Carrol, I. Functional assessment in partial hospitalization. In: J. Maxey et al. (Eds.). *Proceedings of the Annual Conference on Partial Hospitalization (1979).* Boston: American Association of Partial Hospitalization, 1980.

Carter, D. and Newman, F. *A Client-oriented System of Mental Health Service Delivery and Program Management: A Workbook and Guide,* DHEW Pub #(ADM) 76-307. Washington, D.C.: Superintendent of Documents, US Govt. Printing Office, 1976.

Chasin, R.M. Special clinical problems in day hospitalization, *American Journal of Psychiatry,* 1967, *123,* 779-785.

Christmas, J. et al. Report of the task panel on community support systems. In: *Task Panel Reports Submitted to the President's Commission on Mental Health* (Vol. II). Washington, D.C.: Superintendent of Documents, 1978.

Cooper, P. (Ed.), *Health Care Marketing*, Germantown, MD: Aspens Systems, 1979.

Council on Mental Health Services (of The American Psychiatric Association). Position statement on active treatment. *American Journal of Psychiatry*, 1979, *136* (5), 753.

Crossan, M. A treatment evaluation of the community meeting: The implications of merging a social-learning model of mental illness with the medical model. *Dissertation Abstracts International*, 1977, *39*, (9-B), 4668-4669.

Cumming J. and Cumming, E. *Ego and Milieu*. New York: Atherton Press, 1967.

Cutick, R. (Ed.). Guidelines for standards for partial hospitalization. *American Association for Partial Hospitalization Newsletter*, 1979 *4* (3), 6-15.

Daniels, D. and Rubin, R. The community meeting. *Archives of General Psychiatry*, 1968, *18*, 60-75.

Daniels, R. Issues in the origin, organization and operation of a day hospital. In: R. Epps and L. Hanes (Eds.), *Day Care of Psychiatric Patients*. Springfield, Ill.: Charles C Thomas, 1964.

Davenport, B. A cost-effective model for psychiatric day treatment. *Proceedings of the Annual Conference on Partial Hospitalization* (1978) Boston: Federation of Partial Hospitalization Study Groups, 1979.

Davis, H. Management of innovation and change in mental health services. *Hospital & Community Psychiatry*, 1978, *29*(10), 649-658.

Davis, J., Lorei, T., and Caffey, E. An evaluation of the Veteran's Administration day hospital program. *Hospital & Community Psychiatry*, 1978, *29* (5), 297-302.

Davis, J., Schaffer, C., Hillian, G., Kinard, C., and Chan, C. Important issues in the drug treatment of schizophrenia. *Schizophrenia Bulletin*, 1980, *6* (1), 70-87.

de Mare, P.B. and Kreeger, L.C. *Introduction to Group Treatment in Psychiatry*. London: Butterworth, 1974.

Department of Health and Social Security. Better services for the mentally ill: Cmnd, 6233. London: Her Majesty's Stationary Office, 1975.

Derogatis, I. and Melisaratos, N. The Derogatis sexual functioning inventory: A multidimensional measure of sexual functioning. *Journal of Sex and Marital Therapy*, 1979, *5* (3), 244-281.

Deveaugh-Geiss, J. Informed consent for neuroleptic therapy. *American Journal of Psychiatry*, 1979, *136* (7), 959-62.

DeWitt, K. The effectiveness of family therapy: A review of outcome research. *Archives of General Psychiatry*, 1978, *35* (5), 549-561.

DiBella, G. Explanatory text on the problem-oriented record. Brooklyn, N.Y.: Kingsboro Psychiatric Center, 1975. (Mimeographed material, revised)

DiBella, G. Family psychotherapy with the homosexual family: A community psychiatry approach to homosexuality. *Community Mental Health Journal*, 1979, *15* (1), 41-46.

DiBella, G. Mastering money issues complicating treatment. *American Journal of Psychotherapy*, 1980, *34* (4). 510-22.

DiBella, G. Partial hospitalization: Update and overview. *Newsletter of the American Association of General Hospital Psychiatrists*, 1980, *3*(4), 3-4.

DiBella, G. What is the place of partial hospitalization in the total mental health services system? *Newsletter of the American Association of General Hospital Psychiatrists*, In press.

Dincin, J. and Vaillancourt, K. (Eds.). *Newsletter of the International Association of Psycho-social Rehabilitation Services*, Fall 1980, pp. 1-10.

Dincin, J., Selleck, V., and Streiker, S. Restructuring parental attitudes-Working with parents of the adult mentally ill. *Schizophrenia Bulletin*, 1978, *4* (4), 597-608.

Donner, J. and Ganson, A. Experience with multi-family, time-limited outpatient groups at a community psychiatric clinic. *Psychiatry*, 1968, *31*,(2), 126-137.

Dorsey, R., Ayd, F., Cole, J., Klein, D., Simpson, C., Turpin, J., and Di Mascio, A. Psychopharmacological screening criteria development project. *Journal of the American Medical Association*, 1979, *241* (10), 1021-1031.

Dzhagarov, M. (Experience in organizing a half hospital for mental patients). *Neuropathologia Psikhatria*, 1937, *6*, 137-147.

Eckman, T. A. Behavioral approaches to partial hospitalization. In: R. Luber (Ed.) *Partial Hospitalization: A Current Perspective*. New York: Plenum, 1979.

Edwards, C. and Carter, J. Day services and the mentally ill. In: J. Wing and R. Olsen (Eds.), *Community Care for the Mentally Disabled.* New York: Oxford University Press, 1979.

Edwards, D. W., Yarvis, R. M., and Mueller, D. P. Evidence for efficacy of partial hospital data from two studies. *Hospital and Community Psychiatry,* 1979, *29,* 97-101.

Eisen, S., Maynard, L., and Washburn, S. Ongoing evaluation of a partial hospital program. *Proceedings of the Annual Conference on Partial Hospitalization* (1978). Boston: Federation of Partial Hospitalization Study Groups, 1979.

Eisenberg, L. Mental health services: Equity, quality, and constraints. *Hospital & Community Psychiatry,* 1978, *29* (12), 781-787.

Eisenthal, R., Emory, A., Lazare, A., and Udin, H. Adherence and the negotiated approach to patient-hood. *Archives of General Psychiatry,* 1979, *36* (4), 393-399.

Ellsworth, R., Casey, N., Hickey, R., Twemlow, S., Collins, J., Schoonover, R., Hyer, L., and Nesselroade, J. Some characteristics of effective psychiatric treatment programs. *Journal of Consulting and Clinical Psychology,* 1979, *47* (5), 799-817.

Elpers, J. Management and programmatic constraints on community mental health services. *Hospital & Community Psychiatry,* 1978, *29* (6), 369-372.

Emerson, P. and Fagan, J. Integrating mentally retarded clients into comprehensive day treatment programs. *Proceedings of the Annual Conference on Partial Hospitalization* (1976). Boston: Federation of Partial Hospitalization Study Groups, 1977.

Endicott, J., Herz, M. T., and Gibbon, M. Brief versus standard hospitalization: The differential costs. *American Journal of Psychiatry,* 1978, *135,* 707-712.

Endicott, J., and Spitzer, R. Use of the research diagnostic criteria and the schedule for affective disorder and schizophrenia to study affective disorders. *American Journal of Psychiatry,* 1979, *136* (1), 52-56.

Engel, G. The biopsychosocial model and the education of health professionals *General Hospital Psychiatry,* 1979, *1* (2), 156-165.

Engle, R. and Sabin, J. Partial hospitalization. In: H. Grunebaum (Ed.), *The Practice of Community Mental Health.* Boston: Little Brown & Company, 1970.

Ennis, B. and Emery, R. *The Rights of Mental Patients: An American Civil Liberties Handbook.* New York: Avon Books, 1978.

Epps, R. and Hanes, L. (Eds.) *Day Care of Psychiatric Patients.* Springfield, Ill.: Charles C Thomas, 1964.

Erickson, R. and Backus, F. Symptom severity and day hospital admission. *Hospital & Community Psychiatry,* 1973, *24,* 102-104.

Fairweather, G. W. *Social Psychology in Treating Mental Illness.* New York: John Wiley & Sons, 1964.

Fairweather, G.W. *Methods of Experimental Social Innovation.* New York: John Wiley & Sons, 1967.

Farndale, J. *The Day Hospital Movement in Great Britain.* New York: Pergamon Press, 1961.

Feller, K. Art materials as a stage for psychodrama. *Proceedings of the Annual Conference on Partial Hospitalization* (1978). Boston: Federal of Partial Hospitalization Study Groups, 1979.

Fertig, S. and Howes, M. Movement therapy in a day treatment setting. *Proceedings of the Annual Conference on Partial Hospitalization* (1976). Boston: Federation of Partial Hospitalization Study Groups, 1977.

Fink, E. and Heckerman, C. Predicting partial hospital treatment failures. *Proceedings of the Annual Conference on Partial Hospitalization* (1978). Boston: Federation of Partial Hospitalization Study Groups, 1979.

Fink, E., Heckerman, C., and McNeill, D. Clinical variables in treatment setting determination: Partial versus full-time hospitalization. *Proceedings of the Annual Conference on Partial Hospitalization* (1977). Boston: Federation of Partial Hospitalization Study Groups, 1978a.

Fink, E., Longabaugh, R., and Stout, R. The paradoxical underutilization of partial hospitalization. *American Journal of Psychiatry,* 1978b, *135* (6), 713-716.

Finkelhor, D. Psychological, cultural, and family factors in incest and family sexual abuse. *Journal of Marriage and Family Counseling,* 1978, *4* (4), 41-49.

Fontana, V. *The Maltreated Child* (2nd ed.). Springfield, Ill.: Charles C Thomas, 1971.

Fountain House. *A Progress Report for 1979.* New York: Fountain House, 1980.

Fowler, S. and Dunford, P. Music therapy. *Proceedings of the Annual Conference on Partial Hospitalization* (1976). Boston: Federation of Partial Hospitalization Study Groups, 1977.

Framo, J . Chronicle of a struggle to establish a family unit within a community mental health center. In: P. Guerin (Ed.), *Family Therapy*. New York: Gardner Press, 1976.

Frances, A., Clarkin, J., and Marachi, J. Selection criteria for outpatient group psychotherapy. *Hospital & Community Psychiatry*, 1980, *31* (4), 245–50.

Frank, R. Cost-benefit analysis in mental health services: A review of the literature. *Administration in Mental Health*, 1981, *8*(3), 161-176.

Freud, S. Group psychology and the analysis of the ego. In: J. Strachey (Ed. & Translator), *Standard Edition of the Complete Psychological Works of Sigmund Freud*, (Vol. 18). London: Hogarth Press, 1955, pp. 65–143.

Garber, J. The medicaid game. A personal experience in playing and winning. *Hospital & Community Psychiatry*, 1977, *28* (3), 203–206.

Garfield, S. and Bergin, A. (Eds.). *Handbook of Psychotherapy and Behavior Change* (Second edition). New York: John Wiley, 1978.

Garland, J. A., Jones, H. E., and Kolodny, R. L. A model for stages for development in social work groups. In: S. Bernstein (Ed.), *Explorations in Group Work: Essays in Theory and Practice*. Boston: Milford House, 1973.

Gibson, R. (Ed.). *Professional Responsibilities and Peer Review in Psychiatry*. Washington, D.C.: American Psychiatric Association, 1977.

Glaser, F. B. Our place: Design for a day program. *American Journal of Orthopsychiatry*, 1969, *39* (5), 827–840.

Glaser, F. The uses of the day program. In: H. Barten, & L. Bellak (Eds.), *Progress in Community Mental Health*. (Vol. II). New York: Grune and Stratton, 1972.

Glasscote, R. M., Cumming, E., Rutman, I., Sussex, J. and Glassman, S. *Rehabilitating the Mentally Ill in the Community*. Washington, D.C.: Joint Information Service of the American Psychiatric Association and the National Association for Mental Health, 1971.

Glasscote, R. M., Kraft, A. M., Glassman, S., & Jepson, W. W. *Partial hospitalization for the mentally ill: A study of programs and problems*. Washington, D.C.: Joint Information Service of American Psychiatric Association and National Association for Mental Health, 1969.

Goffman, E. *Asylums*. New York: Doubleday, 1961.

Golann, S. and Fremouw, W. (Eds.), *The Right to Treatment for Mental Patients*. New York: Irvington, 1976.

Goldberg, F. The cultivation of a partial hospital treatment team. In: R. Luber et al. (Eds.), *Proceedings of the Annual Conference of Partial Hospitalization*, Boston, 1977, pp. 115–116.

Goldsmith, W. *Psychiatric Drugs for the Non-medical Mental Health Worker*. Springfield, Ill.: Charles C Thomas, 1977.

Goldstein, M., Rodnick, E., Evans, J., May, P., and Steinberg, M. Drug and family therapy in the aftercare of acute schizophrenics. *Archives of General Psychiatry*, 1978, *35* (10), 1169–77.

Gootnick, I. Transference in psychotherapy with schizophrenic patients. *International Journal of Group Psychotherapy*, 1975, *25* (4), 379–388.

Grob, M. C., Washburn, S. L. and Eisen, S. Integration of outcome evaluation in a partial hospitalization program. *Proceedings of the Annual Conference on Partial Hospitalization* (1977). Boston: Federation of Partial Hospitalization Study Groups, 1978.

Gross, R. A., and Kisch, J. Day hospital community meetings. In: J. Maxey, R. Luber, and P. Lefkovitz (Eds.), *Proceedings of the Annual Conference of the American Association for Partial Hospitalization, Inc.*, Boston, 1980, pp. 15–23.

Group for the Advancement of Psychiatry. *The Effect of the Method of Payment on Mental Health Care Practice* (Vol. 9 #95). New York: GAP, 1975.

Guidry, L. S., Winstead, D., Levine, M. and Eicke, J. Evaluation of day treatment center effectiveness. *Journal of Clinical Psychiatry*, 1979, *37*, 221–224.

Guillette, W., Crowley, B., Savitz, S., and Goldberg, F. Day hospitalization as a cost effective alternative to inpatient care: A pilot study. *Hospital & Community Psychiatry*, 1978, *29* (8), 525–527.

Guralnik, D., and Friend, J. (Eds.), *Webster's New World Dictionary of the American Language, College Edition*. New York: The World Publishing Co., 1964.

Gurman, A. and Kniskern, D. *Handbook of Family Therapy*. New York: Brunner/Mazel, 1981.

Guy, W. and Gross, G. Problems in the evaluation of day hospitals. *Community Mental Health Journal*, 1968, *3*, 111–118.

Guy, W., Gross, G. M., Hogarty, G., and Dennis, H. A controlled evaluation of day hospital effectiveness. *Archives of General Psychiatry*, 1969, *20*, 329–338.

Haley, J. Why a mental health clinic should avoid family therapy. *Journal of Marriage and Family Counseling*, 1975, *1* (1), 3–14.

Hall, R., Popkin, M., Devaul, R., Faillace, L., and Stickney, S. Physical illness presenting as psychiatric disease. *Archives of General Psychiatry*, 1978, *35* (11), 1315–1320.

Halpern, W., Kissel, S., and Gold, J. Day treatment as an aid to mainstreaming troubled children. *Community Mental Health Journal*, 1978, *4* (4), 319–26.

Hamill, C. (Ed.) *The Day Hospital: Organization and Management*. New York: Springer, 1981.

Hammersley, D. Congress approves new CMHC act requiring six initial services, allowing sharing between centers. *Hospital & Community Psychiatry*, 1979, *30* (1), 65.

Hansell, N. Services for schizophrenics: A lifelong approach to treatment. *Hospital & Community Psychiatry*, 1978, *29* (2). 105–109.

Hargreaves, W., Attkinson, C., and Sorensen, J. (Eds.). *Resource Materials for Community Health Program Evaluation (Second Edition)*, DHEW Pub #(ADM) 77–328. Washington, D.C.: Superintendent of Documents, US Govt. Printing Office, 1977.

Harrington, J. and Mayer-Gross, W. A day hospital for neurotics in an industrial community. *Journal of Mental Science*, 1959, *105*, 224–234.

Hatfield, A. The family as partner in the treatment of mental illness. *Hospital & Community Psychiatry*, 1979, *30* (5), 338–40.

Hersen, M. and Luber, R. Use of group psychotherapy in a partial hospitalization service: The remediation of basic skills deficits. *International Journal of Group Psychotherapy*, 1977, *27*, 1371–1382.

Hersey, P. and Blanchard, K. H., *Management of Organizational Behavior: Utilizing Human Resources*. New Jersey: Prentice-Hall, 1972, pp. 149–172.

Herz, M. I. Partial hospitalization—Brief hospitalization and aftercare. In: H. I. Kaplan, A. M. Freedman, & B. J. Sadock (Eds.) *Comprehensive Textbook of Psychiatry Vol. III* (3rd edition). Baltimore: Williams & Wilkins, 1980.

Herz, M. I., Endicott, J., Spitzer, R. L., and Mesnikoff, A. Day versus inpatient hospitalization: A controlled study. *American Journal of Psychiatry*, 1971, *127*, 1371–1382.

Herz, M. I., Endicott, J., and Spitzer, R. Brief hospitalization of patients with families. *American Journal of Psychiatry*, 1975, 132 (4), 413–418.

Herz, M.I., Endicott, J., and Spitzer, R. Brief versus standard hospitalization: The families. *American Journal of Psychiatry*, 1976, *133*, 795–801.

Herz, M.I., Endicott, J., and Spitzer, R. Brief hospitalization: A two year follow-up. *American Journal of Psychiatry*, 1977, 134, 502–507.

Herzlinger, R. Fiscal management in health organizations. *Health Care Management Review*, 1977, *2* (3), 37–42.

Hogarty, G., Dennis, H., Guy, W., and Gross, G. Who goes there? *American Journal of Psychiatry*, 1968, *124*, 934–944.

Hollon, S. and Beck, A. Psychotherapy and drug therapy: Comparisons and combinations. In: S. Garfield and A. Bergin (Eds.), *Handbook of Psychotherapy and Behavior Change: An Empirical Analysis* (Second Edition). New York: John Wiley, 1978.

Johnson, C. & Flowers, B. How to make it on the outside. *Proceedings of the Annual Conference on Partial Hospitalization* (1976). Boston: Federation of Partial Hospitalization Study Groups, 1977.

Joint Commission on Accreditation of Hospitals. Chicago: Joint Commission on the Accreditation of Hospitals,
   Standards for services for developmentally disabled individuals. 1977.
   Principles for accreditation of community mental health service programs. 1979.
   Accreditation manual for hospitals. 1980, 1982.
   Consolidated standards manual for child, adolescent, and adult psychiatric, alcoholism, and drug abuse facilities. 1981.

Joint Commission on Mental Illness and Mental Health. *Action for Mental Health: Final Report*. New York: Basic Books, 1961.

Jones, D. and Mowrey, K. Independent living skills workshops as a resource for partial hospitalization clients and pre-discharge hospitalized patients. *Proceedings of the Annual Conference on Partial Hospitalization* (1979). Boston: Federation of Partial Hospitalization Study Groups, 1980.

Jones, M. S. *Social Psychiatry.* London: Tavistock Publications, 1952.

Jones, M. *The Therapeutic Community.* New York: Basic Books, 1953.

Jones, M. *Maturation of the Therapeutic Community,* New York: Human Sciences Press, 1976.

Kadis, A. L. The alternate meeting in group psychotherapy. *American Journal of Group Psychotherapy,* April 1956, *X* (2), 275–291.

Kanter, J. Resocialization in day treatment. In: J. Maxey, R. Luber and P. Lefkovitz (Eds.), *Proceedings of the Annual Conference on Partial Hospitalization* (1979). Boston: American Association for Partial Hospitalization, 1980.

Kaplan, H. *The New Sex Therapy: Active Treatment of Sexual Dysfunctions.* New York: Brunner/Mazel, 1974.

Karasu, T., Waltzman, S., Lindenmayer, J., and Buckley, P. The medical care of patients with psychiatric illness. *Hospital & Community Psychiatry,* 1980, *31* (7), 463–471.

Kellam, S. G. and Chassam, J. B. Social context and symptom fluctuation. *Psychiatry,* 1962, *25,* 370–381.

Kempe, C. H. and Helfer, R. E. (Eds.) *Helping the Battered Child and His Family.* Philadelphia: J. B. Lippincott, 1972.

Kiresuk, T. and Sherman, R. Goal attainment scaling: A general method for evaluating comprehensive community mental health programs. *Community Mental Health Journal,* 1968, *46,* 443–453.

Kjenaas, M. A. A program to improve aftercare in a rural area. *Hospital & Community Psychiatry,* June 1980, 401–403.

Klerman, G. L. National trends in hospitalization. *Hospital and Community Psychiatry,* 1979, *30* (2), 110–113.

Kneale, W. C. The scientific method. In: *The Encyclopaedia Britannica* (Vol. 20). Chicago: William Benton, 1972.

Kopolow, L. and Cohen, G. Milieu therapy: Towards a definition for reimbursement. *American Journal of Psychiatry,* 1976, *133* (9), 1060–1063.

Kraft, A. M. The therapeutic community. In: S. Arieti (Ed.), *American Handbook of Psychiatry,* New York: Basic Books, 1966.

Kramer, B. *Day Hospital: A Study of Partial Hospitalization in Psychiatry.* New York: Grune & Stratton, 1962.

Kris, E. G. Intensive short-term therapy in a daycare facility for control of recurrent psychotic symptoms. *American Journal of Psychiatry,* 1959, *115,* 1027–1028.

Kris, E. G. Prevention of rehospitalization through relapse control in a daycare hospital. In: M. Greenblatt, D. J. Levinson, and G. L. Klerman (Eds.), *Mental Patients in Transition.* Springfield, Ill.: Charles C Thomas, 1962.

Kromberg, C. and Proctor, J. Methadone maintenance; Evolution of a day program. *American Journal of Nursing,* 1970, *70* (12), 2575–77.

Lamb, H. R. Chronic psychiatric patients in the day hospital. *Archives of General Psychiatry,* 1967, *17,* 615–621.

Lamb, H. R. *Community survival for long-term patients.* San Francisco: Jossey-Bass, 1976a.

Lamb, H. R. An educational model for teaching living skills to long-term patients. *Hospital & Community Psychiatry,* 1976b, *27,* 875–877.

Lamb, H. R. and Oliphant, E. Schizophrenia through the eyes of families. *Hospital & Community Psychiatry,* 1978, *29* (12), 803–5.

Lang, E. A rehabilitation model for day hospital. *Proceedings of the Annual Conference on Partial Hospitalization* (1978). Boston: Federation of Partial Hospitalization Study Groups, 1979.

Langsley, D. Community psychiatry. In: H. Kaplan, A. Freedman, and B. Sadock (Eds.), *Comprehensive Textbook of Psychiatry III.* Baltimore: Williams and Wilkins, 1980.

Langsley, D., Stephenson, W., and MacDonald, J. Why not insure partial hospitalization? *Mental Hospital,* 1964, *15,* 16–17.

Laqueur, H. P. Mechanisms of change in multiple family therapy. In: C. J. Sager & H. S. Kaplan (Eds.), *Progress in Group and Family Therapy.* New York: Brunner/Mazel, 1972, pp. 400–415.

Lefkovitz, P. Patient population and treatment programming. In: R. Luber (Ed.), *Partial Hospitalization. Current Perspectives.* New York: Plenum Press, 1979.

Leichter, E. and Schulman, G. L. Emerging phenomena in multi-family group treatment. *International Journal of Group Psychotherapy,* 1968, *18,* 59–69.

Leichter, E. and Schulman, G.L. Interplay of group and family treatment techniques in multi-family group therapy. *International Journal of Group Psychotherapy*, 1972, *22*, 167–176.

Lesser, I. and Friedmann, C. Beyond medications: Group therapy for the chronic psychiatric patient. *International Journal of Group Psychotherapy*, 1980, *30* (2), 187–99.

Levine, C. and Dang, J. The group within the group: The dilemma of co-therapy. *International Journal Group Psychotherapy*, 1979, *29* (2), 175–84.

Liberman, R. P. Behavioral methods in group and family therapy. *Seminars in Psychiatry*, 1972, *4*, 141–156.

Liberman, R., Fearn, C., De Risi, W., Roberts, J., and Carmona, M. The credit-incentive system: Motivating the participation of patients in a day hospital. *British Journal of Social and Clinical Psychology*, 1977, *16*, 85–94.

Lidz, T., Cornelison, A. R., Fleck, S., and Terry, D. Schism and skew in the families of schizophrenics. In: N. W. Bell and E. F. Vogel (Eds.), *A Modern Introduction to the Family*. Glencoe: Free Press, 1960.

Lifshin, J. Child partial hospitalization: A comprehensive treatment approach for high risk children. In: J. Maxey, R. Luber, and P. Lefkovitz (Eds.), *Proceedings of the Annual Conference on Partial Hospitalization* (1979). Boston: American Association for Partial Hospitalization, 1980.

Lindemann, E. Symptomatology and management of acute grief. In: H. Parad (Ed.), *Crisis Intervention: Selected Readings*. New York: Family Service Association of America, 1965, pp. 7–21.

Linn, M., Caffey, E., Klett, C., Hogarty, G., and Lamb, R. Day treatment and psychotropic drugs in the aftercare of schizophrenic patients. *Archives of General Psychiatry*, 1979, *36* (9), 1055–1066.

Linnihan, P. Adolescent day treatment: A community alternative to institutionalization of the emotionally disturbed adolescent. *American Journal of Orthopsychiatry*, 1977, *47* (4), 679–88.

Low, A. A. *Mental Health Through Will Training*. Boston: Christopher, 1950.

Luber, R. (Ed.) *Partial Hospitalization: A Current Perspective*. New York: Plenum, 1979.

Luber, R. Poetry therapy: An introduction to theory and technique. *Proceedings of the Annual Conference on Partial Hospitalization* (1976). Boston: Federation of Partial Hospitalization Study Groups, 1977.

Luber, R. and Wells, R. Structured short term multiple family therapy: An educational approach. *International Journal of Group Psychotherapy*, 1977, *27* (1), 43–58.

MacDonald, W. S. The large group meeting hour. In: G. W. Fairweather (Ed.), *Social Psychology in Treating Mental Illness*. New York: John Wiley & Sons, 1964.

Main, T. F. The hospital as a therapeutic insitition. *Bulletin of the Menniger Clinic*, 1946, *10*, 66–70.

Maratos, J. and Kennedy, M. Evaluation of ward group meetings in a psychiatric unit of a general hospital. *British Journal of Psychiatry*, 1974, *125*, 479–482.

Mardikian, B. and Glick, I. Patient-staff meetings: A study of some aspects of content, tone, speakers. *Mental Hygiene*, 1969, *53*, 303–305.

Maxey, J. (Ed.). *Bibliography on Partial Hospitalization: 1937–79*. Boston: American Association for Partial Hospitalization, 1980.

Maxey, J., Luber, R., and Lefkovitz, P. (Eds.) *Proceedings of the Annual Conference on Partial Hospitalization (1979)*. Boston: American Association for Partial Hospitalization, 1980.

Maxey, J., Luber, R., and Lefkovitz, P. (Eds.) *Proceedings of the Annual Conference on Partial Hospitalization (1980)*. Boston: American Association for Partial Hospitalization, 1981.

May, P. R. A. Rational treatment for an irrational disorder: What does the schizophrenic patient need. *The American Journal of Psychiatry*, 1976, *133* (9), 1008–1011.

Mazur, W. P. *The Problem-Oriented System in the Psychiatric Hospital: A Manual for Mental Health Professionals*, New York: Trainex Press, MEDCOM, Inc., 1974.

McCreary-Jahasz, A. and Kavanagh, J. Factors which influence sexual decisions. *Journal of Sex Education and Therapy*, 1978, *4* (2). 35–39.

McDonough, L. B. and Downing, J. J. The day center as an alternative to the psychiatric ward. *Mental Hygiene*, 1965, *49*, 260–265.

Meltzoff, J. and Blumenthal, R. L. *The Day Treatment Center: Principles, Application and Evaluation*. Springfield, Ill.: Charles C Thomas, 1966.

Memmott, J. and Rees, B. Neurolinguistic programming: A new treatment modality in a day hospital setting. In: J. Maxey et al. (Eds.) *Proceedings of the Annual Conference on Partial Hospitalization (1979)*. Boston: American Association for Partial Hospitalization, 1980.

Michaux, M. H., Chelst, M. R., Foster, S. A., Pruim, R. J., and Dasinger, E. M. Postrelease adjustment of day and full-time psychiatric patients. *Archives of General Psychiatry*, 1973, 29, 647–651

Miller, J. General living systems theory. In: H. Kaplan, A. Freedman, and B. Sadock (Eds.). *Comprehensive Textbook of Psychiatry III*. Baltimore: Williams and Wilkins Co., 1980.

Minskoff, K. A map of chronic mental patients. In: J. Talbott (Ed.). *The Chronic Mental Patient: Problems, Solutions, and Recommendations for a Public Policy*. Washington, D.C.: American Psychiatric Association, 1978.

Mishara, B. Geriatric patients who improve in token economy and general milieu treatment programs: A multivariate analysis. *Journal of Consulting and Clinical Psychology*, 1978, 46, (6), 1340–1348.

Moos, R. *Evaluating Treatment Environments: A Social Ecological Approach*. New York: John Wiley & Sons, 1974.

Morrison, L. Barriers to self-sufficiency for mental health centers. *Hospital & Community Psychiatry*, 1977, 28 (3), 185–191.

Mosher, L. and Keith, S. Psychosocial treatment: Individual, group, family, and community support approaches. *Schizophrenia Bulletin*, 1980, 6 (1), 10–41.

Moss, S. and Moss, M. Mental illness, partial hospitalization, and the family. *Clinical Social Work Journal*, 1973, 1, 168–76.

Mullen, H. and Rosenbaum, M. *Group Psychotherapy*. New York: The Free Press, 1962, pp. 267–285.

National Institute of Mental Health. *A Working Manual of Simple Program Evaluation Techniques for Community Mental Health Centers*. D.H.E.W. Pub (ADM) 76–404. Washington, D.C.: U.S. Government Printing Office, 1976.

National Institute of Mental Health. *Private Psychiatric Hosptials 1974–5*. DHEW Pub #77–380. Washington, D.C.: U.S. Government Printing Office, 1977a.

National Institute of Mental Health. *Resource Materials for Community Mental Health Program Evaluation* (2nd. Edition). DHEW Pub. No. [ADM] 77–328. Washington, D.C.: U.S. Government Printing Office, 1977b.

National Institute of Mental Health. *Guidelines for the Content of Client/Patient Data in Mental Health Information Systems*. Rockville, Maryland: NIMH, March, 1978.

National Institute of Mental Health. (Draft of) *Program Guidelines for the Community Health Centers Act*. Rockville, Maryland: NIMH., July, 1979.

Nelson, C. The administrator's role in quality assessment and control. *Health Care Management Review*, 1977, 2 (1), 7–18.

Nelson, S. Standards affecting mental health care: A review and commentary. *American Journal of Psychiatry*, 1979, 136 (3), 303–307.

New York Codes Rules and Regulations (Title 14). *Proposed part 585; Operation of outpatient facilities for the mentally ill*. Albany, N.Y. (44 Holland Ave Zip 11229): The Office of Mental Health, Jan. 14, 1980.

Nir, Y. and Cutler, R. The unmotivated patient syndrome: Survey of therapeutic interventions. *American Journal of Psychiatry*, 1978, 135 (4), 442–447.

Novello, J. Day hospital treatment of adolescents. In: J. Novello (Ed.), *The Short Course in Adolescent Psychiatry*. New York: Bunner/Mazel, 1979.

O'Brien, C. Group therapy for schizophrenia: A practical approach. *Schizophrenia Bulletin*, 1975, 1 (13), 119–130.

O'Brien, C. P., Hamm, K. B., Ray, B. A., Pierce, J. F., Luborsky L., and Mintz J. Group vs. individual psychotherapy with schizophrenics. *Archives of General Psychiatry*, 1972, 27 (4), 474–478.

Panel discussion: The dilemma of proposition 13. *American Journal of Orthopsychiatry*, 1980, 50 (2), 225–37.

Pardes, H., and Pincus, H. Treatment in the seventies: A decade of refinement. *Hospital & Community Psychiatry*, 1980, 31 (8), 535–42.

Park, C. Partial hospitalization and family involvement: A family member's perspective. In: R. Luber, J. Maxey, and P. Lefkovitz (Eds.), *Proceedings of the Annual Conference on Partial Hospitalization* (1977). Boston: Federation of Partial Hospital Study Groups, 1978.

Pattison, E., De Francisco, D., Wood, P., Frazier, H., and Crowder, J. A psycho-social kinship model for family therapy. *American Journal of Psychiatry*, 1975, 132 (12), 1246–51.

Pattison, E., Llamas, R., and Hurd, G. Social network mediation of anxiety. *Psychiatric Annals*, 1979, 9 (9), 56–67.

Paul, G. and Lentz, R. *Psychological Treatment for Chronic Mental Patients: Milieu Versus Social-learning Programs.* Cambridge, Ma: Harvard University Press, 1977.

Payn, S. Reaching chronic schizophrenic patients with group pharmacotherapy. *International Journal of Group Psychotherapy,* 1974, *24* (1), 25–31.

Peer Review Committee of The American Psychiatric Association. *Manual of Psychiatric Peer Review. (Second Edition)* Washington, D.C.: APA, 1981.

Penk, W., Charles, H., and Hoose, T. Comparative effectiveness of day hospital and inpatient psychiatric treatment. *Journal of Consulting and Clinical Psychology,* 1978, *46* (1), 94–101.

Petyk, M. A. *A Study of Day Treatment.* Ann Arbor, MI: University Microfilms International, 1977.

Pildis, M. Treatment for family members of day hospital patients: A multifamily group in a day hospital setting. *Proceedings of the Annual Conference on Partial Hospitalization* (1977). Boston: Federation of Partial Hospital Study Groups, 1978.

Pines, A. and Kafry, D. Occupational tedium in the social services. *Social Work,* Nov. 1978, *23* (6), 499–500.

Platt, E. S. and Jones, R. E. Creation of a work experience program. *Proceedings of the Annual Conference on Partial Hospitalization* (1979). Boston: Federation of Partial Hospitalization Study Groups, 1980.

Powell, B., Othmer, E., and Sinkhorn, C. Pharmacologic aftercare for homogenous groups of patients. *Hospital & Community Psychiatry,* 1977, *28* (2), 125–27.

Quesnell, J. and Martin, C. A day hospital in a military psychiatric facility. *Corrective Psychiatry,* 1971, *17,* 5–16.

Rapoport, R. *Community as Doctor.* Springfield, Ill.: Charles C Thomas, 1960.

Rathbone-McCuan, E. and Elliot, M. Geriatric day care in theory and practice. *Social Work in Health Care,* 1976–77, *2* (2), 153–170.

Report of the task panel on planning and review. In: *Task Panel Reports Submitted to the President's Commission on Mental Health* (Vol. 2). Washington, D.C.: U.S. Government Printing Office, 1978.

Report of the task panel on research. *Task Panel Reports Submitted to the President's Commission on Mental Health,* (Vol. 4). Washington, D.C.: U.S. Government Printing Office, 1978.

Resnick, H. A social system view of strain. *Administration in Mental Health,* Fall 1979, *7* (1), 43–68.

Roberts, L. M. Group meetings in a therapeutic community. In: H. C. B. Denber (Ed.), *Research Conference on the Therapeutic Community.* Springfield, Ill.: Charles C Thomas, 1960.

Rodgers, R. What is a day center? *Community Mental Health Journal,* 1967, *3* (3), 231–6.

Rooney, M. Is it time for sex: Establishing a human sexuality program in a day treatment center. In: R. Luber, J. Maxey, and P. Lefkovitz (Eds.), *Proceedings of the Annual Conference on Partial Hospitalization* (1976). Boston: Federation of Partial Hospital Study Groups, Inc., 1977.

Rosenbaum, M. and Berger, M. (Eds.) *Group Psychotherapy and Group Function.* New York: Basic Books, 1963.

Roth, L. H. Mental health commitment: The state of the debate, 1980. *Hospital & Community Psychiatry,* June 1980, *31* (6), 385–396.

Rubin, R. S. The community meeting: A comparative study. *American Journal of Psychiatry,* May 1979, *136:5,* 708–712.

Rueveni, U. *Networking Families in Crisis.* New York: Human Sciences Press, 1979.

Ruiz, P. and Saiger, C. Partial hospitalization in an urban slum. *American Journal of Psychiatry,* 1972, *129,* 121–123.

Sacks, M. H., and Carpenter, W. T. The pseudotherapeutic community: An examination of antitherapeutic forces on psychiatric units. *Hospital & Community Psychiatry,* 1974, *25* (5), 315–318.

Sadock, B. J. Group psychotherapy, combined individual and group psychotherapy and psychodrama. In: H. A. Kaplan, A. M. Freedman, and B. J. Sadock (Eds.), *Comprehensive Textbook of Psychiatry III* (Vol. 2). Baltimore: Williams and Wilkins, 1980.

Salzman, C., Strauss, M. E., Engle, R. P. Jr., and Kamins, L. Overnight "guesting" of day hospital patients. *Comprehensive Psychiatry,* 1969, *10,* 369–375.

Satir, V. *Conjoint family therapy.* Palo Alto, CA: Science and Behavior Books, 1967.

Schippits, H. (Ed.) *Proceedings of the Fourth Multi-Disciplinary National Forum on Adult Psychiatric Day Treatment.* Minneapolis, MN: Dept. of Conferences, Continuing Education and Extension, University of Minnesota, 1981.

Schless, A. and Mendels, J. The value of interviewing family and friends in assessing life stressors. *Archives of General Psychiatry,* 1978, *35* (5), 565–67.

Schoenberg, M., Miller, M., and Schoenberg, C. The mind-body dichotomy reified: An illustrative case. *American Journal of Psychiatry*, 1978, *135* (10), 1224–26.

Scholom, A. and Perlman, B. The forgotten staff: Who cares for the care givers? *Administration in Mental Health*, Fall 1979, *7* (1), 21–31.

Schulte, K. and Blume, S. A day treatment center for alcoholic women. *Health and Social Work*, 1979, *4* (4), 222–31.

Schwartz, A. and Swartzburg, M. Hospital care. In: B. Wolman (Ed.), *The Therapist's Handbook*. New York: Van Nostrand Reinhold Company, 1976.

Schwarz, E. A revised checklist to obtain consent to treatment with medication. *Hospital & Community Psychiatry*, 1980, *31* (11), 765–67.

Seawell, L. *Hospital Financial Accounting; Theory and Practice*. Chicago: Hospital Financial Management Association, 1975.

Sharfstein, S. Will community mental health survive in the 1980's? *American Journal of Psychiatry*, 1978, *135* (11), 1363–65.

Silber, S. Strategies for developing multisource funding for community mental health centers. *Hospital & Community Psychiatry*, 1974, *25* (4), 221–24.

Silverman, W. and Val, E. Day hospital in the context of a community mental health program. *Community Mental Health Journal*, 1975, *11*, 82–90.

Simon, J. Marketing the community hospital: A tool for the beleaguered administrator. *Health Care Management Review*, 1978, *3* (2), 11–24.

Simon, H. and Bronsky, T. The day treatment center model at V.A. Center, Wood, Wisconsin. In: H. Schippits and J. Kroll (Eds.), *Proceedings of a Multi-Disciplinary National Forum on Adult Psychiatric Day Treatment*. Minneapolis, MN: Dept. of Conferences, University of Minnesota, 1977.

Skinner, K. The therapeutic milieu: Making it work. *Journal of Psychiatric Nursing*, 1979, *17* (8), 38–44.

Skynner, A. C. R. *Systems of Family and Marital Psychotherapy*. New York: Brunner/Mazel, 1976.

Slavson, S. The nature and treatment of acting out in group psychotherapy. *International Journal of Group Psychotherapy*, January 1956, *VI*, 3–26.

Smith, M. B. The revolution in mental health care—a bold new approach? *Trans-Action*, 1968, *5*, 19–23.

Smith, S. and Cross, E. Review of 1000 patients treated in a psychiatric day hospital. *International Journal of Social Psychiatry*, 1957, *2*, 292–298.

Solomon, M. The staging of family treatment: An approach to developing the therapeutic alliance. *Journal of Marriage and Family Counseling*, 1977, *3* (2), 59–66.

Spiegler, M. and Agigian, H. *The Community Training Center: An Educational-Behavioral-Social Systems Model for Rehabilitating Psychiatric Patients*. New York: Brunner/Mazel, 1977.

Spingarn, N. D. *Confidentiality*. Washington, D.C.: American Psychiatric Association, 1975.

Spitzer, R. and Williams, J. Classification of mental disorders and DSM III. In: H. Kaplan, A. Freedman, and B. Sadock (Eds.), *Comprehensive Textbook of Psychiatry III*. Baltimore: Williams and Wilkins, 1980.

Stemple, J. E. and DeStefane, M. J. Starting a rural partial hospitalization program. In: R. Luber, et al., (Eds.), *Proceedings of the Annual Conference on Partial Hospitalization*, Boston 1978, pp. 87-89.

Stoller, R. Gender identity disorders. In: H. Kaplan, A. Freedman, and B. Sadock (Eds.), *Comprehensive Textbook of Psychiatry III*. Baltimore: Williams and Wilkins, 1980.

Stratas, N. Quality amidst constraints: Creative use of limited resources. *Hospital & Community Psychiatry*, 1978, *29* (6), 350.

Strelnick, A. Multiple family group therapy: A review of the literature. *Family Process*, 1977, *16*, 307-325.

Talbott, J. (Ed.). *The Chronic Mental Patient: Problems, Solutions, and Recommendations for a Public Policy*. Washington, D.C.: American Psychiatric Association, 1978.

Talbott, J. The impact of proposition 13 on mental health services in California. *Hospital & Community Psychiatry*, 1979, *30* (10), 677-83.

Task Force on Electroconvulsive Therapy of the American Psychiatric Association. *Electroconvulsive therapy: Task force report #14*. Washington, D.C.: American Psychiatric Association, Sept., 1978.

Task Force on Nomenclature and Statistics. *Quick Reference to Diagnostic Criteria from DSM-III*. Washington, D.C.: American Psychiatric Association, 1980, 239.

Test, M. and Stein L. Community treatment of the chronic patient: Research overview. *Schizophrenia Bulletin*, 1978, *4*(3), 350-364.

Towery, O. and Perry, P. The scientific basis for coverage decisions by third-party payers. *Journal of American Medical Association*, 1981, *245* (1), 59-61.

Tulipan, A.B. and Heyder, D.W. *Outpatient Psychiatry in the 1970's*. New York: Brunner/Mazel, 1970.

Vannicelli, M., Washburn, S., Scheff, B., and Longabaugh, R. Comparison of usual and experimental patients in a psychiatric day center. *Journal of Consulting and Clinical Psychology*, 1978, *46* (1), 87-93.

Van Putten, T., May, P., and Marder, S. The hospital and optimal chemotherapy in schizophrenia. *Hospital & Community Psychiatry*, 1979, *30* (2), 114-117.

Van Putten, T., May, P., and Marder, S., and Wittmann, L. Subjective responses to antipsychotic drugs. *Archives of General Psychiatry*, 1981, *38* (2), 187-194.

Veil, C. Psychiatric day care units for adults. In: *Outpatient Psychiatric Services: A Mimeographed Report*. Geneva: World Health Organization, 1965.

Vernallis, F. and Reinert, R. The weekend hospital. *Mental Hospitals*, 1963, *14*, 254-58.

Vinter, R.D. (Ed.) *Readings in Group Work Practice*. Ann Arbor, Mi: Campus Publishers, 1967.

Vitale, J. The therapeutic community. In: A.F. Wessen (Ed.), *The Psychiatric Hospital as a Social System*. Springfield, Ill.: Charles C Thomas, 1964.

Washburn, J.D. Utilizing patients as a source of referrals for day treatment centers. *Proceedings of the Annual Conference on Partial Hospitalization* (1978). Boston: Federation of Partial Hospitalization Study Groups, 1979.

Washburn, S., Vannicelli, M., Longabaugh, R., and Scheff, B.J. A controlled comparison of psychiatric day treatment and inpatient hospitalization. *Journal of Consulting and Clinical Psychology*, 1976a, *44*, 665-673.

Washburn, S., Vanicelli, M. and Scheff, B.J. Irrational determinants of the place of psychiatric treatment. *Hospital & Community Psychiatry*, 1976b, *27*, (3) 179-182.

Watts, F. and Bennett, D. Social deviance in a day hospital. *British Journal of Psychiatry*, 1978, *132*, 455-62.

Weed, L. L. The problem-oriented record as a basic tool in medical education, patient care and clinical research. *Annals of Clinical Research*, 1971, *3*, 131-134.

Weiner, R. The psychiatric use of electrically induced seizures. *American Journal of Psychiatry*, 1979, *136* (12), 1507-17.

Weissert, W. Two models of geriatric day care. *The Gerontologist*, 1976, *16* (5), 420-27.

Weldon, E. and Frances, A. The day hospital: Structures and functions. *Psychiatric Quarterly*, 1977, *49* (4), 338-342.

Werlin, S. *Assessing and assuring quality in community mental health centers*. Rockville, MD.: NIMH, 1976.

Werner, A., Campbell, R., Frazier, S., and Stone, E. (Eds.) *A Psychiatric Glossary* (5th Edition). Washington, D.C.: American Psychiatric Association, 1980.

West, O., Casarino, J., DiBella, G., & Gross, R. Partial hospitalization: Guidelines for standards. *Psychiatric Annals*, 1980, *10* (6), 305-312.

West Publishing Co. *McKinney's Consolidated Laws of New York*, Book 34A: *Mental Hygiene Law*. St. Paul, Minn.: West Pub. Co., 1978. (Annotated)

Wexler, D.B. Patients, therapists and third parties: The victimological virtues of Tarasoff. *International Journal of Law and Psychiatry*, 1979, *2*, 1-28.

Whittington, H. *Clinical Practice in Community Mental Health Centers*. New York: International Universities Press, 1972.

Wilder, J., Levin, G., and Zwerling, I. A two year follow-up evaluation of acute psychotic patients treated in a day hospital. *American Journal of Psychiatry*, 1966, *122*, 1095-1101.

Williams, J. The Framingham functional assessment scale. In: J. Maxey, R. Luber, and P. Lefkovitz (Eds.). *Proceedings of the Annual Conference on Partial Hospitalization* (1979), Boston: American Association for Partial Hospitalization, 1980.

Wilmer, H.A. Toward a definition of the therapeutic community. *American Journal of Psychiatry*, 1958, *114*, 824-834.

Wilner, M., Goldberg, F. and Morello, J. Video taping and playback in milieu treatment: Experience in a psychiatric day hospital. *Proceedings of the Annual Conference on Partial Hospitalization* (1978). Boston: Federation of Partial Hospitalization Study Groups, 1979.

Witkin, M. Provisional patient and selective administrative data, state and county mental hospitals, inpatient services by state, U.S. 1976. *Statistical Note #153.* Washington, D.C.: Alcohol Drug Mental Health Administration, U.S.A. Govt. Printing Office, 1979, p. 1.

Witkin, M. Trends in patient care episodes in mental health facilities, 1955–1977. *Mental Health Statistical Note no. 154.* Rockville, Maryland: U.S. Department of Health and Human Services, National Institute of Mental Health, 1980.

Wolf, A. Psychoanalysis in groups. In: M. Rosenbaum and M. M. Berger (Eds.), *Group Therapy and Group Function.* New York: Basic Books, 1975. Reprinted from *Major Contributions to Modern Psychiatry.* Nutley, New Jersey: Roche Laboratories, Division of Hoffman LaRoche, Inc.

Wolf, A. et al., The psychoanalysis of groups. *American Journal of Psychotherapy,* October 1949, *III* (4), 529-558, & 1950, *IV* (1), 16–50.

Wolman, B. B. (Ed.) *The Therapist's Handbook: Treatment Methods of Mental Disorders.* New York: Van Nostrand Reinhold, 1976.

Woolf, H. (Ed.). *Webster's New Collegiate Dictionary.* Springfield, MA: G. & C. Merriam Co., 1975.

Working Group to Define Critical Patient Behaviors in High Blood Pressure Control. Patient behavior for blood pressure control: Guidelines for professionals. *Journal of the American Medical Association,* 1979, *241* (23), 2534-2537.

World Health Organization. Education and treatment in human sexuality: The training of health professionals. *Technical Report Series 572,* Albany, New York: WHO-Q Corporation, 1975.

Zeitlyn, B. The therapeutic community—fact or fantasy. *British Journal of Psychiatry,* 1967, *113,* 1083-1086.

Zwerling, I. The creative arts as "real therapies." *Hospital & Community Psychiatry,* 1979, *30,* 841-844.

Zwerling, I. The day hospital. In: S. Arieti (Ed.), *American Handbook of Psychiatry* Vol. III. New York: Basic Books, 1966.

Zwerling, I. and Wilder, J. An evaluation of the applicability of the day hospital in the treatment of acutely disturbed patients. *Israel Annals of Psychiatry and Related Disciplines,* 1964, *2,* (2), 162-185.

Bibliography

SUGGESTED READINGS FOR CHAPTER 12

Adsit, P. The use of art therapy in a day treatment program. *Proceedings of the Annual Conference on Partial Hospitalization* (1977). Boston: Federation of Partial Hospitalization Study Groups, 1978.

Buckley, L. A case study of an expressive problem solving group. *Proceedings of the Annual Conference on Partial Hospitalization* (1978). Boston: Federation of Partial Hospitalization Study Groups, 1979.

Wolfgram, B. J. Comprehensive implementation of music therapy in a day hospital setting. *Proceedings of the Annual Conference on Partial Hospitalization* (1978). Boston: Federation of Partial Hospitalization Study Groups, 1979.

SUGGESTED READINGS FOR CHAPTER 21

Borriello, J. F. Group psychotherapy with acting-out patients: specific problems and techniques. *American Journal of Psychotherapy*, 1979, *33* (4), 521-530.

DiBella, G. A. W. Educating staff to manage threatening paranoid patients. *American Journal of Psychiatry*, 1979, *136* (3), 333-335.

Hyland, J. The day hospital treatment of the borderline patient. *Proceedings of the Annual Conference on Partial Hospitalization* (1976). Boston: Federation of Partial Hospitalization Study Groups, 1977.

Justice, B. and Justice, R. *The abusing family.* New York: Human Sciences Press, 1976.

Kaminski, R. C. Practice outcome inventory: A treatment technique with an obsessive compulsive in day treatment. *Proceedings of the Annual Conference on Partial Hospitalization* (1977). Boston: Federation of Partial Hospitalization Study Groups, 1978.

Karasu, T. Psychotherapy of the psychosomatic patient. *American Journal of Psychotherapy, 33,* (3), 354-364.

Lesse, S. Behavioral problems masking severe depression—cultural and clinical survey. *American Journal of Psychotherapy*, 1979, *33*, (1), 41-53.

Phelps, R. and Roberts, K. Day treatment for chronic outpatients. *Proceedings of the Annual Conference on Partial Hospitalization* (1977). Boston: Federation of Partial Hospitalization Study Groups, 1978.

Soverno, G. Day hospital treatment of the borderline patient. *Proceedings of the Annual Conference on Partial Hospitalization* (1977). Boston: Federation of Partial Hospitalization Study Groups. 1978.

Spiegel, R. On psychotherapy of patients with problems of hostility. *American Journal of Psychotherapy*, 1980, *34* (2), 178-187.

Steiner, J. Holistic group therapy with schizophrenic patients. *International Journal of Group Psychotherapy*, 1979, *29* (2), 195-210.

Stengel, I. *Suicide and Attempted Suicide.* Middlesex, England: Penguin Books Ltd., 1973.

Turner, S., Jones, D., and Simpson, M. The differential use of groups in a day treatment program. *Proceedings of the Annual Conference on Partial Hospitalization* (1976). Boston: Federation of Partial Hospitalization Study Groups, 1977.

SUGGESTED READINGS FOR CHAPTER 22

Burch, E. A. and Benggio, E. Using personalized consumer charts in a partial hospitalization program. *Hospital & Community Psychiatry*, August 1980, *31* (8), 570-571.

Fay, H. J., & Norman, A. Modifying the problem-oriented record for an inpatient program for children. *Hospital & Community Psychiatry*, 1974, *25*, 28-30.

Gilandas, A. J. The problem-oriented record in a psychiatric hospital. *Hospital & Community Psychiatry*, 1974, *25*, 22-24.

Potts, L. R. Problem-oriented record: Implications for occupational therapy. *American Journal of Occupational Therapy*, 1972, *26*, 288-291.

Rothstein, E. Problem-oriented records for alcoholism programs. *Journal of the American Medical Association*, 1973, *224*, 527-528.

Smith, L. C., Hawley, C. J., and Grant, K. L. Questions frequently asked about the problem-oriented record in psychiatry. *Hospital & Community Psychiatry*, 1974, *25*, 17-22.

Williams, D. H., Jacobs, S., Debski, A., and Revere, M. Introducing the problem-oriented record in a psychiatric inpatient unit. *Hospital & Community Psychiatry*, 1974, *25*, 25-28.

Wogan, M. J. AMR survey shows enthusiasm is key to success with POMR. *Medical Record News*, 1971, *42*, 57-60.

SUGGESTED READINGS FOR CHAPTER 24

Appelbaum, P. S., & Gutheil, T. G. Drug refusal: A study of psychiatric inpatients. *The American Journal of Psychiatry*, March 1980, *137* (3), 340-346.

Ford, M. D. The psychiatrist's double bind: The right to refuse medication. *American Journal of Psychiatry*, March 1980, *137* (3), 332-339.

Gallant, D. M. and Force, R. (Eds.), *Legal and Ethical Issues in Human Research and Treatment: Psychopharmacologic Considerations.* New York: Spectrum Publications, Inc., 1978.

Reiser, S. J. Refusing treatment for mental illness: Historical and ethical dimensions. *The American Journal of Psychiatry*, March 1980, *137* (3), 329-331.

Author Index

Subject Index